OTHER NORTH SHORE BOOKS
BY JOSEPH E. GARLAND

LONE VOYAGER
The Life of Howard Blackburn

THAT GREAT PATTILLO
The Life of James William Pattillo

EASTERN POINT
A Nautical, Rustical and Social Chronicle of Gloucester's
Outer Shield and Inner Sanctum, 1606–1950

THE GLOUCESTER GUIDE
A Stroll through Place and Time

BOSTON'S NORTH SHORE
Being an Account of Life Among the Noteworthy,
Fashionable, Wealthy, Eccentric and Ordinary, 1823–1890

BOSTON'S GOLD COAST
The North Shore, 1890–1929

DOWN TO THE SEA
The Fishing Schooners of Gloucester

ADVENTURE
Queen of the Windjammers

THE EASTERN YACHT CLUB
A History from 1870 to 1985

BEATING TO WINDWARD
A voyage in the *Gloucester Daily Times* through the stormy
years from 1967 to 1973

GLOUCESTER ON THE WIND
A Photographic History of America's Greatest Fishing Port
in the Days of Sail: 1870 to 1938

BEAM REACH
Further voyaging in the *Gloucester Daily Times* with other
miscellaneous musings from 1951 to 1997

The North Shore

A Social History of Summers
Among the Noteworthy, Fashionable,
Rich, Eccentric and Ordinary
on Boston's Gold Coast,
1823–1929

The North Shore

JOSEPH E. GARLAND

Commonwealth Editions
Beverly, Massachusetts

Portions of this work were originally published in
Boston's North Shore (Little, Brown 1978) and
Boston's Gold Coast (Little, Brown 1981).

Library of Congress Catologing-in-Publication Data
Garland, Joseph E.
The North Shore / Joseph E. Garland. — 1st Ed.
p. cm.
Subtitle on cover: A social history of summers among the
noteworthy, fashionable, rich, eccentric and ordinary on
Boston's Gold Coast, 1823–1929.
Includes bibliographical references (p.357) and index.
ISBN 1-889833-04-5 (alk. paper)
1. North Shore (Mass.)—Social life and customs. 2. Boston
Region (Mass.)—Social life and customs. 3. North Shore
(Mass.)—Biography. 4. Boston Region (Mass.)—Biography.
I. Garland, Joseph E. *Boston's North Shore.*
II. Garland, Joseph E. *Boston's Gold Coast.* III. Title.
F73.68.N67G37   1998
974.4'--dc21
98-12940
CIP

Designed by Joyce C. Weston.
Published and distributed by
Commonwealth Editions,
an imprint of Memoirs Unlimited, Inc.,
21 Lothrop Street, Beverly, Massachusetts 01915.
Printed in the United States of America.

CONTENTS

PUBLISHER'S NOTE

It's the rare publisher who gets a chance to help restore a classic. When I met Joe Garland in 1996, his *Boston's North Shore* and *Boston's Gold Coast* were out of print and in demand. You can buy four or five copies of this 1998 edition for what the pair, brought out in 1978 and 1981, still fetch on the used-book market.

We talked about combining them in a single volume. The author said that's what they were supposed to be twenty-five years ago, but after writing twenty-one chapters he had only reached 1890, and his editor at Little, Brown proposed, "We'll publish a first volume, call it *Boston's North Shore*, and if it sells, write the sequel." It sold, and the result was *Boston's Gold Coast*.

"I dunno. Whaddya think?" Joe asked in the first of several dozen faxes we used to hone the idea. I thought we could create a revised edition that would realize the one-volume concept from the early nineteenth century to the Great Crash. Editor Susanna Brougham played a vital role in realizing this approach, and Joe pronounced in a January '98 note: "A better book than the two originals by all means."

Pictorially I dare say it's a better book, too, including a new design, previously unpublished photos, and area maps which I found myself scrambling for whenever I dipped back into *Boston's North Shore* and *Boston's Gold Coast*. To the acknowledgments in the originals I must add the names of those people who eagerly hunted up illustrations for us. Especially helpful were David Goss, Fred Hale, Fred Hammond, and Harold Pinkham of the Beverly Historical Society; Dick Symmes of the society's remarkable Walker Transportation Collection; Slim Proctor and Lotte Calnek of the Manchester Historical Society; Calantha Sears of the Nahant Historical Society; Ellen Nelson of the Cape Ann Historical Association; Cynthia Peckham of the Sandy Bay Historical Society; Eleanor Gaunt of the Ipswich Public Library; Judy Ann Gilliss of the Magnolia Historical Society; the many willing folks of the Marblehead Historical Society; C. G. Rice of the Myopia Hunt Club; and Gordon Abbott, Jr., Fred Bodin, John G. L. Cabot, Peter Freed, Louis Gallo, Tom Halsted and Charlie Shurcliff. I hope to hail you all along the shore.

For the friendship and the laughs and the hope of another book, thanks finally go to Joe and his joyful wife Helen. After ten years at the head of the private publishing concern Memoirs Unlimited, I find myself fairly launched on the waters of commercial publishing with a redoubtable crewmate. You could do worse than go to sea with Joe Garland.

Webster Bull

View from the past. Looking southwest toward Beverly from the veranda of
T. Jefferson Coolidge, Jr.'s, "Marble Palace" in Manchester.
(Manchester Historical Society)

~PROLOGUE~
NORTHEAST OF BOSTON

T HE NORTH SHORE IS NOT WHAT IT used to be, an observer of the fast-passing scene lamented in 1922: certain Boston owners of summer estates are known for a fact to be renting to westerners, and if this were not alarming enough, several properties have actually fallen into the hands of Chicagoans, Detroiters and even a party from Kansas City.

A columnist in that arbiter of all matters Bostonian, the staid old *Transcript,* responded reassuringly. "No doubt this is true, but it is no new tendency. The Listener can well remember when, about thirty years ago, one place on the Beverly shore was occupied by a Chicagoan and the adjoining one by a Washingtonian. And one reason, perhaps, why these people of wealth from the West and South are attracted to the North Shore is that it is so Bostonian. That it still is, and it is to be hoped that it always will be."

Seventy-six years later the object of these solicitudes is still keeping its guard up, or was when a Manchester-by-the-Sea lady from what was then merely Manchester advised me in chilling tones, as the first edition of this book was being written in the 1970s, that to write about the North Shore and not restrict it to Manchester and Beverly—*The* North Shore in her book—was to advance a fraud on the reading public. *Her* North Shore consisted of the dozen social, wealthy and well-walled miles of it that wind from Beverly's Woodbury Point through Pride's Crossing, Beverly Farms, West Manchester and Manchester, terminating at the east property line of the Manchester Bath and Tennis Club just short of Magnolia Point.

That is about twelve percent of the coastline between Boston and Ipswich. Fortunately for the upwardly mobile, however, the mantle of exclusiveness is by self-definition almost infinitely stretchable. The whole cloth, in actual fact, originally covered Nahant; not for years did Beverly and Manchester get even a corner of it. Summer settlers at Eastern Point and Bass Rocks drew another corner down to Gloucester. A third was tugged the length of Argilla Road in far-off Ipswich. The fourth has been draped over most of the horsey countryside that buffers the Myopia Hunt Club crowd from the madding herd, or horde. Amid all this pulling and hauling, the residents of various worthy sections of Swampscott, Marblehead, Salem, Gloucester, Rockport and Essex have claimed their shares of the sacred cloak of ambience, while the remainder of the coast northeast of Boston, including Winthrop, Revere and its beach, Lynn, Danvers and everything and everyone else so far excluded, presumes perfectly legitimately that *it* is part and parcel of the North Shore.

Thus are all the Outs in, and we can get on with the geographically and demographically irrefutable definition of the North Shore of Massachusetts Bay as the hundred or so curious, twisting miles of rock and strand from Point Shirley to Castle Neck where Boston society—capitalist and uncapitalized, castebound and classless—and not a few visitors from a distance have for 175 years found summer resort suited to every civility, every vulgarity, every frivolity and every purse.

In the interests of accuracy it should probably be mentioned in passing that Massachusetts Bay has another shore on the other side of Boston, which holds some pretensions as a watering place, called the South Shore. Languorous and low, this other shore lazes around the shallow bays of Quincy and Hingham, along the graceful spine of Nantasket Beach and down through the friendly towns of Cohasset, Scituate, Marshfield and Duxbury to Plymouth, where Cape Cod takes over. Except where the Cohasset ledges bare their teeth behind the warning wink of Minot's Light, the South Shore is a sandy prelude to the Cape. Its few small harbors, though filled with pleasure boats, are half-emptied by every tide. Miles of flats, marsh and bog provide a haven for waterfowl and avaricious insects. It is simply incomprehensible to the North Shore summerer how his counterpart below Boston can, with evident satisfaction, spend the season sweltering and smacking skeeters while he, enlightened soul, enjoys the ten- or fifteen-degree discount on Fahrenheit with which geography and climate have rewarded his good sense.

Actually, the North Shore is at first nothing much to brag about. Across Boston Harbor there is little in either the Logan International Airport, the no-man's-land of tanks and pipelines known ironically as the Oil Farm or the contemporary aspect of Chelsea to delight the soul. In years gone by, though—before Chelsea was irredeemably devastated by the Great Fire of 1908—a serene summer resort was spread upon the riverbank, and the town occupied a tract of farmland and salt marsh that undulated north as far as the eye could see and oceanward to the four shining miles of what was then called Chelsea Beach.

Settled as resorts of Boston when they broke away from Chelsea, Winthrop and Revere are in fact the beginning of the North Shore, notwithstanding that they alone are in Suffolk, not Essex, County and with Lynn suffered systematic snubbing season after season from that now-defunct synodicon of snobbery, *Who's Who Along the North Shore: Being a Register of the Noteworthy, Fashionable & Wealthy Residents on the North Shore of Massachusetts Bay.* The snooty rural seats of Hamilton, Wenham and Topsfield, on the other hand, extend over some of the most handsome spread in eastern Massachusetts—not an inch of it closer than a mile to salt water—and were season after season baptized and anointed in absentia . . . not without precedent, because the gerrymander, after all, is an Essex County invention.

Once across the Essex County line, the great Chelsea marsh gives way to solid ground. Hanging out to sea from Lynn by a thread of sand, the rocky demi-isles of Nahant portend the geology to come. At Swampscott the rusty ledge breaks through and from Marblehead on rules the coast in ridges, miles of them, erupting and submerging and erupting again in parallel with the long Atlantic swells that seethe upon the shore. Scoured and scarred by the glacial sheet, the bedrock subsides into gullies and swamps and ponds and streams, deep harbors, coves and crescent beaches, and heaves up into bald domes and hard heads, scrawny necks and islands barren of all but boulder and brier, and lurks beneath the wave in silent menace. Along this surf-crashed coast, rock and sea have shaped human destiny.

Beyond Cape Ann the ledge sinks below the billowy borders of Ipswich Bay, and sand takes over again in the dazzling dunes and windy beaches of Wingaersheek, Coffin's and Crane's. Behind them in the marshes and tidal creeks of Essex and Ipswich, where land and water meet uncertainly, the North Shore ends.

From the June day in 1823 when Colonel Perkins threw open the doors of his summer hotel at Nahant to the ocean breeze and invited the upper crust of Boston to come and cool off on his verandas, this patch of coast has been America's most durable seaside resort because it *is* so *Bostonian,* so redoubtably the preserve of Bostonians of all shades of propriety and of successive transfusions of newcomers who have bought, rented or toured their way in, only to turn into the fiercest guardians of them all, as often happens to converts.

Besides Presidents, members of cabinet and congress, and justices of the Supreme Court, there have been victorious and less than victorious generals, an embarrassment of ambassadors, some denfuls of literary lions, heirs and heiresses real and apparent, various princes and princesses of the blood, and one flush fellow who was a Knight of the Bathroom. In the checkered course of its history the North Shore has been the refuge or the hunting ground of crooks and confidence men both high and low, of writers by the bushel and artists by the basket, of idols of the matinee and others who idled all the hours away, of knaves, jokers and jacks of both sexes and of all trades and of none—and the destination for a few weeks or hours of surcease from the baking sidewalks of several million citizens with neither credentials nor pretensions who found respite in their cottages or simply bought ten-cent round-trip tickets to the beach for the day.

Summer styles perforce have changed forever. War, death, taxes, automobiles, the tube, the web and other such markers on the road of time have taken care of that, and of a good lot else. Today most of the more conspicuous monuments to consumption along the golden strip of *the* North Shore have been torn down, truncated or turned over to the tax-exempt (rest assured, though, that if the glitter is gone, some of the gold remains), and Revere Beach's naughty, gilded strip has given way, funhouse by boarded-up arcade, to high-rise apartments.

The liveried carriages, with their haughty coachmen on the boxes, that dashed along the manicured avenues of Pride's Crossing and through the woods of the Big Heater have slipped over the edge of memory. So have the glorious Glidden Tours, the steam yachts with sterling silver toilet pulls and the private Pullmans, followed by strings of boxcars for horses and grooms, that squealed to a stop on the owner's private siding for the season.

Gone is that shadowy line of chauffeurs outside the Casino at Magnolia, awaiting the final wail of the saxophone, cigarettes aglow like fireflies in the night. Gone up in smoke, most of them, are those vast warehouses of hotels with their full-blown piazzas piled one upon another, their fringed horse-drawn barges that met every train when the family arrived for the summer with servants and twenty-eight pieces of baggage. Gone are their billiard parlors, gaslit ballrooms, Thursday night charades, bumpy croquet fields and bathing machines on the beach below the lawn. Long gone over the horizon is the last excursion steamer, jammed rail to rail, brass band blaring away, churning off from the Great Ocean Pier with a white plume of steam and a blast on the whistle that dissolved every spine on board.

So let us revert in time to the recolonization of the North Shore two hundred years after its settlement by a shipload of English fishermen at Gloucester, to its summerization by city people seeking sea-borne surcease from the miasmic emanations of the Back Bay, to its Bostonization town by town with the intrusion of the Iron Monster northward even as it pressed the Frontier ever westward.

We will chronicle our first and last resort in the fullness of its maturity a hundred years ago, then its Belle Edwardian Epoque, its First World War, and its Reasonably Roaring Twenties before the Crashing descent of the Great Depression laid to rest the last ghosts of a lost time, but by no means of a lost place.

J.E.G.

LIST OF MAPS

To Helen

The North Shore

First spotted from Gloucester in 1817, His Snakeship started the summer rush to Nahant. (Nahant Historical Society)

~1~
SUMMER PIONEERS
AT NAHANT

In which a sea serpent, a China merchant, an Ice King and a den of literary lions descend upon the North Shore

Little escaped the curiosity, not to mention the meticulous diary, of Salem's Reverend William Bentley, and when he heard that a steamboat had actually made it from Boston as far as his pastorate of Salem in June of 1817, he must have a ride on her. *Massachusetts* was not a queen, though she breasted the wave with a figurehead. Her enormous, ugly, belching engine cranked a walking beam that somehow caused banks of oars to flail away at the water—a ridiculously ingenious circumvention of the patents of Robert Fulton, whose side-wheeler *North River* had introduced commercial steam navigation on the Hudson River ten years previously. But, by golly, she beat the stagecoach for getting from Boston to its North Shore.

A tour of Boston Harbor and a voyage around Salem Bay convinced the hearty bachelor minister that this odd contraption was safe enough for him to invite his favorite pupil, Miss Hannah Crowninshield of the Salem Crowninshields, for a day's cruise to Gloucester. All went splashingly until a bit of chop kicked up on the return, and "most of us Landmen" were seasick passing Manchester's Kettle Cove.

Cape Ann was still buzzing over the steam monster when Dr. Bentley "heard from Gloucester that a Narway Kraken had visited their harbour within ten pound Island. We have had letter upon letter. Many attempts have been made to kill him. The general representation is that his head is like a horse & that he raises it several feet out of water. That his body when out of water looks like the buoys of a net, or a row of kegs, or a row of large casks. . . . At the last dates he had not been taken."

His usual curiosity failed Dr. Bentley, and he did not trouble himself to confirm or deny with his own eyes these reports of a sea serpent (which he mistakenly referred to as the Norway Kraken, a legendary giant squid). Colonel Thomas Handasyd Perkins, Boston's leading China merchant, did, however, and rode down on August 16 with a friend identified in one account as Daniel Webster. From high on the western shore of Gloucester Harbor the usually sober financier vowed that he saw through his spyglass an undulating, chocolate-colored sea serpent, some forty feet in length, whose flat head, raised a yard or so above the water, was equipped with a single horn in the shape of a marlinspike.

The unquestionably sober Linnaean Society of New England listened gravely to the sworn testimony of a parade of supposedly sober citizens that they had sighted and in a couple of instances encountered the monster along the North Shore. The savants published a scholarly report, solemnly naming the visitor *Scoliophis Atlanticus,* Greek for "Atlantic worm-snake." The craze, thus officially canonized, was on.

Scoliophis (or the single-file school of tuna fish some of the more skeptical old-time fishermen took him for) returned the next summer and was greeted with gunfire and harpoons in Gloucester Harbor; he fled to Salem and then backtracked to Annisquam. His Snakeship, as the newspapers called him, was joined off the North Shore in September by a new steam monster, *Eagle,* smaller than *Massachusetts* but evidently faster and rated for two hundred passengers, which left no room on deck for a lifeboat. With only two passengers *Eagle* thrashed out of Salem September 17, 1817, on the four-hour trip to Boston. Dr. Bentley supposed that her first run would be her last, for "the certainty of reaching Boston in two hours at two thirds of the distance by water, gives every advantage to the Stage."

The steam-powered Eagle. *(Nahant Public Library)*

The Reverend diarist was wrong. That summer *Eagle* inaugurated the first scheduled steamship service in Massachusetts Bay with three round trips a week from Boston to Nahant, alternating with Hingham. For lack of

a pier, passengers were landed and taken on at Nipper Stage Point in dories. Thus did writer James L. Homer first visit Nahant with thirty other excursionists. "The *Eagle* was usually *three hours* in making her trip to Nahant, and the same time back; and she was considered a wonderfully swift boat. Six hours only upon the water out of nine!"

The well-promoted chance of a glimpse of *Scoliophis Atlanticus* while on the Nahant excursion soon doubled *Eagle*'s passenger complement. On the morning of August 13 "the something" (in Bentley's doubting words) obliged off Long Beach before two hundred spectators. James Prince, the highly respectable marshal of the District of Massachusetts, was rolling along the beach with his family and coachman for a few days at Nahant when they caught sight of "an animal of the fish kind" with a bunch of "bunches" on its back, making much wake as it raced back and forth before its fascinated gallery. The marshal said he had a good look through his "famous masthead spyglass," which elicited James Homer's comment that Prince was "a most worthy and estimable old gentleman—a little near-sighted, and at times somewhat passionate and enthusiastic; in a word, he was just the man to see the sea-serpent!" So was Samuel Cabot, who had his family at Nahant and was crossing Long Beach the next morning in his chaise, returning to Boston on business, when the performance was repeated. The Prince and Cabot accounts were published in the papers and revived the sensation a hundredfold. Probably it is only coincidence that Prince was the first treasurer of the Massachusetts General Hospital and a close friend of the chairman of the board, the doyen of sea serpent-sighters, Colonel Perkins, who happened also to be Sam Cabot's father-in-law.

Long of nose and cool of eye, Tom Perkins was fifty-five and the patriarch of an extensive family hierarchy that had been joining him off and on for several summers at Nahant, where the members boarded, usually with Abner Hood. A few weeks of sea air this season had worked such wonders with an ailing Cabot grandson as to persuade the Colonel to stake Sam to land and house on the spot if Perkins could have the occasional use of it. In the fall the Boston tycoon bought from Hood a bluff piece on the north shore of Nahant, west of that wonder of natural hydraulics, Spouting Horn, and overlooking the ocean crag of Eagle Rock, and another lot from the Breeds, and construction began.

Dr. Bentley died of a heart attack on the twenty-ninth of December and with him the era of simplicity whose decline he had bemoaned. The next summer, 1820, the energetic Perkins clan moved into their stone house, the first summer cottage on Nahant, and founded the first enduring summer colony on the North Shore.

Such was the contagion of sea serpent-searching (a shed was built near Faneuil Hall in Boston to exhibit the monster after its expected capture) that *Eagle* extended her thrice-weekly run as far as Salem, and a second *Massachusetts* started a daily schedule connecting Boston, Nahant, Marblehead, Salem and Beverly. This froth of activity was not unnoticed by

the Colonel, relaxing above the sea and Spouting Horn: the single sighting that summer was reported, obligingly, from his terrace.

A born entrepreneur, the China merchant no doubt had perused with interest (if indeed he was not the author) a paean from an unidentified but "very intelligent correspondent" in the *Patriot* of August 14, 1819, the day after Marshal Prince raised his famous masthead spyglass with exclamations of wonder and delight. The writer extolled Nahant as superior to every watering place in New England: "It is only necessary that a hotel and bathing-houses should be erected to make Nahant one of the most frequented places in New England. The advantage of attracting here the company which annually seek amusement or health abroad is prodigious, if calculated only in a pecuniary point of view. A circulation of at least sixty or seventy thousand dollars in specie would be annually derived from the people who frequent any well established watering-place, and with the superior natural accommodations of Nahant, the assistance of a small capital would place it on the most desirable establishment."

A further rationale for going into the resort hotel business on the grand European scale, rather the same that had induced Perkins to build his cottage, was advanced by Dr. Walter Channing, professor of obstetrics and dean of the Harvard Medical School, in *The New England Journal of Medicine and Surgery* in January 1821. Arguing warmly that Nahant's cool summers offered the invalid "a perpetual inducement to exercise," while the beaches were the best on the coast for the sea bathing which so braces the constitution, he asked, "What more is wanted to render this place a most desirable residence for invalids during the excessive heat, the variable atmosphere, the impure air of our summers in town? It wants accommodations."

Moreover, Dr. Channing had learned that a desirable tract was on the market but would be withdrawn by March. He urged its purchase by some-one for the construction of a grand hotel, which, if properly managed, would offer the invalid guest "something positively salutary in the excitement of a gay and happy society. . . . Whatever the plan be . . . none probably will be very successful which does not offer ample accommodation for the healthy, the gay, and the fashionable, as well as for the sick and convalescent. It seems absolutely necessary, that a watering-place should receive the patronage of fashion, in order that its various means of usefulness should be brought into operation. . . . The remedial influences of such places owe much of their power to the intellectual excitement they produce and sustain."

Dr. Channing happened to be married to the Colonel's niece Barbara Higginson Perkins. Uncle Tom required no further urging. That July of 1821, with William Paine, a business associate, he bought nearly all of East Point from Nehemiah Breed for $1,800. While he set about recruiting a syndicate to build the hotel, his observant family was recruiting potential patronage: from their terrace they again spotted the something and so informed the press.

Work started in 1822. Perkins sent prospective backers a testimonial on the medical advantages of sojourning at Nahant. He was chairman and a large benefactor of the just-opened Massachusetts General Hospital, whose founders, Doctors James Jackson and John Collins Warren, were happy to prescribe that "there is not a spot probably on the whole coast of our country which offers so many natural advantages for this purpose as the peninsula of Nahant." Indebted as the Boston profession was to him, the proprietor could anticipate a healthy flow of unhealthy guests referred to the remedial atmosphere of his hotel.

Set upon the crest of East Point high above the crashing surf, America's number one resort hotel flung open its doors on June 26, 1823. The core was stone, like the Perkins cottage. An observation cupola commanded the ocean and the coast. Bold decks of broad porches embraced seventy chambers (most offered "recesses" for beds), a dining room seating 124, and facilities patterned after the continental. The Nahant Hotel cost the Colonel and his associates sixty thousand dollars, an impressive figure for the day. The newspaper puff touted this magnificent establishment as "the most delightful spot on the American coast for health or pleasure. . . . Located in the bosom of the ocean, the air is salubrious and inviting; while the spacious bay continually presenting the fleets of commerce, with the hills, verdant plains, islands, villages and country seats, extending from the heights of Scituate to the peninsula of Cape Ann, form a panorama unrivaled in any country. . . . In truth, Nahant is the chosen domain of the youthful Hygeia, the pleasant summer residence of the invalid and of all those who seek enjoyment or require relaxation from the cares and business of life; whether they flee from the sultry clime of the South, or the 'stir of the great Babels' of commerce, there they can be at ease and KEEP COOL."

There were hot and cold fresh- and salt-water baths and showers, bar, billiard rooms, bowling alleys, sailing, fishing, riding and "a beautiful marine hippodrome," in reality a small and rather pebbly beach. A singular feature of this hippodrome was "a machine of peculiar construction for bathing in the open sea," which may be the first appearance in America of the popular European bathing machine, a bathhouse on wheels that was rolled into the ocean to whatever depth suited the modest occupant desiring privacy and protection from the waves.

Boston had achieved cityhood the previous year, and it would not do for the newly urbane who chose the water route to Nahant to endure ferriage between steamboat and beach in dories, as in former days, like so many quintals of codfish. A road was therefore cut from the hotel to the ledge above Swallow's Cave, terminating at a six-sided belvedere from which steps descended to a wharf and landing just below Joseph's (alias Joe's or Josie's) Beach.

Down at the Boston docks *Eagle* and *Massachusetts* strained at their lines, steam up. On Beacon Hill the best-groomed steeds fretted in their stalls. The Colonel's hotel was primed for the influx. The missing catalyst was His Snakeship. But lo! he surfaced, a fortnight after the opening, before the disbelieving eyes of Francis Johnson, a youthful Nahanter who pursued in his fishing boat what at first he thought was a parade of porpoises near shore until all his old doubts had been dispelled, or so he swore in a deposition that happened into the hands of the press.

And they came, a flood by land, a tidal wave by sea. They drained every drawing room in Boston worth the draining and engulfed Nahant in a Babel of fashion. All that season and the next. Swept along in the stampede to see and be seen were Margaret and Eliza Quincy, daughters of Josiah Quincy, the relentless reformer now beginning his second year as the new city's second mayor. The sisters were bound to make the ball at the Nahant Hotel, notwithstanding reports that Boston was empty and every house at the exciting new resort "absolutely crammed." They left the family home in Quincy on the morning of August 12, 1824. Margaret brought her diary.

Coming down the Salem Turnpike they paused at the Lynn Hotel, where dozens of carriages were pulled up, all headed for Nahant. The road to Long Beach, the beach itself, and the approaches to East Point were clogged with vehicles and promenaders; the hotel grounds were "a forest of parasols, veils, shawls, hats, caps and leghorns"; the piazzas were jammed to the railings with guests; every room was taken.

Five hundred had applied for dinner. The Quincy name found seats for the sisters at three in the afternoon. "The tables were laid in two hollow squares, on the piazza was stationed the six musicians, who had come for the ball, playing with all their might, which, joined to the clattering of knives and forks, the jingling of plates, the screaming to the waiters, the shrieking to one another, and the shouts of laughter formed a concatenation of sounds that was almost deafening."

After the bedlam of dinner Margaret and Eliza strolled to the billiard room, found it packed to the walls, and then were lucky or well connected

China merchant Thomas Handasyd Perkins. (Nahant Public Library)

enough to get a room being vacated. They rested, dressed, and descended to the ball that was by now bursting with a fresh contingent from the steamer. After cotillions, Virginia reels, quadrilles and the like, supper was announced and the couples marched in to be squeezed along tables set up in two drawing rooms. Then more dancing and earlyish to bed soon after eleven because, after all, "the gentlemen informed the ladies in general that they should not be able to serenade them, as Mrs. Dexter was sick and of course it would disturb her, so the house was very quiet after 12 o'clock."

That night the overflow of young eligibles from Boston was stretched out on chairs, tables and floors, in carriages and in the stables. A Mr. Moody told Margaret that "he last night 'wished to *hire* some clean straw, every blade of it was engaged,' 'a tolerably clean bench, not one to be had for love nor money.' 'And what did you do at last,' exclaimed I, in vain endeavoring to keep a decent gravity. 'With much difficulty I hired *part* of

The Nahant Hotel. (From History of Lynn by Alonzo Lewis)

one of those horrible hard sofas in the drawing room, *whereon I stretched my limbs,* but as to sleeping, I never closed my eyes all night, and therefore intend returning in the boat as fast as possible.' Mr. Dawes . . . moaned forth, that he 'took up his quarters over the chicken house, and was serenaded by at least a hundred hens, to say nothing of geese, turkeys and ducks.'"

By 1825 a definite Nahant punctilio had developed. One magazine writer reported that the new resort "bears the marks of rapid improvement. The honest old inhabitants are fitting up their houses, and seem to catch the spirit of courtesy and improvement from their neighbors. . . . There is no aristocracy there—every one is on equal terms, in riding, walking, or in the other amusements,—there is no shunning *this* one and cutting *that.* Gentlemen are found in the fishing boats or bowling alleys together, who never saw each other before. Every one according to the *lex loci* is put upon his own good behavior, and the slightest deviation from the manners of a gentleman, is marked with instant contempt, neglect, or expulsion."

THE BOSTON CHURCH

For the first time in eight years the supposed sea serpent was not reported in Massachusetts Bay in 1825, not even by the Perkinses, nor was he "sighted" again for another eight. The initial two summers of his absence were the Nahant Hotel's third and fourth and were not especially successful. *Eagle* had been sold for scrap and *Massachusetts* relieved of the run. Their places were taken by *Patent,* then *Housatonic.* Steamer service was not what it had been. Perhaps the something, finding smaller and rather more jaded audiences on land and sea, had recoiled and departed in a huff. James Homer, a frequenter of Nahant, conceded that "it has been insinuated—with what truth I am unable to say—that the people of Nahant themselves, the hotel keepers, or some wag of an editor for them, often raised the cry of sea-serpent! when, in fact, his majesty was more than a thousand miles off. I plead guilty to a part of the indictment. And all this was done to induce unsuspecting people to flock to Nahant, to see the monster wag his tail and eat mackerel, while they themselves ate chowder and drank old wine."

Another writer cogitated on the coincidence of the apparition with the opening of the Nahant Hotel and the genteel crowds drawn there. "Whether the serpent was emulous of being reckoned in with such company, or was merely summoned as an outside attraction, it is not the purpose here to enquire. No matter what the envious keepers of other establishments and their friends surmised."

Even the gentle poet John Gardiner Calkins Brainard was unable to suppress his suspicions in an ode to the sea serpent:

> But go not to Nahant, lest men should swear
> You are a great deal bigger than you are.

But His Snakeship was merely a passing diversion. Having been made accessible by the Salem Turnpike and the steamers, and fashionable by Colonel Perkins, Nahant assumed a new life of its own. Let East Point and the hotel contain the glamour; the deeper beauties of the peninsula proper were coming into the possession of the Boston friends of Perkins who followed his lead, one after another, in buying up the shore and building secluded cottages above the sea.

Cornelius Coolidge, a speculator, architect and builder of Beacon Hill mansions in Boston, bought enough Breed and Hood land to lay out streets and sixty-two lots, making him the North Shore's first summer real estate developer. After installing the steamship wharf for the Nahant Hotel, he built a small competitor, the Nahant House, and several cottages before the financial panic of 1829 caught him short.

Nahant's early summer houses verged on the austere. They were rarely more than a story and a half, flanked by piazzas whose supporting posts were half-hidden in rose bushes, and linked sociably by footpaths through field and copse. The usual New England clumps of lilacs in the dooryard bloom'd, but not a tree around. From the cottage colony the gloss of civilized Boston was banned. None of the rich and powerful owners was far from the Yankee dirt of his sires, and the annual removal to Nahant was undertaken as an instructive and refreshing reminder to each family of the fact.

The little stone schoolhouse the Bostonians built before any of them owned a foot of Nahant doubled for divine services until 1831, when some of the new summer residents, led by Colonel Perkins, got up a fund to raise a nominally nonsectarian chapel of distinctly Episcopalian cast ("a modest-

*The east end of
Great Nahant.
From* Atlas of
Essex County,
Massachusetts,
Boston 1884.

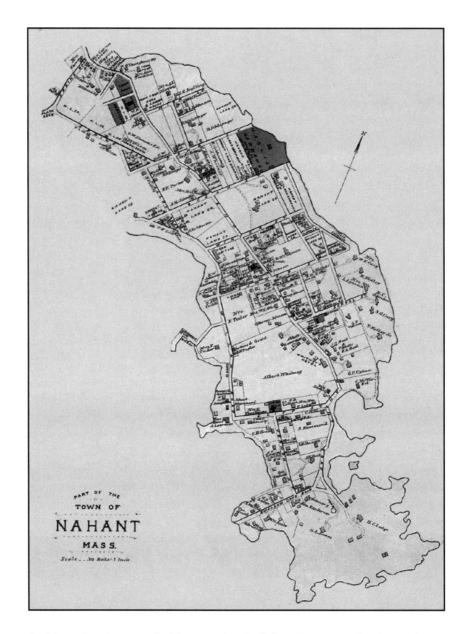

PART OF THE
TOWN OF
NAHANT
MASS.
Scale.. 30 Rods=1 Inch

looking, Grecian temple-like wooden building," wrote a foreign visitor),
ever after known as the Boston Church. With their neighbors, who endowed
it with a bell, they made a fair sampling of the men who were moving New
England commerce, shaking Massachusetts politics and shaping Boston's
cultural influence from their counting rooms and studies in the city, and
from their piazzas by the sea.

There was jovial Abbott Lawrence of infinite energy and shrewdness,
partner with his ailing brother Amos (a Nahant-lover, too) in the firm of
A. & A. Lawrence, the greatest textile manufacturers in America. Abbott
gave the family name to the city he created around his mills. So to Lowell
did the Lowells, represented among the churchly subscribers by John Amory

Lowell, first trustee of the Lowell Institute and grandfather of the cigar-smoking poetess Amy and her brother, A. Lawrence Lowell, Harvard's bricks-and-mortar president.

There was William Appleton, merchant-shipowner who had come down to Boston from New Hampshire "with a small bundle in his hand and a few cents in his pocket," as he liked to recall. William was a cousin of Nathan and Samuel Appleton, mill owners in league with the Lawrences and Lowells; he regarded the Nahant air as a tonic for the chronic dyspepsia to which his daguerreotype bears witness.

Peter Chardon Brooks, penniless apprentice in Boston at fourteen, retired on a fortune in insurance at thirty-six, was another; late in life he tried some very modest yachting, gave it up as an expensive waste of time, and died the richest man in New England. And David Sears, merchant-philanthropist with a cottage on Swallow's Cave Road, a striking, curved business block on Cornhill in Boston called Sears Crescent, and a granite mansion on Beacon Street, now the Somerset Club. And Thomas G. Cary, a Perkins son-in-law and partner. And an Amory and a Codman and a Russell, Boston names to be reckoned with.

There was Dr. Edward H. Robbins, who graduated from Harvard Medical School only to change course for the wool business. Coolidge built him a cottage near Sears. After two lean seasons the proprietors put the Nahant Hotel on the block in 1827, and Robbins, with Perkins as his silent partner, picked it up for less than twelve thousand dollars.

There were the aristocratic Eliot brothers, William H. and Samuel A. The former had a cottage on Vernon Street. His business association with Colonel Perkins in the Nahant Hotel inspired him to promote a landmark in hotel development, the Tremont House in Boston, which opened in 1829. Charles Dickens stayed there in 1842 and reported that it had "more galleries, colonnades, piazzas, and passages than I can remember, or the reader would believe." William Eliot died soon after pledging to the chapel. Samuel built above Bass Beach. He was in the prime of a life of useful public service in politics, music and education, to which his most useful contribution was a son, Charles William Eliot, whose boyhood ABC's, absorbed within the stone schoolhouse (when he might have been down on the beach), paid off in Harvard University's most imperial presidency.

Another subscriber in the Perkins circle was Jonathan Phillips, son of William Phillips, the lieutenant governor around whose legacy the Massachusetts General Hospital was founded. Jonathan was president of the New England Asylum for the Blind when the Colonel decided to follow the example of his late brother, James Perkins, in giving his Pearl Street mansion to the Boston Athenaeum, and presented his own neighboring one to the asylum, provided it raise fifty thousand dollars in endowment. It did so under the leadership of Judge William Prescott and took its benefactor's name as the Perkins Institution for the Blind when it outgrew his home.

Judge Prescott was a subscriber too. He built on Swallow's Cave Road when he retired from the bench in 1828 and shared his cottage with his son,

William Hickling Prescott, already a historian of note. The judge's father, Colonel William Prescott, had commanded the patriots at Breed's (not Bunker, where tradition has misplaced the battle) Hill; his son, through a whimsy of Cupid, had married Susan Amory, granddaughter of the Captain John Linzee whose British sloop of war *Falcon* poured a merciless fire on Prescott's men that hot June day of 1775. The tall, handsome, gracious scholar had been nearly blind since his Harvard days, when he lost the sight of one eye and suffered impairment of the other during a student fracas; he wrote prolifically in a darkened room, relying on secretaries and the illumination of a prodigious memory. The younger Prescott preferred the family homestead at Pepperell ("an acre of grass and old trees is worth a wilderness of ocean"), but summered at Nahant as much out of loyalty to his aged parents, with whom he had always lived, as from love of the place, of which he wrote: "The house stands on a bold cliff overlooking the ocean,—so near that in a storm the spray is thrown over the piazza,—and as it stands on the extreme point of the peninsula, it is many miles out to sea. . . . It is not a bad place—this sea-girt citadel—for reverie and writing, with the music of the winds and water incessantly beating on the rocks and broad beaches below."

Among all the merchant princes on Nahant that summer of the Boston Church, one was monarch, the "Ice King." Frederic Tudor, furiously ambitious, ruthless, creative and, if necessary, charming, was the only one of the four sons of Judge William Tudor not to attend Harvard, and he never got over it. In 1805, when he was twenty-two, he and brother William were seized with the extraordinary notion that they could ship New England ice to southern climes and sell it at huge profits to the native innocents, who had never seen water in such form before. The brothers cut a shipload of blocks from the pond on the family's country place in Saugus, bought a brig, and loaded it for Martinique; Frederic sailed as supercargo to restrain the liquidation of their assets (and to escape the jeers of his friends).

William went his own way, dabbled in business with Colonel Perkins and wound up a man of letters. Fred went it alone, went broke, went to jail for debt, went back to the ponds for more ice and bore with him the motto he adopted when he began to climb: "He who gives back at the first repulse, without striking a second blow, despairs of success, has not been, is not, and never will be a hero in love, war or business." Overcoming a mountain of obstacles, inventing a technology of refrigeration, even designing vessels, Tudor by 1821 had the ice market cornered in Havana and Charleston and in 1833 shipped his first cargo to cool the drinks of the English colonials in Calcutta . . . just in time, as Samuel Eliot Morison has pointed out, to save Boston's East India trade from collapse. The Ice King was a legend before he was fifty.

The Tudors sold their home, "Rockwood," to Saugus for its poor farm in 1822, and Fred's mother, Mrs. Delia Tudor, built a stone cottage at Nahant above Stony Beach, a quarter of a mile west of the Perkins place. Her son bought it from her in 1824 and was off on the avocation that, like everything else he tackled, would grow into an obsession. It would also change forever the face of Nahant.

The Ice King made Euphemia Fenno his queen in 1834. Having shown how to cool drinks in Canton, he launched warmly, at fifty, into the project of fathering six young Tudors. And having entered the age of domesticity, he proposed to demonstrate that what Lynn's historian Alonzo Lewis dismissed as "the barren waste" of Nahant created by the axes of the settlers, now "covered by short, brown grass and tenanted by grasshoppers and snakes" (and the cottages of a small colony of ascetic Bostonians), could be induced to bloom.

Tudor set about buying every piece of land he could get his hands on below his stone cottage on the west side of Great Nahant, including the Great Swamp, which he drained and made largely arable. Colonel Perkins had planted and persuaded a row of elms to survive along the road to the village. The King did him one better: beside the numerous roads he built, and everywhere else his neighbors would let him, he planted balm of Gileads, hoping these brittle poplars would rapidly grow into windbreaks for the slower shade trees, the elms and maples with which he reforested Nahant. It worked, and for the first time in two centuries the windswept peninsula had shade. As for the balm of Gileads, Caroline Curtis in her *Memories of Fifty Years* complained of their "filling the air and covering the ground with fluff. I do not suppose that they committed suicide at his death, but they certainly disappeared."

The Ice King adapted his plan of windbreaks to shelter his orchards of apple, cherry, pear, peach and plum trees with towering fences of vertical slats on rails secured to posts as thick as telegraph poles and as high as thirty

A Civil War-era game of croquet at the Nahant cottage built by Dr. Edward H. Robbins in the late 1820s. (Nahant Historical Society)

Frederic Tudor, the Ice King, who bought every available piece of land on the west side of Great Nahant. (Nahant Historical Society)

feet. His south garden of fruit trees across Nahant Road from his cottage was popularly known as the Brick Garden from the tall slat fence he erected around it, veneered with a basket-weave pattern of bricks. He tried to grow tobacco and some other alien plants without much success, although he refused to employ a professional gardener. He thought insects a great nuisance and hung three hundred bottles of sugar water in his trees, congratulating himself that in a few hours one June, 108,000 (count 'em) flies, bugs and moths were enticed to their sweet sorrow.

Mr. Tudor was "a striking personality with his aquiline face and silver hair," in the childish eyes of another Perkins granddaughter, Emma Cary. The old gentleman with the frigid gaze, in his brass-buttoned blue frock coat, had his eccentricities, cultivated or not, and they were not especially appreciated in the neighboring Perkins-Cary compound. "To arrange a boundary line with Mr. Tudor," Caroline Curtis wrote tartly, "was to expend all you had of time and patience and good sense and good manners—and at the end he got the better by sheer persistence"—which reminded her of his "great gray bull, which was the terror of old and young Nahant, and therefore very dear to his owner, because he had the added pleasure of thinking all the rest of us fools for our fears." Another lady who seems to have run afoul of King Tudor described a sort of moat that he had his men dig so that the sweep of his lawns would remain unmarred by any visible barrier . . . his "Ha! Ha! fence," he called it.

Nahant's historian Fred Wilson had his favorite Tudor story, too, telling how the old man went about hiring a carpenter by first instructing the applicant to shingle the roof of a small shed. "He made the unusual stipulation that the shingles were to be laid upside down, butts up, beginning at the ridgepole. Several job hunters refused to do so foolish a thing, until finally one said 'twas nonsense but he would do it. Next day Tudor found the job done in a workmanlike manner, though wholly useless, and ordered the man to rip the shingles off and put them right, saying he only wanted to be sure he got a man who would obey his instructions."

One more pillar and we are done with the Boston Church. Benjamin Cutler Clark, a rugged, jut-jawed young capitalist, owned a fleet of topsail schooners and clipper brigs in the West Indies and Mediterranean coffee, fruit and wine trades, yet small boats were his passion. This joy in the thrill of a lively tiller, a taut sheet, a galloping hull, a spanking breeze and a wet tail was shared by many of his peers on State Street and his neighbors at Nahant, who had learned the ropes of their businesses from the quarterdecks, and not infrequently forecastles, of their own or their families' vessels on voyages to Canton and Gibraltar. Nahant appealed to Clark as a summer anchorage for small yachts, and when he was thirty-two, in 1832, he built a cottage on the brow of the forty-foot bluff of Bass Rock at the west end of Joe's Beach and dropped a mooring where he could keep an eye on a succession of smart little schooners swinging with the tide and the breeze in the cove below.

Ben Clark was a founder of organized yachting in Massachusetts Bay, and so loved the helm that by keeping fresh horses at Boston, at a stop on the Salem Turnpike and at Nahant, he could reach his landing in an hour in his light sulky. How he thrilled to a patch of canvas, or a cloud of it! In his later years, after the invention of wet-plate photography, he would direct the masters of his clippers when outward bound from Boston to stand in by Clark's Point with every sail flying and have their pictures taken.

Thomas Gold Appleton of the summering Appletons, the sharpest wit of his day, regarded with amusement his neighbors from the city (and himself), congratulating themselves on the simple superiority of life in their simple cottages on Nahant's superior shore, and impaled them collectively on his spit as "Cold Roast Boston." The sobriquet has stuck, but precisely what, one may ask, does it mean? *Cold roast* is slang, long out of fashion, for "something insignificant, nothing to the purpose." So time has left the point but dulled the barb . . . which would probably have relieved Tom Appleton, had he reflected on it, for no one loved Nahant more than he.

LONGFELLOW, HOLMES AND FRIENDS

One day two strangers mistook the cottage of William Hickling Prescott, which perched on a cliff a short stroll from the steamboat wharf and the hotel, for an inn and mounted the piazza, demanding sustenance. The historian's mother graciously obliged. They took their ease, took in the ocean view and an excellent lunch, and when they pushed back their chairs and prepared to pay up were advised crisply by their hostess, "This is Judge Prescott's house and you are entirely welcome to any refreshment it has given you." The judge's almost blind son was so imposed upon by idle lionizers, he wrote, that "I have lost a clear month here by company. . . . Yet how can I escape it, tied like a bear to a stake here? I will devise some way another year, or Nahant shall be 'Nae haunt of mine.'" Some other way he did devise, finally, and in 1853 forsook "Th' Haunt," as the domestic servants called the colony, and its blinding sea glare for a house on the beach at Lynn, where he spent the remaining six summers of his life.

The year previous to Prescott's desertion was marked by the permanent departures of a faded old "Haunter," Daniel Webster, and a brilliant new arrival, the sculptor Horatio Greenough, an early protégé of Colonel Perkins. Greenough was building the cellar walls of his cottage, where the library stands today, when he died suddenly at the age of forty-seven. Webster, on the other hand, had been visiting James W. Paige (a relative whose estate was across the road from Greenough's property) for years, though the Great Man's first loyalty, it must be conceded, was to Marshfield on the South Shore, where he had bought a Tory homestead and turned "a sterile waste of sandy hills to a charming landscape of fertility and beauty."

Webster was the political voice of the summering Lawrences and Lowells and their financial interests, a voice that echoed sonorously if briefly from the aristocratic throat of another summer Nahanter, Robert C. Winthrop, his former law clerk named to Webster's seat when he resigned from the Senate in 1850. Charles Sumner, the ramrod abolitionist who defeated Winthrop in his first run on his own in 1851, was a frequent Nahant visitor in later years. The whole town was invited to the reception Paige gave for Webster after he lost the Whig presidential nomination earlier in 1852. Just before the end, ravaged by drink, the most famous man in America made one last visit to the resort.

The departure of Prescott, literary conquistador of Mexico and Peru, left John Lothrop Motley as Nahant's historian-in-residence. Here he had summered since he learned to read in the stone schoolhouse. Tom Appleton and Wendell Phillips were his boyhood chums in Boston, where Wendell tested his oratory and the three of them shouted poetry and strutted about in finery they found in attic trunks under the eaves of Mot's family home on Beacon Hill. "Cassandra in masculine shape of our long prosperous Ilium," said Dr. Holmes of the terribly handsome abolitionist, twitting affectionately his patrician cousin's "melodious prophecies." In 1840 the Phillips family (Wendell's father, John, was Boston's first mayor) bought the old

Johnson House, archetype of the North Shore summer hotel, and made it their manor, and the west shore of Bass Point, looking across the water to the Point of Pines, their fiefdom. "Old Castle" was torn down in 1903, ending the fears and hopes of a couple of generations of Nahant youngsters that it was haunted by the ghosts of long-gone revelers.

Motley cut as fine a figure as Phillips and took himself less seriously. A sociable scholar, he was frequently tagged for diplomatic missions in Europe and never lacked for invitations to revisit Nahant, sometimes at the cottage of his brother, Edward, near Dashing Rock. While boarding with Mrs. Hood he wrote portions of *The Rise of the Dutch Republic,* a labor from which distractions were not always unwelcome, as he confessed to George Curtis. "After breakfast at Nahant I feel like Coeur de Lion, and burn to give battle to the Saracens. But the brave impulse ends in smoke, and musing and chatting, and building castles in the clouds, you loiter away the day upon the piazza, ending by climbing about the cliffs at sunset or galloping over the beach."

No beach-galloper, Henry Wadsworth Longfellow surrendered sedately

Henry Wadsworth Longfellow with his second wife, Frances Appleton Longfellow, and their two sons, about 1849. (Nahant Historical Society)

to Nahant's Norse beguilements about the time he took Frances Elizabeth Appleton for his second wife, in 1843. He was thirty-six, and she was a sister of Thomas Gold Appleton. After a few years the brothers-in-law built and shared a cottage above Curlew (inevitably renamed Longfellow) Beach. When Captain Arthur Clark, Ben Clark's son renowned in the clipper trade, demonstrated the ocean racing potential of Yankee yachts by sailing Appleton's forty-eight-foot sloop *Alice* from Nahant to the Isle of Wight in nineteen days in 1866, the owner's nephew, Charles A. Longfellow, was a crew member. One summer day when he was a greener hand, young Charlie sailed a small boat across the bay to Lynn to visit his Uncle Tom's brother, Nathan Appleton, but capsized, and was soaking when he arrived. Nathan loaned him a pair of slippers to wear home and next day received from Nahant a parcel on which was written in the poet's hand:

> *Slippers that perhaps another,*
> *Sailing o'er the bay of Lynn,*
> *Forlorn or shipwrecked nephew*
> *Seeing, may purloin again.*

No one relished a glass of claret with Tom Appleton any more than Oliver Wendell Holmes, Sr. The peppery little anatomist and poet had not yet in the 1850s abandoned his country place in Pittsfield for Beverly Farms ("if you would be happy in Berkshire, you must carry mountains in your brain; and if you would enjoy Nahant, you must have an ocean in your soul"); but as the uncommon denominator of the Boston literati, he knew everybody at Nahant and everybody knew him. Dr. Holmes wrote Motley of encountering a barouche one day in Boston "and out jumped Tom Appleton in the flesh, and plenty of it, as aforetime. We embraced—or rather he embraced me and I partially spanned his goodly circumference." Of Appleton's talk, it was "witty, entertaining, audacious, ingenious, sometimes extravagant, but fringed always with pleasing fancies as deep as the border of a Queen's cashmere. . . . I never heard such a fusillade in my life"—praise indeed from Boston's marathon monologist.

Longfellow entertained and walked the beach with Emerson and Whittier, and was entertained by the Ice King and his odd friend, Dr. R. V. Piper, and their talk of planting Iceland with trees, as Tudor had Nahant, thereby turning the frozen waste into one vast wheat field. Piper cut a comical figure in his green sash as surgeon of the Nahant Home Guards during the Civil War—the "Piper Guards"—and thought the Rebs had landed when some jokers dragged a cannon up behind his cottage and fired it off.

In the course of preparing a panegyric on the home life of Longfellow, Blanche Roosevelt Tucker-Macchetta visited the Longfellow-Appleton ménage when her hosts were advanced in age. She found a spacious Italianate cottage girt by a simple garden of roses and sweetbrier. The family assembled for breakfast in the airy dining room at the back which looked out over the porticoed terrace and the sea. On the wall were "some curious painted pebbles, framed in a background of velvet . . . faithful pic-

tures of the surrounding scenery" by Appleton, who sometimes with his daughters (Edith was Mrs. Richard Henry Dana, Jr.) sat across the table from the bard, all in wicker chairs. Longfellow was a light eater, declaring that "most people have a famous appetite at the seashore, but I never had. I think the very sight and sound of it constitute sufficient nourishment." After he had finished, "a general sally takes place through the French window, and the broad balcony is soon peopled with animated faces . . . he sits at a round table drawn up near the edge of the terrace, with a light mantle thrown across his shoulders to protect him from the sea-breeze, which is always strong and brisk at Nahant." Later he took Blanche for a ride around the resort in his open victoria behind his coachman and ebony black horses.

Longfellow was an intimate friend of his Cambridge neighbor, Professor Cornelius Felton. The robust Greek scholar had married Mary Louisa Cary in 1846, the year of the arrival at Harvard of Jean Louis Rodolphe Agassiz. The Swiss naturalist was thirty-nine, his reputation as a zoologist established, his glacial theory more than glacially advanced, and he came to America with all his manic magnetism to explore a new world "where Nature was rich, but tools and workmen few and traditions none." Agassiz and Felton hit it off from the start. Mrs. Agassiz had remained in Europe, too ill to accompany her husband, and died in 1848. Louis in the meanwhile was introduced to Felton's sister-in-law, Elizabeth Cary, and to the Nahant beloved by their circle. In 1850 the widower and Elizabeth were married.

Nahanters both, Jean Louis Rodolphe Agassiz was a legendary Swiss naturalist, while his wife, Elizabeth Cary Agassiz, helped found Radcliffe College. (Nahant Historical Society)

Four years later the sisters' venerable grandfather, Thomas Handasyd Perkins, the founder of the Nahant summer colony, died at the age of eighty-nine, spurning all entreaties that he take to his bed: "Certainly not. I have always proposed to die dressed and sitting in my chair." And so, they say, he did. His stone cottage near Spouting Horn went to his daughter Mary and her husband, Thomas G. Cary; they moved a foursquare house, the "Butter Box," onto the family land above the bluffs and turned it over to their daughters and their learned husbands.

Almost surrounded and deeply eroded by the ocean, Nahant was an ideal natural laboratory for Louis Agassiz's studies of geology (in 1851 he discovered fossils in the slate and limestone by which the strata were proved years afterward to be Lower Cambrian) and marine zoology. A small lab was tacked onto the "Butter Box" for him, so near the ocean that he had a constant supply of salt water for his aquarium and a cornucopia of specimens from the local fishermen, who brought him their exotic catches. "It is said the finny tenants of the sea already know the philosopher, who has done so much to sound their fame all over the world," Professor Felton joshed. "They surrender themselves cheerfully without hook or bait, bob or sinker, for the good of science, into his hands. . . . All the odd fish, star fishes, sea urchins, shovel sharks and the like find the way to the workshop of Agassiz, but none of them get back again. Perhaps they chose to remain; perhaps they prefer their lot; for they are forthwith thrown into bottles or casks and continue in liquor the rest of their days."

The great Agassiz would hole up for hours in this seashore laboratory; yet, as Emma Cary remarked, "he could come out of this state of absorption and join in the merriment of the young people like a boy free from care and responsibility." The gentle scientist radiated warmth, and but for the season of his residence, it equally could have been said of the "Butter Box" that "one has less need of an overcoat in passing Agassiz's house than by any other in Cambridge." Dr. Holmes regarded Elizabeth Agassiz "so wonderfully fitted to be his wife that it seems as if he could not have bettered his choice if all womankind had passed before him." As a measure of her devotion to the compulsive collector, she was dressing one morning while they were traveling and discovered a small snake in her shoe. "What, only one?" cried her husband. "Where is the other six?"

Cornelius Felton, too, loved the company of family and friends at Nahant, but like Agassiz he must have time for study and contemplation. The classicist was most content lolling upon the brink of the cliff, where he could watch the sails crossing the horizon and "the play of purple, blue, green, and the flash of the foaming waves as they break along the rocks; the march of the clouds across the sky, and now and then a fog-bank slowly and majestically sweeping landward and hiding all behind it like a solid wall." In the consummation of his career Felton was appointed president of Harvard in 1860, but he was in poor health and died in 1862. Louis Agassiz died in 1873. His widow then helped found Radcliffe College and presided over it from 1894 to 1902.

On September 12, 1861, five months to the day after the bombardment of Fort Sumter and the onset of the Civil War, the Nahant Hotel caught fire ("as empty mortgaged buildings sometimes do," in the skeptical words of Henry Cabot Lodge, who inherited the real estate on which it had stood since Colonel Perkins put it there) "and after making a most magnificent blaze for the benefit of onlookers along miles of coast, was burned to the ground."

That was the utter end of the hotel period at Nahant. Along the rest of the North Shore the breezy days of piazzas measured by the mile were in the offing, over a dark horizon, somewhere beyond the approaching firestorm of war. The storm descended, and in the midst of it one of the summer people returned and reflected as if in a dream: "Nahant is very solitary and deserted this year. I stood looking down at the steamboat landing opposite—not a fishing boat, not a human being in sight; then the ghostly little steamer comes in, and the phantoms go over the hill towards the ruins of the burned hotel, and all is still and lonely again."

*The Eastern had linked Boston through the North Shore to Maine by 1842,
thoroughly sooting its passengers through the open windows of summertime.
An iron monster indeed. (Peabody Essex Museum, F. B. C. Bradlee collection)*

~2~
ENTER THE
IRON MONSTER

*Outrunning the stagecoach, the railroad roars
through Salem and helps colonize Swampscott*

Never one to be left standing
at the station, Colonel Perkins in 1826 had bankrolled the first railroad in
America, the Granite Railway Company, to horse-haul the stones for the
Bunker Hill Monument from his Quincy quarry over rails of wood to the
Neponset River, whence they were sailed to Charlestown. In four more
years he was promoting a steam road between Boston and the textile mills
of Lowell, in which he held a large stake. By then the rail age was hissing
down the track.

So it is no great surprise to find the builder of the country's first seaside
resort hotel at Nahant, as a stop on New England's first steamship line, asking the Massachusetts General Court in 1832 to charter the first train service in Essex County, between Boston and Salem. But the five hundred
horses of the Eastern Stage Company were pulling seventy-seven thousand
passengers a year over that route alone. Its stock was at double par and
nowhere higher than under the golden dome of the State House, where the
sympathetic legislators stopped the incursion of the "Iron Monster" into the
stagecoach's territory in its tracks.

This transient triumph of oats over steam evaporated with the opening
of three different railroads out of Boston in 1835. When a group headed by
the Danvers-born financier George Peabody proposed that year to lay a
fourth line of tracks through Salem to Newburyport, the General Court
approved the line; thus the Eastern Stage gave way to the Eastern Railroad
Company the following spring. Rail passengers were shuttled by steam ferry
from Boston's Lewis Wharf to East Boston. From there, tracks coursed
north in a nearly straight line over the expanse of salt marsh behind great
Chelsea Beach, over the Saugus River, through the heart of Lynn and the
west of Swampscott, and on to Salem. Gangs of Irish laborers dug and piled
the bed and laid rails "chaired" high above the ground to prevent their
blockage by snow.

Disgorging clouds of smoke and showers of sparks from its wood fire,
the Eastern's inaugural train clattered and jerked with high fanfare into the
Salem depot on August 27, 1838. Although they were the first to boast

ladies' and toilet rooms, the twenty-four passenger cars were so loosely chained together that anyone standing up when they started and stopped was thrown to the floor. Time from Boston's Lewis Wharf to Salem, including the obligatory ferry ride across the harbor, was thirty-five minutes. The fare was fifty cents, half that charged by the stage company. Six trains a day. Before most departures from Salem, Corporal Joshua Pitman, a one-legged local character who claimed to be a Revolutionary War veteran, clanged the bell in the station's belfry.

The corporal's bell tolled for the stagecoach. Already the Boston and Lowell railroad had penetrated to Haverhill, and now the Iron Monster threaded its way through Essex County, "enfolding in his fatal coils," as Salem historian Robert S. Rantoul put the matter, "the poor struggling Stage Companies whose nightly dreams were disturbed by the scream of the whistle." Eastern Stage dashed into runaway bankruptcy on June 26, 1838, two months before the railroad had even got up a full head of steam.

Pushing on through Salem, Irish laborers dug a huge trench along Washington Street and laid up a granite arch inside, 718 feet long, which they covered with earth for a tunnel. Past the city, the tracks bridged Beverly Harbor, traversed the meadows and glens of Beverly, Wenham and Hamilton, reached Ipswich at the end of 1839, then Newburyport in the summer of 1840, and Portsmouth, New Hampshire, on New Year's Eve, linking in 1842 with the Portland, Saco and Portsmouth Railroad, which became the Boston and Maine in 1843. Meanwhile, with their prospering fisheries and nascent shoe factories, Marbleheaders subscribed enough Eastern shares to finance their own branch from Salem, which opened on December 10, 1839.

There were the dissenters like the mossback who groused about the giant that had "laid a hand of iron upon the bosom of Essex County." But not Salem's Robert S. Rantoul, who rejoiced that "if Boston is the Hub, the Railroads seen from the State House dome are the living spokes, which bind it to an outer circle of social and business relations. If these have carried off our men of enterprise in search of a larger market, they have brought back the wealth they accumulate, to beautify our estates and elevate our culture, and make of Massachusetts Bay, from Plymouth to Cape Ann, one great suburb in which the arts of cultivated life are brought to aid the native charms of country living."

ESCAPING A VERY BAD SMELL

The railroad penetrated the North Shore just as the charms of country living were looking increasingly attractive to Bostonians of means. Again, Thomas Handasyd Perkins was behind it. Back in 1814 he had led a move in the General Court to build a milldam westward across the middle of the Back Bay (the mucky Charles River tidal basin directly west of Boston proper) as a source of waterpower for factories that would presumably spring up in response. His intention was not to drive his wealthy friends to the beds and bars of his Nahant Hotel, for that had not yet taken shape in his mind; yet the fruition of the project provided the push for the railroad's pull that populated the resorts of the North Shore.

The colonel did not carry all with him on this one. As a clairvoyant reader wrote in the *Boston Daily Advertiser*, "What think you of converting the beautiful sheet of water which skirts the Common into an empty mudbasin, reeking with filth, abhorrent to the smell, and disgusting to the eye? By every god of sea, lake, or fountain, it is incredible." All the same, the Milldam was completed in 1821.

Hardly a hope of its backers, and all the fears of its foes, materialized. Built across the flats as an extension of Beacon Street, the Milldam failed to provide significant waterpower, and although it gave the city another land access as an alternative to Boston Neck, it shut off most of the cleansing tidal circulation of the Charles River and created a stinking swamp. This sorry state coincided with the influx of European immigrants into the area and the gradual displacement of the Boston establishment, which escaped westward down the only route it trusted, Beacon Street, which now led straight through the muck.

By 1849 the Board of Health was condemning the Back Bay as a "nuisance, offensive and injurious to the large and increasing population residing upon it." To Justin Winsor it was in "an abominably filthy state . . . an open cesspool, receiving the sewage of a large community." Public pressure (and the dreams of speculators) forced the issue; the state intervened, and the famous filling that turned the melancholy miasma into Commonwealth

The Back Bay photographed from the dome of the State House in 1857. The Milldam, later an extension of Beacon Street, separates the miasma from the Charles River. (Boston Public Library, Print Department)

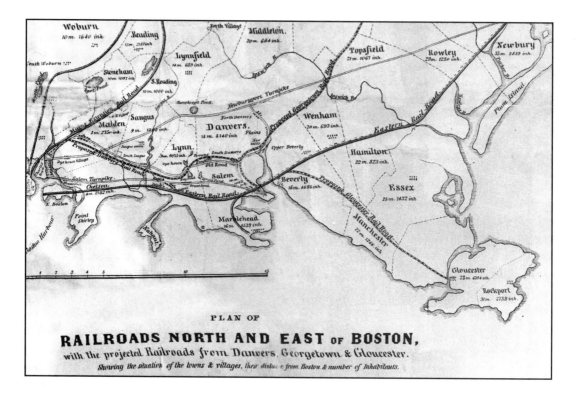

PLAN OF
RAILROADS NORTH AND EAST OF BOSTON,
with the projected Railroads from Danvers, Georgetown & Gloucester.
Showing the situation of the towns & villages, their distance from Boston & number of Inhabitants.

Alonzo Lewis's map of about 1845 shows the Eastern Railroad line when it still connected with Boston by ferry, as well as the proposed Gloucester and Georgetown branches. (Peabody Essex Museum)

Avenue, Copley Square, and the Fens began in 1858 and continued for several years, the building upon it for many more.

Until it was completed, the southwest air of summer, hot as blazes, drifted torpidly over the flats before assailing the nostrils of Beacon Street, where residents had been escaping to the North Shore in such numbers that Cold Roast Boston's capacity to contain them had long since been exhausted. The first to grasp the railroad's potential for opening up the frontier of the North Shore mainland to summer colonizing on a scale that would leave Nahant behind was not a Beacon Streeter, but the proprietor of a well-known restaurant in Theatre Alley (now Devonshire Street), William Fenno.

THE SWAMPSCOTT SHORE

Eastern Railroad's petition was before the legislature in the summer of 1835 when Fenno and a friend went fishing one day in a boat off the shore of Swampscott, then a mere borough of the city of Lynn. As they passed Phillips Point, the northern headland of Nahant Bay, the restaurateur remarked that it would make a fine location for a summer resort. On September 14 he bought nineteen acres of the point known as New Cove from the heirs of Walter Phillips for sixteen hundred dollars; on a rise commanding the Atlantic he built the Ocean House, the first summer hotel on the mainland of the North Shore.

The infrequent summer visitor had been lodging in Lynn's picturesque fishing and farming village of Swampscott since 1777, when William Allen sojourned above Phillips Beach; there were only five houses in the center then. Farmer Jonathan Phillips put up his first guest at Phillips Point in 1815, and in 1830, west a mile at Blaney's Beach, Mrs. Jonathan Blaney took in a Medford family who grumbled at paying her three dollars a week and having to wait on themselves. James L. Homer boarded at Phillips Beach in his youth. "The old lady who made the chowders and fried the fish," he wrote, "will ever live in my memory, for I remember that she wore spectacles, that she was an excellent cook, that her tumblers and wine-glasses were always wiped with a clean napkin, and that it delighted her to see a visitor enjoy a good cigar."

William Fenno and the Eastern Railroad put Swampscott on the summer map. He ran his Ocean House for two years, then leased it out and built a second hotel nearby, Fenno Cottage. After wining and dining old friends their host would invite them down on the beach if it happened to be low tide. At a certain spot he would clear away the sand and gravel, revealing a hidden spring into which he would empty a flagon of Hennessey's best brandy "and bid them drink it before it became diluted, and they generally effectually did it."

An early Ocean House guest, Philo S. Shelton of Boston, bought land on Whale Beach bordering Phillips Point on the west and built probably the first summer cottage on the North Shore mainland inside of Nahant. Other pioneer summer residents of the North Shore "off Nahant" were Benjamin Tyler Reed, financial angel of the Episcopal Theological School in Cambridge, and Enoch Redington Mudge. Reed put up his cottage on Ocean Street (now Puritan Road) above Blaney's Beach on land he bought in 1842 from Joseph Ingalls, who was haying when the philanthropist approached him:

"Good afternoon, sir. Is this your land?"

"Yes, sir."

"Will you sell it?"

"Yes."

"I will give you four hundred dollars per acre for it."

The owner threw down his rake in astonishment. "Do you mean it?"

"Yes, sir." And Farmer Ingalls straightway hustled off to a lawyer to have the deed drawn for fear that the crazy man from the city would change his mind.

The scenario would change but the dialogue would oft be repeated up and down the rural North Shore over the next decades. A mere forty years later Reed's land was worth eight thousand dollars an acre.

Enoch Redington Mudge possessed flowing side-whiskers and features as stalwart as his name. In 1843, at age thirty-one, he bought the 130-acre Burrill estate above King's Beach for eight thousand dollars and built a Gothic stone summer cottage on the upland. He brought with him the four members of the slave family he had owned since 1840 and freed them. Mudge wintered in New York and then Boston, after taking up the textile business in 1845. With its tree-lined drives, fountains, and Paradise Road (which Mudge cut through his forest for public use), "Elmwood" was an early North Shore showplace long before its owner died in 1881.

On the heels of Reed and Mudge, the Bates and Curtis families settled Fishing Point and the adjacent Cedar Cliffs for the summer. Addison Child got hold of a tract at Beach Bluff at the east end of Phillips Beach and catalyzed a cottage development around the old Jacob Phillips farmhouse, which he enlarged into an estate and leased to Chickering, the piano manufacturer. On Phillips Point Dr. G. H. Lodge acquired "John's Field" from the heirs of Farmer Phillips in 1847 and made a summer estate of it, while the same year his neighbor, James L. Little, Boston dry goods importer, bought up the northeast head of the Point and built "Blythewood," the nucleus of a family compound of summer mansions he raised as he enlarged his holdings—"Greenhill," "Grasshead," "Shingleside," "The Cottage," "Beach End," and "Brier Gate"—until, at last, his end of it had to be known as Little's Point. Most families left their best carriages at their winter homes lest the salt air tarnish them.

The railroad was raising not only Swampscott's land values but its consciousness as well, all reinforced by the mass descent on September 6, 1844, of twenty-five thousand Massachusetts Democrats, who assembled at the depot in Lynn and marched to Clambake Hill. It was the year of James K. Polk's successful Democratic campaign for the Presidency against the pride of the Whigs, Henry Clay.

A mile of marchers and bands and banners were led by a platoon of Swampscott fishermen in red shirts and sou'westers. Up on the hill overlooking the ocean, seven pits awaited the faithful, each ten feet across and hot enough to roast a dozen Whigs; in the absence of the enemy, 170 barrels of clams and a thousand lobsters were tossed in for starters. In the eye of the maelstrom stood a stage in the guise of a rural temple, garlanded with wreaths and flowers and dedicated to the Genius of Democracy. Order was called at one o'clock. Robert Rantoul shouted out an oration, followed by numerous high-spirited toasts. Pretty heady stuff for the "droll, queer place" described by one visitor at about this time.

Swampscott's transformation was hastened by the ambitions of its parent, Lynn, which in 1850 declared itself a city. Swampscott by then was a coming resort of the affluent and the influential, resented relegation to mere ward status and proclaimed itself a separate town in 1852. Independence called for another parade, more oratory, and an encore of fireworks which all encouraged Nahant to go and do likewise the next year.

These defections stripped Lynn of three quarters of its finest coastline and of any significant future as a watering place. But Lynn had always been stodgy. One July afternoon in 1851 a bevy of young ladies from Boston romped off the train in bloomers, just then all the rage, prompting local historian Alonzo Lewis to comment that they created "considerable observation if not admiration by their short tunics, full trousers, bright sashes and jaunty hats. Quite a number of the young ladies of Lynn arrayed themselves

in the new style, but such a strong prejudice against the innovation began to manifest itself, that they soon laid aside the unappreciated garments."

Nor would Lynn lift a finger to encourage the nearest to godliness of all the attractions of the shore. "There are many people in Lynn," chided its impatient historian, "who never washed themselves all over in their lives, and who would as soon think of taking a journey through the air in a balloon, as of going under water. . . . Some of these water haters a few years since made a law that boys should not bathe in sight of any house; yet they have furnished no bathing houses; and there are no secluded places, excepting where the lives of children would be endangered. . . . Perhaps nothing is more conducive to health than sea bathing."

Swampscott was as tolerant as Lynn was tight-lipped. One Bostonian in 1846 rejoiced that ladies from the city enjoy a sea bath at Swampscott Beach "in just such costumes as they please, in elaborate costumes or in old cast-off dresses, without fear of talk."

Enoch Redington Mudge's "Elmwood" in Swampscott was an early North Shore showplace. (From History of Lynn *by Alonzo Lewis.)*

The cottage of Richard Henry Dana, Sr., Manchester's first summer resident, presides comfortably on the crest of Graves Beach, about 1850. From Houses of American Authors *by L. V. Hunt.*
(Courtesy of Gordon Abbott, Jr.)

~3~
BEVERLY AND MANCHESTER ARE ALL BUT SUBDUED

"Let him throw away his money if he wants to!"

WITH EVERYBODY COMPLAINING about the terrible service on the steam ferry that shuttled North Shore–bound passengers across Boston Harbor between the city's Lewis Wharf and the Eastern Railroad's terminal at East Boston, the Eastern's new president in 1851 threw his weight behind an alternative pathway out of Boston which exited the city via Causeway Street and, once across the Mystic River Bridge, continued entirely overland through Charlestown, Somerville, South Malden (now Everett) and Chelsea.

The new route opened in 1854 over the objections, this time of a stockholder minority, that it was both circuitous and dangerous: the new right-of-way crossed the tracks of both the Boston and Maine and the Fitchburg railroads; moreover, Eastern's Boston terminal was so small that arriving locomotives had to be uncoupled and switched off the main line a half a mile away, letting the passenger cars roll into the station on their own momentum.

These were the bold days of railroading. At the end of the Beverly bridge, for instance, the Gloucester Branch coaches were uncoupled from the noon train bound for Portland. The engine and the Maine cars steamed into the triple-track Beverly depot. At just the right moment the switch was thrown. The Gloucester cars were shunted off onto the middle track and coupled with their waiting locomotive. The spare cars were then separated from the Gloucester train (everything still rolling along); another switch was thrown with split-second timing, and the spares swung onto the third track, from which they were switched a third time to a spur to await pick-up for the trip back to Boston. Eventually, such sleight-of-hand was outlawed.

From Beverly on, Eastern's tracks ran due north for Newburyport, bypassing the Beverly, Manchester and Cape Ann shores and all the verdant saltwater farm and woodland that drifted and tumbled down to the sea. Here at first the Iron Monster was no more than a distant whistle wafted in on a westerly breeze. Life went on as ever for the farming and fishing families, uncomplicated by contacts with Boston and Salem rendered the more

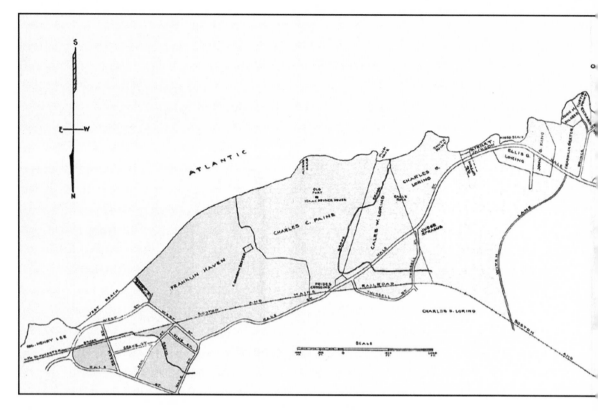

distasteful to country people by the high toll at the Beverly bridge, for they were perfectly content with the scraps of news dropped in his passage by Jake Winchester, the Gloucester stage driver.

Such was the Farms section in the east part of Beverly when Mary Larcom Dow was a girl in 1840. The long green fields and deep woods skirted the shore, a peaceful hamlet inhabited by kind and honest folk and here and there an Uncle Jimmy Woodberry, who wrote a letter to the rats that had taken over his barn, informing them that there was more and better corn in David Preston's across the road. Uncle Jimmy kept watch and "on a beautiful moonlight night had the satisfaction of beholding a long line of rodents with an old gray fellow as leader, crossing the road on their way to Uncle David's."

That was a good story, and not a few firmly believed that not only barns but woods and beehives were haunted, and spirits were all about. When John G. King, a Salem businessman, first brought his family to board at Beverly Farms in the summer of 1840 at the Isaac Prince homestead above West Beach, his daughter Caroline was impressed that the beehives around the place were draped with black bows, "the belief being universal that if on the death of a member of a family, the bees were not told of it, and their hives put in mourning, they would fly away."

One afternoon, Caroline related, her father arrived with the news from Salem, to which he commuted by stagecoach, that the children's music teacher was bringing the Manchester Brass Band out to serenade them that

evening. Expecting twenty musicians, Mrs. King divided her only cake into as many slices and concocted a well-watered "sangaree" with her only bottle of claret. Meanwhile, the eight Prince children carried word of the great event to all corners, so that by seven-thirty the surrounding fields were filled with country people, who, to pass the time away, sent a deputation to the house with the request that Miss Gusty give them a tune on the "argin" (the piano the Kings had brought from Salem—a mystery to the neighbors, who had never seen one before). Sister Augusta obliged until the arrival of the band in a huge hay wagon.

"Oh, Miss King, ma'am says there are twenty-*six* men!" reported a little Prince girl, rushing into the parlor. "Much to our amusement," wrote Caroline King, "my mother instantly cut six of the largest wedges of cake in two, and drowned her claret with another pitcher of water." The band arrayed itself before the house, and in half an hour, when its repertoire was exhausted, partook with satisfaction of Mrs. King's cakes and wine. "Then to make some return for the compliment they had paid us by offering this 'serenade' (Heaven save the mark!) William Story stood forth on the doorstep and sang as loudly as he could 'A Life on the Ocean Wave' and 'The sea, the sea, the blue, the fresh, the ever free,' which were received with great applause from Band and neighbors. Then the Band brayed out 'Auld Lang Syne,' . . . the haycart was brought round, and amid a chorus of thanks and goodnights, the Manchester Brass Band departed."

Genial and courtly John King was credited by Warren Prince, a contractor who built many summer cottages, as the first to bring the beauties of the Beverly shore to the attention of "the cultivated people from our cities," such as other Prince farm boarders in the early 1840s. These included the sculptor William Wetmore Story—the answering serenader—and his close friends (all authors) James Russell Lowell, Thomas Wentworth Higginson and the newlywed Dr. Oliver Wendell Holmes.

On April 29, 1844, attorney Charles Cushing Paine of Boston bought the Prince farm of 101 acres with its half a mile of ocean frontage for $5,500, and for another $500 the house, tools, chickens, stock, old Charley the horse, and a yoke of oxen that Farmer Prince threw in to ease his conscience. Prince remarked that "these Boston fellows don't know anything about values." Paine was the grandson of Robert Treat Paine, a signer of the Declaration of Independence; his own son, R. T. the second, who made a career of giving the

family's money away, claimed years later that this germinative acquisition came about after "the previous summer [when] Father took some of us boys on a drive from Marblehead around the Beverly Farms shore and so on to Gloucester. . . . Father made the pioneer purchase, selecting the most beautiful mile of sea-coast in Massachusetts, the side lines converging to a point where now is Pride's Crossing station. . . . Thus our family were the first settlers by purchase on this justly famous and now too fashionable shore."

Paine's was the pioneer purchase of summer property on the North Shore east of Swampscott, if one excepts John Cushing's premature acquisition of Eastern Point at Gloucester, but only barely. Three weeks after the Prince farm changed hands, John King bought John Thissell's house and five acres above Mingo Beach (named supposedly for a black slave, Robin Mingo, who once had a shack there) on Hale Street half a mile back toward Beverly, for nine hundred dollars.

On the fifth of October another Boston lawyer, Charles Greely Loring, did likewise; for four thousand dollars he relieved Benjamin Smith of twenty-five acres on Plum Cove and Smith Point adjoining Paine's new property and engaged Warren Prince to build Beverly's first summer mansion. Loring wanted to establish friendly relations with his neighbors and, when his house was in frames, had Prince stage an old-fashioned raising, to which he invited all who lived along the Beverly shore. The house continually attracted curiosity-seekers from as far as Marblehead, who poked around the grounds and peeked in windows.

Charles Cushing Paine sliced the Prince farm into building lots and offered them at auction in 1846; the bids were not satisfactory, so he abandoned speculation, farmed the estate in gentlemanly fashion, and kept it intact until its subdivision in 1875 after his death. Up the road Charles Greely Loring built a huge barn and hung swings from the loft for the local children. He kept horses, put up hen houses, and built sties with a room and yard for each pig, which got a brushing every morning and a hot bath on Saturdays. He imported Norway firs, Chinese fowl, and Alderney stock and swine from the Royal Farm at Windsor, and he shared their progeny with his neighbors. Of his land he gave away none, save to his son Caleb William Loring, lawyer and trustee of Boston.

Before he died in 1868 Loring owned a hundred acres, gathered in with the object, as he calmly told a friend who chided him for his acquisitiveness, that "I never want any land except the piece next to my own." Every worthy cause in Beverly had his support, and he was respectfully known as Squire Loring. Warren Prince had the squire in mind when he reflected that "although these families were all accustomed to wealth and its comforts, the poor were always remembered; no stain of ostentation or snobbery ever emanated from their escutcheons; these were the true nobility."

THE TRACKS PUSH ON

Ever since the Eastern Railroad was extended to Newburyport in 1840, an offshoot to Gloucester was in the cards. In September 1844, three weeks before Loring bought the Smith land, a meeting of citizens convinced the railroad, and surveyors laid out the Gloucester Branch, extending from the main line (via multiple switchings and shuntings) just north of the Beverly depot.

Next May builder Warren Prince was the go-between in the sale of twenty acres west of Mingo Beach, adjoining John King, to Franklin Dexter of Boston, a noted trial lawyer and the U.S. attorney for Massachusetts. Samuel Obear, the owner, thought Dexter's offer was too high, and his conscience drove him to seek the advice of William Endicott, Beverly's leading citizen:

"Here's a Boston man wants to buy my land for two thousand dollars. 'Tain't worth it. What am I to do?"

"I think he knows what he wants. Let him have it."

"But it ain't worth it."

"Never mind. Let him throw away his money if he wants to."

Prince built a stone mansion for Dexter, who kept Sam Obear on as his caretaker. Mrs. Dexter was the sister of William Hickling Prescott, the historian and Nahant summerer, and had lived in England. "I want to have a lawn like an English lawn," she instructed the former owner. "It must be watered, rolled, and cut regularly." "Well," said Sam, "if you will send out your maid to hold up the grass, I will undertake to cut it with a pair of scissors."

After Franklin Dexter, the next to succumb to the Beverly shore was the textile tycoon Patrick Tracy Jackson, Newburyport-born, cofounder of the city of Lowell, and organizer of the Boston and Lowell Railroad. In

September 1845 he paid Peter Obear eighteen hundred dollars for ten acres on Hale Street east of Mingo Beach and hired Warren Prince to build his cottage, which served him but two summers, for he died there of dysentery in September 1847. The ink was hardly dry on Jackson's deed when John Amory Lowell, the Boston philanthropist, abandoned Nahant for a premium piece of Woodberry (later Woodbury) Point, next on from Hospital Point to the west of Beverly Cove; he was joined on the east by son-in-law William Sohier in 1854. Lowell anchored the west flank of the Beverly colony beyond the Cove. Three days later P. T. Jackson's brother-in-law, Colonel Henry Lee, idealistic (and unsuccessful) merchant, shy (and unelected) politician, staked out the eastern limit with three acres on the other side of West Beach. It remained for Franklin Haven, president of the Merchants National Bank of Boston, to nail down the rest of West Beach with twenty acres, for which he paid Josiah Obear five hundred dollars in April 1846, a beachhead he and Franklin, Jr., had quadrupled before the century was over.

The Gloucester Branch pushed on from Beverly to Manchester in August 1847 and to Gloucester on December 1. The initial stop for the convenience of Beverly's shoreside summer residents was first designated West Beach, then Beverly Farms. Three quarters of a mile to the west the tracks transected Hale Street near the north corner of the Paine estate, at the colonial seat of the Pride family, and the crossing was given this name. (Brenton H. Dickson of Manchester suggests that long before the railroad the area of the crossing took its name from a Pride who ferried travelers in a small boat across the sand-duned entrance of a tidal cove that existed behind West Beach, long since blocked off by sea walls.) It is difficult to ascertain when the depot at Pride's Crossing was built—no later than 1871 anyway—and for years it was a private flag stop tended by a superannuated Pride, stone deaf and so indifferent to the approach of the train that boarding passengers had to flag it down themselves.

In the early days of the Gloucester Branch, the railroad company touted the Beverly shore to one and all, its "excellent conveniences for sea-bathing, the invigorating sea-breezes, together with the charming views, walks, and rides. . . . As a proof of the wholesome moral tone of Beverly, it has been said that no conviction for crime has occurred within its limits for five successive years."

Another Beverly panegyric flowed from the pen of James Russell Lowell, commenting on Beverly Farms to Miss Jane Norton, a young friend, in a letter dated August 14, 1854. The dislodged Prince farm boarder, who had lost his wife the previous October, was staying at "Underhill": "Now in order that you may not fancy (as most persons who go to Rhode Island do) that Newport is the only place in the world where there is any virtue in salt water—I will say a word or two of Beverly. Country and sea-shore are combined here in the most charming way. Find the Yankee word for Sorrento, and you have Beverly—it is only the Bay of Naples translated into the New England dialect. . . . We are in a little house close upon the road, with the sea just below, as seen through a fringe of

cedar, wild cherry, and barberry. Beyond this fringe is a sand-beach where we bathe. . . . We are at the foot of a bay, across the mouth of which lies a line of islands - some bare rock, some shrubby, and some wooded. These are the true islands of the Sirens. One [Cat Island] has been disenchanted by a great hotel, to which a steamboat runs innumerably every day with a band—the energetic *boong! boong!—boong! boong! boong!* of the bass drum being all we hear. . . . [At sunset] every evening the clouds and islands bloom and the slow sails are yellowed and the dories become golden birds swinging on the rosy water."

Franklin Haven's house on West Beach. (Beverly Historical Society)

"I would not have told you," Lowell continued, "how much better this is than your Rhode Island glories—only that you Newport folks always seem a little (I must go to my Yankee) *stuck up*, as if Newport were all the world, and you the saints that had inherited it. But I hope to see you and Newport soon, and I will be lenient. You shall find in me the Beverly grandeur of soul which can acknowledge alien merit."

Money picked off the loose lots along the shore—the city wealth of Captain Israel Whitney, Boston merchant and one-time East India shipmaster, of Ellis Gray Loring, abolitionist lawyer, of Augustus Lowell and Benjamin Franklin Burgess of the West Indies trade and father of the yacht designer. John H. Silsbee and William Dudley Pickman, Salem shipmasters, bought up vantages "from which they could watch their ships as they came into midship channel from any old port of the world, at any time," in the words of their grandson John S. Lawrence. "With a horse and chaise ever ready, they could drive to Derby Wharf in Salem, and then attend to the merchandising of their cargo while their families remained at the beach."

In 1860, sixteen years after Charles Cushing Paine's coup of the Prince farm for fifty-five dollars an acre, Richard T. Parker of Boston bought an acre and a few poles of Curtis Point for three thousand dollars, and the last of Beverly's coast from Mackerel Cove to the Manchester line, five miles of it, was the domain of the rich men from Boston and Salem. Seventy years after that, the 101 acres and house for which Paine paid six thousand dollars were assessed, with their "cottages," for $2,144,325.

The poet's appreciation of their shore, and the rest of the Boston men's, had been miscalculated by the country Princes, Thissells and Obears, to the sorrow of their descendants, one of whom, Frederick A. Ober, would lament of his ancestors in his town history of 1888: "This 'fatal gift of beauty,' which was to them a thing imponderable, attracted strangers to their birthright, and it passed from their possession."

THE WILD SHORE OF MANCHESTER

Like that of Beverly, Manchester's coast was captured by city Yankees following the trail cindered along the North Shore by the Gloucester Branch. But not so rapidly. Manchester was more remote, rustic, and inbred, and the spectacle of the country Yankees across the town line so shrewdly bargaining off their birthrights gave the natives pause to reappraise their own. Perhaps a further deterrent lurked deep in the majestic, mysterious woods behind, so densely populated with rattlesnakes as late as 1844 that they fetched a bounty of a dollar each.

Manchester was "discovered" by Richard Henry Dana, the poet and essayist of Boston and father of the author of *Two Years Before the Mast*. Actually Dana had earlier leapfrogged the town and discovered Rockport in 1840, the year of John King's discovery of Beverly. The fresh granite quarries of Pigeon Cove and Sandy Bay had been bestowing moderate prosperity and such a sense of independence upon the northeast coast of Cape Ann that the same year the two villages seceded from Gloucester as the town of Rockport. The retiring and aloof Dana found the retreat he was seeking in an old tavern on the south side of the hamlet that clustered around and above the rockbound pocket of Pigeon Cove. He was joined in the summer of 1842 by his friends William Cullen Bryant, the poet and editor, and the sculptor Edward Augustus Brackett, who did a bust of Bryant.

While at Pigeon Cove a summer or two later, Dana was induced by the Reverend Oliver A. Taylor of Manchester to visit the town, according to Richard Henry Dana III. "My grandfather then drove up and down, and hearing the sound of the surf, he said, 'There must be a beach,' and following up an old wood road he came to the spot which he afterwards selected."

That spot was a tract of wild land and shore between the old Gloucester-Salem road and Graves Beach. On April 9, 1845, Dana's lawyer-author son, Richard Henry Dana, Jr., bought all thirty acres on his behalf from the Allen family for $225. The elder Dana, then age fifty-eight, built a simple, square, gray cottage on the bluff above the beach and moved in as Manchester's first summer resident. By 1877, two years before his death, the venerable pioneer's desire for privacy had swelled his thirty to a hundred uncultivated acres.

Manchester's second summer settler, Charles Frederic Adams, trailed Dana by three years. The Gloucester Branch had just extended to the town in 1848 when Adams bought Crow Island from William Hooper and built a summer cottage on the nob of this small sentinel of five acres, not far east of the Dana estate. Like Charles Greely Loring of Beverly Farms, the island's new proprietor made a point of courting his neighbors, and it was said that "in cases of sickness he would often with his own hands supply such articles as he thought might be needed in the sick room. Frequently on the approach of winter he would distribute flannel among the more limited for their personal comfort." Adams died in 1862 and left Crow Island to his daughter Emily. It remained in the family's possession until 1935, when E. Hyde Cox made a year-round estate of it.

That most singular of the singular among Bostonians, Robert Bennet Forbes, was the third to find summer harbor on Manchester's wild shore. In April 1856 he bought seventeen acres near the Beverly line from Israel F. Tappan for $800 and set his cottage on the hill west of Black Cove Beach; he called it "Masconomo" after the last sagamore of the Agawams and moved in on July 24, 1857. "Black Ben," as dark-complexioned Captain Forbes was hailed in his youth, had been a shipmaster in the China (and opium) trade under the aegis of his uncle, Thomas Handasyd Perkins. He

In this 1870s photograph, Manchester's first summer resident, Richard Henry Dana, Sr., poses with his grandson and his son, the author of Two Years Before the Mast. *(National Park Service, Longfellow National Historic Site)*

made, lost and regained a fortune, devised all kinds of improvements in vessel design, sailed a relief ship to Ireland during the famine of 1847, plumped for better lifesaving methods and shipwreck patrols, organized a farsighted though premature coast guard at the outbreak of the Civil War, threw himself into sport and yachting as commodore of the first informal boat club at Boston in 1834, and at last wrote up his adventures, achievements and even a few failures with energetic immodesty in his *Personal Reminiscences.* Strange for a born seafarer, Captain Forbes in 1865 sold his Manchester estate (to B. G. Boardman, a merchant who paid him in gold as a hedge against wartime inflation) and then moved his summer residence to Milton, one of the coming country suburbs south of Boston. One year later, Boardman's purchase, by his own account, had doubled in value.

Also in 1856, John Crowninshield Dodge, a Chicago native, picked up two lots behind Old Neck Beach. Adjoining him, Dr. Jedidiah Cobb built his cottage in 1857. Dodge built on the upland and sold his beach frontage in 1861 to Russell Sturgis, Jr., son of Captain Forbes's salty old ex-partner in the shipping and mercantile firm of Russell and Company of Boston. Major Sturgis built in 1863, war or no war. At the height of it, in 1864, Benjamin W. Thayer, a Boston real estate broker who had been boarding in Manchester for thirteen seasons, talked Andrew Ruffin into selling him his land and boardinghouse on Old Neck Beach, whose sands when walked upon beguiled the ears with such a sweet, strange music that its new owners renamed it Musical Beach.

The end of the Civil War found the courtly outsiders in complete control of the Beverly seaside and holding down most of Manchester's except

"Masconomo," the West Manchester summer home of Robert Bennet Forbes, first occupied in July 1857. (Manchester Historical Society)

Robert Bennet Forbes. (From his Personal Reminiscences.)

for a few holdouts such as the Smith family, who had refused sixteen thousand dollars for their thirty-two acres of farmland on the east of the harbor, which they claimed was worth twice that. "Next to gold, for certainty of value both present and prospective," declared Thomas P. Gentlee, the railroad's land agent who himself had heavily invested in the North Shore, "I had rather hold such land now than any other property I know of."

Gentlee was not the only speculator who spotted gold onward and eastward in the granite of Cape Ann. The rush to the North Shore had only begun.

To the left of a theatrical spot of sunlight under a thunderhead rising over Gloucester's harbor in 1852 stands the new Pavilion, the town's first summer hotel, and to the right, the old Revolutionary fort—all caught by the magic brush of Fitz Hugh Lane. (Cape Ann Historical Association)

~4~
GLOUCESTER KEEPS ON FISHING

The stout-hearted camper and the sly investor meet
the stoic native, and summers will never be the same

THE MOST IMPRESSIVE APPROACH
to Cape Ann by land has always been along the shore road that Jake
Winchester's stagecoach traveled from Salem, winding through Beverly and
Manchester with enticing glimpses of the ocean across beach and cove, then
plunging inland into the West Gloucester wilderness of swamp and forest,
as dank and dark as if a thousand miles from the fresh breath and sparkle
of the sea.

The clattering coach encounters Sawyer's Hill. The sound of surf and
the salt smell tinged with the iodine pungency of seaweed quicken the pulse.
The horses labor up the grade. Abruptly at the crest the woods give way to
pasture. The stage leaps into the sunlight, and there under the canopy of
blue sky sparkles Freshwater Cove, pocketed within wooded Dolliver's
Neck. Beyond is the shimmering sheet of Gloucester Harbor, rockbound
behind the thrust of Eastern Point, and, beyonder still, the dazzling Atlantic.

In a few seconds the stage sways down the slope in billows of dust, and
the electrifying vista evaporates into roadside rock and brush. Then, as suddenly again, the curtain parts to reveal the arc of Cressy's Beach bit up
against the ledge of Stage Head and, upon its brow, the grassed-over fort of
the Revolution. Now the whole of Gloucester Bay spreads forth, crisscrossed with a hundred sail tacking through the lee of Eastern Point. There,
to the east, is little Ten Pound Island, abaft of it the thumb of Rocky Neck,
and across from it the inner harbor's Watchhouse Point, crowned with
another grassy fort.

Some summer in the early 1830s that vision stopped a visitor in his
horse's tracks, and Freshwater Cove was adopted as their summer campground by the stout hearts of the Boston Pioneer Seashore Club. They were
young businessmen of a musical turn, a score of them, and they brought
flutes, trumpets, accordions, tambourines, Jew's harps, clappers and snare
drums, besides their camping outfits and tents.

Charlie Sawyer had two wharves on Freshwater Cove where a pair of
pinky schooners landed their fares; he cured and sold fish, ran a fisher-

Freshwater Cove from Dolliver's Neck, 1870s. (Procter Brothers, Howard collection)

man's outfitting store, stocked West India goods, and owned a cluster of fish houses just above the tide. The Pioneers pitched their tents on his land, and Charlie let them inhabit one of the fish houses during their month-long stay. In part payment for this hospitality, the Boston boys played evening concerts that drew Gloucester people from miles around, but particularly the belles of the Cove Village, whose nightly presence resulted in the following pledge to Mr. Sawyer: "The girls will always be welcome here as our guests, and we assure you, sir, that they will be in the best of company for reputation, honesty and protection under the name of the Boston Pioneer Seashore Club!"

After a few years the campsite of the Pioneers was inherited by a fraternity of Charlestown merchants and politicians, the 999th Battery, which camped in style, bringing tents, tables, chairs, beds, cooking utensils and a brass fieldpiece. The members carried on the Pioneer tradition of concerts and entertainment for the locals, not without the cooperation of one of their number who was a wealthy distiller. Their signal cannon awoke Gloucester at every dawn, proclaimed high noon, and shot down the sun resoundingly.

Nonetheless, the Batterymen of Freshwater Cove, like the Pioneers before them, were summer soldiers, who struck their tents and left no wounds except on the hearts and eardrums of the local populace. Furthermore, the subsequent land grab under cover of the smoke and cinders of the advancing railroad lost steam with every mile as the tracks pushed toward what many regarded as the bitter end of the North Shore. And it must be admitted that for all Gloucester cared—preoccupied with the comings and going of the fleet, the weather, the price of fish and its cost in lives and fortunes, and bastioned from the rest of humanity behind the wilderness of the West Parish and the moat of the Annisquam River— Boston, save as a market, could be a thousand miles away.

Under such unfavorable circumstances, investment in summer property on a relatively distant coast whose climate, albeit cool, was not so cool as the welcome of its inhabitants, was undertaken by few, and they were intrepid. They were also farseeing: the imminence of the Gloucester Branch and the diminishing supply of available remaining shoreline were the inducement.

THE FIRST REAL ESTATE DEALS

George Hovey, for one, was a Boston wholesaler, perhaps a Seashore Pioneer, who is thought to have summered at Freshwater Cove for the first time in 1843. But it was his brother Charles, a dry goods merchant in the

With some changes in fashion, tenting at Freshwater Cove in the 1830s may have looked much like this West Gloucester scene photographed in the 1870s. (Procter Brothers, Howard Collection)

city, who on March 10, 1845, paid the town seven hundred dollars for a piece of pasture on the slope south of Granite Street, midway above the curve of Gloucester's frontal beach, on what is now Hovey Street. Nine months later George followed suit by giving Charles and Samuel E. Sawyer four hundred dollars for the Lookout Lot, so called, on Sawyer's Hill commanding Freshwater Cove and the harbor. The summer houses the brothers built, sumptuous for Gloucester, were the first on Cape Ann. Charles's sons wheeled through the dirty streets of Fishtown in a willow carriage behind a brisk team of ponies. George in time bought up Dolliver's Neck and adjoining Mussel Point, which made Freshwater Cove practically his private anchorage, and took up yachting.

At the same time, an astute Gloucester Surinam trader with business connections in Boston and an ear for the approach of the railroad train was laying out the handsome sum of fifty dollars for the first of

Thomas Niles, the author's irascible great-great-grandfather, who snapped up the entire Eastern Point farm for five thousand dollars in 1844. (Author's collection)

many tracts of pasture he would gather to himself in the Bass Rocks section of Eastern Point. George H. Rogers would patiently assemble his great holdings in a series of sorties.

South of him, Thomas Niles, a Boston livery-stable owner who also heard the whistle in the distance, purchased the four hundred acres of the Eastern Point farm, comprising the entire end of the peninsula (except for the acre on which the government's lighthouse stood) for five thousand dollars and some small real estate in the city. This was in July 1844. A naval veteran of the War of 1812, the buyer was my great-great-grandfather (by the coincidence of his daughter's marriage many years later to John Kimball Rogers, my great-grandfather) and a great-grandson of the Gloucester merchant Daniel Rogers, who by further coincidence had owned the very same farm after the Revolution.

Thomas Niles intended his coup of Eastern Point as a long-term investment in seaside summer property which would hatch in its own good time, with good husbandry in the meanwhile. He herded his numerous brood (fifteen children, eventually, by three successive wives) aboard his sailboat, so the family story goes, like Noah embarked upon the flood, and took possession of the weathered farmhouse between the harbor beach and the freshwater pond that is separated from the sea on the other side by a membrane of sand; beach and pond now bear his name.

What could have possessed Thomas Niles—clean-cut and handsome in his youth, fearsomely bearded in his prime—to transplant his loved ones from the amenities of Boston to a distant and deserted demi-island several miles removed even from the rough fishing port, a primitive saltwater farm of transcendental loveliness in the warm months, but desolate and gale-swept during the cold? "I designed to make it my home, and I did so," he reflected with laconic firmness in his twilight, "believing that on my death my children would inherit in it a sure fortune by its steady enhancement in value."

The sole clue as to why he chose such a remote target for the rustication of his family may lie in the identity of the quite as extraordinary party who sold him the farm, John Perkins Cushing. Ten years previously Grandsir Niles sold Cushing two horses for four hundred dollars in cash and cancellation of a seven-hundred-dollar note for which, the great Boston merchant admitted to his diary, he "never expected to get anything."

"Ku-Shing," as his Chinese admirers called him, had returned to Boston in 1831 after twenty-eight years representing the mercantile interests in Canton of his uncle Thomas Handasyd Perkins so efficiently that at the age of forty-four Cushing was rumored to be worth seven million dollars. First this most eligible bachelor in New England and perhaps all of America lost this singular distinction. Then he built an opulent mansion in Summer Street. And then (and here we must again rely on the account of Thomas Niles) Cushing "proposed to make a sea-side estate which should surpass in beauty of situation and in completeness of detail any other in the United States. For this, after careful examination of a great part of the coast of New England, he had finally selected Eastern Point as best adapted to his purpose."

Eastern Point Light from the 1871 sketchbook of Thomas Niles's granddaughter Sarah M. Rogers. (Author's collection)

Cushing abandoned the idea almost immediately. Instead of North Shoreward, the following August he moved inland from Boston to Watertown, where he built a perfectly splendid country manor with all kinds of neo-Oriental overtones. For the rest of his life Colonel Perkins's nephew lavished his fortune on "Belmont," importing shiploads of flora from the world over and supervising every detail until his gardens were the

horticultural wonder of the eastern United States. Three years before his death in 1862, portions of Watertown, Waltham and West Cambridge were incorporated and named Belmont in tribute to their grandest taxpayer.

On his far more inspiring property at Eastern Point, John Cushing did little more than build a boundary wall of fieldstone that still stands between the harbor and the east shore of Brace Cove on the Atlantic. Evidently Eastern Point was too distant from Boston; for a vacation by the sea, like the rest of his clan, John Perkins Cushing preferred Nahant, where he put up his family at his uncle's hotel in the summer of 1836 and visited a half dozen times.

Whatever moved Thomas Niles to relieve "Ku-Shing" of the cares of absentee ownership that July of 1844, he set about with all the energy of the newly arrived gentleman farmer at the age of forty-seven, clearing and plowing and fertilizing his acres with seaweed ("sea manure") from his beaches, planting vegetables, orchards and shade trees, raising stock, and cutting ice from the pond for the Gloucester and Boston markets.

The irascibility of my ancestor is family legend. Trespassers infuriated him; he ordered the townspeople (including farmer Isaac Patch to his north, long accustomed to harvesting "sea manure" for his fields) to keep to their side of the Cushing Wall or face him in court. The antipathy was mutual, since Gloucester folk had always freely roamed the fields and woods and shores of the point. Resentment mounted. His barns were burned, and a farmhand was tried for arson. He shut off visitors to the lighthouse and expelled picnickers from his beaches. In the end he prevailed. After six years of acrimonious litigation between Niles and Patch, the Massachusetts Supreme Court in 1859 ruled that his land, roads and beaches were his private domain, to the mean low-water mark of Gloucester Harbor, securing for him and his heirs and generations of summer residents to come the famous exclusiveness of Eastern Point.

All this hard-won privacy didn't last very long. In 1863, the War Department seized fifty-three acres of the high ground of Eastern Point, piled up an earthen fort for the defense of Gloucester against Confederate gunboats, armed it with seven cannon, and moved in a rollicking company of artillerymen. They remained until 1865, when the Confederacy collapsed. Farmer Niles had been grinding his teeth all this time and late that year filed a claim against Uncle Sam for $64,980 in rent and damages.

While presenting his case before the War Claims Commission in 1866, he persuaded several leading North Shore summer residents to testify to the spectacular rise in coastal property values and the potential of Eastern Point, if the United States would only dismantle its fort and evacuate. His witnesses agreed with gravity that most of the best available shore between Boston and Cape Ann had already been taken up and that Eastern Point was among the few promontories on the coast that jutted out sufficiently to benefit from the water-cooled southwester; indeed, it might even surpass Nahant as a watering place but for its distance from Boston, which none regarded as an immutable bar to development.

Finally the War Department gave in and returned his land to Thomas Niles in 1869. Not until 1890, long after his death, did Congress pass a special act indemnifying his heirs (who by then had disposed of their inheritance) to the scaled-down tune of $6,050.

THE FIRST SUMMER LODGINGS

A terrible gale, perhaps a hurricane, in September 1846 cost Marblehead ten vessels and sixty-five men and boys, as well as its place of importance in the fishing industry. Thereby Gloucester was left unrivaled, with a fleet of 127 schooners and a busy waterfront that expanded rapidly around the inner harbor, giving rise to the village of East Gloucester, as differentiated from the rest of Eastern Point—a designation henceforth restricted to the Niles farm and pond.

The rest of the world first found out about East Gloucester's cool combination of rural ebb and tidal flow from Joseph Kidder, a Boston druggist who in 1843 came with his family to board at the home of young Mrs. Judith Wonson on Wonson's Point, between Niles Beach and Rocky Neck.

Ernest L. Blatchford photo of the Niles farmhouse at Eastern Point, about 1900. (Cape Ann Historical Association, Gordon W. Thomas collection)

THE "SEA BREEZE" POLKA BRILLANTE.

Bathers at Gloucester's Pavilion Beach, 1856. (Peabody Essex Museum)

The Kidders brought their friends, and their friends brought theirs, and they overflowed across the road to Mrs. Mary Wonson's place, "The Fair View," which still offers a fair view of the harbor to its guests. Thus was founded the East Gloucester summer colony. "There were ducks and chickens raised on the place," wrote George Procter of Judy Wonson's fare, "together with fresh vegetables, apples, pears and currants from the garden. . . . A cow supplied butter and cream. Lobsters and fish were plentiful. . . . The cooking was done by an open fire on the hearth, and there was one of the old style brick ovens which turned out delicious brown bread and beans, Indian pudding, pies and berry cakes."

The extension of the Gloucester Branch of the Eastern Railroad in 1847 put the town in the business of swapping salt fish for summer folks. As the trade increased, the first strictly summer hotel, the Pavilion, opened on June 29, 1849, halfway along the town beach (Pavilion Beach ever since). A welcome sight from land or sea was this window on the harbor, its tiers of arcaded porches mounting to the roof, then up, up, to the glassed-in cupola, topped by the house flag.

One August afternoon in 1853 a large party of Gloucester natives and Pavilion guests (and some "strangers," presumably gate-crashers) converged upon Eastern Point by carriage and boat on the surprising invitation of Mr. Thomas Niles, Esquire, who was making an unaccustomed effort to improve his public image. Back of the stone wharf near the quarry and the lighthouse was pitched a spacious tent. On the beach below, an oven of flat stones had been assembled, wherein clams and sweet corn tucked in blankets of seaweed exuded tantalizing clouds of steam. There were chowder and fried fish and other viands, singing and dancing to the clarion strains of Procter's Band, and speeches of appreciation for Mr. Niles. The host's purpose seemed to have been more than amply accomplished until several days later, when he declared heatedly through the newspaper that in offering the use of his property for the gala he had supposed its organizers understood it was to be a Dutch treat.

A town whose streets were as narrow and twisted, some claimed, as its inhabitants. This view toward Peach's Point was taken from Bailey's Head in Marblehead in the late nineteenth century. (Marblehead Historical Society)

~5~

MARBLEHEAD SUCCUMBS AS SWAMPSCOTT HUMS

A town of crooked streets, a summer colony on the Neck and an uneasy alliance between neighbors

On a Sunday morning early in their classic cruise down east the summer of 1858, that ever-curious, ever-amused journalist Robert Carter and his companions sailed *Helen* into the long and rockbound harbor of Marblehead. They dropped anchor and rowed across to inspect the Neck, the port's partially protecting promontory, a breezy pasture.

After a swim the argonauts made for the shade of a stand of elms above the water, lit their cigars, and contemplated a prospect that Carter thought could have no rival between Rio de Janeiro and Bar Harbor, their destination on the Maine coast. A magnificent harbor, as they could see, quite safe against all winds except from the northeast, as they had been informed and as was demonstrated in a few hours when a violent thunderstorm from that quarter almost hove their sloop upon the rocks.

"We went ashore to take a look at the town, which has always been reputed one of the queerest places in New England," wrote Carter, a New Yorker who found the streets as narrow and twisted as the inhabitants. "The people were formerly the most uncivilized in New England," he had been told, "and the boys so rude and turbulent as to be a terror to strangers, whom they were accustomed to stone, or, as they themselves expressed it, to *rock*, for amusement. But of late years the place has much improved." Carter did not explain how or why Marblehead had improved, and his parting compliment implies that the visitors had escaped a rocking.

THE SIX LIVES OF CAT ISLAND

Creeping civilization had so weakened the independent fiber of the town since fishing gave way to such lubberish pursuits as shoe-making that mainland Marblehead would be able to hold off the summer invasion of the *strangers* for only another ten years, until after the Civil War. Sneaking up by sea, strangers had already captured the town's little Cat Island, a mile northeast of the Neck, without so much as a rocking. When earlier aliens had built a smallpox inoculation hospital on Cat Island (named for Robert Catta, the first owner) back in 1774, 'Headers knew what to do: they rowed out and burned it down. Now they just grumbled when the Salem Steamboat Company, organized for the express purpose, bought Cat's fifteen scrabbly acres in 1851 as a holiday resort for mill workers from Lowell.

Actually, the acquisition of Cat Island was part of a larger and rather ingenious speculation. The previous summer the same strangers had started the Salem and Lowell Railroad in the quixotic dream of restoring Salem's lost commerce as the port for the fast-growing inland textile city. The offshore resort was to be an attraction for passenger traffic. They built the Island House, with a hundred rooms, dining hall and bowling alley. A thousand Lowell people were entrained to Salem on the new railway for the opening in August 1851, then shuttled by steamer to what came to be called Lowell Island for a mass picnic.

The Island House in its prime was nearly as big as Cat Island. (From History of Catta Island off Marblehead *by Richard W. Searle.)*

Fishing, sailing, sea bathing and the inevitable divine services mill owners supposed were uplifting for those faceless employees called "operatives" were among the attractions. Spirits were not, with the result, as the management rejoiced, that "rowdies have taken a disgust at Lowell Island because they can find no intoxicating liquor there. Their absence will not lessen the satisfactions of decent people with the place." The novelty of the first full season of 1852 was a regatta of eleven boats sailed over a course of nine miles, Marblehead's first such contest. The summer ended with a dance lasting until three in the morning.

But Salem disappointed its promoters as Lowell's port. The railroad only limped along, and in 1857 the steamboat company was forced to sell the island to Colonel Gorham L. Pollard of Lowell, who renamed it after

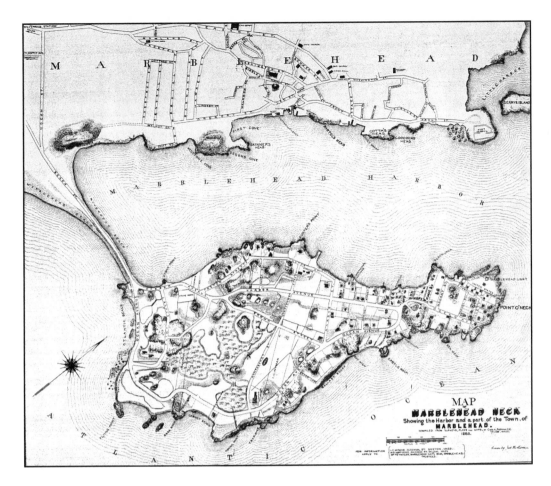

himself and ran the hotel until 1869, when a Bostonian bought him out. Cat Island it was again, until in 1878 it fell into the hands of Samuel B. Rindge, a merchant-banker of Cambridge whose son, philanthropist Frederick Hastings Rindge, converted the hotel into the Children's Island Sanatorium, fulfilling Cat Island's therapeutic destiny, wrenched from it by Marbleheaders fearful of the pox so near their shore. For sixty years the sanatorium did its good work, until funds ran out in 1946. But Cat Island had more lives, and its sixth is as the Marblehead YMCA's summer camp for children.

Map of Marblehead Neck, 1883. (Marblehead Historical Society)

TENTING ON THE NECK

Defining the Neck as part of mainland Marblehead stretches the point because in the days before its "discovery," like Nahant and Gloucester's Rocky Neck, it was an island at high tide and quite impossible to gain dry-shod across the sandy isthmus, sometimes called Riverhead Beach, at the head of the harbor. The natural insularity of its three hundred acres was reinforced by the cultivated reclusion of the villagers, whose reaction when the late Jesse Blanchard's executors tried to auction off his 130-acre farm

Benjamin P. Ware. (From Standard History of Essex County, Massachusetts.)

there for a summer resort in 1835 can be imagined. A summer resort at Marblehead! The executors advertised that the ocean view equaled Nahant's: "To the sportsman and angler it presents the greatest of facilities for the prosecution of their sports. In the summer season, pearch and tautog are caught from the rocks in abundance; plovers and curlews abound in the pastures. Persons disposed to obtain summer residences will find, in the Neck, capabilities equal to those of Nahant, with the additional conveniences of being nearer Marblehead and Salem. . . . A Public House might be erected here, which would make the Neck a fashionable resort for people from all quarters, as soon as the beauty of its situation and its other attractions became more generally known."

The enterprising executors were thirty years ahead of their time. No resort-minded bidders took the bait, and Ephraim Brown added the Blanchard farm to his other holdings on the Neck until he had 240 acres under cultivation and was marketing produce as far away as New York.

Not until the end of the Civil War released a surge of yearning for fresh air and good times was Marblehead breached, and then not from Boston, the expected quarter, but by Lowell, with reinforcements from neighboring Nashua over the line in New Hampshire, and from Peabody. The strangers struck almost simultaneously along the portion of the coast of Marblehead next to Swampscott always known as the Farms, now frequently called Clifton, and on the harbor shore of the Neck.

Supposedly Clifton was named for the Clifton House, Marblehead's first small summer hotel, built by Benjamin P. Ware on the water side of his farm in 1846, the year before his marriage to Hannah Clifton of Salem. Ware was a sturdy son of the soil (not Marblehead's but Salem's, to his disadvantage locally), who with his father and brother brought back to life the farmed-out Hinkley farm they had acquired in 1831. Being a stranger himself, Ben Ware was not heir to the native suspicion of the outside world. Quite the opposite; he welcomed out-of-towners, and their cash, so heartily and pushed so energetically for Marblehead's future as a resort, that he incurred, in the carefully chosen words of one admirer, "many criticisms of doubt expressed by short-sighted and narrow-minded men."

The year after Ware opened the Clifton House, the Marblehead and Lynn Branch Railroad Company was incorporated to run tracks along the shore from Marblehead to connect with the Eastern at Swampscott. This would have turned the Ware farm into a gold field (of which Clifton House was no doubt built in anticipation), but the attempt failed for insufficient capital. Almost twenty years passed before the proposal was revived by Marblehead interests that wanted a more direct communication with Boston than that offered by the existing branch, which backtracked through Salem. However, Swampscott, looking to itself, countered with a rival effort to get the county to push a shore boulevard through its own potentially rich seaside, stopping at the Marblehead line. Ben Ware was behind the railroad scheme or an extension of the boulevard through his adopted town—he didn't really care which—and it was at this juncture, around 1866, that people from nearby Peabody discovered Clifton (with his prompting) and pitched the tents of Peabody Camp.

All this road-and-railroad agitation, coming on a wave of postwar euphoria, shook up even the proprietors of Marblehead Neck. After farmer Ephraim Brown's passing in 1861 the heft of his acreage was leased by his trustees to Martin Ham. In the summer of 1866 farmer Ham sublet patches of shore on the ocean side of the Neck opposite Tinker's Island to campers from Lowell and Lawrence and rented a shanty near the head of the harbor to a group of men from Nashua.

The next spring, on the initiative of Judge Thomas Pearson, the Nashua crowd bought a small lot on the harbor from John Gregory, divided it six ways, framed cottages and barns in New Hampshire, brought

Benjamin Ware's Clifton House. (From Atlas of Essex County, Massachusetts, *Boston 1884.)*

them down to Marblehead, assembled them, and moved their families into the first permanent summer houses on the Neck on the Fourth of July, 1867. Theirs were the only buildings on the entire peninsula from the Ham farmhouse by the beach to the lighthouse at the entrance to Marblehead Harbor. The breezy Neck drew them to its shores under the same atmospheric conditions that a few years earlier had driven off an ancient female native, who in frustration finally moved across the harbor to town because "I wish to die sometime, and people never die on the Neck, it's too healthy there."

Judge Pearson succumbed to nostalgia when he thought back, only ten years after he planted his colony, how "it was no uncommon sight on Sunday evening, in 1869, to count between fifty and seventy-five dories on the Nashua shore. Those were the most enjoyable days for rest and fun which the settlement has ever known. White vest and neck ties, silk hats and kid gloves, trailing dresses, Valenciennes laces, button gloves, and high heeled shoes, banged hair (except what the wind banged), were laid aside and tried to be forgotten in the universal desire to be happy!"

The tenting craze had given the ocean shore of Marblehead Neck by 1870 "the appearance of an encampment of a small army," with the familiar wooden floors, rococo furnishings, cooking tents and domestic tents, and tents combined with cottages. This fresh, newly discovered summer life, with the broad blue bay to seaward, the harbor so full of interest to the inlander and the queer, twisted village across from it, brought a new light to the lives of the summerers after the dark tunnel of the long war—and a happy release from the Victorian restraint of the city.

It was a free life out on the Neck, scrambling over the ledges, rambling the fields, swimming and rowing. Blue flannel shirts were the passion, wrote a visitor—"the booths and cozy little shanties are in full bloom, dainty city damsels may be seen bereft of fashion's folly and conducting themselves in a manner that would shock the sensitive nerves of a sojourner at Newport or Saratoga; and stiff and stern paterfamilias frees himself entirely from the meshes of his ledger and bank account, and roams about the Neck, reveling in the freedom he encounters at every step."

When the first road to the mainland was built over Riverhead Beach in 1870, the Hams converted their place nearby into Riverhead House, later the Atlantic House of fish dinner fame; but even after the first horse-drawn barges began running between the Neck and the railroad depot, dories remained the pleasanter way of getting across the harbor.

A MODERN RESORT

Bewhiskered Ben Ware's espousal of "modern ideas" was half vindicated with the completion of the Swampscott section of Atlantic Avenue in 1870 and its grudging extension by Marblehead through Clifton and Devereux to the center soon after. His triumph was complete when the Eastern Railroad opened its shore branch between the two towns in 1873, escalating the

boom in summer property and more than repaying the adjoining landowners, who had agreed to foot the bill for the depots at Phillips Beach, Beach
Bluff, Clifton and Devereux. The prophet of course was not honored by his
townspeople, who during the bitterest rounds of the fight against his modern ideas had raised the cry "Be-ware B. Ware!" and muttered on the street
corners that "the first thing you know you'll go down town and meet someone you don't know." When it reached the point where Ware would emerge
from church to find insults daubed on his carriage, he coolly transferred to
a church in Lynn.

Atlantic Avenue made Swampscott the late afternoon promenade for
the smart turnouts of the North Shore. The Boston *Times* reported that it
was "graded to perfection, broad and hard, while its recent extension to
Marblehead gives a glorious ride of nine miles, with a sea view all the way
on one side and the groves and highly cultivated farms all about." As much
elegance and as great diversity in horses and vehicles as could be seen anywhere, wrote James Newhall—"the gay nag pranced with the lordly
equipage, and the rawboned roadster with his rattling gig." He estimated
that Swampscott was host to eleven thousand visitors during the summer of
1872.

The host at the old Swampscott Tavern, S. H. Wardwell, had regarded
with approval the swelling rush of summer traffic past his door and bought
the Marshall House near the end of Fishing Point to increase his trade.
Adjoining, on the very tip of the point, he built and opened the Lincoln
House, named for the president, in 1864, the year the Ocean House happened to burn to the ground on Phillips Point. S. H.'s brother, E. N., then

*Quiet elegance
was the mark of
the first new
Ocean House
above
Swampscott's
Whale Beach,
photographed in
1880. Two
seasons later it
burned to the
ground.
(Lynn Historical
Society)*

bought the Beach House, moved it from Phillips Point to Whale Beach and renamed *it* the Ocean House. After a few years E. N. sold out and joined S. H. in the management of the Lincoln House, which doubled and tripled in size though the Wardwells stuck to their claim that since it was "completely removed from the rush of travel and traffic . . . its worst disturbing sounds are the rattle of dory oars against thole pins, or the whirring of halliard blocks as the fishermen round up to their holding ground in the lee of Dread Ledge."

Rather less than catastrophically, the new Ocean House followed the fate of the old and burned down in 1882, only a year after its purchase by R. W. Carter of Boston, who in 1884 rebuilt and reopened a *new* new Ocean House, which he called the New Ocean House. This raised the room count in the town's sixteen summer hostelries, large and small, to six hundred and made Swampscott the North Shore's leading hotel resort of the day. By the turn of the century the New Ocean House, which might better have been named the Phoenix, was one of the grand spas of the New England coast. And so it remained until the middle of the twentieth century, when it, too, met its fiery fate.

Like dominoes, one after another of those highly cultivated farms along the shore from Fishing Point in Swampscott to Marblehead's Peach's Point tumbled onto the market in the decade after the Civil War. After the first Ocean House fire on Phillips Point in 1864, Charles W. Galloupe and three associates bought the twenty acres of the grounds and subdivided, Galloupe taking the commanding share for his elegant summer mansion. Galloupe's Point, as the western bluff of Phillips Point became known, was obviously jinxed; his "Bay View Cottage" went up in flames in 1876 for a $60,000 loss, and in four more years his "Summit Villa" was in ashes too.

Over in Marblehead, with Atlantic Avenue and the railroad headed right for the heart of them, the Horace Ware estate at Clifton and the 110 acres of the George A. Smith farm in Devereux surrendered to subdivision in 1870. Francis B. Crowninshield sniffed the trend and, with the sixth sense that had concentrated so much of Salem's wealth in his family's hands, bought most of Peach's Point on Marblehead's northeast shore for $9,500 in 1871. F. B. built his own summer cottage the next year on this rocky pasture first occupied by the fisherman-settler John Peach, then one for his son Benjamin (who in 1875 gathered in most of the rest of the point for another $21,000), and before he died in 1876 a third for his daughter Mrs. Josiah Bradlee. Benjamin tightened the Crowninshield grip with four more, plus a stable for the family compound and water tanks up on Pitman Hill.

A small but dramatically situated leftover portion of Peach's Point somehow slipped through the grasp of the Crowninshields and into the hands of Samuel Rindge in 1880, two years after the Cambridge banker bought Cat Island, which he decided was not to his taste. After the Rindges moved to California to enjoy the proceeds of their speculation in some of the land on which Los Angeles was built, they continued to return to Peach's

Point summers until abruptly one day they walked away forever, "leaving the house as if they were merely going out to tea," according to one report.

James I. H. Gregory, Marblehead's homegrown Seed King and father of the "Mother Hubbard Squash," erected the first large cottage on Naugus Head, facing Winter Island across Salem Harbor, in 1876. President Garfield, it is said, reluctantly declined Mr. Gregory's invitation to make the place his summer White House in 1881; had he accepted, he might have avoided that fatal bullet from the revolver of Charles J. Guiteau in the Washington railroad station on July 2. From the Seed King's benign spadework sprouted a tent and cottage colony and a popular picnic, dance and band concert spot, Naugus Head Grove.

The most far-reaching effect of the construction of Atlantic Avenue and the prospect of Eastern Railroad's Swampscott branch was the decision of the trustees to sell the 230 acres of the Ephraim Brown farm, with its two miles of coast. Thus was one of the North Shore's three most dramatic peninsulas auctioned off on January 11, 1872, to the Marblehead Great Neck Land Company for $250,000. The deal prompted the railroad to go ahead with the shore line to Marblehead. After thirty-seven years the aspirations of Jesse Blanchard's farseeing executors to rivalry with Nahant seemed about to be fulfilled. (Some of the shareholders in the land company, Junius Brutus Booth and Benjamin W. Thayer, will reappear in a later chapter.)

The new owners of the Neck built Ocean Avenue, laid out 250 lots ranging from a half to two acres, and suggested pointedly to the lessees of

"Strodehurst," of forty rooms, was Charles W. Galloupe's response to the fires that leveled his two earlier summer mansions on Phillips Point, Swampscott. (Louis A. Gallo collection)

the Lowell Camp, who had been enjoying some of their best ocean frontage courtesy of Farmer Ham, that they buy or be gone. A few paid up and improved their cottages, but the majority pulled up, and the next season, 1873, they set up a camp at Juniper Point on Salem Neck.

Hard times in the wake of the financial panic of 1873 dogged the overextended promoters of Marblehead Neck. Land sales fell off, and in 1878 came the inevitable foreclosure and reversion of the balance of the farm to the Brown estate. The trustees completed the circumferential avenue, added connecting roads, and resumed land offerings, with reserve clauses guaranteeing right of public (meaning Neck residents) access to water frontage. This Neck clubbiness went back to 1866 when Judge Pearson and his Nashua friends prevailed on a Congregational divine from upstate New York, who was camping with his family, to hold a Sunday service in a large "boarding-house tent," as the judge called it. About fifty summer people brought their chairs and dropped three dollars and eight cents in the hat passed by His Honor after a "very well written, earnest, Christian sermon." They made do here and there until 1876, when the Marblehead Neck Hall Association was organized to build a hall for socials and the Sabbath.

By 1880 there were seventy summer cottages on the Neck; like those on the Marblehead mainland, they were unpretentious. According to one contemporary judgment, none but a handful of the most recently built could rival the summer architecture of Swampscott and Cape Ann for splendor— the reason being that people who selected Marblehead, wealthy and cultured as many were, came for recreation and rest, not for show.

The new Neckers had chosen to be in a world of their own, and it was perhaps their wish to be different from Marblehead, which was different enough itself, that motivated a rather humorless campaign to rename the Neck "Manataug," which some pedant claimed the Indians had called the place. The old 'Headers naturally would have nothing to do with such pretentious nonsense. Assuredly it was the desire of the Neckers to have the best of *both* worlds that motivated Captain A. Allen Pitman to launch transharbor service to the town in the summer of 1880 with the steam ferry *Lillie May*. His landing was not far from the depot, and he made twelve daily round trips, which gave him twenty-four opportunities a day to inflict his infamous two-liner on his captive passengers:

City feller: "Say, does this train stop in Marblehead?"

Conductor: "Wal, if it don't there's gonna be one helluva splash."

After only three seasons of quips and trips, Captain Pitman turned the run over to Philip B. Tucker, who had been ferrying the harbor with a string of dories and sailboats for years and now continued with steam.

The single event that only fifteen years after its settlement crystallized the character of the Neck and to a great degree charted the future course of the town was the decision of the Eastern Yacht Club to locate permanently at Marblehead. Almost since its inception in 1870 the club had been the largest and richest in New England, and the construction of its first clubhouse midway on the harbor shore of the Neck in 1881 established Marblehead as the yachting center of the Northeast. Next year a hotel of eighty rooms, named the Nanapashemet after a North Shore Indian sagamore as if in vengeance for the rebuff of Manataug, was built high on an ocean bluff across from the new clubhouse, probably as a support facility. (For more on Marblehead yachting, see chapter six.)

A PETITION FOR SECESSION

Benjamin P. Ware, who had done so much for Marblehead, was now doing his damnedest to undo it all by changing the map. The earth started shaking in the fall of 1884 when Ware led an agitation to break off the Neck, part of Devereux, and all of Clifton from Marblehead, and Beach Bluff and Phillips Beach from Swampscott, and make a new town of them. To that end he and his co-secessionists put in twin petitions to the state legislature. The shore was in an uproar, and the alarm was revived: "Be-ware B. Ware!"

Ben Ware, with his modern ideas for the Farms, pushing for Atlantic Avenue and the shore branch of the railroad, had succeeded too well. New summer cottages were rising one beside and behind another, along with boardinghouses and several hotels, of which Ware's Clifton House, now managed by his son and namesake, was not the least, for he could take in 125 guests, feed them from his own large vegetable garden and fruit farm and herd of thoroughbred Ayrshires, and divert them with riding, billiards, bowling, croquet, baseball, picnics, bathing and boating.

Look, the petitioners exclaimed, what we have done for our respective towns! And look, they complained, at what is being done to us! In return for carrying twenty-four percent of the tax load, in the case of Marblehead, they got back one percent in services—scant fire protection, hardly any policing, very little road work, but with so much more than their share of liquor licenses and resort permits that "the roads and stores are infested with disorderly persons, who frighten ladies, children and the timid with unrestrained ribaldry."

Not much was said by the secessionists about tax-dodging, an issue coming to the fore with the public revelation that many a wealthy Bostonian was ducking high city taxes by claiming his summer home on the North Shore, where taxes were low, as his legal residence.

The recent invasion of the horsecars, predecessors of the electric street-cars, was likewise soft-pedaled by the petitioners. The Lynn and Boston Street Railroad had extended service to Swampscott every fifteen minutes in 1881, and then on to Marblehead in June of 1884, a few months before the secession movement surfaced, and with startling results, conveying as many as three thousand passengers a day. A few weeks later the Naumkeag Street Railway started running *its* horsecars off for Marblehead.

Would the developing shore from Phillips Point to Marblehead Neck be trampled by the thundering herd, dumped off the "bobtails" before every private gate at five cents a head? There was a popular ditty going the rounds already:

> *Hail! today cheap transportation*
> *Comes in triumph to our station;*
> *Bearing in its train the story*
> *Anti-monopoly, the people's glory!*
> *Roll it along, through all the town,*
> *The people's right—cheap transportation!*
> *See the people come to meet us!*
> *At the station many greet us!*
> *All take seats with exultation.*
> *Glory in cheap transportation.*

As far as Marblehead was concerned, the proposed amputation would give the new town most of the parent's area and seven of its thirteen miles of coastline. Injury enough. The insult, which the town fathers carefully brought to the notice of the legislature's committee on towns during the hearings in 1885, was enough to kill the proposition outright: while the Farms and the Neck accounted for $1 million (a figure inflated by double, claimed the petitioners) of Marblehead's $3,270,000 real estate valuation, only 61 of the 1,930 registered voters resided in the area in dispute, and but 19 of 1,405 pupils attended the Farms school. Ben Ware and his cabal tried to revive their secession in 1886, but the steam had gone out of it.

This time around, 'Headers were dead right in bewaring Ben Ware. They could ill have afforded the loss of the cream of their summer colony.

On Christmas Day, 1888, a fire swept through the town center. It destroyed fifty buildings, including a number of the new shoe factories. Two thousand were put out of work. A comeback was attempted, but many of the unemployed had been forced to leave town for other work, and the disaster was the death knell of Marblehead's shoe industry, just as the terrible gale of 1846, which took ten vessels and sixty-five crew members and decimated the fleet, had been the beginning of the end of its fishing industry.

As the 1880s closed, population dropped to the lowest level since the September gale, and the proud and independent citizens of old Marblehead turned to a future quite largely dependent upon the foibles of the summer strangers and the fortunes of those whose fleets of shining yachts had captured their harbor.

The catboat ferry takes on passengers for town at the post office landing on Marblehead Neck, 1887. (Peabody Essex Museum)

Ben Clark drives his new schooner yacht Young Raven *on a spanking breeze, probably 1857 off Boston Bay. Attributed to Clarence Drew. (Peabody Essex Museum)*

~6~

YACHTING
GETS SERIOUS

*Salem pleasure craft, early regattas and yacht clubs,
and Marblehead's defense of America's Cup*

Sɪɴᴄᴇ ᴛʜᴇ ꜰɪʀsᴛ ʙɪʀᴄʜ ʙᴀʀᴋ canoe assayed the waters of the bay, boating—just boating—has been the joy of anyone with access to anything that floats. Yachting, at the other extreme, was imported as an indulgence of royal governors, not all of whom had salt water in their veins; the seat of provincial power was temporarily at Salem in the summer of 1774 when Governor Thomas Gage, who was a general and not an admiral, spent his leisure hours cruising about Wenham Lake in a pleasure barge.

When William Bentley was settled as pastor of Salem's East Church right after the Revolution in 1784, "only two Sail Boats had any claim to the name when their construction was considered in regard to amusement." Seventeen years passed before a third was sufficiently yachtlike to draw his attention. On the fifteenth of June, 1801, three months into the first administration of Thomas Jefferson, "Capt. G. Crowninshield junr carried me in his remarkably fast sailing Boat from Salem into Beverly Harbour. We made the whole course in 15 minutes & returned in 34, wind fresh at S.W. We made no tack in going, & one in Salem Harbour upon our return. I never did sail so much at my ease in any other boat."

George Crowninshield was a short and wiry bachelor of thirty-five; he had recently settled ashore to run the family's extensive business affairs after commanding various of its vessels in the world trade. The Crowninshields were ardent partisans of Mr. Jefferson (who made George's brother Jacob his Secretary of the Navy), and when George launched this fast sailer within a few days of the inauguration in March, he named her after the new President. This first North Shore yacht was thirty-six feet long and very burdensome by modern standards, displacing twenty-two tons. *Jefferson* is said to have been sloop-rigged originally and doubtless followed the lines of the small fishing vessels that were common on the coast.

Having loaned his name to the launching of the North Shore's first yacht, President Jefferson gave a whole fleet of pleasure boats a mighty shove when he persuaded Congress in 1807 to adopt the Embargo Acts, by which he hoped to set America on a par at sea with England and France. Salem ship owners were reasonably conscientious in forgoing their foreign trade, which left many the master and the mate on the beach with time on their hands. As Dr. Bentley observed the following August, "Since the embargo almost every person fond of sailing has purchased a sail boat & a great variety of experiments have been made upon the form of the boat & the manner of rigging, & these experiments have discovered great ingenuity with various success. . . . The Crowninshields, Derbys, Gardners, &c. & most of our enterprising Masters of Vessels have something of this kind they call their own & most of our Ship & boat builders & several of our townsmen who live at their ease."

The War of 1812 ended the yachting experiments of the seafaring class on the North Shore and enlisted little *Jefferson* in the privateering fleet of the Crowninshields. When his father died in 1815, George Crowninshield, Jr., retired from business altogether, as sons and heirs are sometimes wont to do under such circumstances, and devoted himself to spending their profits from the late war, no way more flamboyantly than on his latest enthusiasm, the hermaphrodite brig *Cleopatra's Barge,* eighty-three feet on the waterline and generally regarded as the first large private yacht built in America.

The *Barge* had all her owner's flair, fifty thousand dollars' worth of it, which was a lot of money in those days. From afar she presented the profile of a warship, which was belied, as she hove into closer view, by her multicolored stripes on one side, and when she tacked, by a herringbone pattern on the other, all set off with colored rigging. The main saloon was nineteen by twenty feet, mahogany and bird's-eye maple, upholstered in red Genoese velvet and gold lace, with gilded mirrors, a chandelier, custom glassware, china

John Perkins Cushing's schooner Sylph, *first of the racing yachts. (Peabody Essex Museum)*

and silver service. In 1816 Crowninshield sailed her to the Mediterranean, where she was a sensation and visited by thousands of the curious. But he died suddenly on his return to Salem in 1817, and his gorgeous creation was sold to King Kamehameha as Hawaii's royal yacht, only to be wrecked by the royal sailors.

Except as the plaything of a Crowninshield, a *Cleopatra's Barge* was shockingly rich for Yankee sporting blood. Anything approaching the North Shore tradition of yachtiness was another fifteen years in coming, when Benjamin C. Clark, the young shipping magnate who summered in Nahant, built *Mermaid,* a small schooner said to have been the first Boston-owned "yacht" to be adorned with that badge of degeneracy, a deck.

John Perkins Cushing had returned home from China with his fortune in 1831, the year previous to *Mermaid*'s debut. Having more money than he knew what to do with, Cushing too must have a yacht. His much younger cousin and protégé in business, Captain Robert Bennet Forbes, was also fresh from the China seas. Though not yet thirty, Forbes was a master among mariners, having shipped before the mast at thirteen and assumed his first command at twenty. Cushing commissioned the construction of a fifty-eight-foot schooner yacht to be called *Sylph,* which was built up the Mystic River at Medford during the winter of 1833.

Sylph was launched in the spring of 1834, and that summer in Boston Forbes and friends launched the Boat Club, whose only boats were row-boats. Next spring the Forbes circle, most of whom were young Boston merchant-shipmasters cradled on the ocean wave (by which they had avoided being rocked to sleep at Harvard), bought the forty-foot, thirty-ton schooner *Dream* in New York and upgraded the Boat Club to the Dream Club, the first American yacht club on record.

Not satisfied with *Sylph*'s performance, John Cushing had instructed the builder to lengthen her by eight and a half feet that winter. She proved perceptibly swifter on July 8, 1835, winning an informal race from Boston to Nahant and back against the smaller *Dream* and the big new brigs *Henry Clay* and *Isidore.* In another trial with *Dream, Sylph* didn't come off so well, unless the account is apocryphal. This time Colonel Thomas Handasyd Perkins, Jr., and Captain Philip Dumaresq, who would be one of the great masters of the clippers, sailed *Dream* against *Sylph* around a buoy outside Boston Harbor; it was agreed that the crew of the lead schooner would drive a boat hook into the buoy while going by, the runner-up to bring it back. *Dream* rounded first; Perkins hove his gaff home, and they finished ahead.

At the end of July 1835, John Cushing, with his cousins, captains Forbes and William Sturgis, shipowner R. D. Shepherd (who had sold him the land for "Belmont"), Sam Cabot (Uncle Tom's serpent-sighting son-in-law) and Captain Daniel C. Bacon (another old China hand and Forbes's close friend and business partner) embarked in *Sylph* on a cruise around Cape Cod. Off Nantucket they fell in with the larger schooner yacht *Wave,* ninety-two feet, owned by John Cox Stevens, future founding commodore

of the New York Yacht Club, "and got handsomely beaten by her," as Cushing noted in his diary. Near Woods Hole the tide carried them aground, and the owner, figuring his *Sylph* was a goner, sold her on the spot for a quarter of her cost to Forbes and Sam Cabot—a transaction that he did not note in his diary. But with help from a government cutter the wily Ben floated his prize. Homeward bound, they fell in again with the *Wave* for a race down Vineyard Sound and were gaining when the rising wind decided Stevens to give it up and bear away for Tarpaulin Cove on the island of Naushon. Samuel Eliot Morison called this the first American yacht race of record, although one and possibly both of *Sylph*'s bouts with *Dream* might take the precedence.

Sylph was sold as a Boston Harbor pilot boat, and in 1837 Commodore Forbes, Captain Dan Bacon and William H. Boardman built the thirty-ton schooner *Breeze,* fifty-one feet long, doubling the fleet of the Dream Club. That summer they raced to Marblehead. *Dream* arrived first and anchored. *Breeze* came up and tied alongside. Forbes hospitably invited the rival crew into his more spacious cabin for lunch and, when they were below, slipped aboard *Dream* and induced their cook to pass his guests' own food and wine over and down his forehatch. Upon the conclusion of this deception, *Breeze* cast off first and got under way. Forbes hoisted a well-drained champagne bottle (one of *Dream*'s) to his main gaff and maintained his lead back to Boston (so he claimed) by tossing empty bottles and strawberry boxes overboard, causing the still-hungry Dreamers, who had unwittingly shared their lunch, to heave to and pick up what they supposed, with by now astonishing naïveté, was good wine and good fruit.

That first American yacht club and most of its commodore's fortune evaporated in the financial crisis of 1837, and Forbes returned to China to recoup. Yet, though the shore east of New York remained clubless for thirty more years, the building of the fast little schooners and the informal matches had had their effect; the sport of yachting, as distinct from messing about in boats, had caught the imagination of a slowly growing number of those who could afford to buy, staff and maintain their own private sailing vessels.

Robert Bennet Forbes was a superb sailor, where John Cox Stevens, the inventor-engineer-yachtsman, was merely first-rate, but when Stevens and friends celebrated the dawn of recovery from the 1837 depression by organizing the New York Yacht Club aboard his new schooner *Gimcrack*, anchored off the Battery on July 30, 1844, it stayed organized. A month later the New York squadron put in to Newport on its maiden cruise and rendezvoused with Captain Forbes in the chartered Boston pilot schooner *Belle* and Colonel William P. Winchester's sixty-seven-foot schooner yacht *Northern Light*. With David Sears of Nahant they were enlisted on the spot as the club's first New England members; thus was sanctioned the long and frequently amiable rivalry between North Shore and New York yachtsmen.

THE CRAZE HEATS UP

Yachting excitement built to a peak in 1851, when the New York Yacht Club's 102-foot schooner *America* sailed across the Atlantic and in the most important, if not most exciting, race of the century beat Britain's best and brought home the Royal Yacht Squadron's Hundred Guineas Cup. *America*'s victory stunned Britannia and gave a further push to the already burgeoning interest in yachting on the East Coast of the United States, where there was money to spare as the 1850s basked in the sun of prosperity.

The first regatta to be held off Marblehead in 1852 merely divided the entries over and under fourteen tons. The next such meet on the North Shore verged on the chaotic. Gloucester, where children were weaned on brine, put on an extempore "regatta" in its own unique style on August 16, 1855, when fifteen boats simply tacked out the harbor and back. The Gloucester *Telegraph* thought the exercise "a very fine, yet rather singular scene, scarcely any two being rigged alike, or carrying the same amount of sail. . . . It would be difficult to state the winning boat, as no measures were taken to make due allowance for tonnage, nor any rules laid down for guidance, and as far as we can learn no judges were appointed to decide." No prizes and few spectators.

However, it all comes out of the hold, as the Gloucester saying goes. Fishing was prosperous, and a little fleet of local yachts reflected the fact. The second attempt at a regatta succeeded splendidly, a sweepstakes in four classes according to length of waterline, with time allowances between boats. Eighteen started off Pavilion Beach on September 3, 1858, and sailed outside Eastern Point over ocean courses, the shortest eight miles. Significantly, the most spirited match of the day was provided by the class of centerboard sloops led by Captain Robert Bennet Forbes, age fifty-four,

From Winthrop northeast to Cape Ann, the North Shore has always provided ample challenge for sailors of all stripes. (Author's collection)

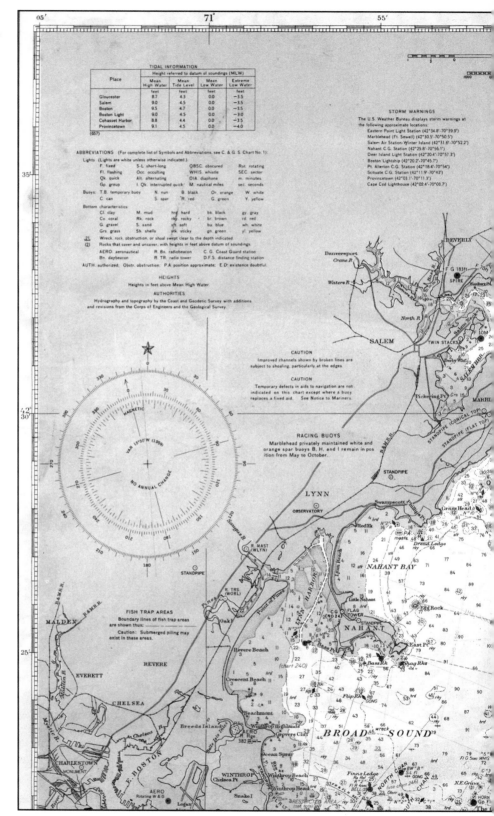

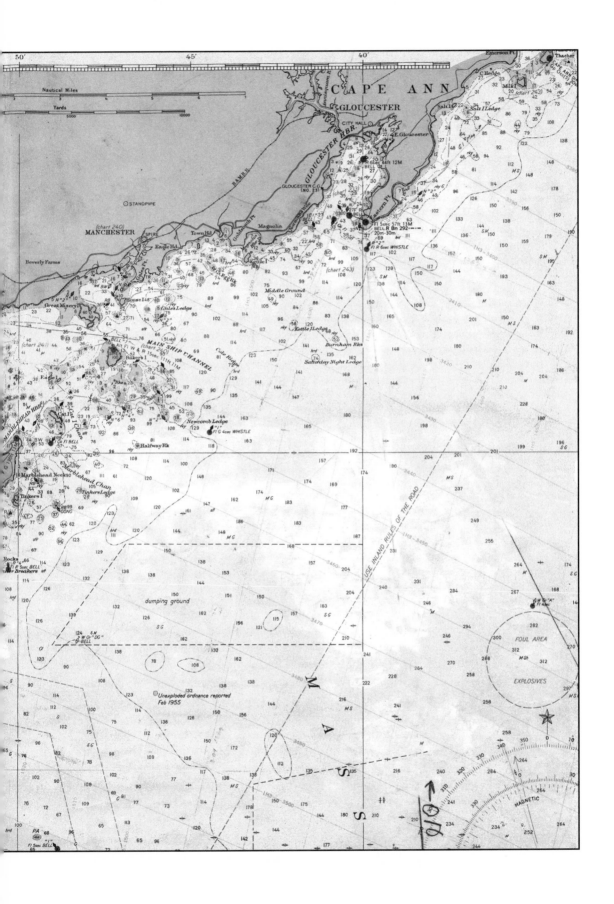

at the tiller of his twenty-four-foot *Grace Darling,* which won eight dollars and "the commendations of all by her very superior performance."

The name was a characteristically Forbesian choice. A noted heroine of the period, Grace Darling braved a stormy sea in an open boat with her father, an English lighthouse keeper, to rescue survivors of a wreck off the coast of Northumberland in 1838. Her American admirer evidently felt a kinship: in 1849 the steamship *Europa,* on which he was a passenger for Liverpool, rammed and sank the barque *Charles Bartlett* in mid-Atlantic; Forbes leaped into the ocean and helped save several survivors.

When the second Gloucester sweepstakes was run off on August 17, 1860, the owners of the three local centerboard sloops lost to summer people. This time the raiders were Franklin Burgess and his younger brother, Edward, or Ned, who was twelve, in *Cassie.* Summering on Woodbury Point in Beverly, the Burgesses would become famous in the annals of yachting. Ned never forgot that race: "We beat around the outer stake-boat so far ahead of the local boats that the patriotic keepers of the stake-boat cut her adrift, after we turned, so as to lessen the distance the other boats had to make!" Fishermen's tricks.

Captain Forbes returned to Stonington in 1859 and ordered the larger centerboarder *Scud* for himself and the keel sloop *Mist* for cousin John Cushing, both thirty feet on the waterline. Neither kept his boat more than a season or so; Cushing was seventy-two anyway and sold *Mist* to Francis E. Bacon.

On July 6, 1861, just as her new owner and *Mist* were embarking for a day of sailing on the bay, Captain Seth Simmons and a reporter for the Boston *Herald* identifying himself modestly as "E. B. H." clambered into a wicker basket. The lines were let go, the crowd huzzahed, and the hot-air balloon *Queen of the Air* ascended above Boston Common until, in a trice, "the horse cars crawled beneath us like flies." High over the harbor they floated on the wings of the southwesterly and across the bluffs of Winthrop so far below, and then, as the bag cooled, the *Queen* began her regal descent, rather to the consternation of her passengers, who had counted a bit recklessly, considering the direction of the wind, on a dry landing.

There was Nahant, two miles off, and the broad Atlantic below and all around, and rising up with alarming rapidity. Ahead, the only two craft in sight, dead ahead in fact, were a schooner and a sloop. The basket struck, scooped up a load of sea water, lifted as the breeze bore the bag along, surged above the waves with its soaked and gasping occupants for a couple of hundred yards, then dipped and dunked them again.

Captain Simmons, with strength born of desperation, hove himself up and opened the air valve a turn or two just as his runaway craft missed the sloop by a hair (it was *Mist,* of course, which had barely succeeded in luffing out of the way) and sailed into the fore rigging of the schooner *Atlantic,* bound down east. Simmons was hurled from the basket onto the deck, while E. B. H. splashed into the sea and was left astern. *Atlantic*'s crew immediately lowered away for him, but the boat swamped and dumped one of them overboard. They bailed their boat, cast off, and rescued the fellow, while *Mist* came up on E. B. H. (who fortunately was a strong swimmer, for he was half a mile astern by now), plucked the reporter from the briny, gave him a change of clothes, chowder and champagne, and set him ashore at Nahant with something to write about. The *Queen of the Air,* having done her mischief for the day, worked clear of the schooner's rigging and soared off and away.

THE EASTERN YACHT CLUB

Yachting was one of the lesser casualties of the Civil War. During the peaceful summer of 1866 Captain Arthur H. Clark took a crew of professionals and amateurs, which included Henry Wadsworth Longfellow's son Charley, in Uncle Tom

The Eastern Yacht Club's founding commodore, John Heard. (Eastern Yacht Club)

Appleton's forty-eight-foot sloop *Alice* on a precedent-making, record-breaking sail from Nahant to England in the smashing time of nineteen days. That December the schooner *Henrietta,* owned by James Gordon Bennett, Jr., copped a ninety-thousand-dollar stake from *Fleetwing* and *Vesta* in a daring winter race to Cowes under the burgees of the New York Yacht Club.

Before the year was over the Boston Yacht Club had materialized out of this postwar burst of yachting excitement. Although the club was the first in Massachusetts Bay since the Dreamers, its North Shore members fretted from the start over the distance of the station at City Point, South Boston, from their own piazzas. Impatient Beverly sailors activated the Essex County Squadron for impromptu sweepstakes off Marblehead in 1868 and 1869; eight of the squadron's sixteen member schooners and sloops were based at Beverly, four at Swampscott, two at Manchester, and one each at Gloucester and Nahant. By now upwards of fifty substantial pleasure craft were afloat in Boston Bay.

The racing cauldron stirred up by the Essex County Squadron boiled over into a cabalistic session of Boston Yacht Club dissidents on the evening of March 5, 1870. Meeting furtively at the Park Street home of John Heard, these disloyalists created the Eastern Yacht Club and elected their host as their commodore and Franklin Burgess as their vice commodore. Heard was a nephew of Augustine Heard, the China merchant. For some years before his return to the States and his settlement for the summer on Ober's Point east of Beverly Cove, Commodore Heard had been the family firm's managing partner in Canton, where he owned and raced yachts, probably from the Canton Regatta Club, started by Bostonians on the Pearl River in 1837.

The Eastern Yacht Club, about 1890. (Peabody Essex Museum)

In no time Eastern had a roster of eighty, a set of bylaws, sailing regulations, a uniform, and a burgee . . . but no fixed home. So a room was hired on India Wharf in Boston for convivial purposes.

Eastern beat out the Lynn Yacht Club as the first on the North Shore by only two days. The yachtsmen of the shoe city organized on March 7, 1870, and actually went on to sail the North Shore's first club regatta with a fleet of fourteen over a seven-mile course on June 17.

Lynn was strictly a local club, whereas Eastern represented Boston money and the North Shore. It, too, sent fourteen yachts to the starting line of its first regatta on July 12, twenty-five days after Lynn's. But the course was forty miles from Marblehead Rock to Minot's Ledge and return, and the fleet was convoyed by a steamer laden with flag officers, women spectators and musicians. At the end of the month the Easterners headed east to Mt. Desert Island for a fortnight's cruise, and by the end of the season there were sixteen schooners, nine sloops and one steam yacht in the squadron.

In a well-meaning plagiarism of the New York Yacht Club charter, the Eastern Yacht Club was incorporated in 1871 "for the purpose of encouraging yacht building and naval architecture, and the cultivation of nautical science." And what an encouraging sight it was as the billowing sails of the New Yorkers hove into view from the westward for the first joint regatta of the two clubs off Swampscott on August 11! The Easterners sailed out to meet them behind Commodore Heard's flagship, the schooner *Rebecca*, whereupon the visitors separated with fine precision into two divisions on a signal from Commodore Bennett's *Dauntless* and engaged in a sequence of faultless maneuvers (that is, their professional sailing masters and crews did).

The fleets were on the point of exchanging the traditional salutes when a small sloop slipped tipsily out from under the lee of Nahant, displaying strings of empty bottles in the rigging in place of pennants. She headed, after a fashion, for *Dauntless,* to the rising consternation of those on board, when at the last moment she bore off with shouts and graphic gestures of welcome from her carefree crew. It was Eastern's *Daisy,* whose owner, Captain William C. (Billy) Otis, "having considered the reception as planned somewhat too formal, had decided to inject an element of frivolity and good fellowship to relieve any possible stiffness from the occasion. . . . The joke was taken in good part all around and keenly enjoyed, dispelling at one stroke any risk of too much ceremonial."

That evening the Eastern yachts and bands on board two towboats combined to fill the sky with fireworks and the night with music. In the morning the tugs conveyed a joint party of members to Point Shirley, where they were photographed in attitudes of obvious satisfaction on the porch of Taft's Hotel. On August 14 hosts and visitors raced through a tangle of spectator boats for cups put up by Eastern and the town of Swampscott; it was the largest regatta of large yachts in American waters to date.

MARBLEHEAD IN ITS YACHTING GLORY

When the Eastern Yacht Club was founded in 1870, the dories belonging to the Nashua campers were about the most pretentious pleasure craft at Marblehead. Appreciation of the harbor's potential as a yachting base was late in awakening and was not wholeheartedly encouraged by 'Headers. The

Greely Curtis with three of his children aboard Dream *out of the Eastern Yacht Club. (Curtis family collection)*

extension of the railroad and the highway up along the shore from Swampscott represented one flank of the summer invasion, and the slow subversion of the Neck by the outside world served as the other. Easterners found the deep harbor a convenient anchorage midway along the North Shore but were divided over its merits as a candidate for their home station. Not until 1880, after nine years of debate, did the club agree to settle down at Marblehead and build a conservatively gingerbreaded house half along the Neck.

Opening day on June 10, 1881, was to be a blast (and why not, for what is so rare as a day in June?), but it turned into another sort of blast not soon forgotten, a blast of wind and rain from the northeast. Members and guests huddled aboard their pitching yachts in the anchorage, peering at the festivities ashore (such as they were) through the portholes, or got a thorough drenching rowing in. And those disappointed souls from Beverly who had fought to locate the clubhouse closer to home in Manchester Harbor or even the lee of Misery Island, secure from the whims of the northeaster, shook their heads and growled, "We told you so!" But it was too late. The mantle of destiny had descended on Marblehead Neck.

No sooner had the Eastern Yacht Club settled in its new clubhouse than the porch was taken over by a self-elected auxiliary to the flag officers, comprised largely of elderly bachelors, known as the Piazza Committee, who passed judgment upon all matters of nautical protocol and etiquette. For example: should the rustle of skirts intrude on these manly precincts? The debate on this question was reported by C. H. W. Foster, president of Chickering, the Boston piano manufacturer, and a summer resident of Marblehead Neck, who at an advanced age compiled *The Eastern Yacht Club Ditty Box: 1870–1900,* a chronicle of the early years. From the outset, he wrote, "man was supreme but, as is usual, the fair sex began to win its way and finally some member under female domination offered a motion that would open the clubhouse to the general use of ladies. Our Piazza Committee was furious, but the motion was carried and what do you suppose happened? Three of the elderly bachelors soon became married! Ah, you sailor men know how it is: 'Tis the old rope that is the easier spliced."

Almost without exception the schooners and sloops that dominated the Eastern Yacht Club squadron were thirty feet or more of waterline length, most of them much more. Many members also owned boats too small for racing under the club rules. To make a home for these poor relations, Ned Burgess and other North Shore sailors active in Eastern started the Beverly Yacht Club early in 1872.

The Beverly's espousal of small-boat racing sparked such enthusiasm across Boston Bay among South Shore yachtsmen that in seven years it was running a union regatta clear around Cape Cod off Monument Beach in Buzzards Bay. Two more years, and most of its fleet hailed from the South Shore and Buzzards Bay. In 1895 the rest of the camel followed the nose and reestablished itself at Pocasset. In 1913 the Beverly Yacht Club moved to

Marion, where it remains, name unchanged, to the mystification of the uninitiated.

This gradual desertion of the small-boat sailors of the North Shore left behind Eastern, which disdained anything under thirty feet on the waterline, and a few scattered local clubs—Lynn (1870), Salem Bay (1879), West Lynn and Gloucester's Cape Ann (1880), Winthrop's Great Head (1881), Rockport's Sandy Bay (1885) and Manchester (1892). (The Nahant and Annisquam dory clubs would not be born of the craze for the Swampscott sailing dory until the mid-1890s.)

At this juncture, by defending the America's Cup on the one hand and popularizing the art of small-boat sailing on the other, Marblehead established itself as the yachting center of the Northeast. In 1885 a group led by C. H. W. Foster and Benjamin W. Crowninshield organized the Corinthian Yacht Club for sailing craft between sixteen and thirty feet water-

Legendary yacht designer Edward (Ned) Burgess. From Harper's Weekly, *October 1, 1887.*

line and bought part of Jack's Point near the lighthouse on Marblehead Neck, where they erected a clubhouse in 1888. Their dual objective was to advance the design of small boats and racing by amateurs (hence *Corinthian*, amateurism in the tradition of the sailing aristocracy of ancient Corinth). And on the sound theory that good young sailors grow up to be better older ones, the Pleon, the first junior yacht club in America, was also founded on the Neck (for males only, to be sure). Thus Marblehead laid the groundwork for a brilliant future in yachting.

Corinthianism was imported to Marblehead, where few Easterners dreamed of raising their own sails. At Gloucester, which had long relished its reputation as the saltiest port in America, it was the only way. Sporadic pick-up regattas commencing in 1860 ultimately produced the Cape Ann Yacht Club in 1880, which for several years "sailed" out of the practice room of the Gloucester Cornet Club on Main Street. Uniquely, small-boat racing here was the home-grown, after-hours sport of local small businessmen, working-men and fishermen, grown-up wharf rats who just loved to sail.

BURGESS'S *VOLUNTEER* RULES BRITANNIA

Since losing the Hundred Guineas Cup in 1851 to *America* and the New York Yacht Club, the British Empire had tried four times to win it back; England sent schooners to New York in 1870 and 1871, Canada a schooner in 1876 and a sloop in 1881, all to no avail. Then in 1884 the Irish designer J. Beavor-Webb challenged with a pair of promising ninety-ton cutters—*Genesta*, with a successful season behind her, and *Galatea*, not yet built—proposing that if one were defeated, the other would be given a crack the next time around. The two were of somewhat different dimensions, of advanced construction,

*On board
Puritan. (From
Harper's Weekly,
September 12,
1885.)*

HARPER'S WEEKLY.

JOURNAL OF CIVILIZATION.

Vol. XXIX.—No. 1499.
Copyright, 1885, by Harper & Brothers.

NEW YORK, SATURDAY, SEPTEMBER 12, 1885.

TEN CENTS A COPY.
$4.00 PER YEAR, IN ADVANCE.

and so much longer than its largest candidates that the New Yorkers set about to build a defender of matching size, entrusting the design of *Priscilla*—with firm orders that she be a conventional centerboard sloop—to A. Cary Smith, who had lined off the club's 1881 cup winner, *Mischief*.

The owners of the top boats in the Eastern Yacht Club had raced the New York squadron's finest during its cruises to Marblehead in 1882 and 1883 and were satisfied that nothing their convention-bound brethren might throw into the defense of the America's Cup stood a chance against Beavor-Webb's challengers. Figuring that Boston's day might be dawning,

General Charles J. Paine and Vice Commodore J. Malcolm Forbes, son of former commodore John Murray Forbes, formed an Eastern syndicate to build their own candidate for the defense in 1885.

General Paine was a lean, balding, hawk-eyed, down-to-earth Bostonian with a sweeping mustache, who had commanded a division of black soldiers and been wounded in the Civil War. He managed a family fortune in railroads and owned a summer estate in Nahant, and his dual membership in the Marblehead and New York clubs qualified the syndicate's entry.

Of the other members of the Boston group, Malcolm Forbes had the new keel cutter *Lapwing*. His brother William H. Forbes sailed the keel sloop *Hesper*. Eastern Commodore Henry S. Hovey the previous year had launched his 109-foot *Fortuna*, which Captain R. F. Coffin, the leading yachting writer of the day, considered the fastest keel schooner in the world. Harry Hovey, the bachelor son of the late George O. Hovey, the Boston dry goods merchant, wintered on Beacon Street and summered in his father's luxurious cottage on the bank above Gloucester's Freshwater Cove with his sister Marion. The house burned in 1878, and they rebuilt in 1881 in the modish half-timbered style. Rear Commodore William F. Weld, of another Boston family in the shipping business, had already cruised abroad in his handsome new keel schooner *Gitana*. The sixth of the syndicate, William Gray, Jr., was a good amateur sailor who had designed his own keel sloop, *Huron*. Augustus Hemenway of Manchester, Boston merchant scion, owned the keel cutter *Beetle*. The remaining backers were Francis Lee Higginson, J. Montgomery Sears, and John L. (Jack) Gardner, the husband of Boston's flamboyant patroness of the arts, Isabella Stewart Gardner.

For the Eastern Yacht Club to mount such an effort called for boldness. To design their entry, which would be called *Puritan*, the members of the syndicate engaged the club's secretary, Ned Burgess, who was unfettered by preconceptions and unspoiled by success since he was just setting up practice as a professional yacht designer. His father's business failure in 1879 had forced Ned to go to work as an instructor in entomology at Harvard, but the summer of 1883, spent observing English yachts at Torquay and the Isle of Wight on the Channel, decided him to abandon bugs for boats.

On their return to Boston in the fall of 1883, Ned and his younger brother Sidney started the Eastern Yacht Agency on the strength of Ned's thorough avocational acquaintance with design and his drafting skill. No one beat down their doors, and Sid quit the partnership.

When caught between extremes, boldness may be the middle course. Burgess's plans for *Puritan* were a compromise between the deep English keel cutter and the shallow American centerboard sloop, even striking a balance between the relative rigs and sail areas. His aim was to combine in a new design what he considered the better features of each as to safety, speed, and weatherliness.

Indeed, the approach had already been tried and had worked brilliantly, but with no evident effect on the traditionalists. Back in 1871 Nathanael G.

Herreshoff designed and his brother John built for a New Bedford owner the initial tentative compromise between the Anglo-American extremes, the remarkably fast centerboard sloop *Shadow,* thirty-three and a half feet waterline, definitely deeper than the "skimming dishes" and equipped with a "railroad" for shifting ballast athwartships—an early sign of her creator's genius. Nat was three months Ned Burgess's senior, and the two had been friends since the 1860s, when the Herreshoffs first launched yachts for the Burgesses from their shop at Bristol, Rhode Island. Herreshoff had become wholly preoccupied with steamboats and engines soon after *Shadow*'s appearance, however, and was not to resume his interest in sailing craft until 1890.

Puritan was launched from South Boston on May 26, 1885, ninety-four feet overall, eighty-one waterline, with the plumb stem and counter of the cutter. The New York press called her a "bean boat" and sneered that she'd be all right for carrying bricks on the Hudson River.

With a well-drilled Corinthian crew (all friends of Paine and Burgess) under Captain Aubrey Crocker, a Cohasset professional, the bean boat jolted New York by beating *Priscilla* in the Goelet Cup Race off Newport in August 1885 (the prize, a silver tankard, was presented to the Eastern Yacht Club by the winner as the perpetual Puritan Cup, the prime trophy thereafter for major yachts in Massachusetts Bay). In the official trials that followed, *Puritan* finished off *Priscilla,* one, two, three.

Meanwhile Sir Richard Sutton's *Genesta* had arrived from England, flying the signal of the Royal Yacht Squadron. On September 14 and 16 *Puritan* outpointed and outfooted the traditional cutter off New York Harbor to retain the America's Cup in two straight races, the second extremely close. In so doing, she catapulted Marblehead to the top of the yachting world, carried off a middle-of-the-road revolution in yacht design, and transformed her creator from a relative unknown into the first of the great professional sailboat designers on the western shore of the Atlantic. In boyish celebration (as he did for all his victories where there was the deck room), Ned Burgess turned a double somersault as his masterpiece crossed the finish line.

Burgess was now beset with orders. As agreed, Beavor-Webb's *Galatea*, owned by British navy Lieutenant William R. Henn of the Royal Northern Yacht Club, was to have a crack at the Cup in 1886. This time General Paine alone engaged the Beverly designer to improve, if he could, on *Puritan,* which the syndicate had sold to J. Malcolm Forbes. *Mayflower* was the result, rather larger than her predecessor but along the same lines

Sketches made during the Volunteer-Thistle series. From Harper's Weekly, October 1, 1887.

and also built by Lawley at South Boston. The new Burgess boat was actually defeated by *Puritan* in the early 1886 trials, but a shift of ballast here, and a sail and rig change there, soon brought her up to trim. *Mayflower* sailed to New York in August and drubbed *Puritan*, an altered *Priscilla* and the new sloop *Atlantic*, built as a contender by members of the Atlantic Yacht Club of New York in an attempt to incorporate Burgess's design novelties.

On August 1, 1886, *Galatea* hove into Marblehead Harbor under jury rig from England and was greeted with fireworks, bonfires and salutes, a reception at the Eastern Yacht Club, more fireworks and a serenading by the Salem Cadet Band. The mutual amiability survived *Galatea*'s one-sided defeat off New York on September 7 and 11. Burgess turned his somersaults.

Wasting no time, the leading English designer, George L. Watson, visited America in the autumn of 1886 to see what ideas he could discreetly borrow. That winter he returned home and drafted the steel cutter *Thistle* for a syndicate of Scots from the Royal Clyde Yacht Club. She was faster than anything afloat in her home waters, as she proved, and great things were expected.

As soon as *Thistle*'s dimensions were published (the New York Yacht Club had amended the Deed of Gift of the America's Cup to force the challenger to show something of his hand in advance), General Paine commissioned Burgess to outdesign her. *Volunteer* was rushed through construction and set maiden sail on July 21, 1887. In her trials the latest magic from the Burgess board left her parent *Mayflower*, as *Mayflower* had *Puritan*, far, far astern.

Thistle crossed with all the hopes of empire riding on her wake. Her design and construction had been shrouded in secrecy, and she had been a veritable terror amongst the British yachting fleet. The first Cup race was sailed through an armada of spectator boats on September 27 over the thirty-eight miles of the New York Yacht Club inside course. The stunning white *Volunteer* simply walked away from the gallant pretender, passed her in the opposite direction on the homeward run, and finished nineteen minutes ahead. The second race on the thirtieth was a formality; the Burgess double somersault set off eleven minutes and fifty-four seconds of whistles and cannon fire before *Thistle* crossed the finish line. There would not be another challenge for six more years.

Volunteer sailed in triumph for Marblehead, and while a tugboat towed her the windless last few miles into the harbor on the evening of October 7, the City of Boston held a packed reception for her designer and owner in Faneuil Hall. The briefest of the panegyrics was the best, from the absent Dr. Holmes, who could not resist writing from Beverly Farms, "Proud as I am of their achievement, I own that the General is the only commander I ever heard of who made himself illustrious by running away from all his competitors."

Later in the evening the half-encircling shore of Marblehead Harbor blazed with bonfires, and every yacht was illuminated. Into this eerie

amphitheater puffed the steamer *Brunette*, towing a serpentine procession of fifty dories strung with Chinese lanterns. As they completed their encirclement of *Volunteer* the harbor exploded with skyrockets, Roman candles and red fire. Then, on a toot from the steamer, every church bell in town pealed furiously and the shores echoed with the blasts of cannon from the squadron. The Lynn Cadet Band burst into a medley of patriotic airs from *Brunette*'s deck, and Town Clerk Felton stepped aboard the third-in-a-row Marblehead defender of the America's Cup with resolutions of congratulation from the selectmen.

Ned Burgess did not live to see the best of his more than two hundred designs utterly overshadowed by Nat Herreshoff's great forty-six footer *Gloriana*, first of the rule-beaters with her long overhangs and "spoon bow" that stretched so extraordinarily her measured waterline and her speed, when heeled—as inventive in her construction as she was radical, yet sound, in her lines. The North Shore designer died of typhoid fever on July 12, 1891, having just turned forty-three. "He might have designed the world's handsomest yachts if he had lived to an age of greater maturity, for in my opinion he was a great artist." So wrote the Marblehead designer L. Francis Herreshoff of his father's close friend.

The torch passed silently from Edward Burgess to Nathanael Herreshoff that midsummer day of 1891, from the pragmatic bugologist and his faithful North Shore friends, who broke with tradition and brought Yankee sense to yacht design, to the genius who raised it to its glory.

Thus dawned the golden age of yachting.

Volunteer runs in from Sandy Hook to win the first day's race. Thistle can barely be seen at extreme right. (From Harper's Weekly, *October 8, 1887.)*

The Nahant House failed as a hotel but, beginning in 1837, served as a home to generations of Peabodys and Fays before burning in 1958. The "tower" was added in 1876 to enhance the view of Boston Harbor.
(Nahant Historical Society)

~7~
NAHANT OUT-BOSTONS BOSTON

Unamused by amusements, Cold Roast cold-shoulders Newport and takes to the tennis court

Aɴʏ ɴᴏᴛɪᴏɴs ᴏꜰ ᴍᴀᴋɪɴɢ another Newport of Nahant went up in smoke with Colonel Perkins's hotel that September night of 1861, putting a spectacular *coup de grâce* to the last rambling reminder of *la vie gaie* and leaving the North Shore's first resort utterly in the clannish (and clammy, some said) grip of Cold Roast Boston. Nahant had already achieved the distinction among observers of the social scene of being more quintessentially Boston than Boston itself. In the Hub, Henry Cabot Lodge asserted with satisfaction, "everybody knew everybody else and all about everybody else's family." Since Nahant had but a twentieth part of the city's everybodys, the interfamiliarity was in inverse ratio.

Just to show how unfair, let alone inaccurate, was John Collins Bossidy's parodic toast to "The home of the bean and the cod / Where the Lowells talk to the Cabots / And the Cabots talk only to God," John Ellerton Lodge had returned to Boston with a New Orleans cotton fortune and plans for an early retirement at the age of thirty-five when Henry Cabot's daughter Anna deigned not merely to talk to him in 1842 but to marry him as well. The bridegroom's curly fringe of chin whiskers and air of poetic contemplation belied his driving nature; not content with one fortune, he was soon pursuing another in shipping. During the gold rush of 1849 one of his vessels paid for itself in freight charges before its maiden voyage; by 1853 Lodge had three clippers in the service to 'Frisco.

The family vacationed in the Cabot cottage on Cliff Street in Nahant. In 1862 John Ellerton Lodge died unexpectedly at fifty-five, leaving Anna, their son Henry Cabot Lodge and their daughter Elizabeth. Cabot, as the boy was known, was eleven and worshipped his father. Fortunately he had supportive friends and was a Cabot as much as a Lodge, and everybody in his world, after all, knew everybody else.

Among his chums was William Lawrence, eighteen days his junior. He too was a young sprout in Nahant's genealogical hothouse, his roots intermingled with those of the other well-established families. Young Bill, the Episcopal bishop-to-be, was a son of Amos A. Lawrence, the textile capitalist. Although the family had old Nahant connections, Amos did not gain a foothold there until 1864, when he forsook his summer place on the Lynn shore of Nahant Bay and bought the Clark's Point estate of that vigorous early yachtsman, Benjamin C. Clark.

Bill's mother, Sarah, was a daughter of the dyspeptic merchant William Appleton, who owned the former David Sears cottage on Swallow's Cave Road next to the sailing General Paine, Cup defender. The Appletons and Searses were of course related, and Mrs. Sears was a sister-in-law of Dr. John Collins Warren, who had helped colonize Nahant with his endorsement of its therapeutic properties. Dr. Warren's second wife was the sister of that other senator from Nahant, Robert C. Winthrop; his son, the third in the medical dynasty, Dr. J. Mason Warren, had married Annie, a daughter of Benjamin W. Crowninshield of Salem, who had a summer cottage on Swallow's Cave Road. As his brother Jacob was Jefferson's Secretary of the Navy, Benjamin was Madison's; brother George had his own private flagship in the form of *Cleopatra's Barge*. The Mason Warren cottage was back of Joe's Beach. A second Crowninshield daughter, Mary, married Dr. Charles Mifflin, and they bought the old Eliot cottage behind Bass Beach, where the president of Harvard spent the summers of his youth; it was later owned by their son George, head of Houghton Mifflin, the publisher. Elizabeth, the third Crowninshield daughter and a great beauty, married the Reverend William Mountford; *their* house overlooked the sea next the Prescotts. The late historian, by the way, was married to a sister of William Amory, who was married to a daughter of David Sears. Dr. Mason Warren's daughter Rosamond married Charles Hammond Gibson (the Gibsons and Hammonds were behind Cedar Point), while his sister married Thomas Dwight and lived on Cliff Street west of the church. The Dwight boys, James and Thomas, studied medicine; later, across the road from his parents, Dr. Tom bought the Charles Amory place from the heirs of Elizabeth Clarke Copley Greene. "Madame Greene," the daughter of John Singleton Copley and wife of Gardiner Greene, the artist's agent in Boston after he had gone to England, lived there many summers.

Thus were intertwined the everybodys of Nahant and Boston, root, branch and twig.

With the Civil War's end, Bill Lawrence and his brother Amory moved sailboats and horses from the old cottage at Lynn to the new one on Clark's Point. Other summer activities stuck in Bill's memory. "As the bowling-alleys and stables of the old hotel were still standing, we boys, Cabot Lodge, Frank Chadwick, Sturgis Bigelow, and Frank Amory, amused ourselves smashing the windows and were chased over fence after fence by Cabot's gardener."

Near East Point and beyond sight of the road was a deep inlet marked by Cupid's Rock. Here, in the properly clothed remembrance of the bishop, "all Nahant boys and men in the garb of nature bathed and dived." Every Sunday after the internal cleansing in the Boston Church, the summer male population headed for Cupid's Rock for a cold dash of the external. One

such morning the dignified commission merchant Patrick Grant had stripped himself of all but nature's garb, or so he thought, and was about to plunge into the sea when someone shouted a warning and he stepped back to discover that he was still topped off with his tall beaver hat.

These weekly baptisms continued for years, surviving even the disapproval long afterward of Probate Judge Rollin E. Harmon, who one afternoon observed the rite while on his way to supper with Patrick Grant's son, the jurist-novelist Robert Grant, and complained to the Nahant police. The bathers had to supplement nature until Judge Grant wrote his stiff-necked colleague, "You were within your rights, to be sure, but it is really my bailiwick. I know Nahant better than you do." Judge Harmon retreated, and the garb of Cupid was permitted at Cupid's Rock for a few more years until the prying tourists in their motor cars got too thick along the shore.

In the early 1870s Cabot Lodge and his sister Elizabeth, who had married George Abbot James, divided the East Point estate and built their houses there; Cabot shelved his library in the Greek Revival temple that had been the hotel's billiard hall. East Point was his base for the rest of his life, as indifferent lawyer, as enthusiastic writer and historian, as shrewdest of politicians first elected state representative from Nahant in 1879, then congressman, finally U.S. Senator for thirty-one years, in which capacity he belonged to a club only slightly less exclusive than his Cold Roast bastion by the briny blue. The aristocratic squire with his cool eyes and clipped

Dr. J. Mason Warren with family and friends on the porch of his Nahant cottage, August 1866. (Nahant Historical Society)

beard, arising every morning to split wood for an hour, riding his horse about town with a nod here and a faint smile there, though the course of his career shook nations, was the personification of Nahant to itself and to the world.

THE ICE KING'S GRAND FINALE

Nahanters who had sighed with relief over the demise of the ugly, tasteless barrack of a hotel in their midst in 1859 might better have held their breaths. The Ice King was even then thawing out a disagreeable surprise, his ultimate eccentricity. Now seventy-six, Frederic Tudor chose the occasion to create possibly the first full-fledged amusement park in America. Amused, his neighbors were not. Most everyone had been delighted when the snowy-bearded tycoon with the frosty eyes had made their windswept peninsula bloom with trees and vegetation; but now he proposed, in the words of a maverick who applauded his plan, to offer a refuge in the heart of the resort for the public, "who would otherwise be deterred by the fear of trespassing upon private grounds, where some unhospitable sign-board forbids eating your luncheon if you are hungry, or of overstepping certain imaginary boundaries if adventurous."

Unfortunately for the peace and quiet of his abutters, the awkward truth was that the open pasture behind North Spring's clear, cold trickle at the shore edge of Tudor's property, where he chose to launch his latest enthusiasm, was a public chowder and stamping ground by tradition. Furthermore, it was adjoined on the west by Cadet Field, which every July for a decade at least (and as it would be for another fifteen years) had been the tenting and marching ground of Boston's First Corps of Cadets, of which several prominent summer residents were members. Here the governor's honor guard paraded in brilliant uniform, put on band concerts and evening collations, and flirted with the flower of Nahant, the whole colorful excitement of Cadet Week climaxing with the appearance of His Excellency on Governor's Day for review.

Tudor bought the North Spring pasture between Ocean and Pond streets about the time a second freshet was discovered on the shore to the east of it. He built a circular wall around this new spring in 1859, called it the Pool of Maolis (a transposition of Jerusalem's Pool of Siloam) and Maolis Gardens, the curious project that for the remaining five years of his life engaged his whimsy and his furious energy.

Around his pasture Nahant's master of the unexpected erected a ten-foot slat fence with entrance gate (adults five cents, children three). Inside, he planted trees and flower beds and built a restaurant on the edge of the cliff overlooking the ocean, a dance hall, a small hotel, several open pavilions that could be hired for picnics requiring cooking and an ice cream parlor. His men installed seesaws and swings, one of which was fifty feet high with a collective seat. Flying horses were added, and a shooting range, a croquet field, bowling alleys, wheels of fortune, a Punch and Judy show, caged

The Witch House at Maolis Gardens, about 1870. It stands today, though no longer guarded by a stone lion in his lair. (Nahant Public Library)

animals and two tame bears with the Civil War–inspired monikers Ben Butler and Jeff Davis, which took their keeper to the beach for dips. Indians from Old Town, Maine, sold baskets and trinkets, and concessions were let to the balloon man, the candy man and the tintype artist.

Was the Fun King in his second childhood? The teahouse of Maolis Gardens was a temple-like pavilion of marble, tiles and seashells. Nearby was an octagonal fancy of similar construction sheltering a pool in which stood the spouting statue of a boy covered with shells; a third pavilion consisted simply of a tilted circular roof, the Parasol. He blasted a den out of a cleft in the ledge and had a local mason carve a stone lion that glared out from behind the iron bars of its cage. A painted clay bull menaced little children from its pen under the trees. Everywhere was strange statuary, and on every surface playful paintings and murals such as a depiction of the sea serpent, which writhed across a hundred feet of slat fence and appeared and disappeared as one walked by.

Frederic Tudor was eighty when he died in 1864. It was said that he spent no less than thirty thousand dollars a year the last thirty of his life on his eccentric projects at Nahant. His widow carried on valiantly after the Civil War and is credited with inventing the barge, the horse-drawn conveyance for guests familiar to every summer hotel, when she bought a boatsleigh called *Cleopatra's Barge* and had it put on wheels to carry passengers from the Lynn depot to Maolis Gardens. By 1882, however, the crowds had shifted to Revere Beach, and that June, when Mrs. Tudor's amusement park opened under the strict temperance management of the Lynn Reform Club, it presented a "ragged appearance" to a visiting reporter, and the speakers almost outnumbered their hearers.

Before her death in 1884 the Ice Queen willed Maolis to the town of Nahant, but it was more than the taxpayers would support, and they refused the gift, settling eventually for Tudor Wharf. In 1892 most of what was left was removed. Today there remains a single intact monument to the driving, driven Despot of the Ice Trade, who wanted possibly more than all else to be loved by his fellows en masse. This is the Witch House, last remnant of his midway, standing on a private estate near the corner of Marginal Road and Ocean Street. Eight fieldstone columns support the octagonal gabled roof. Time has stripped away most of the weird carved ornaments and doodads, and it broods above the sea, a pseudo-Druidic put-on left there by Nahant's most extraordinary, and unfathomable, citizen.

Sphairistike, or lawn tennis, swept all other distractions aside for James Dwight, who imported the game from England to Nahant. (From Harper's Weekly, September 17, 1887.)

Frederick R. Sears, Jr., was Jim Dwight's cousin, neighbor and earliest tennis opponent. (From Harper's Weekly, September 17, 1887.)

THE TWANG OF CATGUT

After reluctantly selling his summer house in the Berkshire town of Pittsfield because it was too far from the city and too expensive to maintain, Dr. Oliver Wendell Holmes lit upon Nahant in the summer of 1871, when he stayed with Senator Charles Sumner. He returned for three or four years with Mrs. Holmes, renting the Charles Amory cottage near the Lawrences; to Bill Lawrence, in his early teens, the Autocrat of the Breakfast Table's talk was "like the running of a mountain brook, fresh and inexhaustible. He dropped in upon the piazza and talked and talked."

Dr. Holmes wrote his old friend John Lothrop Motley, then in Europe, a gossipy letter from Nahant on August 26, 1873. As a diplomat first appointed ambassador to Austria by President Lincoln in 1861 on Senator Sumner's urging, the historian had had his ups and downs, having been named envoy to Great Britain by President Grant in 1869 (again on

Sumner's initiative), only to be fired after a year by Grant out of pique at the Massachusetts senator's opposition to his Santo Dominican policy. Holmes: "I write, you see, from Nahant, where I have been during July and August, staying . . . in the cottage you must remember as Mr. Charles Amory's . . . playing cuckoo in the nest, with my wife, who enjoys Nahant much more than I do—having had more or less of asthma to take off from my pleasures . . . Many of your old friends are our neighbors. Longfellow is hard by, with Tom Appleton in the same house, and for a fortnight or two Sumner as his guest. . . . I have dined since I have been here at Mr. George Peabody's with Longfellow, Sumner, Appleton, and William Amory; at Cabot Lodge's with nearly the same company; at Mr. [George Abbot] James's with L. and S., and at Longfellow's *en famille,* pretty nearly. Very pleasant dinners . . . Nahant is a gossipy Little Pedlington kind of a place . . . prattling and speculating . . . "

Motley returned to Nahant in 1875 for a last summer, crushed by his wife's death. He was frail and sick; Holmes spent hours with him. Their friend, the haughty Sumner, had died the previous year, embittered by political setbacks. Motley died in England in 1877. Dr. Holmes in his jaunty way had enjoyed the company at Nahant but not its ocean dampness, which aggravated his asthma, and now the company was dwindling. Probably "Th' Haunt" evoked too many old associations. For the season of 1878 he rented a cottage near the depot at Beverly Farms. There, with the warm land at his back, the anatomist of the human frame and spirit was to taper off his own remaining summers.

When the Holmeses stayed in the Charles Amory cottage, Mr. and Mrs. Thomas Dwight and family were across the road. Tom, Jr., had studied anatomy with the doctor at Harvard Medical School and in 1874 was assisting him in the teaching of it. His younger brother Jim was graduated from the college that June and would be attending their famous neighbor's lectures himself in the fall; old Holmes was the liveliest professor in the university, but the prospect of the long medical course was sobering nevertheless, and a summer of diversion was not unwarranted, even for a Bostonian.

It so happened that Mrs. William Appleton's son-in-law, J. Arthur Beebe, returned from England in August 1874 with the equipment for a new outdoor game that was sweeping all other distractions aside. It was called "sphairistike" by its inventor, an Edwardian-looking cavalry major by the horsey-sounding name of Walter Clopton Wingfield. Beebe's set consisted of spoon-shaped, thirteen-ounce racquets made by Malings of Woolwich, several rubber balls of the sort children played with, a net and rules.

Jim Dwight and Frederick R. Sears, Jr., one of his nearby cousins, measured off a level stretch of lawn on the east side of the Appleton estate on Swallow's Cave Road and strung up the net, taking care to taper the court twenty-six feet on either side back to what the rules called service lines. Racquets in hand, they sallied forth. Their first try was a fiasco. Neither could keep the ball in play. "We voted the whole thing a fraud," in Dwight's words, "and put it away."

Time, however, hung heavy in the somnolence of a Nahant summer, and a month later the cousins again tried "sticky," which was merely Major Wingfield's adaptation to a lawn of the ancient sport of court tennis. Each won a game this time, and they played all afternoon in the rain, in rubber coats and boots. The since-epidemic bug had bitten.

Dwight and Sears at the time had every reason to suppose that they and Arthur Beebe were introducing lawn tennis to America. In reality they were not. Miss Mary Ewing Outerbridge of the Staten Island and Bermuda Outerbridges had played sticky with the British officers of the Bermuda garrison the previous winter and brought a set home to New York in February. That spring, two or three months before Nahant declared the game a delusion, her brother, A. Emilius Outerbridge, laid out a court, indisputably the first in the country, at the Staten Island Cricket and Baseball Club.

For two summers while he was a Harvard medical student Jim Dwight and his cousins (Bill Appleton and Bob Grant, besides the Sears boys) and friends (Cabot Lodge among them) played obsessively as the informal "Nahant Tennis Club" and in August of 1876 held their first handicapped tournament on the Appleton court, with fifteen entries. Fred's younger brother, Richard D. Sears, tried the game the next summer when he was fifteen, practicing against a barn door with rubber balls that his mother had stitched around with pieces of old flannel shirts. The Nahanters had their third tournament in 1878, when they used modern tennis scoring and ventured to take on "strangers" in a match at Newport. Bill Lawrence helped canonize the fad on his Aunt Emily Appleton's lawn; fifty years afterward at The Country Club in Brookline, an old-fashioned racquet was pointed out to him, with the inscription: Racquet Used by Bishop Lawrence in the First Lawn Tennis Game in this Country. Among the first, anyway.

Dick Sears was a natural at what a letter writer to the *Harvard Crimson* in 1878 derided as "a seaside pastime . . . well enough for lazy or *weak* men, but men who have rowed or taken part in a nobler sport should blush to be seen playing Lawn Tennis." In 1881, when he was nineteen and a junior at Harvard, Sears won the first U.S. national singles championship at the Newport Casino, a feat he repeated six years running. With Jim Dwight, Sears captured five of his six consecutive national doubles championships. In 1884 they traveled to England, two clean-cut, mustached young Boston-Nahanters in white trousers, shirts with rolled-up sleeves, striped blazers, striped belts and striped caps, and Dwight was the first Yank to play on the sacred green of Wimbledon.

Jim in the meanwhile found the spare time to graduate from Harvard Medical School in 1879 and was entering the practice of obstetrics when he was taken ill. Though he recovered completely, he abandoned the active pursuit of medicine, leaving that to brother Tom, who went on to distinguish himself as the successor in the chair of anatomy at Harvard of their revered old Nahant neighbor, Dr. Holmes, who—to make a nice cycle of it—had succeeded their grandfather, Dr. John C. Warren. In 1881 Dr. James Dwight organized the U.S. National Lawn Tennis Association and was primarily responsible for bringing order out of chaos as the game swept the land; he served a total of twenty-one years as its second president and was gratefully ordained during his lifetime as "the Father of American Tennis."

THE NAHANT CLUB: A NICE SECURE FEELING

In view of the fact that the Eastern Yacht Club had been organized back in 1870, one may wonder why the Nahant Club didn't materialize in the old Tudor mansion until 1889. The reason is that there was no need for it; all Nahant beyond the Great Swamp was one water-bound club. But subtle encroaching changes may have influenced Abbott Lawrence's son-in-law, Francis Peabody, Jr., to lead the move to rent the Tudor field in 1888 and put in several tennis courts and a baseball diamond that led, the next year, to leasing the whole place as the inner sanctum within the outer.

A newspaper commentator suspected the resort was a trifle passé—lowering the bars just an inch. It used to be, he wrote, that "about Nahant there existed an atmosphere that beat the band for exclusiveness and frigid social life. The very name was synonymous then with all that made Beacon Hill the fashionable centre, for to obtain a cottage in that blest region was to attain the right to social recognition anywhere on earth, or at least that was the accepted creed in Boston. . . . New blood and new money were kept at bay for years."

The Nahant Club drew the circle tighter. To the colony's delight it revived the amenities of the ghostly Nahant Hotel without the vulgar necessity of sharing them with all comers. In the 1890s once again the bowling alley, the smoke-filled billiard room, the stables and the ballroom came alive. The Ice King's parlors served for whist and lavendered letter writing, his dining room as the setting for the private luncheon party and the candlelit champagne dinner. Afternoon tea for the ladies every day, and every Saturday a band concert. And of course, tennis, the ultimate sport of the

elite, of the effete, of the Anglophilic easterner, of the blazered Ivy Leaguer, played with strenuous flair before a gallery of parasols and bowlers upon a velvety turf that only the Nahant Club and the likes of Aunt Emily could afford to have and to maintain, played on and on in the lengthening shadows of the perfect summer afternoon, where it all *really* began.

Members of the Nahant Club. Not to be meddled with. (Nahant Historical Society)

In the summer of 1893, the year he was appointed a Suffolk County judge of probate, jurist and novelist Robert Grant had charge of entertaining the officers of a pair of visiting Russian warships at Nahant. He arranged to have them brought by tugboat from Boston for a very posh reception on the great lawn of the Nahant Club. All the members, who numbered among them some veteran topers, of course hoped their guests would topple like dominoes, and of course the Russians refused nothing, round after round.

When the last cork had popped, Judge Grant surveyed the scene: "The lawn looked somewhat like a battle-field, but with the victors in dignified retreat. The sea dogs had more than held their own." Their chaperone shepherded his czarist charges aboard the waiting tug. The sea shimmered under the shining moon, while, "gathered in a rug at the stern with their commander in the centre, they indulged in a repertoire of sentimental and patriotic songs worthy of a return from a Sunday-School picnic."

Contrasting with amiable detachment America's two most distin-

Lawyer, writer, historian and politician, Senator Henry Cabot Lodge was Cold Roast personified. (From Town and Country, *May 23, 1903.)*

guished resorts back in the middle of the century, George William Curtis had observed that "the repose, the freedom from the fury of fashion, is precisely what endears Nahant to its lovers, and the very opposite is the characteristic of Newport."

Forty years later, on the threshold of the 1890s, the two stood in the same relative positions, only more so. "The tendencies to more frivolous and more luxurious habits of life in New York," declared a writer in the Boston *Sunday Herald* in August 1890, "are at Newport highly accentuated, the season of the latter growing, indeed, more and more to be the climax of the winter gayeties of the metropolis; while Nahant, on the other hand, maintains the pristine dignity and aristocratic quality which have given to Boston her fame among cities.

"Nahant may be said to be even more characteristically Boston than Boston itself. So generally is this felt with respect to Nahant, that the unappreciative frequently make the charge of its being snobbishly exclusive. To one, however, who sees and feels how dreadful is the trend of our modern

American life, this preservation of the old and the true is particularly to be cherished. And it is a pleasure to know that there is a place where people are not in a rush and turmoil over hunts and parades and sumptuous entertainments, but where they live in quiet ease, having indeed entertainment, but not such as puts life to confusion.

"There are probably more people here, than in any other similar place in America, who may have true claims to aristocracy by reason of cultivation and wealth possessed for generations, back to the first days of the colonies."

Indeed, the practice of the wealthy, most of them from Boston, of evading the general personal property tax in their winter quarters by taking up legal residence in the outlying suburbs, where the rates were incomparably lower, started in Nahant in 1870, and there was not much the Boston assessors could do about it. The dodge was perfectly legal, and because valuations were based on demonstrable holdings, tangible property such as real estate carried the burden while the elusive stock certificate on which the greater wealth was based escaped any detection at all except by the most sophisticated city assessors. Tax collectors in the small suburbs and resorts like Nahant were only too happy to provide havens for the rich commuters and summer residents, assessing them at face value for what they were permitted to see with their own eyes, leaving the hidden intangibles to the owner and his conscience.

The result of Nahant's discovery by the tax-dodgers was that the valuation rose from $2,900,000 in 1869 to $6,000,000 in 1872, while the tax rate dropped from $4.50 to $2.50 per thousand. When the rate commenced to creep back to its former level, one prominent summer resident wangled a sizeable abatement of his $800,000 assessment and died a few years later leaving millions. Other probate returns likewise opened the eyes of the assessors—too late. In 1908, after the death of Frederick R. Sears, father of the tennis players, the Nahant assessors were directed by the state tax commissioner to go after certain large sums owing in local taxes that had been discovered in probate, and when they were finally collected after a long legal battle they paid most of the cost of the new town hall.

Of course the inequity of these evasions, as they crept into one North Shore resort after another, was as visible to the townspeople as the untaxed intangibles were invisible to the local collectors; as Fred Wilson observed of his native Nahant, "the working man, with only a house and lot, was assessed for a far greater proportion of his total wealth than the wealthier residents, most of whose property was not in plain sight of the assessors."

What if the taxes of the summer resident with no children in the local school did subsidize the education of the natives and enable the town to build town halls and provide services it could not have otherwise? Was it worth it, being the object of that special, super-cooled Boston brand of *noblesse oblige* based on family, friends and education, on occupation or the absence of it, and on the possession of an iceberg of wealth of which only the slight eminence above water showed on the tax rolls?

"Thunderbolt Hill," the Manchester summer home of Boston publisher James T. Fields, hurler from on high. (Manchester Historical Society)

~8~
THE GOLD COAST

*Of autocrats and actors, a perspicacious pastor
and a civil civil war along the shingled shore*

JAMES T. FIELDS WAS THE LEADING
book publisher in Boston and the Daniel among its literary lions, and he did
so well by them, and they by him, that he retired in 1871 at fifty-four and
went on the lecture circuit, titillating audiences with anecdotes of his expe-
riences in the den. Two years later he bought Thunderbolt Hill in
Manchester and in 1874 built his summer house on it. After a while he and
his beautiful, brilliant second wife Annie invented "Manchester-by-the-Sea"
and started printing it on their stationery.

Besides steering countless mail, freight and travelers away from the
other five Manchesters of New England, the Fieldses succeeded in stamping
their chosen retreat as an upper-crust watering place pervaded with a vague
air of Englishness and with distinct undertones of class. Manchester's
tradesmen, desirous of conveying the assurance that they were fully as discriminating as their clientele, soon were adding their own "by-the-Seas" to
their by-your-leaves.

The publisher's friends reacted irreverently, however. Dr. Holmes had
taken a cottage near the Beverly Farms railroad station and replied to Fields
from "Beverly-by-the-Dépot," and John Greenleaf Whittier wrote from
"Haverhill-by-the-Hollyhocks." At Cape Ann someone muttered,
"Gloucester-by-the-Smell." But Manchester-by-the-Sea stuck, in spite of the
jibes, showing that Mr. Fields knew how to pick a catchy title. The angli-
cism—dare one call it an affectation?—has recently been canonized as the
town's official name.

Fields was a child of four in Portsmouth, New Hampshire, when his
father, an improvident shipmaster, died. Want stunted the boy's formal education but not his curiosity. He read everything in sight and got a job clerk-
ing in Boston in William D. Ticknor's Old Corner Book Store at Washington
and School streets. The rest is literary history. He rose to partnership and
then to ownership of the publishing firm on the strength of his almost infal-
lible judgment of America's reading tastes in a day when America read.
Fields profoundly influenced American literary history as book publisher
and as editor of the *Atlantic,* for his authors included Holmes, Emerson,
Hawthorne, Thoreau and other members of Boston's Society for Mutual

Admiration. He tolerated outsiders like Mark Twain and Bret Harte, as well as the English Victorians, whom he introduced to this country. Most of his den loved their great, hearty tamer in his Scottish tweeds, with his shaggy beard and roaring laugh—"guardian and maintainer of us all," as Emerson called him. When Fields retired in 1871, Dr. Holmes expressed mock doubt that without his friend's praise and encouragement he would ever "write anything more worth mentioning."

The travel writer Bayard Taylor looked in on them in August of 1875, the Fieldses' first full season in their "quaint, old-fashioned residence," and was bowled over by the view of the coast and the ocean from the veranda. "We have but to turn our heads and we see the inlet, the village, the bluff, and swelling waves of forest, melting into distant grays and purples under a sky which (just now at least) is more English than American. There is a perpetual breeze, with strength enough on its wings to refresh and not exhaust."

In Boston James and Annie, who was seventeen years younger and a literary figure in her own right, resided at 37 Charles Street, the foot of Beacon Hill, where international celebrities paraded through their guest room. Dr. and Mrs. Holmes for some years lived a few doors off at number 21. No great coincidence, then, that three years after Fields moved to Manchester-by-the-Sea, Holmes popped up at Beverly Farms. On September 22, 1878, he wrote James Russell Lowell, who had been appointed minister to Spain by President Hayes as reward for his political support, "We are at a small wayside house, where we make ourselves comfortable, my wife, my daughter, and myself, with books, walks, drives, and as much laziness as we can bring ourselves to, which is quite too little, for none of us has a real genius for the *far niente*. [*Dolce far niente*, 'sweet doing nothing,' was an expression then in vogue.] All round us are the most beautiful and expensive residences, some close to the sea beaches, some on heights farther back in the midst of the woods, some perched on the edge of precipices; one has a net spread out which she calls a baby-catcher, over the abyss, on the verge of which her piazza hangs shuddering."

A sometime neighbor of the Holmeses-by-the-Dépot was the Beverly-born poet Lucy Larcom, a large, good-humored unmarried woman who had relinquished teaching for the wider didactic opportunities of publication. She padded out a sparse living with sentimental effusions on nature such as (from *Wild Roses of Cape Ann*): "I never knew the world in white / So beautiful could be / As I have seen it here to-day / Beside the wintry sea"—verses, as one gentle biographer put it, "of the kind that pass with the generation to which they belong." Dr. Holmes, being of Miss Larcom's generation, wrote her after thumbing through a presentation copy of *Wild Roses* in 1880, "My wife and daughter were sitting opposite to me, and I had to shade my eyes with my hand that they should not see the tears shining in them." Whittier wrote Holmes that *Wild Roses* gave Larcom "a right to stand with the rest of us."

But time would have its toll on this summer community—"as if an autumn wind were tearing away the last leaves all around me," the doctor lamented to Lowell. Richard Henry Dana, who had led off the summer march to Manchester, died in 1879 at age ninety-one. Fields died in 1881; his widow and the Maine author Sarah Orne Jewett became almost inseparable companions, traveling abroad, wintering at the Charles Street salon carried on by Annie, summering on Thunderbolt Hill. In 1882 Emerson and Longfellow died, and Dr. Holmes retired from guiding generations of Harvard medical students through the twists and tunnels of the mortal coil. About this time he pulled out of his cottage by-the-Dépot and rented one recently built by the

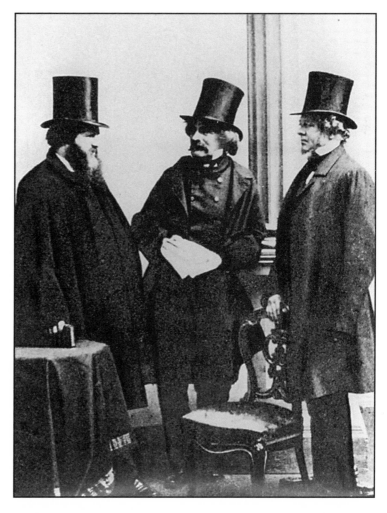

James T. Fields, Nathaniel Hawthorne, and the author's close friend and publishing partner of Fields, William D. Ticknor. (Peabody Essex Museum)

Marshall family on Hale Street, within sound of the surf on West Beach.

In the spring of 1884 roistering, rotund old Tom Appleton died, and the blows redoubled. That summer Holmes lost his younger son, Edward, then his wife, Amelia, in 1888; and the next year, his eightieth, his daughter, Amelia Sargent. Stoically, the old man surrendered himself to the care of his surviving son, then a justice of the Massachusetts Supreme Court, and his daughter-in-law, Fanny.

In his last years Oliver Wendell Holmes was without rival the most famous figure on the North Shore, and because his birthday fell on the twenty-ninth of August, when he was invariably in their midst, everyone made much of it. Flowers and fruit were heaped within the cottage with letters and telegrams, adulatory poems and loving cups. The newspapers sent reporters, the summer people called, the neighbors came by, and each year the schoolchildren of Beverly Farms—scrubbed and dressed in their holiday best—were admitted en masse by Judge and Mrs. Holmes to recite their greetings and then ushered out, each with a remembrance of the occasion.

MANCHESTER'S THEATER LANE

Soon after his retirement, Dr. Holmes was drawn under the marquee of the elegant Boston Theatre by the twin billing of the great English players Ellen Terry and Henry Irving. The Oliver Goldsmith of Boston made his way backstage, "and while I was talking with them a very heavy piece of scenery came crashing down, and filled the whole place with dust. It was but a short distance from where we were standing, and I could not help thinking how near our several life-dramas came to a simultaneous *exeunt omnes*."

Well-nigh all the stars of the day graced the Boston Theatre, which filled the block between Washington and Mason streets and seated 3,140. When one of the brightest chanced to be drawn slightly out of orbit one summer by the fascination of Manchester's heavenly shore-by-the-sea, others followed until every season a galaxy of them clustered there, as reported in the New York *Dramatic News:* "Hidden snugly among the pine woods and granite rocks of the Eastern shore of Massachusetts is a romantic spot beloved by many members of the profession, a quiet retreat to where they can hide and dream away the summer months in *dolce far niente*. It is currently reported that this Lotus-land was discovered by the eminent tragedian, Joseph Proctor, who with his characteristic unselfishness introduced other actors to the scene, until regularly, every off season, there came a full company to the Old Neck."

Joseph Proctor was a lofty presence in the romantic theater. He specialized in Shakespearean heavies and had snarled, growled, threatened, roared, wept and expired his way all over America and Britain since emerging from the country town of Marlboro at age seventeen. Some measure of his polemic ability was his frequent appearance as the tattered and wild-eyed Jibbenainosay in *Nick of the Woods,* a ridiculously melodramatic role that he was able to lift to the verge, so it was claimed, of tragedy. In 1864 the Jibbenainosay was forty-eight and a sure box-office draw when he bought

the snug, colonial Sally Samples House on Sea Street, at the tip of a finger of Manchester Harbor, for a summer place.

Why Manchester? In 1856, two years after the Boston Theatre was built, Joseph Proctor had made his first appearance there. The theater went broke in the financial panic of 1857. One of its reorganizers the next year was the Boston real estate broker Benjamin W. Thayer. In 1864 Thayer acquired part control, and he and Proctor acquired their summer cottages at Manchester a quarter of a mile apart. Thayer's Old Neck Road neighbor on his other side, almost to Eagle Head, was Samuel H. Bullard, who had built the previous year; he too was an incorporator of the Boston Theatre. The Manchester theatrical plot was thickening.

Enter Junius Brutus Booth.

On April 14, 1865, five days after Robert E. Lee handed his sword and his beaten army to Ulysses S. Grant, John Wilkes Booth—considered by some critics the most brilliant, and certainly the most erratic, of America's most erratically brilliant family of actors—shot Abraham Lincoln in the President's box at Ford's Theater in Washington. John and his older brothers, Edwin and Junius, had last acted together in *Julius Caesar* at the Winter Garden in New York the previous November. Ned and June had argued violently with Johnnie over his fervor for the Southern cause and his raging hatred of the President, whom at that moment—if they had only known—he was plotting to abduct.

Edwin Booth was playing at the Boston Theatre when he heard the news of John's latest aberration. Junius, the eldest and the spitting image of their late glowering, heavyset actor-father of the same name, was playing in Cincinnati. A mob stormed his hotel. He was smuggled out and sheltered by friends, made his way to Philadelphia, and on April 26 was arrested by federal agents who suspected him (by erroneous interpretation, as they later learned, of a letter he had written to his deranged brother) of complicity.

Theatre Lane dominated the Manchester skyline in this view looking east from the Congregational church steeple in about 1876. Joseph Proctor's house is behind the trees at left; Fred Conway's massive place dominates Ocean Hill; that of his sister-in-law, Mrs. Bowers, is lower to its right; "Thunderbolt Hill" sits squarely on the ledge; and at right is the Booths' cottage just before they made it the Masconomo. (Manchester Historical Society)

Aboard the train to Washington and prison, Junius told his guard, "I wish John had been killed before the assassination, for the sake of his family." That peacetime summer was the worst in a lifetime of nightmares for the Booths.

Edwin fled into anguished seclusion after the assassination, but 1866 found him back in Boston with his sister's actor-husband, John S. Clarke, leasing the Boston Theatre from Benjamin Thayer and his partner. Junius was forty-five and had been several months out of jail; he joined Edwin and Clarke in Boston as acting and stage manager. One of the female leads in the company was Agnes Perry, the widowed daughter of a British army officer, and she and Junius fell in love. Within a year Booth's brother and brother-in-law turned over the lease and management of the Boston Theatre to him. He married Agnes and was feeling flush enough to buy a piece of land above Old Neck Beach in Manchester from Thayer; in 1869 they built a cottage on it. The new Mrs. Booth was twenty-five years younger than her husband and younger by three than his oldest daughter by his first wife.

Enter John Gibbs Gilbert.

A leading comedian, this polished Bostonian recited the dedicatory poem at the opening of the Boston Theatre on September 11, 1854, then walked back on as Sir Anthony Absolute, one of his virtuoso roles, with his actress wife, Maria, in Sheridan's *The Rivals*. They reappeared periodically until her death in 1866. Reserved and solemn offstage, Gilbert remarried and in 1868 bought a summer cottage on Old Neck Road between Bullard and Thayer.

Enter Mr. and Mrs. Frederick B. Conway.

Though a familiar figure on tour in America, this English actor had never appeared at the Boston Theatre when he and his better-known second wife, an actress, bought land and built a summer mansion on Ocean Hill above Sea Street in 1868, next to Joseph Proctor. A year later they moved into their summer mansion.

Conway in 1852 had married the daughter of a Methodist minister, Sarah Crocker, who with her sister Elizabeth had taken up with the naughty world of professional theater. The Conways toured together until 1864, when, like

John Wilkes Booth as Mark Anthony, Edwin Booth as Brutus and Junius Brutus Booth, Jr., as Cassius in Julius Caesar *at the Winter Garden, New York, November 25, 1864. (Harvard Theatre Collection)*

The actress sisters Sarah Conway and Elizabeth Bowers. (From History of the Boston Theatre.)

many other actors hungering for a larger bite of the box office, they leased the Park Theatre in Brooklyn, put their name on the marquee, and played to the popular madness for melodrama and romance, appearing on most of the bills together and debuting their daughters, Lillian and Minnie.

In Conway, who was a large man, what struck one critic as pomposity impressed another as burlesque. One summer day in 1870, as a newspaper correspondent reported with great relish, Mr. Conway was at Manchester "in a dory with his son and servant off some distance from the shore, when suddenly the boat was upset and over they went into the 'vasty deep.' The boat came up, but Mr. C., immense in weight, was floundering about—as I had the story—like a whale harpooned and hampered, 'swilled with wild and wasteful ocean.' He 'blew' at last—the actor was the father here—and out of the engulfing brine the gurgling cry came up from the cave of Aeolus: 'Save the boys, the boys; I'll shift it for myself!' The boat took up the boys—the father would have swamped it in an instant—and he had the presence of mind to see it. So resting his right hand on the bow, he was towed, still floundering through the water like a captured whale, or huge leviathan, in safety to the shore, and amid the acclamations of the audience the curtain fell. Mr. C. is, by the by, very much of a gentleman, and highly respected by the citizens of Manchester."

Two years after Fred's death, in the evening of December 5, 1876, fire broke out backstage during a crowded performance in Conway's Theatre, and 297 people died trying to get out.

Enter Mrs. D. P. Bowers.

Elizabeth, that other daring daughter of the Reverend Mr. Crocker, married David P. Bowers, a Philadelphia actor, in 1847 when she was sev-

The Manchester cottage of Junius Brutus Booth before its transformation to the Masconomo House. (Manchester Historical Society)

enteen. He died in ten years, but not before she was well launched on the stage as a popular actress with pretty eyes and, so said a critic, "a voice of fascinating sweetness, a refined manner and a cultivated mind." In 1866 she played Romeo to her sister's Juliet at the Winter Garden; three years later they switched roles at the Boston Theatre. Having surely paid many an off-season visit on her sister and brother-in-law (her second husband, a chemist, died in 1867), Mrs. Bowers bought a cottage a few rods down Old Neck Road from the Conways in 1873 and so completed the already famous actors' summer colony known by then as Theatre Lane.

Junius Brutus Booth, in the meantime, had become involved in North Shore summer property speculation, joining others of the actors' colony in a land company hoping to purchase Marblehead Neck for $250,000 in January 1872. Edwin had built the lavish Booth's Theatre in New York in 1868 (Mrs. Bowers played Lady Macbeth to his Macbeth there) but ran into such financial problems that at last, early in 1873, Junius agreed to give up the management of the Boston Theatre and to take on his brother's opulent white elephant in order to free the Prince of Players for the road, where the real money was. Then all were engulfed in the panic, and in January 1874 Edwin Booth was forced into bankruptcy.

Junius must not have made out so badly amidst these alarums, because in the spring of 1877 (the Marblehead Great Neck Land Company even then was on the brink of foreclosure) he embarked in his own spectacular fashion on the summer hotel business in Manchester. And since he proposed to tack an enormous dog on the tail of the cottage he and Agnes had occupied for eight years in the heart of the summer colony, the reaction of their neighbors was mixed. (As one observer said, all such ventures had hitherto been held at bay by Manchester "with a view to keeping the society somewhat select.")

Edwin had settled in Boston on Beacon Hill and wrote a friend that "June is building a hotel at Manchester—sits still—smokes and bewails his hard lot. Aggy *jobs* and looks as though her hair dye had affected her health." In other words, Agnes was doing acting stints to help with the mortgage. Their inspiration in this hotel venture may be inferred from the observation in the New York *Dramatic News* that summer that the Manchester colony had entertained "almost every actress and actor of note, many of whom would have been delighted to purchase summer residences in this earthly paradise, but, as usual, no sooner was it known to the world, than every foot of land was bought up, and Manchester has become a select seashore resort for a number of wealthy persons and a few artists and literary men."

The Masconomo House, invoking the name of the last sagamore of the Agawams, opened for the season of 1878. Someone joked that a guest who tried to pronounce it "died the following day of complications resulting from lockjaw." Presiding over twelve acres of lawn that rolled sedately down to Old Neck Beach, the Booths' greatest production extended 240 feet from their cottage with 106 rooms. At four corners of an octagonal hall in the center were four mammoth fireplaces "that glow merrily with their great log fires on cold and stormy days." Above the roof the chimneys bounded an eight-sided observatory. A guidebook likened it to one of "those charming hostelries to be seen around the shores of the Swiss lakes."

June and Aggy's bowling alleys and billiard tables were joined by tennis courts, then by bathhouses above the high-water mark of Singing Beach, for-

Masconomo House, about 1880. Note the former Booth cottage at the right end. (Manchester Historical Society)

merly Musical Beach, originally plain Old Neck Beach, whose sands beguiled the ear with a strange music, described as follows by one who walked there: "As you step briskly over it, a distinct and somewhat clear, shrill note is heard, which seems to be upon the key of C of the treble scale [others claim B]. By scraping or shuffling the foot over the sand, the tone may be prolonged; and it is loudest, I have noticed, when the sand is dryest." Contrarywise, some Canadian scientists have concluded that the common feature of singing beaches appears to be the friction produced by walking over smooth-surfaced grains of sand weakly bonded by quite pure sea water. Various other explanations have been advanced for the music of the sands— "some wise," in the words of a local historian, "and some otherwise."

Overnight the Masconomo was a hit. Of course it was, for how could it have flopped in such a setting, with such management, such a company, and such guest stars?

Junius Brutus Booth exited for the last time in 1883 after only five flush seasons of his final extravaganza and was elaborately interred in Manchester. In 1885 Aggy Booth married her third husband, John B. Schoeffel, owner of the Tremont Theatre in Boston.

Under the Schoeffels the Masconomo House kept right on flourishing. They knew how to put on a show, all right. One summer night in 1886 it was *A Midsummer Night's Dream*, outdoors under the stars. Special trains steamed into the Manchester depot from Boston, and by early afternoon the audience was streaming onto the grounds. That evening, before an enthralled throng on the great lawn that rolled down to the twinkling sea, Shakespeare cast his spell under the glow of novel electric lights, Chinese lanterns, and a score of locomotive headlamps, all to the swelling sounds of a full orchestra and chorus above the murmur of the surf.

By the dawn of the 1890s those romantic, bombastic, melodramatic, comic and tragic players on Manchester's charming Theatre Lane were in the wings or in their graves.

Exeunt omnes.

THE MANCHESTER REAL ESTATE EXTRAVAGANZA

The land-grabbers from the city, whose cohorts had captured the Beverly shore before the Civil War, discovered more distant Manchester during the brief postwar boom. Poet, publisher and player publicized its potential as a resort, but with land values on the verge of explosion, it was the perspicacious and powerful who populated it.

Down from Boston came Greely Curtis in 1868 to buy up the headland just east of Dana's Beach, long called Sharksmouth for the undercut cliff by the shore resembling the upper jaw of a shark. Curtis was married to Tom Appleton's sister Hattie, Longfellow to another sister, Fannie. Addressed by friends as Colonel Curtis (having risen from captain to brigadier general), though he achieved no fame in the Civil War he was admired by those who served under him and was characterized by his tentmate Robert Gould Shaw as "the boldest man I ever knew." Driving by the Curtis mansion, travel writer Bayard Taylor was impressed with his "castle by the sea, built of gray stone, and of a very original design, an Italian *loggia* being combined with Norman-Gothic features. . . . Around it the roughness of the native pine forest has been softened in the most admirable manner, turf borders melting naturally into huckleberry thickets, and geraniums growing amicably in the midst of ferns."

Greely Curtis and five of his children emerge from the porte cochere at "Sharksmouth." (Curtis family collection)

Close on the spurs of General Curtis trod John Henry Towne, a wealthy Philadelphia industrial engineer; in 1869 Towne bought Eagle Head (formerly Old Neck, at the tip of the actors' colony) from John Murray Forbes, built a summer mansion above the surf, and put together an estate of seventy-five acres before dying in Paris six years later. Forbes had influenced the naval conduct of the Civil War, and Towne had made engines for several Union vessels, including the ironclad *Monitor.* At about the time he acquired Eagle Head he set up his son Henry in partnership with Linus Yale in the manufacture of Yale's patented locks. After the elder Towne's death, the University of Pennsylvania created the Towne Scientific School for engineering studies to recognize his benefactions.

John Henry Towne's daughter, Mrs. Alice Towne Lincoln, started a fund-raising campaign among Manchester and Beverly summer residents in 1879 to acquire a strip of land on either side of the country road through the thick Essex Woods from Manchester to Essex. Through purchases and gifts of land, most of this road came under public protection and, with Essex and Western avenues, was adopted as the third leg of the "Big Heater," a popular pleasure drive connecting Manchester, Essex and the Blynman Canal at Gloucester, resembling on the map a triangular horse-drawn snowplow, a "heater," or, as some held instead, a flatiron.

The fast-pedaling author of the bicyclist's guidebook *In and Around Cape Ann,* John S. Webber, Jr., while exploring Theatre Lane one summer day a few years after Towne's death, wheeled toward Eagle Head, where "we soon enter the private grounds of Mrs. J. H. Towne of Philadelphia and continue over the well kept avenue to the turn-off, where a politely worded sign-board tells us that 'Strangers are requested to turn here,'" which he did. Mrs. Towne died in 1892, and in three years Eagle Head was sold to James McMillan, the rich and powerful senator from Michigan, for upwards of $200,000, they said.

The third of the strangers to invest heavily in the Manchester coast after the Civil War was Cyrus Augustus Bartol. Diminutive, whimsical, learned and literary, Dr. Bartol was the Unitarian pastor of the Old West Church on Cambridge Street in Boston. Up until around 1870 his flock had supposed him to be preoccupied with the transcendentalist abstractions of the Emersonians, of whom he was a leading spirit. Under this impression, someone, probably a parishioner, remonstrated with him for impractically sinking his spare dollars into shoreline down at Manchester when he should be stashing them in a sound Boston bank, where they belonged, like the prudent but impractical man of God everyone knew him to be.

"Ah, my friend," the shepherd is said to have responded with a knowing shake of his snow-white locks, "you and a lot of other folks seem to forget that the Lord Almighty has stopped making sea coast."

Perhaps getting his tips from On High, Dr. Bartol took his baptismal plunge into seaside real estate in 1870, at the age of fifty-four, when he bought for a modest sum the long stretch of magnificent shore in West Manchester called the Glass Head Pasture. The seller was Lewis N. Tappan, a native who was considered an especially astute real estate man.

On the choicest elevation of Glass Head, Dr. Bartol built his mansion and, on a nearby bump the natives proudly called The Mountain, his observatory and study. When the spirit took hold of him he would ascend to the summit of his Sinai by a spiral staircase and through a trapdoor in the floor, which he was wont to shut after him and sit upon in his easy chair so as not to be disturbed as he contemplated his earthly domain and how a man of God should be so mysteriously blessed with the best of both worlds. When, in another twenty-five years, Dr. Bartol did move on to the next, his daughter sold Glass Head to Gordon Abbott, president of the Old Colony Trust Company in Boston, reportedly for $135,000.

While he was overseeing the construction of his manse in 1871, Dr. Bartol looked out across the water and sighed for what he saw (it was not his nature to *covet*)—the seventy-five acres of the Great Pasture, that is, most of Smith's Point, which provides Manchester its harbor. The tract was, in the words of a New York journalist, "dotted with juniper and barberry, gay with wild roses and goldenrod, an immense green pasture of hill and dell lying open to the ocean, whose cliffs are its utmost bounds." And so Dr. Bartol gladly paid the $600 an acre that Williston Smith was asking for the family's seventy-five on Smith's Point and laid out a road; before long he was sharing his new corner of the temple with converts eager for niches at from $10,000 to $12,000 apiece. For good measure he picked up House

Island, half a mile offshore. In 1872 he gave David Leach $1,225 for Norton's Point, inside Tuck's Point (which he bought too) on the western shore, rocky and barren of all but a gnarled cedar standing near the tide. As the opportunity presented, he added to these holdings.

Such was the bread that Cyrus Augustus Bartol cast upon the bay. Years later, when it had come back to him ten- and a hundredfold, he surveyed the results and pronounced in benedictory tones that "Manchester has become in our day a splendid watering place, known as such throughout the United States; so she finds gold eagles stitched into her dress"—and into the clerical cloth. An unlikely colossus, Dr. Bartol—and yet, there he stood astride the entrance to Manchester Harbor in 1872, one foot firmly fixed on Glass Head, the other on Smith's Point.

Augustus Hemenway and Thomas Jefferson Coolidge, two titans of Boston finance, in the same year descended on the prime remaining seacoast unaccountably unbought by the pastor. Hemenway picked up Pickworth Point, the smaller jut of pasture-crowned ledge east of Smith's Point, but he had short use of the house he built above Bellyache Cove, for he died four years later.

Coolidge, on the other hand and at the east end of town, lopped off the old Goldsmith Farm that occupied the whole of the kettle-shaped peninsula east of kettle-like Kettle Cove and behind Kettle Island, which does not

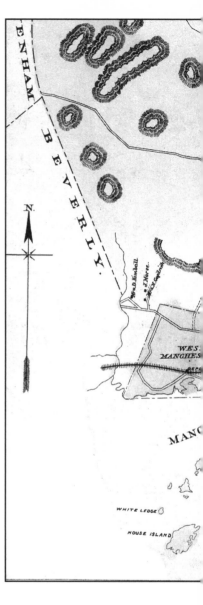

resemble a kettle at all but was named after a family of Kettles. Old man Gifford Goldsmith was an original; he grew tobacco and claimed the sun circled the earth, figuring from the length of the shadow of his cane that it was only three thousand miles away.

In the mansion he built on Coolidge Point, the textile-banking-railroad capitalist spent most of his remaining forty-eight summers until his death in 1920 at eighty-nine. T. J. was old Boston through and through. After Harvard, he set his cap for money and a daughter of William Appleton and got both. He was as honest, they said, as he was shrewd, which makes a hard bargainer. In later life, after he had built his pile, Coolidge served Harvard and country as overseer and minister to France. His gift to Manchester of its public library (he would not have his name over the door)

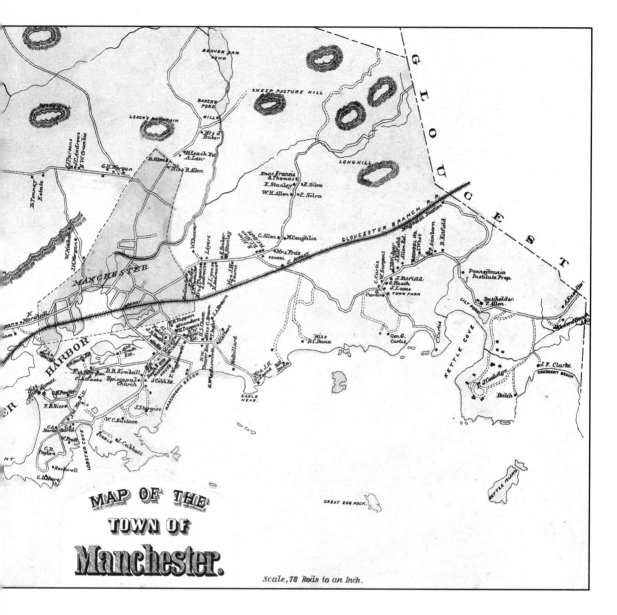

MAP OF THE TOWN OF Manchester.

Scale, 78 Rods to an Inch.

was in hopeful, if partial, retreat from the political creed of his youth, a creed that would have grieved his great-grandfather Jefferson: "I believed myself to belong to a superior class, and that the principle that the ignorant and poor should have the same right to make laws and govern as the educated and refined was an absurdity." The Coolidge purchase in the lee of Kettle Island, as the Louisiana Purchase had been for his farsighted ancestor, proved to be one of his characteristically sagacious deals and remains under conservative restrictions.

The doldrums in the wake of the financial storms of 1873 took some of the wind out of luxury land sales, and it was four years before Cyrus Bartol's initial subdivision of Smith's Point produced any summer cottages. The first of these were J. Warren Merrill's, sited on the hill above Lobster Cove and

The Manchester shoreline. From Atlas of Essex County, Massachusetts, Boston, 1884.

jokingly dubbed "The Extinguisher House" by his neighbors in reference to his tower, and E. E. Rice's on the harbor shore above Long Beach.

Dr. Bartol's third buyer, as clever an actor as any on Theatre Lane, was "Professor" Orson Squire Fowler, who in 1878 built on the Point of Rocks at the north end of Long Beach. Fowler was then sixty-nine years old and at the peak of his fame and fortune as a practitioner of phrenology and what he termed "physiology," by means of which, he claimed to believe, every problem known to man could be solved.

No professor (though an Amherst College graduate), "Doctor" Fowler lectured widely and published a prodigious array of pseudoscientific mish-mash, such as two volumes, which went to forty editions, extending *Important Directions and Suggestions to Lovers and the Married,* and advice on *Amativeness: or, Evils and Remedies of Excessive and Perverted Sexuality.* He was married three times and after he was seventy fathered three children, so it may be unjust to state, as one unsympathetic biographer has, that only Orson Fowler's conceit saved him from deliberate charlatanism.

The professor had published *A Home for All; or, the Gravel Wall, and Octagon Mode of Building* in 1849. The book started a fad in eight-sided houses as cheaper to build, easier to heat and light, space-saving and step-saving.

THE SHINGLED SHORE

Every kind of "cottage" was to be encountered along the North Shore in the 1870s, from the rude tent on the beach to Major Henry Lee Higginson's "Sunset Hill" at West Manchester, described wonderingly by one guidebook as "a sort of Schönburg castle." Somewhere in between, for the plain people, was the "piano box," a type of plain cottage typically rented for a few weeks. (Why not stay home and move into the attic, grumbled a disenchanted vacationer, for there one can "enjoy open stud construction and one layer of boards between the occupant and the almighty sun, and never have to pay for the temporary change of address"?)

If there was a denominator of design common to the open-stud piano box and the gingerbreaded atrocity, it was the "stick style" that sawed and hammered the most plentiful building material in the land in a practical compromise between mid-Victorian hearts and flowers and the requirements of domestic routine. The stick style was all planes and awkward angles of boards, battens and braces, dull at best and prone to unpredictable eruptions of vogue as in the Eastern Yacht Club on Marblehead Neck, whose piazza columns and fence posts were of debarked tree trunks bristling with the naked stumps of lopped-off branches like sloppily assembled hat racks (see page 76).

Nosing around Cape Ann for *Harper's* in 1875, the restless writer-painter Samuel Greene Wheeler Benjamin liked the sea, the natives and the scenery and scoffed at the cottage architecture that was typical of most of the North Shore. "The weather-worn and quaint gambrel-roofed farmhouses are turned for the nonce into villas. They are garnished with new porches, lace curtains, and croquet grounds; and cottages presenting a cross between an Italian villa and a Chinese joss-house are perched on the hill-tops and planted among the buildings of the early settlers, not always with perfect success as regards effect."

Thirty years earlier Alonzo Lewis had dreamed of a day when the summer cottages of the North Shore "shall appear to grow out of the rocks and to be born of the woods." Now the day was at hand, and it belonged to Henry Hobson Richardson, master of the third dimension. The great Boston architect was supervising the construction of massive Trinity Church in Copley Square when he designed in 1874 a large cottage for Watts Sherman in Newport that was like nothing seen before in America. Spacious and pleasant, with stately gables and fluted chimneys, aproned roofs, wide bay windows, masonry below and half-timbered above, and an open, interconnected interior layout emanating from a central living hall, Richardson's creation applied to the New England coast the innovative Queen Anne style revived in Britain by Richard Norman Shaw, substituting plain wooden shingles for the English architect's tiles to impart a sense of flow to his exterior planes.

Before the decade was out, Watts Sherman adaptations had sprung from the boards of other architects into suburban and seaside settings, showing ever more shingle, fewer distracting doodads and pleasing spatial effects. With the Morrill cottage at Bar Harbor sheathed in shingle from sill to eave, the enchanting, fleeting "Shingle Style" had arrived. Here was a house of cool

"Betsy's Inducement," a shingle-style house built on Norton's Point in Manchester by the Reverend Cyrus Bartol from a design by Arthur Little. (Manchester Historical Society)

dreams above the ocean, at ease with ledge and lawn, every window thrown open to a vista of beguilement, every ceiling ashimmer in watery reflections, a languid sprawl of space wrapped in an undulation of shingle roasted in the sun and seasoned to a silver gray by the salt of the winter spray.

During the early 1880s, William Ralph Emerson and other architects planted an experimental crop of shingled cottages at Manchester, Beverly and Swampscott that the architectural historian Vincent J. Scully, Jr., cited as prime examples of the genre in his definitive study, *The Shingle Style and the Stick Style.*

First to sprout were two by Emerson in 1881. The Queen Anne manse designed for Alexander Cochrane at Pride's Crossing was rambling and refined, with flat surfaces, scalloped shingling above a touch of brickwork, and Palladian and eyebrow windows. The other was so well sited that it appeared to have been summoned forth from the sheer ledge on which it crouched. Owner Charles Greely Loring of Pride's Crossing, a man of superb taste and the son and namesake of Squire Loring, Beverly's original summer settler, was a Harvard graduate of delicate health and independent means who, instead of entering business or a profession, toured Europe, dabbled in Egyptian archaeology, and later assayed to farm the family summer estate in gentlemanly fashion. But a life of pleasant underachievement was not for a Loring. He joined General Ambrose Everett Burnside's staff in 1861 and overcompensated for his retiring nature so thoroughly that he emerged from the Civil War a major general himself. He returned to Egypt and so schooled himself in archaeology and the arts that when the Boston Museum of Fine Arts opened its new building in Copley Square in 1876, the modest, goateed general was invited to be curator and thus served the museum until shortly before his death in 1902.

The third shingled affair to break North Shore ground in 1881 was "Shingleside," a bastardized colonial saltbox of ungainly proportion with indented porches and an awkward pepper grinder of a bay built on Swampscott's Little's Point by James L. Little to the design of his son, Arthur, who was twenty-eight and had studied at Massachusetts Institute of Technology and in Paris. Little's first commission had been a successful colonial revival house, "Cliffs," which he designed in 1879 for George Dudley Howe, who had bought his commanding lot on Smith's Point from Dr. Bartol in 1878. Although the design of "Cliffs" proved influential, Little characteristically abandoned it and turned to shingle with enthusiasm. After "Shingleside" he designed "Grasshead" nearby for his father the next year, more satisfactory in shape, marred only by the same stick-style piazza posts that discouraged leaners at the Eastern Yacht Club.

Cyrus Bartol had done so well as a speculator in land that in 1883 he built three speculative shingle cottages to Little's plans on Norton's Point in Manchester, "River," "Barn" and "Fort" (on the site of an 1812 earthworks); two others on Smith's Point probably bore Little's stamp as well, since he is known to have designed one that year at Lobster Cove. Arthur Little was mastering the new style, adapting it by sections to conform to rugged seaside terrain and sculpting the shell with towers, turrets, bays, nooks, walkways and peekaboo windows to take in the most striking vistas, then shingling it all together.

Augustus Hemenway's death in 1876 had left his widow Mary, always regal, rich as well, and she was not chary of spending her mite. A determined philanthropist, she gave $100,000 to help save the Old South Church in Boston from destruction and introduced cooking instruction and physical education to America by way of the Boston public schools. In 1883 Mrs. Hemenway commissioned William Ralph Emerson to design a shingle-above-stone cottage for her daughter, Mrs. W. E. C. Eustis, on Pickworth Point at Manchester.

McKim, Mead and White of New York (McKim and White were Richardson alumni) raised the style to its zenith in the late 1880s and then moved on to other forms. Arthur Little swung with the times and turned out vast Georgian piles for the filthy rich buying their way into Pride's Crossing.

It is tempting to associate the shingled homes with the easy noblesse of those early arrivals from Boston, the Lorings and the Paines and their friends and their children, who were much too secure to succumb to the anxious exclusiveness that gripped each successive newcomer. Size and show were the new clients pounding at the door. The age of pretension swaggered in with the 1890s, and our first try at wrapping our houses lightly and loosely around the angularities of our lives was over.

A NEAR-SECESSION IN BEVERLY

As late as 1879 Hill and Nevins could get away with suggesting in their guidebook to the North Shore that since few of the estates between Pride's Crossing and Beverly Farms could be seen from the train, tourists should get off at the first depot, proceed on foot or otherwise, and resume the ride at the next. "These 'mansions by the sea,'" they advised, "are surrounded by extensive natural forests, meadows, fields, lawns, and flower gardens interspersed with ponds, streams, carriage roads, bridle paths and footpaths. . . . These private grounds and the roads through them are mostly open to the public in summer, and a drive or walk through them should not be omitted. But in doing so the visitor should bear in mind that the least recompense he can make for so much pleasure is to conduct himself decorously and not stray from the beaten paths picking flowers, trampling the lawns, or breaking the limbs of tree and shrubbery. He ought at least to be as considerate as his English cousins who, year after year, travel through the broad acres of the 'Lord' without ever stepping to one side or the other, thankful that his more favored fellow being shares with him thus much."

Unhappily for the Lords of the Shore, base ingratitude toward the more favored fellow was growing into the curse of the eighties in America. The western farmers were rising up against the eastern "interests," the Knights of Labor were breaking their lances upon the walls of capitalism, and, worst of all, the Democrats were running things.

As for the North Shore, those conveyers of the masses from the ovens of the city to the seaside, the horsecars, had already been insinuated into Swampscott and Marblehead, raising the threat of conquest by a fifth column. In March 1885, even as cries of "B-Ware!" were being raised in the streets of Marblehead and Swampscott, the Naumkeag Street Railway proposed to extend the route of its horsecars from Beverly Center to Pride's Crossing and Beverly Farms. "A mere entering wedge!" expostulated Thornton K. Lothrop, retired lawyer and summer resident. If the cars came, he warned, "a great many of Beverly's citizens would avail themselves of a fine ride and visit the beaches and drives," and the value of shore property would go all to hell. Let us control our own destiny, said he, by incorporating as a separate town.

Lothrop persuaded his Pride's neighbor, John T. Morse, Jr. (Dr. Holmes's nephew), that disaster impended. The two were among some ten out of the seventy summer residents of the Farms and Pride's Crossing who paid their general property taxes in Beverly, which entitled them to vote locally. The natives were all for lower taxes; many of them, having bartered their birthrights to the lords, were by way of being their lieges anyway. A petition was got up; a bill for the incorporation of Beverly Farms was filed in the General Court, and in due course it was rejected in March 1886 (not for the first time; back in 1717 the Farms, on account of some now-forgotten gripe with Beverly, had tried without avail to unite with Manchester).

John I. Baker, chairman of the Beverly selectmen, veteran local politician and business leader, a patriarch long of beard and sharp of wit, cut the ground out from under the Boston lawyers. Regard the summer people, he declaimed to a committee of the legislature (where he had served as state representative for eighteen years)—driving their fancy turnouts over town roads and running town water from their taps (as a matter of fact, summer taxes made possible the public water supply, the library, extension of roads and better schools and police and fire service, but never mind). Now they propose to pull out and throw the whole tax burden on the rest of us!

Furthermore, argued Selectman Baker (and here is where he cut the ice with his old cohorts on Beacon Hill), these fellows are nothing but Boston tax-dodgers, whose real aim is to set up their own private summer colony as a tax haven. Unless you stop them short, the epidemic of tax evasion for the benefit of the rich and privileged that started at Nahant will infect the entire North Shore! Not for nothing did they call John Baker "King of Beverly."

In retaliation against the defeated summer secessionists, the Beverly assessors raised valuations wholesale along the shore, uncovering in the process nearly two million dollars concealed in paper assets, including nine hundred thousand dollars of Lothrop's. This draconian sweep naturally caused the residents of the Farms and Pride's Crossing, summer and year-round—"the first-rate, native, old-fashioned Yankee population" to whom John Morse appealed—to rise up almost to a soul in righteous wrath.

A Farms committee (with Lothrop and Morse keeping a low profile this time) went to work on the legislature in an extraordinary lobbying campaign financed with a slush fund of eighteen thousand dollars raised by a Boston-based committee of summer people. Charges and countercharges flew during the winter of 1886, and the Beverly separation issue threatened to blow the dome off the State House. The Beverly Farms–Beacon Street axis put the pressure on the state government, which the Republicans had always presumed to be their private preserve.

But King Baker had long since split with the Republicans over the temperance issue, having run twice as the Prohibitionist candidate for governor, and this garnered him little support in the legislature. And the most he and the forces of union could raise for lobbying and sundry purposes was thirty-five hundred dollars, which did not go very far when competing with division lobbyists who buttonholed House members to "bet" them two hundred dollars that they would vote against division. That spring of 1887 a thoroughly cozened legislature bestowed its tentative blessing on this second fierce campaign to keep the horsecars off Hale Street.

There was a most terrible stink. Traffic in votes was charged. Committees of both branches held hearings and condemned corruption, but released no evidence, if they found it. The votes held firm, and the division bill was finally passed over the objections of no less a figure than U.S. Senator George Frisbie Hoar, the Republican leader of the state, and sent to Governor Oliver Ames.

The governor's blood was as blue as any that coursed through the veins of the separationists, and he was in their camp, but it was all too much; his friends had gone too far; the reputation of the party (and the outcome of the next election) was at stake. He vetoed the bill to incorporate Beverly Farms,

"King of Beverly" John I. Baker, here addressing his townspeople as the city's first mayor, led the fight against the tax-dodging summerers who were swinging their weight around on the Gold Coast. (Beverly Historical Society)

declaring that to sign it would be "to excuse and encourage a monstrously bad and corrupt practice."

Governor Ames's veto was sustained. The Beverly assessors relented and passed around some downward revaluations in the right places. And of course the charges of tax-dodging and the well-publicized slush fund and the scandalous lobbying were an awful embarrassment to the summer residents of the Gold Coast, who were mightily relieved at last to be out of an adventure upon which they had embarked, as John Morse sighed, "with scant foresight."

THE PRIVILEGED MAKE THEIR MARK

Emmanuel Church, built by Russell Sturgis in 1880. (Manchester Historical Society)

The cynical and roughshod tactics of the rich men from Boston failed to split the town on the map, but they succeeded in drawing class lines where before few on either side were disposed to bear witness to their existence. "Nobody can bring back the beautiful fields, stretching from the woods to the sea, where cows and oxen grazed," grieved the old schoolmistress Mary Larcom Dow, who could not conceal her bitterness over the transformation of the Farms. "Nobody can bring back the roadsides bordered with wild roses."

At Manchester, which was not involved in the controversy except by

empathy, the lines were also drawn, as they were across the land. On his estate near Lobster Cove, in 1880 Russell Sturgis built Emmanuel Church, a half-timbered Episcopal chapel, for the use of his summer neighbors. The Reverend D. F. Lamson, who had been called up from Hartford as pastor of King Baker's Baptist church and later was commissioned to write Manchester's history, described this more or less friendly rival as "a churchly little building, with lych-gate, mantling ivy and 'storied windows richly dight,'" which during the summer season "receives within its walls more wealth and fashion and culture than are often found in churches of much larger size and greater pretensions. It is viewed, however, rather as an exotic by some of the permanent residents." Of his own parish Mr. Lamson said only that "it has never been a strong one in numbers or in wealth."

Looking about him as his adopted town entered the final decade of the century, Lamson concluded that as a noted resort, Manchester "has lost much of its individuality, greatly to the regret of its older inhabitants who remember it as a place which had life in itself. . . . From the first Richard H. Dana to the latest representative of the new aristocracy, from senator, ex-governor and minister plenipotentiary to champion golf player and imported flunkey, from 'tally-ho' to donkey cart, from Russian wolf-hound to my lady's lap-dog—an influence has been exerted upon the town by its summer population. It has furnished a new social problem.

"[This] will be considered by some the period of the town's prosperity and glory, and by some the period of its decline and decay. It must be left to some future historian fully to tell the story, and to strike the balance between the advantages and disadvantages of a modern summer resort."

"Eaglis," the summer home of Edward E. Paramore on the tip of Gale's Point in Manchester, as it appeared near the turn of the century. (Manchester Historical Society)

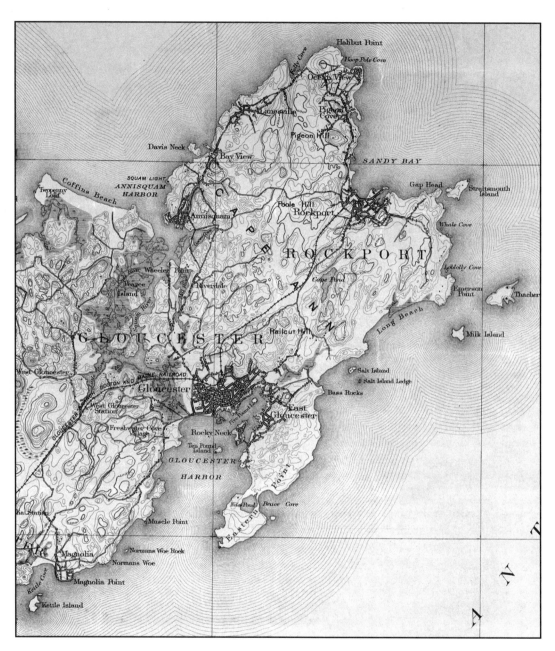

Too far from Boston for most summer invaders, much of Cape Ann in 1893 was still open for discovery and investment. (Sandy Bay Historical Society)

~9~
'ROUND THE CAPE

From Magnolia clear around Cape Ann,
the shore succumbs to the summerers

Only along her flanks, open to the ocean and hence unclaimed by the fisheries, was Gloucester exposed to the nips of the land-hungry pack that ranged the North Shore in the wake of the Civil War. The nearest straggler for the picking-off was the snoring hamlet of Kettle Cove, which lay partly along the shore of Gloucester a mile and a half west of the harbor, partly within the easterly limits of Manchester. This coastal anomaly consisted of the twin points of Coolidge in Manchester and Magnolia in Gloucester, of nearly equal size and separated by a fine crescent of beach inside Kettle Cove, named not for a kettle but for a family of them that settled there in colonial times. Kettle Cove was so far from both town centers that it was of no great interest to either, and the natives were left by both to their own vices and devices—small farming, slight shore fishing and less lobstering, and the heroic consumption of rum on every excusable occasion.

Magnolia Point took its name from the exotic flowering shrub common to the South but found in Massachusetts in its wild state only in the swampy ravines of the forest behind the West Gloucester and Manchester shore. This stretch from Freshwater Cove to Kettle Cove is all bold red ledge, during winter storms a continuous explosion of white water, in summer offering safe harbor only for a few small craft. The railroad was a mile from Kettle Cove, and even the shore road through Manchester to Gloucester passed it by, so that the first summer boarders (the Day family from Boston in 1861) had the warm sands of Crescent Beach and the sleepy upland of the point to themselves.

Like its twin across the cove, which had been owned originally by the Goldsmiths, Magnolia Point was the family farm of the Knowltons until 1867, when they sold most of it to Daniel W. Fuller, who had witnessed the transformation of his home town, Swampscott, into a prosperous resort and foresaw similar possibilities farther along the North Shore. East-west across its shoulder Fuller laid out Hesperus Avenue in honor of the imaginary ship that Longfellow wrecked on the very real rock of Norman's Woe a mile alongshore toward Gloucester; with increased traffic this new road took over the ancient cart path, Master Moore's Lane (after a famous teacher of navigation to local sea captains, whose house still stands at the head of it), above the ledges that tied in with Western Avenue behind Freshwater Cove.

North-south from Lobster Lane (later extended around the point at the water's edge as Shore Road) Fuller cut through a namesake road to Hesperus Avenue. The tenting craze was in full pitch, and he encouraged campers; to some he sold lots, and to others he sold or rented cottages that he built himself. In 1873 this enterprising developer opened a café at the corner of Hesperus and Fuller, in charge of Mrs. Maria H. Bray, a West Gloucester housewife.

Magnolia, as the village of Kettle Cove was renamed, developed rapidly during the 1870s into a hotel resort second only on the North Shore to Swampscott. Up behind the cove Allen Knowlton opened the small Crescent Beach Hotel in 1873, enlarged it year by year and soon had 150 guests. Success gave him grander ideas. In 1877 he dusted off and elaborated on a project his father, James Knowlton, had vainly pushed in 1847 when he attempted to get Manchester to annex Magnolia Point from Gloucester. Allen petitioned the legislature to carve a new town of Magnolia out of Gloucester and Manchester, but the son fared no better than the sire.

Behind the east end of Crescent Beach, Allen's brother-in-law, Barnard Stanwood, fixed over the Knowlton homestead into Willow Cottage and hired Mrs. Bray to run it in 1876. Her hospitality and its location on the crest of a meadow that rolled down to the ocean soon brought waves of vacationing celebrities to the comfortable summer boardinghouse, set so invitingly in the shade of giant trees at the end of a driveway fenced with the bones of a stranded whale.

Halfway out on the point, on Hesperus Avenue, Daniel Fuller built the Hesperus House in 1877; it was so popular that after only two seasons he matched it with a wing seventy feet to the west and joined the two with a

Lobster Lane (now Shore Road) in Magnolia before the summer onslaught. (Procter Brothers)

covered walkway that bulged at the middle in an eccentric Chinese pagoda entered through a porte cochere, which was the latest thing under which to arrive, especially for those arriving by private conveyance, with coachman up. The Hesperus was Magnolia's first definitely fashionable hotel and long retained the loyalty of quiet Bostonians of breeding, perhaps due in some measure to its practice of feeding children with nurses at separate hours.

The Hesperus House in its early days, about 1883. (Magnolia Historical Society)

The winter after he doubled the Hesperus House, Fuller traveled to the young state of Colorado to visit Lewis N. Tappan, the Manchester real estate man, who in his younger days had pioneered the territory and owned an interest in underground real estate at Leadville, where the friends descended into the Virginius silver mine. The founder of Magnolia was being hoisted back up in the ore bucket when it let go as he neared the surface and dropped him 140 feet to his death. A few hours later Tappan died of shock.

By the 1880s the rocketing popularity of Magnolia kept six summer hotels filled, including the Oceanside, which opened as a homey boarding-house with a sweeping view of the sea and betrayed no hint of its future glitter as the North Shore's preeminent pied-à-terre. Excursion steamers sometimes touched at the Kettle Cove wharf, and the Eastern Railroad built a depot to serve East Manchester and Magnolia, bringing the point within a twenty-minute trot by hotel barge. Stamped by Baedeker as "a pleasant little watering-place," the resort soon also had its own postal substation to keep Magnolia in touch with the world.

The wealthy summer people built a library for the resort in 1889. Previously its books had been shelved in a small church on Magnolia Avenue and supported by the proceeds of an annual fair, also run by the summer folks. *Magnolia Leaves,* the summer monthly founded by the energetic Mrs. Bray, observed that by making it available to the natives (who really had no use for it), its sponsors had invested the library with the necessary flavor of charity.

Fashion frequently follows fame, and in 1877 a figure both famous and

This 1887 map of Magnolia shows the Hesperus House to the left of Lexington Avenue and the Oceanside to the right. (Magnolia Historical Society)

fashionable doubled the effect on the resort. Bearded, bald and bearing a spectral palette, William Morris Hunt had captured Boston on his return from Europe a score of years earlier with an exciting portfolio of paintings, his enthusiasm for Millet, and the novel techniques of the Barbizon School. He married a granddaughter of Thomas Handasyd Perkins and, when he felt so disposed, charmed the city's innermost circles. But Boston charmed him not, less so than ever after he lost his studio and much of his work in the Great Fire of 1872.

Hunt roamed to remote places like Newport, his native Vermont, the sun-splashed Azores and North Easton, Massachusetts, where his friend Henry Hobson Richardson was creating architectural monuments to the Ames family of shovel fortune. The inland heat in the summer of 1877 drove him to sea-cooled Magnolia on the invitation of another architect friend, William Ralph Emerson, who had a small cottage above Crescent Beach for the season. The two searched lucklessly for a fish house or shed whose owner would let them cut a studio skylight through the roof, until "a cultivated lady from Gloucester" assured Barnard Stanwood, who owned an old barn across the road from Willow Cottage where Hunt was staying,

that the artist was a great man and his choice of Magnolia for painting would be "the making of the place."

Hunt bought Stanwood's barn and adjacent carpentry shop that July. Emerson oversaw its conversion into a studio; they christened it "The Hulk." The barn was doubled in length for horse stalls, painter's van, buggy and dogcart. In a nod to the nautical they hung davits and swung ropes here and there and screwed a sundial to an outside wall with the spoilsport legend NOW IS THE TIME.

The artist probably had some late-season use of "The Hulk" in 1877 but was dissatisfied with the loft as a studio and made what he called a barracks of it for himself and visitors, doing his painting in the carpentry shop. Every morning he set forth in his van with a student and a driver. Once upon the scene, as one of them told it, he "would leap from the van, take a camp-stool and a block of charcoal paper, and, with a stick of soft charcoal seize the salient points of the subject to be rendered. The assistant would . . . 'lay in' the first painting— reproducing the effect of the charcoal-sketch, while Hunt would watch intently for the right moment . . . when he would seize palette and brushes, and perhaps complete the picture in one sitting." To ward off kibitzers he is said to have worn sandwich boards advising I CAN'T TALK and I CAN'T HEAR.

For the 1878 season Emerson and Hunt perched a one-man gazebo on a pole thirty feet above the ground, reached from "The Hulk" by a catwalk with a drawbridge by which the artist could isolate himself. From this nest he surveyed Magnolia Point, the sea and Eastern Point, and sketched and meditated in lofty loneliness. But for most of that summer he was kept in Boston, drafting the murals for the Albany State House, and he broke away to Magnolia for only a few weekends. Almost prostrate with overwork, Hunt fled the next summer to the Isles of Shoals off the New Hampshire coast to visit with his friend Celia Thaxter, the poet. On September 8, 1879, his body was found in a tidal pool. He was fifty-five. Whether he had died by suicide or accident was never satisfactorily resolved.

Five months after the artist's death an auction of his unsold works in Boston revealed that the painting van had not ranged far from "The Hulk";

William Morris Hunt. (Peabody Essex Museum)

the shore had inspired the culminating production of his life. Of twenty-one canvases and charcoal drawings, all but two or three were set in Magnolia. The best was *Gloucester Harbor,* shimmering through a windless midsummer haze, a large oil painting now in the Museum of Fine Arts, Boston, which sold for three thousand dollars. He dashed off this masterpiece in an afternoon and sized it up with satisfaction: "I believe that I have painted a picture with *light* in it!"

Its distinctive light was what had attracted William Morris Hunt to Gloucester, and it shines through the works of his predecessors there. The native Fitz Hugh Lane produced calm, glowing, suspended animations of the harbor and its shores (though he could paint a coaster wallowing through a sloppy swell to make a stomach somersault). Lane died a dozen years before Hunt's arrival; no painter since has matched his achievements with atmospheric light, and he stands with Winslow Homer as the greatest of American marine artists.

Homer painted Gloucester as early as 1871, six years after Fitz Hugh Lane's death. His first stay of any duration was in the summer of 1873, when he undertook to tackle watercolors seriously. He returned in 1880, the summer following Hunt's mysterious demise, literally getting inside his subject by boarding with the lighthouse keeper on Ten Pound Island in the middle of Gloucester Harbor. The artist was rowed back to the mainland in a few weeks with fifty or more watercolors of haunting beauty that attest to his absolute mastery of the medium and to the harbor's theatrical effect on the painters to come, for whom Lane, Hunt and Homer raised the curtain—or lifted the veil.

GLOUCESTER'S ENCHANTED VISITOR

In 1880 Elizabeth Stuart Phelps, a popular author from Andover, built a cottage in Wonson's Field at the north end of Niles Beach on Eastern Point, calling it archly "The Old Maid's Paradise." From her window Miss Phelps was seduced by the sunset breaking through the scudding clouds at the end of a storm: "All Gloucester harbor tossed against it. The bows of the anchored fleet rose and sank angrily. The head-lights came out one by one, and flared, surging up and down. Ten Pound Light flashed out for the night; but her blinder was on, towards us. The little city, glorified now, forgiven of her fish, and her dust, and her bounding roads, loved and dreamed over, and sung in heart and pen, melted all through her pretty outlines against the massive colors of the west."

But by the light of day Miss Phelps had regained her underlying irritation with Gloucester's imperturbability. "Her summer guests may come and go, may pay or not, may criticize or adore, but her fish bite on forever. The result of my own observation has been that Gloucester, in her heart of hearts, regards her large summer population with a certain contempt." Of course, the more the lady criticized, the more she adored and, like all unrequited lovers, the worse she was rebuffed.

The train ride down from Boston, for instance, took an hour by the clock, but the local public conveyance until almost 1890 was the stagecoach since Gloucester people never went anywhere, being already there. The extension of the rails to Gloucester in 1847 had driven the Salem stage off the old colonial shore road, though the coach still clattered from the depot across the cape until 1861, when the first train steamed on to Rockport. The stage line from the Gloucester station to Annisquam and Lanesville was not finally forced to give way until the trolley cars scared the horses off the road.

Excursionists by sea fared no better when the bay was bumpy. In 1859 the Boston and Gloucester Steamboat Company was organized and put *Mystic* in regular year-round service. A succession of steamers during and after the Civil War carried fish from the company's wharf on Duncan's Point for the Boston market and general cargo on the return from Central Wharf.

Some effort to accommodate the summer excursion trade was made during the late 1860s, pausing long enough in Gloucester for passengers to take a swim at Pavilion Beach, down a fish dinner at the Pavilion or the Atlantic House, and have a quick look around the waterfront before the reboarding whistle sounded. Eleven more steamers, mostly sidewheelers—five of them operated by a rival company in the early 1870s—plied the thirty-two miles along the North Shore, sometimes touching in summer at Magnolia or Salem, until the Boston and Gloucester settled down in 1876 with the sturdy 108-foot screw steamer *George A. Chaffee*—"The Bed Bug"—which remained in service for nineteen years.

The real heroine of the run was the line's first custom-built steamship, the 142-foot *City of Gloucester*, with the profile of a warehouse topped off by two masts and a single stack, yet as squat as a tugboat, slow, powerful and unbelievably ugly. The *City*'s trial trip from Gloucester on July 28, 1883, was planned as a gala to Nantasket; the large and happy party of local men and women on board was to indulge in a catered collation to the strains of the Gloucester Cornet Band. But the day broke stormy, and the waves capered uncooperatively. Wrote the reporter for the *Cape Ann*

Advertiser, "A spirit of uneasiness was manifest. Some of the ladies and gents whose smiles and laughter added much to the pleasure of the occasion began to look pale. . . . Vainly they tried to overcome it, a praiseworthy effort, but it proved a failure, and the seasick victims paid tribute to Father Neptune and felt all the better after the account was settled." And very much better after the captain mercifully put about at Halfway Rock and returned to harbor, where the collation was brought out in the calm lee of Eastern Point.

That was the first and very nearly the last time the *City of Gloucester* reneged on a trip in forty-two years. Only the dirtiest weather daunted her. She endeared herself to generations of year-round and summer folk such as Gloucester native Theodore S. Ireland, who remembered the boyhood thrill of the 3:30 a.m. departure for Boston: "At the wharf bright stars . . . then the churning of water as we slid away from the dock, and later the sun coming up out of the ocean. A mug-up from the galley with coffee and donuts. . . . I doubt if any ship had a whistle like the *City.* It was single tone and I believe high C. Just after daylight on a thick foggy morning it was really something to hear the *City* leave the harbor, blowing every 20–30 seconds."

Most guests booked for the few summer hostelries on Cape Ann arrived by train and were met at the depot by the hotel barge. Those bound for camp or cottage on the cape's more distant shores had to wait for the stagecoach that four times daily lurched over the dusty road skirting the Annisquam and Mill rivers to Squam and on to the back of the cape on Ipswich Bay. Vacationers to the handful of small hotels and boardinghouses of East Gloucester and Rocky Neck shared the delight of a four-cent ride across the busy harbor on the midget steam ferry. Or they could make one of the hourly trips behind the pungent wharves in the lumbering horse-drawn omnibus, of which the *Advertiser* reported one June that "when a very fat lady got in last week a passenger grumbled, 'Omnibuses were not made for elephants.' To which she retorted with a twinkle, 'Sir, omnibuses are like Noah's Ark, intended for all kinds of beasts.'"

Miss Phelps was not fat, nor did she come upon East Gloucester by omnibus. Daughter of Professor Austin Phelps of the theological seminary at Andover, Elizabeth, like countless other girls, had lost the boy she loved in the Civil War. Her novel *The Gates Ajar,* in which she laid bare her own spiritual torture and recovery, appeared in 1868 when she was twenty-four and sold seventy-eight thousand copies. Not long after, she jounced in her buggy on an exploratory trip over that abhorrent dirt road, past the snowy acres of split salt cod curing in the sun above the wharves where the fishing schooners nudged and creaked, paused on the crest of Patch's Hill, "and drew the breath of unexpected and undreamed-of delight. We had discovered Eastern Point . . . the fairest face of all the New England coast." After boarding with the Wonsons for a few trial seasons, the author in 1880 built "The Old Maid's Paradise."

Over the years a lengthening litany of vessels, most of them Gloucester schooners returning from fishing, had piled up on the rocks of Brace Cove in night darkness or storm or fog, mistaking the small of Eastern Point's back for its head, beyond which lay safe harbor. In 1880 several veteran mariners suggested that because the light and bell at the end of the point frequently could be neither seen nor heard under adverse conditions, a loud whistling buoy, activated by the tossing of the waves, should be moored a mile offshore to guide vessels away from Brace Cove and into Gloucester Harbor.

Elizabeth Stuart Phelps. (From her autobiography, Chapters of a Life.*)*

This prudent advice raised a tempest of hysteria. One alarmed opponent wrote the *Advertiser* that when a whistler was moored off Newport, an ailing summer visitor "died raving for want of sleep" and reminded landholding readers that Beverly property owners had recently blocked attempts to locate one of the dreadful things off their shore; he (or she) warned that the bellowing buoy would most certainly drive summer visitors away and result in depreciation of land values from Eastern Point clear around to Magnolia.

And so nothing was done. Two years later, after several more wrecks, the wise heads of Gloucester again brought up the whistler and this time brought down on themselves a regular hurricane of letters and petitions from the shore owners, real estate agents and summer visitors. The Lighthouse Board ordered a heavier hammer for the fog bell at the Eastern Point lighthouse. Another year passed. A returning mackerel schooner drove ashore in the night.

At last Washington acted, and late in 1883 "Mother Ann's Cow" was moored, over the groans of the summer people, half a mile south of Eastern Point Light, where it has remained to this day—except during the vacation seasons from 1885 through 1888, when Miss Phelps, a chronic insomniac with friends in high places, had it removed.

Luckily for the lowly fishermen, the old maid just then finally found the paradise she pined for in the Reverend Herbert Dickinson Ward, seventeen years younger than she. The knot was tied by the father of the bride in October 1888; soon after, the Boston *Record* reported that "since her marriage Mrs. Ward is much better, and the officer who had to remove the buoy has put it back with the assurance that next summer he will have no orders to disturb it."

How much of this hue and cry against Mother Ann's Cow, this scare talk about sleepless nights and ruined land, can be laid to what might rightly strike the reader as the preposterously irrelevant imminence of the twenty-first birthday of my grandmother in 1882?

My great-great-grandfather, Thomas Niles, had died in 1872 at the age of seventy-five. He had seen the worth of his Eastern Point farm increase tenfold since 1844, and with fifteen children between the ages of sixteen and forty-seven among whom it would be divided, he counted on his investment to continue upward under the rising pressure on shore property. Therefore in his will Farmer Niles had forbidden his executors to divide the four hundred acres until his youngest granddaughter, Sarah McClennen Rogers, had reached her majority. Meanwhile two of his sons managed the farm. My grandmother was twenty-one in 1882. The executors immediately published a subdivision plan; no satisfactory buyers approached, and since the taxes then were only about $720, they bided their time.

A quarter of a century after they had first rattled north from Boston into Lynn, the horsecars finally breached Gloucester's unconcern about such conveniences in 1886, and it appeared that inevitably (as it was, in three more years) proper public

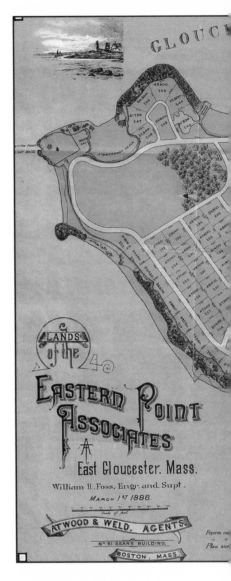

transportation would be extended from the Eastern Railroad depot around the harbor through East Gloucester Square and probably as far as Rocky Neck, which was but a short trot from the Niles gate. In 1887 the Niles executors sold the entire farm to a syndicate of American and Canadian capitalists, lawyers and entrepreneurs, the Eastern Point Associates, for $100,000.

The key to the deal may have been the syndicate's clerk, A. Spalding Weld of the real estate firm of Atwood and Weld, the only member who did not subsequently build. Weld lived in the Jamaica Plain section of Boston, where also resided his friends Charles F. Farrington, a businessman, and David S. Greenough, an importer. David and his brother John, a New York railroad financier, had first come to Gloucester as boys in 1855, when they stayed at the Pavilion with their family; they would row across the harbor

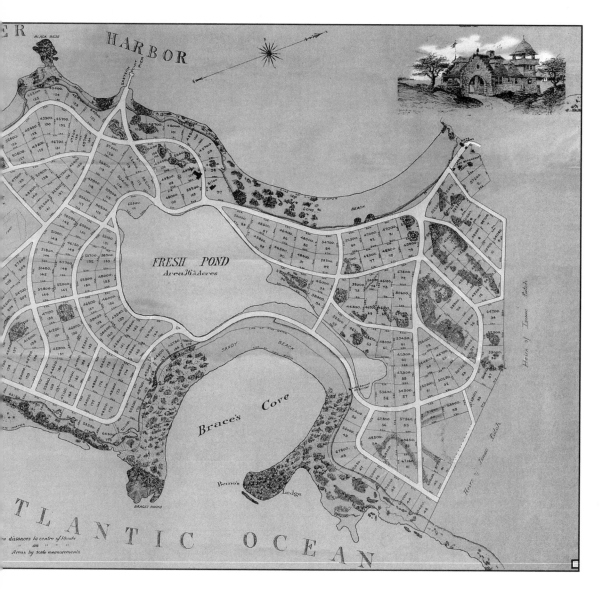

to Eastern Point and "spy out the land," taking care to keep clear of Mr. Niles, and they vowed that someday they would build their summer homes on its Black Bess Point. This they did in 1888. The three Canadians were from Toronto: Henry J. Scott was a retired merchant and Member of Parliament; J. Hamilton Kane was a banker; Walter Barwick was an attorney who had been vacationing at the small Seaside Hotel on Niles Beach for several years. The Greenoughs must have had a strong hand in engineering the deal through their friends Weld and his partner, L. P. Atwood, who bought one of the first cottages to be built as did Barwick in bringing in the Canadian money.

During the fall and winter of 1888, eleven pleasant shingle-style cottages, incorporating native fieldstone and schoonerloads of lumber from Maine, were strung out along the outer harbor shore and up the dirt road

Some plans, like this subdivision of Eastern Point drawn up in 1888, are better left undeveloped. (Cape Ann Historical Association)

that led to the abandoned Civil War earthworks on the point's highest elevation, which they called Fort Hill Avenue. Barwick, Kane and Benjamin S. Calef, a Boston insurance executive, had Arthur Hooper Dodd design their houses, grouped around an old water-filled quarry on the nubbin of ledge below the lighthouse, at a cost of seven thousand dollars each. On the end of Quarry Point across the small cove from the lighthouse, John V. Lewis, Cincinnati Standard Oil magnate, built the grandest (many years later the house of the Eastern Point Yacht Club), a spacious twelve-thousand-dollar cottage designed by Appleton and Stephenson of Boston, who that same winter created the Gate Lodge at the north end of Niles Beach; here the Associates' porter was stationed to screen all who entered their private sanctum through the lodge's stone arch. John J. Stanwood, Gloucester fish dealer and land speculator, built on the rise behind Niles Beach, and Captain Albert Lewis, owner of Lewis Wharf in Boston, raised his cottage next to Farrington on Fort Hill Avenue.

The Eastern Point Associates had more in mind than an "exclusive" colony of 250 cottages. The center of it all was to be the classiest summer hotel on the North Shore, presiding over Gloucester Harbor from behind the embrasures of the old fort. Guests and summer residents were to have direct steamer service to Gloucester and Boston from a three-hundred-foot pier they built from the harbor end of Fort Hill Avenue. While they worked on the financing, they bought the diminutive Seaside Hotel opposite Niles Beach as a stopgap and refurbished it as The Beachcroft. And then with splendid flourish they brought a boatload of prime prospects down from Boston on the *City* for a catered *dejeuner à la fourchette* under a striped tent, followed by a tour of their magnificent resort-to-be by horse barouche. But the well was dry. Not a shingle of the syndicate's fortress hotel materialized. The steamship stop at their pier was abandoned from lack of patronage. Although a few lots were sold, not one beyond the first dozen was built on for five years, and in 1892 the Eastern Point Associates declared themselves bankrupt and reorganized on less ambitious lines.

"The scheme was doomed to failure from the beginning," reflected a later summer resident. "There were no water mains, no gas mains, no electric wires, no telephones. Purchasers for such land could not be found." The clouds of dust and lurking potholes that beset the wayfarer on the road through East Gloucester, predicted the *Cape Ann Advertiser,* "will down more summer visitors than the cars and steamboat will bring to town."

THE FARTHER REACHES OF THE CAPE

As the Eastern Point Associates learned to their ultimate benefit, Cape Ann was no ripe plum for the picking, while all of West Gloucester beyond walking distance of the depot and the four marshy miles of the Annisquam River estuary had scarcely any roads at all and on a hot and windless August day were ambushed by squadrons of greenhead flies with the jaws of crocodiles, armies of bloodthirsty mosquitoes and legions of tiny midges.

All travelers approaching Gloucester proper and Rockport by road had to squeeze across the Blynman Canal that had connected Annisquam (or "Squam") River and the fishing port since colonial days. This extraordinary feat was accomplished over the drawbridge (when it chanced to be shut) that was installed over the "Cut" in 1868. Once in Gloucester, the summer visitor discovered that the stagecoach was the sole public conveyance to the shore almost until the advent of the electric trolley cars in the 1890s. Add to these natural obstacles the indifference of the native population, and grand ventures for summer colonization had a way of foundering on the Cape Ann shore like lost ships in the night.

The mile and a half of Coffin's Beach, as an example, was simply a sand-bar cast up between Two Penny Loaf and Farm Point by a few millennia of storms sweeping across Ipswich Bay. On his deathbed the old Revolutionary hero Peter Coffin had gathered his sons and cautioned them to husband the stand of timber that held the vagabond sand from drifting over his fields. But the trees went to the mill anyway, and the farm went to hell.

Superb as it was and is, the beach was miles from the main road, much too far from anywhere to serve the pleasure of any but Gloucester folk fowling, wading and digging for hen clams. In the 1870s and 1880s the solitary year-rounder on the several hundred acres of the deserted Coffin farm was Solomon T. Trumbull, a quarry owner who sold off a few lots for summer camps. Where the cart track dignified as Atlantic Street disappeared amongst the dunes he put up a rough-and-tumble roller-skating rink that doubled as a dance hall and clam chowder canteen.

The Cut Bridge was the only road to Gloucester proper and Rockport until the post–World War II extension of Route 128. (Cape Ann Historical Association, James B. Benham collection)

In about 1888 Edward C. Hawks, a Buffalo lawyer, came upon this wasteland by the sea, so clean and beautiful in its very barrenness, bought Trumbull's land and several smaller abandoned farms, and integrated the titles. Far out on Two Penny Loaf in 1890 he built a pair of "castles" of granite barged to the beach from a local quarry and dragged up to the site on sand sleds by oxen. With a faint smile, one imagines, he called this outpost "Hawksworth Hall." Later he was joined by his brother, James D. Hawks of Detroit, an engineer then runging it up the ladder to the presidency of the Detroit and Mackinac Railroad; James built his own castle, "The Bungalow," at the other end of the beach on Farm Point.

Did Edward Hawks grow lonely in the solitude of his splendid spit of sand, or merely land-poor? In the 1890s he cut Two Penny Loaf into 106 slices around the core of "Hawksworth Hall" and chopped the beach into another 50, all with results as barren as his real estate. No one wanted to build an isolated summer house on sand, exposed to storm and sea. Local speculators carved the land below Farm Point into yet another hundred lots; they named the small pond there Sleepy Hollow Lake, and their dream resort Willoughby Park. Sleepy it all remained, and hollow the hopes, and they tiptoed away, most of their land unsold.

James Hawks survived his brother and summered at Coffin's Beach for thirty years. At one time he owned about a thousand acres, of which he restored a hundred to cultivation, and he planted ten thousand Austrian pines on the dunes in atonement for the prodigality of the Coffin boys. In 1924 his widow donated Wingaersheek Beach, the stretch southeast of Farm Point across the river from Annisquam, to the city of Gloucester, and not until the breakup of the Hawks estate did summer cottages finally sprout on the sands.

The variety of transport that George H. Procter had to use in order to commute summers to Merchant's Island six days a week from his *Cape Ann Weekly Advertiser* in downtown Gloucester suggests why more of the Annisquam River cottagers were not from out of town until the first motor car crossed the Cut. Pearce's Island it was originally, about midway along the Squam River, owned and farmed by Captain Elias Day and James Thurston until 1864, when the farmhouse burned and they sold out to Simeon Merchant, a Gloucester man recently returned from the California gold rush. Twice a day the tide swirled back and forth around the island; behind it and Rust and Ram islands, clear back to the West Parish woods and the Coffin farm, Jones Creek filled and drained through two miles of marsh where the farmers cut and stacked the salt hay, which they poled across to Gloucester in gundalows. Uncle Sim resumed the farming, and after the war his produce, meat and sundry supplies attracted Gloucester people to tent on his island. In 1869 he built several small summer cottages for rent. The Procters were among his first tenants.

To get to town from Merchant's Island the editor rowed his dory three hundred yards across Squam River to Brown's landing (or was ferried by his children to the flats if the tide was out) and hiked through the fields a half a mile to catch the Gloucester-bound stagecoach from Annisquam. Returning, if he'd not been able to leave the dory, Father would hail the island across the quiet of the water and soon hear the thump of oars in tholepins and much juvenile excitement as the family boat approached. At the end of his six-day week editor Procter bought the Sunday groceries, boarded the last Annisquam coach, trudged through Brown's field with his basket to the landing, shoved off in the waiting dory or shouted for it, and slid across the tide to his island retreat.

Merchant's Island was made for memories. Lobsters then abounded around the scattered rocks in Jones Creek, and the flats were gorged with clams. Uncle Sim initiated the boys in the art of bobbin' for eels and dispatched them in the dory with instructions to anchor by the light of the moon over a certain spot in the creek. In an hour one night they hooked fifty of the critters; Uncle Sim skinned the lot, and the island had an eel fry the next day. And the annual mackerel run: one afternoon two of the boys hooked, split and salted a whole barrelful, hove it aboard their dory, rowed to Squam the next morning, and sold their catch to a dealer for $3.50. In the 1870s Lloyd Lewis, father of my uncle Phil Lewis, came down from Lynn as a young fellow with a pal to camp on the island and shoot game birds in the marshes for the city market; the day's bag was taken into Gloucester and handed to the Eastern Railroad station agent, tagged for delivery to the chef of the famed United States Hotel in Boston.

There was never anything fancy about summer life on the Annisquam River. The cottages that cropped up on the shores of Merchant's and Rust islands and Wheeler's Point—later at Wolf and Ferry hills, Riverview and Thurston's Point—were solidly middle-class, inexpensive and unplastered, with piazzas that gave sweeping views up and down the river to Squam and its blinking lighthouse, the line of Coffin's snowy dunes and Ipswich Bay beyond.

THE VILLAGE OF ANNISQUAM

East of the sand-swirled mouth of the river on Ipswich Bay the village of Annisquam jealously guarded its peninsular privacy, part of Gloucester but a world removed from the hustle and clatter of the port four miles away. In early colonial times Squam's narrow Lobster Cove was as busy with fishing and shipbuilding as the harbor, but the maritime activity naturally gravitated to the larger, leaving the village's fishermen, clammers, lobstermen, sometime smugglers and farmers to their twisting lanes and weathered cottages, which suited them just fine.

For several summers during the Civil War "a party of ladies and gentlemen," as described in the Gloucester *Telegraph,* tented on a rise of pasture near the old Village Church at the head of Lobster Cove. August of 1865 saw "quite an accession to their numbers, and they have three tents and quite a spacious camp ground. They have also a fine little yacht and a fancy row-boat moored in the cove, below the bridge, and a span of horses stabled

in the vicinity." Next summer the contagion of canvas had spread to Wigwam Point on Ipswich Bay and Squam Point on the cove.

Pioneer Annisquam cottagers, the "Cambridge Settlement," came from Cambridge to Babson's Point above the village, leaving their mark on Cambridge Beach and Cambridge Avenue. In the 1870s Isaac Adams, the wealthy inventor of a nickel-plating process, set his summer mansion on "Adams Hill," where beds of shells told of Indian clambakes, and walled up nearby springs to make a goldfish pond. On the bank of the Squam River at the end of Cambridge Avenue, Pennsylvania steel magnate Luther S. Bent placed his "bungalow" and decreed that gardens bloom among the rocks; after his demise his son Quincy, vice president of the Bethlehem Steel Company, tore the place down and in 1921 substituted a $250,000 Italianate villa.

Another early summer Squammer (though a little off-Squam on the south shore of Lobster Cove) was the Harvard marine zoologist Alpheus Hyatt, disciple of Louis Agassiz and curator of the Boston Society of Natural History. In 1878 Professor Hyatt bought the 1664 Norwood house, where he set up the first oceanography laboratory in the United States. The location did not quite suit him, however, and after two or three years he and his associates founded the marine biological laboratory at Woods Hole in Buzzards Bay. When not aboard his research schooner *Arethusa*, the professor sailed a boxlike catboat with name lettered in Chinese characters; the neighbors called it "Hyatt's Old Tea Chest." One of his two sculptress daughters, Mrs. Anna Vaughn Hyatt Huntington, created and had cast several triumphant equestrian statues of Joan of Arc, one of which prances through New York's Riverside Park, another through Gloucester's Legion Square, immortalizing the East Gloucester firehorse she used for her model.

The summer colonies of Norwood Heights and Rockholm rose out of the windy pasture above the Ipswich Bay shore around the turn of the century; but Annisquam village, with its intimate lanes, compact old houses and air of snug security against the sea, never surrendered to the twentieth century.

BAY VIEW

After he was relieved of his command at New Orleans in 1863, that colorful political general of the Civil War, Benjamin F. Butler, happened upon the expanse of rocky pasture that tumbles down from the wilds of Dogtown Common to Hodgkins and Diamond coves east of Squam. A man of quick decision, he forthwith bought forty-seven acres and camped out with his two sons before embarking on a second inglorious tour of duty terminated by his second relief by President Lincoln in January 1865. Back in Gloucester next year, Ben was elected to Congress, though a Lowell resident, campaigning "while I lived in a tent on the beach." In 1869 he enlisted his former aide, Colonel Jonas H. French, in organizing the Cape Ann Granite Company, granite being in great demand for public works authorized by Congress. They built stone mansions on the high slope above Hodgkins Cove and Ipswich Bay and called their domain Bay View.

Between Davis Neck and their granite-loading pier at Hodgkins Cove Congressman Butler moored his beloved schooner yacht *America*, winner of the America's Cup, which he acquired from the Navy in a cozy deal in 1873. For the remaining twenty years of his life *America* was his pride, his joy, his relaxation from the cares of politics and legal practice, especially after the death in 1876 of Sarah, the actress wife he worshipped, when he all but abandoned Bay View to his daughter and her family. He maintained *America* to the nines under a smartly uniformed crew, dressed ship at the slightest excuse, was ever on the lookout for a race, and cruised with his sons and friends as far off as Labrador and Havana. Under sail as in politics, he had a stout pair of sea legs and reveled in tempestuous weather. On advance notice from the Coast Survey of an approaching storm he would hurry to sea out of pure zest for the battle, ordering his sailing master to "hold her to it." Small wonder the Butlerian advice to the prospective guest aboard that a yachtsman must "be able to eat and drink unlimitedly, not be seasick more than one-half of the time and keep goodnatured under difficulties."

Benjamin Franklin Butler, once described by a fellow general as "a cross-eyed cuttlefish swimming about in waters of his own muddying," died in 1893 in his seventy-fifth year, still going strong. He left Bay View and *America* to his only daughter, Blanche, and her husband, General Adelbert Ames, whom she had married in 1870. Ames was a West Point graduate and winner of the Congressional Medal of Honor for bravery in the First Battle of Bull Run. In Virginia he served under his future father-in-law, the citizen major general who at every opportunity had made a point of scorning Pointers since having been politically passed over for admission as a boy. Ames rose to general, commanded a military department in the South after the war, and was appointed to the Senate from Mississippi in 1871 at a time when Congressman Butler enjoyed great influence with President Grant. In 1874 he was elected governor of the former slave state. At the head of a corrupt carpetbag government and caught up in the forces that were tearing Reconstruction apart, Governor Ames was impeached by the whiteliners when they regained control of the Mississippi legislature. Butler got a smart ex-Confederate lawyer to defend his son-in-law, and the charges were withdrawn in exchange for his resignation. Adelbert and Blanche returned north for good, summering at Bay View with their children, and the Ames Estate, where General Butler ran for Congress from a tent on the beach, has remained in his family ever since.

OVER IN ROCKPORT

About the time Butler and French were settling into Bay View, the Fish Oil King from Swampscott, Eben B. Phillips, was mapping the North Shore's first extensive summer subdivision across the top of Cape Ann on Andrews Point in Rockport. Back in 1855, when there was talk of extending the railroad from Gloucester to Rockport, Phillips had shrewdly bought a large section of pasture and woodland north of Pigeon Cove, to which he added acreage east of the Babson Farm in partnership with George Babson, finally gathering in almost all of Andrews and Halibut points. A hard worker and player, Phillips made his money in salt fish, cod-liver oil and real estate. In his time he had gone fishing, farming (dug a hundred bushels of potatoes one day), gunning (once bagged nineteen pigeons out of a flock of twenty), rowing (for miles in subzero temperature) and yachting (as a familiar figure, bearded, bald and broad of beam at the helm of his schooners *Moll Pitcher* and *Fearless*). Taciturn yet restless and keen of mind, a devotee of the poetry of Alexander Pope, he was by the admission of an admiring biographer "a very peculiar person."

Eben Phillips bided his time and around 1870 launched into a well-publicized summer development of Andrews Point as "Ocean View," which he subdivided into 225 building lots crisscrossed with roads linked to a mile-long peripheral boulevard, Phillips Avenue. In 1871 he opened a small summer hotel, the Ocean View House, at the south entrance to his project, sold a few lots, and built a few cottages along the shore; he was planning a large hotel at the very tip of Andrews Point when he died in 1879.

Pigeon Cove and the rest of Rockport owe no mean debt for their calm and sober atmosphere to two hundred determined women armed with hatchets who marched on Dock Square on July 8, 1856, at the instigation of one Hannah Jumper and noisily chopped their way through fourteen illegal rum shops; thereby they established, possibly forever, the moral tone that almost ever since has sustained the voters of Rockport in their resolve to remain publicly dry.

Eight days after this smashing victory over the demon, Ralph Waldo Emerson arrived at the Pigeon Cove House for a week of contemplation that must not have been sundered by any distracting revelry, judging by his journal entry of July 23: "'Tis a noble friendly power, and seemed to say to me, 'Why so late and slow to come to me? Am I not here always thy proper summer home? Is not my voice thy needful music; my breath, thy healthful climate in the heat; my touch, thy cure?'"

Be such sentiments as they may, Robert Carter and his shipmates in the cruising sloop *Helen* spent an un-Emersonian evening over claret two summers later, locked in behind Pigeon Cove's quarry pier with the fogbound fishing fleet. They had rowed through the thick all the way from Rockport, where they had resolved not to remain another minute, for the stench of rotten fish in that tight little harbor had rendered it "so unpleasant on deck that, immediately after supper, we had lighted our cigars and closed the cabin doors, to smother with the fumes of tobacco the fishy odors from the shore." Anchored there in Pigeon Cove, as the drinks were about to give out they mixed and poured a final round with the toast "Confusion to the fog

Fishing at Pigeon Cove in the early 1870s was for gentlemen in full attire. The favored spot was Singer's Bluff, also known as Angling Point. (Procter Brothers, Howard collection)

The Pigeon Cove House, 1870s. (Procter Brothers, Howard collection)

and success to the last of the cocktails"—only to discover in the midst of a general spluttering that in the dark of the cabin someone had reached for the jug of lamp fluid.

Such foggy antics were barred from shore, where Pigeon Cove, in the words of the Reverend Henry C. Leonard, a summer habitué, "though not departing from simple, unfashionable ways, donned a habit somewhat new, and became widely known as a watering place. Gentlemen, whether with or without families, came to Pigeon Cove, not to waste their substance and wear their life out in excesses and follies, but for rest and quiet and healthful pastimes."

After the Civil War the Pigeon Cove House changed hands and in 1871 was moved to another site and replaced by a large new house. Down on the shore, bathers of both sexes waded and paddled in the Bath (there was also a Gentlemen's Bath at Hoop Pole Cove), a natural basin in the ledge, behind ropes tied to bolts driven into the smooth rock. "Here they come tripping down with bathing-dresses on arm and bathing-hats on head," wrote one female guest fascinated by the ritual. "A few moments suffice for change of dress, and then they come forth from the bathing-houses a merry company. Some bathe from a sense of duty, others for pleasure and excitement. You can tell the different motives of the bathers at a glance. The former go into the water as they would into a dentist's chair."

The absentee landowner Eben Phillips developed Ocean View as an out-and-out speculation, gambling on the extension of the railroad to Rockport. Ten years earlier, at the other end of Cape Ann, Thomas Niles had been similarly motivated by the prospect of train service to Gloucester in buying the Eastern Point Farm. George H. Rogers must have been seized with the same idea when, a few months after plans were announced to push the rails on to Cape Ann in 1845, he started quietly buying up the ancient colonial "cow rights" to the pastures north of the Niles and Patch farms, on the ocean side of East Gloucester overlooking some of the boldest coast on the North Shore, whose most prominent feature is Bass Rocks at the southern end of Little Good Harbor Beach.

George Rogers was a merchant of Gloucester, genial and generous, humorous and outspoken, with an insatiable appetite for real estate. He commenced his career as an apothecary, but rolling pills was not for him.

A reflective group of guests on the porch of the Pigeon Cove House, 1870s. (Procter Brothers, Howard collection)

After the death of George H. Rogers in 1870, porches were added to his house and it was renamed the Bass Rocks Inn. (Procter Brothers, Howard collection)

With a small stake he got in on the ground floor of Gloucester's profitable trade with Surinam on the north coast of South America. When that showed signs of flagging during the darkening years before the Civil War, he pushed his surplus into real estate, with such verve that they called him the Great Conveyancer, and moved buildings over land and water so offhandedly as to be the Great Remover.

Rogers paid fifty dollars for the first of his cow rights in the Bass Rocks section and by 1862 owned all fourteen, for which he was out of pocket $1,359.98. His investment was described as "completely wild, abounding in swamps, rocks and berry bushes, presenting as rough a piece of territory as could be found on the Cape." He spent $120,000 clearing forty acres for tillage and mowing and four miles of roads, kept forty head of cattle, sold milk and vegetables, planted three hundred fruit trees, and put in a large grapery, peach house, greenhouse and conservatory. On the heights above Bass Rocks he laid the foundation for his summer house, which he bought in Boston and brought up on one of his vessels. Across the road Rogers assembled from parts of demolished Boston mansions a combined board-inghouse and sanatorium, Whiting House.

Apparently overextended, the Great Conveyancer in 1868 offered fifty summer building lots for sale. But there were few buyers, and when George Rogers died broke at sixty-eight in 1870, his 250-acre investment went on the block against $85,000 in debts. Henry Souther, a Boston brewer, headed a syndicate that took it over for $46,000 and had the controlling hand in the casual development of Bass Rocks over the next two decades until his death in 1892.

Souther's friends thought Bass Rocks a poor business venture, but he saw it as an investment for his grandchildren and let the farm continue to dominate. The Rogers home was converted into the Bass Rocks Inn. Whiting House became the Bass Rocks Hotel until an incendiary took care of that. The Pebbly Beach House built on the shore also burned suspiciously in 1884 and was replaced after ten years by the Moorland Hotel.

Among the more interesting of the few cottages of the era is the cupolaed landmark of Judge Edgar J. Sherman of Lawrence, a former state attorney general, who was a trustee of the development after Souther's death. The house is literally bolted to the highest ledge of Bass Rocks, and with reason. John Webber paused there on a bicycle circuit of Cape Ann in 1885 and looked down from the veranda, where "seventy odd feet beneath us the 'sad sea waves' dash with terrific force against the huge jagged rocks, sending a thick blanket of snow-white foam afar out over the restless surface of the little cove. To see Bass Rocks in its glory one must visit the place during a storm; then the waters roll up in mountainous waves, and breaking against the rocky shore send thousands of tons of water completely over the dwelling on the cliff above."

And what befell these grand strategies to honeycomb the Cape Ann shore with summer colonies? Willoughby Park and the dreams of Edward Hawks to make the desert bloom never got off the paper; the myriad cells of Ocean View were integrated into substantially larger estates by 1900; likewise a similar attempt of the Southers at Bass Rocks. Reality sundered the web of paper lot lines entangling Eastern Point, likewise a plan to slice Rockport's Emerson Point into two hundred summer parcels in 1889. The Rockport group bought up five hundred acres behind Loblolly Cove and on Emerson Point, which they renamed Lands End after its opposite across the sea. They laid out streets with quaint Cornish names such as Wessex Road, Tregony Bow and Penrhyn Lane and actually built a three-wing, three-story hotel above the cove, the Turk's Head Inn. But like the rest, the Lands End Association threw in the towel. Cottages refused to spring from checkerboards. Land prices were too high, locations too remote, ledge too prevalent, services too primitive for the buyer of average means.

But the wealthy scooped up the lots by the handful, and before the end of the century most of the prime shore frontage on Cape Ann, from Magnolia along Gloucester Harbor through the Annisquam River and all the way back around by the sea to Eastern Point, had fallen to the summer people, by design or by default.

All aboard for Revere Beach on the Lynn and Boston Street Railway. Giddyap!
(Revere Public Library)

~10~
YOU CAN HAVE
ALL YOUR CONEYS

Just take her to Wonderland,
but behave yourself at Salem Willows

Breezy mansions by the shore, tennis courts and yacht races were all right for the Brahmins of Beacon Street, who only lightly perspired, but what respite for the working people in a supposedly classless society who sweated out their summers in the teeming, steaming tenements of industrial Greater Boston?

Ah, but their moment was at hand at last, and the man for it was Alpheus P. Blake, Barnum and Vanderbilt rolled and stretched into one, a tall, spare speculator who came down a poor country boy from New Hampshire and made his first fortune developing the Hyde Park section of Boston's Dorchester. Looking for further frontiers to bring within the orbit of the city, he lit upon the bypassed, population-barren territory of the lower North Shore. Around 1871, the year North Chelsea became Revere, he formed the Boston Land Company, bought up a thousand acres of East Boston, Winthrop and Revere, and conceived of their development as a great recreational and residential region to be fed from Boston and Lynn by cheap-to-build, cheap-to-run and cheap-to-ride mass transportation, namely a narrow-gauge railroad.

The time was right for taking on the Eastern Railroad, which had disdained any extension of branch service to this unprofitable region. Moreover, the road was embroiled in a depot war with Lynn over the inadequacy of its Central Square station and haughtily refused to run trains on Sunday, leaving travelers to contend for seats on an ancient stagecoach that made one round trip daily between Salem and Boston. Furthermore, Eastern had also lost public confidence after its infamous Revere Disaster on the foggy evening of August 26, 1871, when the Bangor Express plowed full speed into the rear of a Beverly local at the Revere station, killing twenty-nine and injuring fifty-seven—all because of chaotic dispatching, the railroad's inadequate double-tracking and the superintendent's outrageous refusal to use the telegraph between stations.

Lynn's smoldering dissatisfaction with the Eastern first flared up in 1861 in the form of the Lynn and Boston Street Railway, a horsecar line its founders trusted would "prove no small regulator of the freaks and follies of the great steam corporation." The horsecars had been the darlings of Boston for five years, and soon the first of these pleasant anomalies to appear in Essex County was clattering along between Lynn and Scollay Square via Chelsea Bridge, and via a branch track to a restaurant above the sands of great Chelsea Beach. The larger cars carried a conductor on a rear platform; the smaller, platformless, were called bobtails. Long or short, they rattled about their business on absurdly abbreviated wheel bases that gave them an especially teetery look when loaded with portly gents hung with ponderous watch chains, headed for office, factory or beer parlor. The operators got the better of temporarily immovable obstacles by driving off the track and around them. Winters along the steppelike Lynn and Revere marshes were miserable, but then came spring, and the fancy-painted open cars with their running boards were wheeled out of hibernation. Up rolled the curtains, and it was off to Chelsea Beach, with the sea breeze blowing through, all joy and jollity.

Nevertheless, Alpheus P. Blake had a vision, and bobtails hauled by plodding nags were not part of it. He looked to bring Land Company's thousand acres within commuting time of Boston and to transport sweltering Bostonians by the tens of thousands to the beach for a few hours of relief. On April 8, 1872, the Boston, Revere Beach and Lynn Railroad was organized. Construction moved rapidly along the eight miles from Lynn across the marshes, on trestles over the Saugus River and along the Point of Pines and the great beach, to Beachmont, across more marsh past Belle Isle Inlet to Orient Heights, thence on fill and trestles to Harbor View, Wood Island and Jeffries Point, where the tracks shot through a four-hundred-foot brick tunnel to the company's East Boston ferry slip for the passage on its steamers across Boston Harbor to Rowe's Wharf.

Along the crest of the beach, according to one account, the sand "kept sinking under the ties and what was infinitely worse, getting into the workers' beer. This caused a two-day strike until the situation was remedied." When a Revere crowd, grumbling "we don't want all the riffraff of Boston at our back doors," blocked the link-up of the two work gangs on the Point of Pines, the boss snuck his men out that night and laid the rails before dawn.

On its first day, July 29, 1875, the Narrow Gauge carried 1,078 passengers—the opening freshet of the flood to come. The slim coaches were elegantly appointed (seats in plush, with silver-plated mountings), some closed, some open after the manner of the summer horsecars. They flew behind the sturdy little locomotives in black and gleaming brass, delivered for $7,000 apiece. The entire "Little Wiggler," including two steam ferries, was completed within its capitalization of $350,000.

The impact on Revere (formerly Chelsea) Beach was explosive. Blake had tapped wells of yearning, drilled a summer safety valve into the simmering subterranean frustrations of a mass of city people, and run an outlet, round trip twenty cents, to the sea.

WINTHROP'S SHORT-LIVED RESORT

Hanging off to the southeast of the direct new line to the beach, Winthrop was at first circumvented by the Narrow Gauge, a slight for which the citizens soon enough were grateful.

During a downpour on the Fourth of July, 1874, while the Narrow Gauge was still abuilding, Mr. George E. Woodman set out to explore the shore road to Point Shirley and came upon the grand, empty expanse of Winthrop Beach. He hurried home and returned with a three-family tent colony under the banner "Atlantic Wave." The superintendent of the horse railroad that served Winthrop at the time was a former Union Army surgeon, Dr. Samuel Ingalls. An operator in more ways than one, Dr. Ingalls regarded the tents and listened to the distant sounds of spikes being driven up and down the Narrow Gauge's right of way and purchased fifty-five acres of Winthrop Beach. "Ocean Spray" he christened his investment and in 1875 commenced to parcel it out at two cents a square foot (shortly up to eight cents), insisting upon a no-liquor clause in each and every deed. Trim summer cottages sprouted along the bank above Winthrop Beach. Ocean Spray hung red and green lanterns the evening of its third anniversary clambake in August 1878, and ten thousand turned up to hear the Winthrop Brass Band sound out its brand-new stand. Ten thousand. Quite beyond the capacity of the Boston steamers that touched at Point Shirley and of Winthrop's moribund horse railroad, but not of an offshoot of the Little Wiggler at Winthrop Junction, just entering service that spring, nicknamed the "Peanut Train," more proudly, the Boston, Winthrop and Point Shirley Railroad.

The "Peanut Train" poses with its keepers about 1883 at Winthrop's Cottage Hill depot. (Winthrop Improvement and Historical Association)

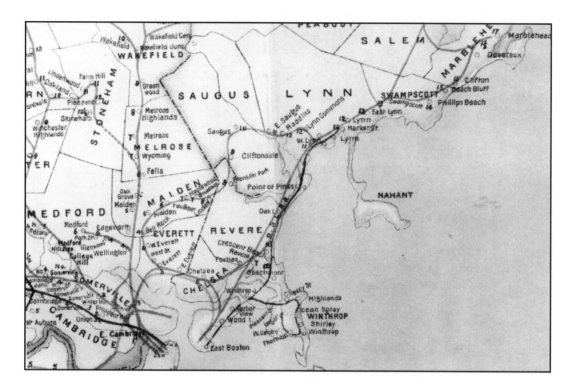

The network of
narrow-gauge
railroads serving
the lower North
Shore, in a map
of 1891.
(Peabody Essex
Museum)

The Narrow Gauge was the making of Winthrop as a resort for Boston. Boston was its unmaking. In 1888 the railroad looped the town with more than thirty summer trains a day, augmented by an hourly steamer schedule. The cottagers streamed in, and many remained the year round, twenty-seven hundred in 1890 and six thousand by 1900, when only half the houses were closed for the winter. The construction of the sea walls and boulevard of the Winthrop Shore Reservation quarantined Winthrop Beach from commercialization. At the end of its yard-wide lifeline to Boston, the town slipped cottage by cottage into suburbia.

REVERE BEACH THRIVES

A torrent of superheated Bostonians boiled along the tracks of the Boston, Revere Beach and Lynn Railroad that opening summer of 1875 and spilled across its first outlet on the four miles of the beach, Beachmont, whose slopes blossomed with a colorful crop of tents sown by Alpheus P. Blake's syndicate.

The company three years earlier had picked up 160 acres of the Sale family farm and marsh at Beachmont for $23,000. From its summit, Blake and his lieutenants could survey the rest of their promised land, stretching north in a carefree arc of shining sand and surf, mile after practically deserted mile to the Point of Pines. The only way into Beachmont had been over a carriage road from the town center. Came the Narrow Gauge, and suddenly it was a ten-cent ride from Boston. The first summer of the railroad the land company auctioned off lots at two and a half cents a foot and threw in a five-year pass to every buyer who promised to build. Tents by the score whitened the slopes above the shore. Within eight years the land was up to fifteen cents a foot, and Beachmont had 173 dwellings, three more than all of Revere in 1871.

The next influx came half a mile farther on at Crescent Beach. Here at the foot of Beach Street the railroad built the New Pavilion Hotel on the site of the old, which had been moved a quarter mile south near the Cove House, a weathered oasis of chowder and rum. The New Pavilion doubled as the depot for seven years before it was moved a few feet closer to the ocean (and France) and renamed the Vue de l'Eau (pronounced *voodle-oo*).

After puffing out of the hotel the Little Wiggler embarked upon Revere Beach, which to the end of the Point of Pines is nothing more than a barrier reef of sand hove up by wave and current. A string of summer shanties, bath shacks and bistros clung to the dunes. Surrounded by salt marsh midway behind Revere Beach were the twenty-three acres of Oak Island, the next stop on the Narrow Gauge. Set off from the mainstream, Oak Island developed as a haven for social clubs and ethnic fraternal organizations.

Entering the isthmus between the Pines River and the ocean, the Narrow Gauge dropped unaccustomed prosperity on the bleached piazza of the Neptune House, the second oldest beach hotel, and chugged on, hugging the dune. The roadbed broadened into the Point of Pines, the mile-long spit of sand and pitch pine that brings Revere Beach to an end in the Saugus River. Here the pint-sized train paused at the Ocean House, the beach's oldest and most remote and, with a hiss of steam, clanking driver wheels and a couple of long toots on the whistle, headed for the trestle bridge and Lynn.

Then in 1881 the Chelsea Beach Company bought the prime two

Pines Hotel, early 1880s. (Madeline Berlo Rhea)

The Great Ocean Pier from Beachmont, about 1883. (H. T. Wing photo, from Henry L. Nicolas)

hundred acres of the Pines and also the Ocean House, which it refurbished and renamed The Goodwood. Immediately the company began construction of The Pines, a resort hotel of five stories in the Queen Anne style, three hundred feet long, girdled by a thirty-two-foot veranda, containing three hundred chambers and two dining rooms with a capacity of two thousand, and advertised as the biggest on the New England coast. Simultaneously there arose a steamboat wharf, a racetrack and a bandstand illuminated by 182 gaslights in white globes. They built bathhouses and boathouses, cottages and a café, planted lush lawns, trees, shrubs and beds of flowers, pitched a striped tent, festooned Chinese lanterns everywhere overhead, stocked an arsenal of fireworks, hired the Germania Band, and opened in time for the Fourth of July, 1881.

And the city came, by boat, bicycle and buggy, atop the swaying barge, crowding the rails of the steamers, stuffing into the horsecars, and overflowing even the Narrow Gauge into the capacious coaches of the Eastern Railroad, which that summer belatedly bid for a piece of the beach trade with a branch leaving the main line at Oak Island. That first season sixty-two trains a day, each way, stopped at the Pines station. One hectic Sunday the Narrow Gauge alone carried 16,321 passengers.

The merits of a steamship connection with booming Crescent Beach and Beachmont had been obvious enough, but there was a problem: the

slope of the beach kept all passenger vessels at bay for a third of a mile out. The solution was the Great Ocean Pier, thrust seventeen hundred feet into Broad Sound from Roughan's Point over Cherry Island Bar, claimed to be the longest in America. Two thousand piles were secured in wooden caissons filled with mud and stones on the underlying ledge; a worn-out barge was loaded with rock and sunk as the foundation of the terminal. The pier was twenty-two feet wide and roofed over; dance halls bulged midway and at the outer end. The *John Sylvester* and *Eliza Hancox* made eight round trips daily from Boston. The Great Ocean Pier wanted only rail service to the entrance, and this the ubiquitous Alpheus P. Blake supplied by organizing the standard-gauge Eastern Junction, Broad Sound Pier, and Point Shirley Railroad as a connection. After a series of consolidations of smaller railways during the 1880s, Blake ruled the rails from Point to Point by 1891.

The concurrent opening of The Pines and the Great Ocean Pier during the summer of 1881 rocketed Revere Beach into the popular fancy, and it overwhelmingly outgrew and outdrew the old-fashioned amusements across Boston Bay at Hull's Nantasket Beach. Nantasket was, in fact, much the senior resort. Its sidewheel paddle steamers had been shuttling excursionists from Boston for half a century. But except for gambling and drinking in the hotels, the fun and games at Nantasket couldn't hold a candle to the garish splendors of The Pier and The Pines, nor could its steamship and rail service compete with the ferry and the Narrow Gauge.

Charles H. Thayer, master of the extravaganza, ran the amusement park at the Point of Pines. He opened in 1881 with two set fireworks pieces anchored off the beach, representing the Union and Confederate ironclads *Monitor* and *Merrimac;* their no-win duel of the Civil War was still fresh in the minds of older spectators and a thrilling episode of recent history to the youngsters. Young and old by the thousands gaped at the crude silhouettes exchanging flaming trajectories of bombs, which exploded in showers of stars in the eerie light and drifting smoke of recreated battle.

Night after night of Thayer's second season the sky over The Pines was a screaming, hissing, thudding spectral blaze—five thousand star shells one night, culminating in a mushrooming bouquet of a thousand rockets. Mr. Barnum's circus paraded by (the Big Top was in Lynn in July, attendance twenty-five thousand). In climax Admiral Farragut's fleet hove up under full sail and reenacted the attack on the fort at New Orleans to the delight of the fans.

Summer's spectacle of 1883 at The Pines was a reenactment of the Civil War battle for Roanoke Island under the supervision of the Lynn post of the Grand Army of the Republic, fought by a thousand uniformed veterans armed with muskets, sixteen fieldpieces and unlimited stores of black powder and red fire before the eyes of twenty-five thousand.

Baldwin's Boston Cadet Band was engaged and played before standing-room crowds so ringingly that after eight seasons the leader bought out his employers. In 1885 The Pines presented a six-day music festival that drew 108,000 riders on the Narrow Gauge; on the evening of August 12 it

Even the electric trolley must stand aside as Barnum circus elephants lumber through Central Square in Lynn, 1904. (Beverly Historical Society, Walker Transportation Collection)

touched off "Five Miles of Fire," an illumination of the entire beach by hundreds of bonfires, fireworks and colored fire and lanterns, with music by eleven bands avidly enjoyed by forty thousand pyrophiles. Showman Thayer came up with Revere Beach's first figure-eight roller coaster. (He got his inspiration from a "jolly-go-round" at Coney Island, where he had been snooping about for ideas.) The five-hundred-foot ride took eighteen seconds and cost a nickel.

Combining the pageantry of a sham battle with pyrotechnic props, Thayer in 1886 gave the world the "pyrorama," in a repeat of "Monitor versus Merrimac." Concealed crews moved the adversaries around the racetrack past a fort and lighthouse; other wooden warships stood off in the distance, while a cast of soldiers and sailors dashed about under a fury of rockets, chemical fire, stars and bombs. A few more great battles followed, and "The Apaches," allegedly with real Indians. The Narrow Gauge ran pyrorama specials to The Pines, and pyrorama parties were the rage. Thayer imported a Coney Island-type carousel and produced an eight-day music festival.

For less than fifty cents, the Boston *Daily Record* advised readers, you could get out to The Pines from the city, hear the music, eat, and return, "probably a happier man for the trip than the man of wealth who makes a tour to Saratoga and wears himself and a $50 bill quite out."

Entertainment at the Great Ocean Pier was pitched to the younger set, which accounts for the metamorphosis in 1883 of one of the dance halls into a roller-skating rink boasted by the management as the largest in the world, a quarter of a mile around, with twin bands playing the same music at both ends. The owners of Oak Island Grove had a finger to the wind too and turned their dance emporium into a roller rink. With a new and larger ballroom, bowling alleys, shooting galleries, swings, flying horses, roller coaster (straight grade, half as fast as the figure eight at The Pines), boats, menagerie and aviary, Oak Island catered to blue-collar outings. During a typical midsummer week in 1881 it was visited by picnicking members of the Boston YMCA and their girls, the Daughters of Rebecca, the Olive Branch Lodge of Odd Ladies, the Celtic Association of Lowell, the Lawrence Irish Benevolent Society (several senior members danced the jig as it should be danced) and a party of eighteen Scandinavians who arrived by barge. Fifteen thousand packed the Oak Island park to cheer on four champion European horsemen clad in armor, whacking away at each other with broadswords (a vogue then current) for a fifteen-hundred-dollar purse put up by the hotelmen. By way of contrast, two prizefighters mixed it up for five hours and seventy-two rounds to a draw behind the blackened windows of the guarded, crowded stable of the Atlantic House.

The novel electric lighting supplied by its generator was so popular at The Pines that in 1884 the North Shore Company was organized to extend it to the rest of the beach. When five years later it lit the whole town, Leo Daft, a pioneer in the development of electric street railways, was there. None was yet in practical use anywhere, but he installed a demonstration line in 1884 and next year, in advance of the Fourth, had the diminutive

Daft Electric Railway (powered from a third rail) whirling along, carrying curious beachgoers on a half-mile run.

Another twist in the novelty, as the Revere *Journal* reported, was "bathing by the electric light at the Vue de l'Eau." Sea bathing, by day or night, more surely than satire, helped loosen the grip of Victorian convention on its victims. Preparing for the water, ladies divested themselves (never "undressed") of swaths of mysterious raiment: button shoes, corsets, petticoats and unmentionables, billowing blouses, mushrooming hats and black parasols that were de rigueur on dry land, in exchange for flannel or woolen dresses, bloomers, long stockings and floppy oilcloth caps. The gents were no better off, stepping out of stiflingly fashionable haberdashery into what looked like one-piece pajamas or woolen union suits.

These bathing outfits were commonly rented catch-as-catch-can from bathhouse operators. They were so loose-fitting and at the same time so airtight, in spite of moth holes, that in the water they exhibited "the tendency to billow out like half submerged balloons, giving the general appearance of blue cabbages floating wrong side up," according to one description. The phenomenon may account for the Revere *Journal*'s report that "a man reading a newspaper, while floating on his back in the water at Crescent Beach on Wednesday afternoon, attracted much attention."

Bathers at Revere Beach. (Peter McCauley collection)

Getting in and out of your bathing costume was a complicated and protracted procedure requiring the privacy of a bathhouse, whether you were a day-tripper or staying at a hotel. (A hotel guest padding across the lobby in swimsuit, dry or dripping, would have been subject to summary expulsion;

but such a performance was utterly unthinkable.) In the late 1880s a guidebook touted the amenities of one such establishment at Revere Beach: "The elegant bathrooms are free from the objections of many other bathhouses on the beach, being retired and free from the curious gaze of strangers." For the ultrasensitive, across from Oak Island a Lynn man operated a wheeled bathing car that he moved up and down on portable tracks with the tide, thus affording his custom the minimum of public exposure.

By the mid-1880s the flood let loose by Alpheus Blake had presented Revere with some serious problems related to overpopulation and, in some cases, the wrong kind of population. At Beachmont the cottages crowded thick upon one another, and tents still clung to the slopes and fields overlooking Broad Sound. Many were decked with wooden floors and furnished with rugs, settees,

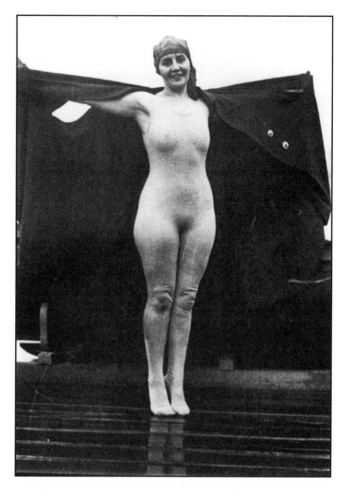

Distance swimmer Annette Kellerman in the one-piece suit she made famous, at Revere Beach shortly before her arrest for overexposure. (Peter McCauley collection)

chairs, afghans, doodads of the period and beds behind gossamer barricades of mosquito netting, frequently with the family servant or local hired girl set up in a separate cook tent.

More and more of these beach habitations, however, were "cots" (a euphemism for shanties), and as the 1890s approached they were squeezed in among cheap bathhouses, eateries, bars, beer joints (the nickel beer was ubiquitous), galleries and arcades. The crowding was closest at Crescent Beach and Beachmont, whose residents in 1887 were assured by a sanitation expert that a fifteen-inch sewer pipe carried to the end of the Great Ocean Pier would solve any problems along that line to which they were privy and be "no detriment" to bathers.

Within a dozen years of Revere's penetration by the Narrow Gauge, hundreds of thousands of innocents—and many pickpockets, confidence men, fancy ladies and hoodlums—were swarming in on Alpheus Blake's iron horse of Troy and every other conveyance to seek their pleasures and ply their trades at Boston's Coney Island. A few of Revere's staunch old residents, for whom footprints on the sand were once objects of curiosity, wondered if a devil's compact had not been made and tried to check the

unbridled sale of liquor; but year after year, overwhelmed by the threats and blandishments of the hotel owners who ruled the beach, their townsmen voted for licenses.

One July day in 1884 eight young drunks pulled up in an express wagon outside a photo gallery at Crescent Beach and demanded to have their pictures taken. When the two owners tried to bar them at the door, they pushed in, beat them up, and assaulted the assistant, Miss Maggie O'Neil, who, "although of slight build, was active and full of pluck, cutting the face of one assailant with stones which she threw with unusual precision." The ruffians broke the windows of the shop, smashed the camera, and drove off. No one in the crowd outside came to the assistance of the victims, and there were no police officers around.

A couple of years later the Revere police chief was suspended after he boarded a horsecar while drunk, knocked the conductor into the street, and struck a woman passenger when she declined to give up her seat to him.

A thrill a minute. That was Revere Beach, right from the word go.

THE GREAT INVASION OF SALEM WILLOWS

When Lou Collins and George Hardy wrote the music and lyrics of the "Salem Willows for Mine Waltz" in 1919, they struck just the note of good clean fun that had marked it as the healthy prototype of the all-American small-city amusement park for forty years:

> *It's not very far from old Salem
> And from Lynn it's a half an hour's ride.*

You don't mind the trolley because you can jolly
The nice little girls by your side.
On moonlight nights, Gee! it is dandy,
And on Sundays it's simply divine.
You can have all your "Coneys,"
To me they're all phoneys,
But Salem Willows for mine—it's mine.

By 1919 the Age of Innocence was on the skids, and so was the amusement park, no thanks to world war and the Tin Lizzie; but the merry-go-round and the midway and the trolley party, and all they evoked of that grandest of small-time, small-town larcenies, the stolen kiss, lingered on in the afterglow of the national self-image. Naughty Revere Beach was the creature of the big bad city, dismissed by the American Baedeker as "a popular holiday resort of Boston's lower classes." While old Salem's mini-resort lacked the attractions of the beach, the Willows was as handy as it was dandy, only twenty minutes from town, and it lay firmly within the grasp of the municipal authorities and the horsecar company that operated one of the first of the hundreds of amusement parks organized by the street railways of the United States.

Salem sticks its Neck a mile into the bay between Beverly and Marblehead. Out at the end of it is Juniper Point; toward Marblehead hangs Winter Island from a causeway. When the colony was founded in the seventeenth century, the Neck and Winter Island were forested to the water's edge. The settlers stripped off the timber; there was deep water up to shore then, and Winter Island was Salem's fishing and commercial base. But northeast storms ripped across the lowlands that were no longer buffered by forest, eroding the soil and shoaling the coves until Winter Island had to be abandoned for deeper water.

After the waning of its maritime activities, the Neck was used for other purposes. Three convicted murderers were hanged there, the first in 1772, when twelve thousand spectators in holiday mood ignored the January cold, munched their box lunches, heard a highly satisfactory sermon on the wages of sin, and watched Bryan Sheehan collect his. In response to wars and scares of war, a number of forts were built on the Neck. Juniper Point and Winter Island also served as good vantages from which to watch for returning East India merchants—and a Spanish silver dollar for the winner of the race in to Derby Wharf with the good news. Later Winter Island was adopted as a training ground for the militia.

A mile out of town in the bay and "cleansed" by the breezes off the water, the Neck pasture was regarded as a likely location for the pesthouse, erected halfway along the northwest shore of what came to be called Hospital Point; thence were ostracized the victims of smallpox and other contagious diseases, to die in isolation. In 1801 a conscience-stricken board of health had forty willows planted nearby "in such direction as they may think will be most conducive to the comfort and convenience of the sick." The hospital burned in 1846, but the trees held their ground, grew stately and o'erspreading, and around 1858 the Willows was embraced by the Salem park system.

The Neck was already becoming a locus for joy and jollity. By the 1850s the Massachusetts Volunteers' annual displays of preparedness for come-what-may attracted vast throngs to Winter Island. The citizenry followed the drills and the parades, fraternized with the volunteers, settled down with their lunch baskets, and listened to band after band. The champion, of course, was the Salem Brass Band, whose members arranged themselves on the grass and read their music, like coal miners, by the light of miniature oil lamps affixed to their caps.

The volunteers and their bands marched off to the Civil War, then straggled back, but the surrender of Salem Neck to its destiny did not begin until the year 1873. This came about when the land company that had gobbled up most of Marblehead Neck advised the summer colony of Lowell people who had been leasing their camps there since 1866 to buy or get out. Most chose the latter course, snooped out some available land on Juniper Point in 1873, and transplanted themselves there.

That was the start of it. Two years later Daniel B. Gardner of Salem purchased the Neck Farm and divided the forty-two acres into summer cottage lots. The evictees from Marblehead were joined by friends from Lowell and by others from Salem and Peabody. Roads were laid out and shade trees planted; Wenham Lake water was piped in, fountains were installed, and a boating basin was seawalled up to Winter Island. In the early 1880s the Neck was the base for the Salem Bay Yacht Club. By 1884 a growing colony of a hundred summer cottages had taken hold.

The exodus of the Lowell campers from Neck to Neck in the summer of 1873 coincided with the appearance at the Willows of the restaurant of François, a black chef who specialized in fish dinners, and an influx of outings and picnic parties. City dwellers were just awakening to the possibilities of the North Shore "pic-nic." Consequently, when the Naumkeag Street Railway was incorporated in the summer of 1875 on the foundations of the Salem Street Railway, which had been running horsecars through town since 1862, the owners were quite aware of the nickel-and-dime potential of traffic in picnickers and outdoor enthusiasts.

The Eastern Railroad's next move pointed the way for the Great Invasion of Salem Neck. After years of backing and filling, Eastern in 1872 had consented to run a branch line from Wenham to Essex, skirting the shore of Chebacco Lake, where the icehouses were expected to be a decisive source of freight. It occurred to an imaginative official of the railroad that the Neck, a stretch of lake shore of great beauty owned by the Low family, might make an ideal picnic spot for city people, and he set the wheels in motion. Eastern leased Essex's Neck from the Lows for ten years, named it Centennial Grove (this was 1876), built a dining room, dance hall and shooting gallery, laid in a fleet of boats for hire, let in one of the earliest of the "flying horses" (a couple of crosspieces with wooden horses at either end, pushed around by hand), and opened in the spring.

After its lease expired the railroad turned the park over to the owners to manage, having demonstrated brilliantly how a transportation company could attract passengers by creating the attraction; one record summer two locomotives labored into Centennial Grove with a single picnic party that required forty-two coaches in two sections for the hauling.

Hospital Beach at Salem Willows, 1891. (Peabody Essex Museum)

If the railroads could do it, the horsecars should be able to at a fraction of the cost. Centennial Grove had hardly opened when the Naumkeag Street Railway sought and secured its franchise, laid tracks out to Salem Neck, and dispatched the first bobtail car to the Willows on June 10, 1877. Patrick Kennealley followed with his peanut stand—yes, Pat Kennealley, inventor of the amazing, the one and only "double-jointed" peanut. And then the picnickers, happy droves of them.

Naumkeag owners within the next few months bought land at the end of the new line and built the Willow Park Pavilion, with dance hall on the ground floor, a restaurant seating three hundred upstairs, decks of piazzas, an observation tower and a theater. They planted gardens and persuaded the city of Salem to spruce up its adjoining park. Finally, they stocked up on fireworks and opened to the public with a smashing debut on the tenth of June, 1880, three years to the day from the first horsecar's inaugural trip to the Willows.

By 1882 Willow Park had signed on the new Salem Cadet Band for Sunday concerts and the steamer *Three Brothers* for daily excursions. Horsecars ran from Salem every ten minutes. Fifty cents covered a complete fish dinner with choice of chowder. And a thin dime admitted the curious into the camera obscura, which "brings into striking prominence objects within a circuit of 20 miles." This centuries-old forerunner of photography may have been sited in the Pavilion's observation tower, from which by means of a mirror a rotating lens would cast an inverted panoramic image of the countryside and seascape down onto a white table placed in the middle of the darkened room below. A more conventional camera was employed by Harry Esbach, who invited the sitter to enjoy the garden outside his studio while the tintype emerged.

From the very start the Willows was a smash hit on the North Shore. If you could get to Salem by train or horsecar, the trip out on the Naumkeag line was a breeze. The simple attractions drew great crowds, as many as eight thousand a day. The Shore's largest public resort outside of Revere Beach was cheap, wholesome and well run. It was also well regulated by the city, which took a proprietary attitude toward its traditional hanging and marching ground.

Its bold stroke in devising an end for its own means contributed largely to the financial success of the Naumkeag Street Railway. Expanding east to Marblehead and north through Beverly, the line brought its bobtails to Asbury Grove via Wenham, causing one resident of that secluded nook of rural Essex County to complain that "with the first car which jangled down the quiet elm-shaded street, the peaceful calm of the town was ended, and in its place, the clang and hurry of modern life was to be for ever more." The effect on the campground of this so much more accomodating supplement to the steam railroad was a second boom. Crowds of "rounders" hustled aboard Naumkeag's ten-bench, fifty-passenger cars at Salem for an afternoon at Asbury at thirty cents a head. The summer population of the Grove leaped to two thousand, and the count of rented cottages under the tall trees to nearly four hundred; camp meetings drew as many as fifteen thousand faithful, so that it became necessary for this unique summer community of seventy-five acres in the woods of West Hamilton to provide, besides the chapels and the tabernacle of the religious revivial, a small hotel, stores, restaurants, an express office and its own post office.

THE COMING OF THE TROLLEYS

The horse railroad reached the top of the hill in 1888, when more than six thousand nags clip-clopped through the streets of Boston. Then, suddenly, it plummeted into oblivion.

As early as 1885 Leo Daft had used electricity to run his queer little trams along Revere Beach, and late in 1887 the Lynn and Boston had tried an electric car on its Highlands circuit. But it was not until February 1888 that Frank J. Sprague, a genius in electronics, got the world's first practical citywide electric streetcar system operating in Richmond, Virginia. Horsecar executives (having their tracks already laid) grabbed the first train for Richmond to see for themselves. Boston's biggest horsecar line, the West End Railroad, made the decision to go electric, and the stampede was on.

On June 2 the Revere Electric Street Railroad was organized. Six weeks later its two trolley cars, which looked to idle bystanders like ordinary bobtails, gave a demonstration over the tracks above the beach, reaching the breakneck speed of thirty miles an hour and frightening several horses. On August 2 the Naumkeag Street Railway started regular electric car service to Salem Willows. On August 25 the Revere line was officially in business, carrying excited passengers the mile, almost, between Crescent Beach and the Great Ocean Pier in three thrilling minutes.

After only twenty summers of free enterprise, unrestrained by zoning law, building code or health ordinance, enjoyed every day and abandoned every night by sixty or seventy thousand escapees from urban suffocation, a Boston guidebook found Revere Beach in the mid-1890s "a queer colony . . . a place of low-browed, cheap, unlovely structures, in a crowded row on either side of the tracks, with narrow promenade, protected from them by wire fences. It was picturesque, if shabby. . . . Prices ruled at the lowest, and all its ways were democratic."

And they all dispensed their trash and sewage with an equal abandon that advertised Revere Beach to the world, with the help of the midsummer sun. This ample muck for the raking lay in the course of the metropolitan planning movement just then taking shape behind the pioneer landscape architect Frederick Law Olmsted, who had already turned the Back Bay into the wondrous Charles River Fens park. The state legislature in 1889 established the Metropolitan Sewerage Commission, connecting the thirty-three communities of Greater Boston, then three years later the Metropolitan Parks Commission.

The voters of Revere accepted the Parks Act in 1894 with relief, and the new commission moved in with the new broom. A correspondent for the *Boston Evening Transcript* was mildly excited by the prospects: "The sights are many though not edifying, but it is easy for one to see what this beach was 20 years ago, and what it is soon to be again under the State park control. The project is to remove all the unsightly pasteboard structures from the beach, to move the railroads back and to construct a boulevard on what is now the roadbed of the narrow gauge line, the reservation to include the entire sweep of the sands from the Pines to Beachmont. . . . It is difficult to realize today that this was once a favorite shore resort for the best class of people."

By 1896 every trace of shantytown between the Great Ocean Pier, which was the southern anchor of blue-collar respectability, and the former white-collar bastion of the Point of Pines—now descended to more proletarian pleasures—had been swept clean away. As if by a tidal wave, Revere Beach had been purified.

The sea-bathing rituals changed with the times. In former days some of the "bathing shanties" that rented swimsuits sold liquor under the counter. "Business was good," according to one source, "even when the ocean water was too cold for bathing and many of the suits were returned as dry as when given out." To get to the beach, unsteady patrons bent on getting wet outside as well had to dodge the trains hurtling along from both directions; the moving of the tracks and the banishment of the shanties by the Parks Commission took care of that. In their place a stately brick bathhouse was opened in 1897, stocked with suits for both sexes and black hose for the ladies, enough for five thousand, and dressing facilities for a thousand at once.

But while the metropolitan planners dreamed of a model seaside park above the beach, the hundreds of thousands of the bored and the super-heated who flocked there from Greater Boston were less interested in immersion than diversion, the more spectacular the better. Overnight a new shantytown-in-the-making arose on the sands from which the old had just been stripped. By 1901 Crescent Gardens, the largest open-air dance hall in New England, and its rival, the Casino, had opened. The heart-stopping Loop-the-Loop had been added to the roller coaster's sickening third of a mile. For beachgoers who enjoyed watching others risk their necks, there was a motorcycle racetrack, and for those who cared for neither, Hurley's Hurdlers, billed as the world's most elaborate carousel.

Each colossal new attraction had to outdo the last. In 1902 the sensa-tion of the season was a water ride inside an enormous wood-and-tarpaper structure called The Old Mill that went up in flames after only two seasons; the customers escaped simply by pushing out through the tarpaper walls. The wettest shows, for some reason, burned the best: The Johnstown Flood was a macabre recreation of the burst dam that had drowned 2,009 in that Pennsylvania mining town in 1889; it opened in 1903 on the biggest stage in the Boston area, with a thousand seats, and was in ashes in 1905.

The summit of silliness was scaled in the summer of 1904 when the management of the Point of Pines Hotel and associated amusements pro-posed to celebrate the Fourth with the head-on collision of two antiquated steam locomotives. So great was the public excitement that crashers stormed the gates, there was a riot involving forty thousand, and the pro-moters refused to let the show go on, whereupon a mob tried to get the engines moving, in vain. Six weeks later the Great Bash was restaged, but the crews who were supposed to leap from their cabs at the last second lost their nerve and applied the brakes; the locomotives merely stopped and hissed at each other.

WONDERLAND

Pushed by press exposures of its political corruption and wickedness in general, Nantasket challenged Revere by building Paragon Park in 1905, under the aegis of the Metropolitan Parks Commission, with a new menu of laundered attractions. The North Shore's reply, a total put-down, was Wonderland Park, the all-time Revere Beach extravaganza. It opened in 1906, admission one dime. Both were straight steals from Coney Island and, in the case of Wonderland's mammoth shoot-the-chutes ending in a mighty splash and glide over the lagoon, from the St. Louis Exposition of 1904 as well. Wild Bill Kennedy's Wild West Show and Indian Congress arrived with a hundred genuine cowboys and Indians, forty horses and a

tent camp, and they put on a raid, stagecoach holdup and buffalo hunt every half hour.

As if the beach hadn't fires enough, a show called Fighting the Flames was staged daily before a grandstand seating thirty-five hundred, with a cast of 350, a twelve-piece ladder company and thirty horses—"a marvelously realistic and soul-stirring reproduction of the conflagration in a city block," and quite enough to satisfy, or inspire, the most ardent firebug. As a popular song beckoned:

Wonderland, Wonderland, that's the place to be!
Each night when I call on my sweetie, she says to me:
"Let's take a trolley ride to the oceanside
Where the shining lights are grand."
If you want to make good as a true lover should,
Just take her to Wonderland!

But there were too many cowboys, Indians, Oriental villagers, monkeys, trained horses, wire-walking elephants, high-diving dogs, miniature railroads and brass bands per thin dime. Attendance peaked, and overhead peaked higher. After two sensational years Wonderland faltered . . . and was reorganized on the brink. Three more seasons and the entire flamboyant fantasy tottered, midway in time between Frederic Tudor's Maolis Gardens at Nahant and an animated cartoonist's Disneyland. In 1911 Wonderland Park closed its gilded gates forever. Twenty-three years later a nearby dog track appropriated the magic name of Revere Beach's crowning achievement and took the site as its parking lot.

Between the fall of shantytown and the rise of honky-tonk, for a few

The Lightning Roller Coaster at Revere claimed speeds of a mile a minute. (Peter McCauley collection)

Wonderland REVERE BEACH MAY 30 TO SEPT 9

FIGHTING THE FLAMES

One of Wonderland's more extravangant attractions. (Peter McCauley collection)

summers at the turn of the century, reformers hoped that their clean-cut "American Brighton" could thrive untainted despite laissez-faire building regulations. "The masses of the people," reflected the *New Ocean House Reminder* from the portico of the grand summer hotel a safe distance away at Swampscott, "have the benefit of beautiful outdoor surroundings where they are free to enjoy but restrained from any abuse of the attractions, and where manners and morals are required to be on a par with the high character of the scenery and the well kept roads and grounds."

This briefly idealized Revere Beach was discovered in the summer of 1896 by the great impressionist Maurice Prendergast, that shy, mustached bachelor Bostonian who parted his hair gravely in the middle and wore a high collar and cravat even while working. The miles of glaring whiteness were populated, judging by his sketchbook and watercolors, by ladies swathed from the sun, wearing hats almost as broad as their parasols or perky little affairs with flowers, watching in desultory preoccupation over beribboned and sunbonneted young girls lifting their skirts above black-stockinged ankles to tiptoe from rock to rock above the shining tide pools, and by well-behaved boys in striped bathing suits, and by portly autocrats of their supper tables, properly suited and derbied, hands thrust in pants pockets, staring out over the American Sea.

Too soon the artist's idealized vistas and leisurely women were overwhelmed by crowds in the hundreds of thousands. Promoting a descending denominator of taste, the proprietors vied for the cheapest thrills, the most mindless spectacles. It was downhill most of the way after the failure of Wonderland Park in 1911, bottoming out (with extraordinary flair, it must be admitted) in 1927 with the Great Marine Bonfire.

The perpetrators of this mayhem anchored a decrepit three-masted schooner off the beach, loaded her with wood scraps and a thousand old railroad ties, hung her with fireworks, drenched the sails with oil, dumped gunpowder on the decks, torched her off, and abandoned ship. A million suckers showed up, jamming the roads for miles. Two hundred thousand couldn't get out afterward and had to spend the night on the beach. A helluva spectacle all right, except that the old hulk failed to burn below the waterline for some strange reason, and it cost the promoters twenty thousand dollars to clean up the mess.

As mass entertainment, Revere Beach never outgrew its own pimply adolescence and hadn't a chance against the motorcar and the movies. It remained a hand-cranked thirty-ring circus and tried to hang on to the sunburned, roller coastering, dance-marathoning, hotdogging, love-tunneling, gum-chewing, Kewpie doll-winning trade, as it drifted into sorry, shambling senility. In its raucous heyday, though, The Beach was a national symbol of American energy, restlessness, extravagance and unquenchable optimism.

MELLOW AT THE WILLOWS

Salem Willows was an intimate (what is more intimate than a holiday crowd of twenty thousand?), cool, shaded but in no way shady, provincial (locally owned and properly policed), refined (roughhousers were expelled) picnic and playground featuring a lively, more or less yokel-oriented amusement park. No beach to speak of, hence no mass bathing, and no liquor. Jake Alpert offered seventeen kinds of temperance drinks to parched bicyclers.

The most sensational crowd-catcher of 1897 (though not enough to pay its own way for more than a couple of seasons) was a shoot-the-chute, ten years in advance of Wonderland's, that hauled the car-boats up a funicular tramway, then loosed them down the long slide with their shrieking cargoes to surf through a lagoon that is now the junction of Fort and Columbus avenues. The most durable crowd-pleaser that year was Joe Brown's steam-driven "Flying Horses," one of the oldest and most colorful merry-go-rounds in the United States. His carved steeds were vintage examples of the art, some of them sculptures of famous racehorses. Music for the "over a mile in every ride" was provided by a twenty-four-piece mechanical orchestra. An "automatic village" in the hole of Brown's whirling doughnut had houses, church, gristmill, swan pond, fort, lighthouse, miniature trains, merry-go-round and circus parade, all going to beat the band.

The most elevated crowd-thrillers of 1897 were Professor Bonette and his family, who arose above the Willows in twin hot-air balloons to an altitude of six thousand feet, then parachute-raced back to earth. Thirteen years after that, to celebrate the Fourth in his own unique fashion, the iron-jawed Professor Ullven's "Slide for Life" (all true daredevils in those days

The gazebo at Hospital Point, Salem Willows, 1891. (Peabody Essex Museum)

were "professors") had all agape as he scorched down a tightwire strung from the top of the Pavilion tower to the stone beacon off the steamship pier, hanging from a traveling block by nothing but his teeth.

Or you could pay your penny and catch Edison's Kinetoscope, a primitive motion-picture peepshow featuring "The Seminary Girls' Pillow Fight" and "The Irwin Kiss," or buy a basket from the Indians and get your fortune told, or gawk at that party of kite-flying Chinese. Harry Esbach, the tintype photographer, was attracting custom with his tank of live alligators that he brought up from his Florida winter quarters, while F. J. Tree taught ballroom dancing and ran a soft-drink stand called "The Only Poplar Tree at the Willows."

Over it all watched the sleepless keepers of the quiet. Midsummer of 1905: "Tommy Hyde, the Willows cop, had a good taste of roughhouse with a party of young men under the influence of the ardent fluid, Saturday evening last. It is needless to say that Tommy came out on top although he was presented with a beauty upper cut which nearly knocked him out." A few nights later: "The roughs 'wid der loidy friens' who visited the Willows on Wednesday evening last didn't find our blue coâted guardians of the peace such 'easy marks' as they expected. They were on the contrary rushed away from here about 11 o'clock while the Willows assembly piped out in chorus 'Good Bye My Blue Bells.'"

What makes the world go round, on the other hand, was less summarily dealt with by the blue-coated guardians, as on one Sunday evening in August of 1906: "A spooning match was held on the oval opposite the band stand. Two couples, old enough to know better, took a prominent place to show their affection. . . . The match was ended by the appearance of one of the park police. The attention of the officer was called and walking over in front of them he threw his 'bug' light on the faces of the quartette. This did not shame them, but simply served to bring the bold visitors to their senses. They gathered up their traps and went on their way, leaving behind them sounds of laughter. Perhaps if the Charles River 'sit-up' law were enforced at the Willows, the conditions would be improved for the visitors who do not care to run into such surroundings."

Eventually Salem's intimate park found room for four thousand gasoline-driven demons. Like the last of the original willows, two or three attractions hang on, as yet another century turns. The breezes still caress, and Salem Neck welcomes strollers and, as always, spooners.

And that, to revert to waltz time, is why

The place that I long for,
The place that I'm strong for,
Is sure to be in the race.
The boys who will meet you,
The girls who will greet you,
Will all have a smile on their face.
The dear ball-room floor is the place I adore,
The waters with nice shady views.
The music is grand, makes you dance, understand,
It's the place where you'll never feel blue.
It's not very far from old Salem,
And from Lynn it's a half an hour's ride.
You don't mind the trolley because you can jolly
The nice little girls by your side. . . .

As the merry-go-round turned at Nahant, so turned the century.
Maurice Prendergast, 1900. (Museum of Fine Arts, Springfield, Massachusetts)

~11~
THE CENTURY TURNS

While society papers cling to the past, the future is already here aboard the electric trolleys and horseless carriages

B<small>Y THE END OF THE CENTURY</small> the North Shore was Boston's Riviera, a settled and mature summer society whose reaches were now extending onto Cape Ann. In the view of one prominent insider, the Nahant syndrome—marked by the sameness of faces, winter and summer, due to everybody's knowing everybody—was coming to define the whole resort—the whole, that is, as defined from the inside, rather like Jonah describing the whale. One such Jonah was a Harvard overseer and Suffolk County Judge of Probate, Robert Grant, better known in his day as a novelist and the boyhood summer chum of Henry Cabot Lodge at Nahant. Judge Grant in 1894 published a pleasantly patronizing inside story on *The North Shore*, which according to his book was the "fringe of aristocracy" that held down the coast from Nahant and Swampscott as far as Cape Ann—since "civilization properly ceases before you come to Gloucester."

With its unique advantages, wondered novelist Grant (not the least of which was "its freedom from either democratic or plutocratic crowds"), why hadn't *his* Shore attracted more than a handful of summer residents from elsewhere than Boston? "Perhaps the reason is to be found in the argument that it is too near Boston, which is a polite way of expressing reluctance to invade the sacred precincts of the most critical society in America for fear of not pleasing. . . . The society is so exclusively Bostonese. The families from a distance are almost to be numbered on the fingers of one hand, and you meet in your walks and drives and social intercourse the self-same people with whom you have dined and slummed, or whom you have seen at the Symphony concerts all winter."

Robert Grant accurately reflected the proprietary attitude of Boston's upper crust toward its North Shore. The jurist obliquely alluded to the rise of social barriers along with fences, walls and hedges on the coast: "Those who regard the continued individual ownership of large tracts of land, or even of an acreage sufficient to keep one's neighbor at a respectful distance, as inconsistent with true democratic development, will be likely to look askance at the beautiful estates along the North Shore. It may be that in a few generations we shall all live cheek by jowl with one another in houses built and painted after a stereotyped model. [This was 1894!] . . . Such a

period may become necessary in the process of giving all men an opportunity to enjoy equally the fruits of the earth and the fullness thereof. But whatever the dim future may bring to pass in this regard . . . at present, the beautiful seaside estates . . . are among the most precious of human possession, and the class of people seeking them is increasing in direct ratio to the growth of refined civilization over the country."

STILL EXCLUSIVE, BUT CHANGING

Along the North Shore thus narrowly defined by the owners who had acquired it, if not for a steal then practically for a giveaway, there was by the 1890s a definite defensiveness tinged, as Judge Grant's conscience betrayed, with a faint streak of Victorian guilt.

No longer now did the leading guidebook to the Shore invite the curious outsider to rubberneck along the private drives between Pride's Crossing and Beverly Farms, with a caution not to pick the flowers or trample the lawns but like his English cousin (note the ethnic assumption) venturing on the turf of the local lord, to be "thankful that his more favored fellow being shares with him thus much." Indeed, after the Civil War the wealthy increasingly used summer residency to dodge city taxes and strove to shelter themselves from the encroachments of hoi polloi-ridden horsecars.

As the nineteenth century wound down, more social barriers rose, enforced by the posting of estates, individually and collectively, behind gatekeepers and constables; the privatizing of beaches once considered accessible to all; and the yacht clubs, hunt clubs, country clubs, garden clubs, kennel clubs, outing clubs, golf clubs, tennis clubs and beach clubs.

To reassure upper-crust summerers of their secure place within the smart set, J. Alexander Lodge (a "herring-choker" from Newfoundland, of *all* people!) founded the *North Shore Breeze*, a periodical that with a perfect fit kept a gentle finger to the pulse of the North Shore summer elite. An astute observer of his adopted scene, he knew his readers and adventurers better than they knew themselves and played to their assumed rules. From 1904 on, nary a breath of scandal was borne on the *Breeze*, nothing satirical (God forbid), a hint of the sardonic now and again and, once comfortably ensconced, occasional brief editorials by Mr. Lodge indulging "healthy" self-criticism of a social nature. In the society news that filled each issue, the publisher invited his readers to take ingenuous joy in the mention of one's house, one's garden, one's pink-cheeked children, one's hat, one's horse, one's yacht, one's club and one's guests—and if accompanied by a photograph, sheer bliss! Such was the success of the *Breeze* that advertisers pumped it up to as many as ninety-six pages a week; off-season it was a monthly. Suspended briefly during World War I, the periodical survived the Depression and continued for three years after the death of its founder in 1939.

Rocklike in this seasonal stream of Comings, Doings and Goings stood the *North Shore Blue Book and Social Register*, more inclusive geographically than Judge Grant's close-drawn sanctum sanctorum, but discriminating enough to maintain a buffer against *outs* wanting *in*. As if one such *Burke's Peerage* wasn't protection enough for such a brief fringe of coastline, the *Blue Book* was joined in discreet competition by *Who's Who Along the North Shore: Being a Register of the Noteworthy, Fashionable & Wealthy Residents on the North Shore of Massachusetts Bay*. Cannily masterminded by the *Breeze*'s Lodge, it allowed another thousand or so outs in.

Yet, for all its artifice and jockeying for social position, nowhere was the *style* of our belle époque, with its relaxing patresfamilias, its delicious little girls in their bonnets and ginghams, its full-blown Edwardians, its incredible tycoons, its beachgoers, its climbers and its plungers, played out in more kaleidoscopic tableau than along the North Shore of Massachusetts Bay, in the afterglow of Boston's Golden Age as most self-assuredly the Athens of America.

But the ground was shifting. Cold Roast Nahant and Phillips Beach, Marblehead Neck, Beverly Cove and Eastern Point could hear only too well the sounds of the circus on a midsummer night when the wind was right (or wrong), and they blinked at the garish lights of the promiscuous parks at Revere Beach and Salem Willows. Another and overwhelmingly larger world out there was pressing in by land and sea. The frustration of a city baking in the oven of August could not be contained. The celluloid-collar workers and the brawny blue collars and their crinolined wives and chattering children, the Catholics, the Protestants and the Jews, the Irish and the Yanks, the Italians, Swedes, Greeks, Germans, Poles, Russians and the rest of Boston's sweltering melting pot poured forth along the rails and roads and seaways to the beaches and meccas of merriment with their nickels and dimes.

Almost literally overnight, live wire replaced horseflesh, and the trolley car swept across the landscape like a bolt of lightning. In 1885 Leo Daft had run his queer electric trams above Revere Beach, so it was wildly appropriate that one of the first trolleys anywhere in regular service should rattle along the beach at thirty miles an hour in June 1888. In two months Naumkeag electrified its Salem Willows line. When the owners of Boston's sprawling West End Railroad fired their horses, the rush was on; by 1899 two hundred systems were operating or under construction.

The speed with which the trolley lines spun their web across the face of the North Shore was a phenomenon in itself. Within two years of its first run to Revere Beach in 1891, the Lynn and Boston Electric Railway had plugged into the West End network of Scollay Square in Boston (five cents and forty-five minutes to Revere Beach), inland as far as Woburn and down the North Shore to Hamilton, letting riders off at a dozen and a half resorts and parks on the way. In two more years it connected with the independent Gloucester trolleys running to Rocky Neck and Annisquam since 1890. Few would take exception to the Lynn and Boston's enthusiastic guidebook boast that "in its annual mission of taking thousands from the heated cities, into the pure, refreshing scenes of the country and seashore, the electric car has proved itself one of the greatest blessings mankind has ever known. It is the universal vehicle, as comfortable and convenient for the well-to-do as it is economical and available for the less fortunate."

By 1899 the Lynn and Boston was the biggest spider in Essex County and ready for the eating by a bigger one, the Massachusetts Electric Company, which in its turn was swallowed in 1901 by the Boston and Northern, a combine of twenty-three independents north of Boston. That was the nadir of expansion for the electrics. The screeching, swaying, sparking, clanging, careening little trolley cars were creating suburbanism and metropolitanism and interurbanism, providing everybody with wheels to everywhere for pocket change. Round trip by trolley car from Scollay Square to Gloucester and all the way around the Cape Ann shore and back to Boston, for instance, consumed nine and a half hours and one dollar.

At the Gloucester end of Rockport's Long Beach a midway in miniature was so completely the creation of the local street railway that when one died, the other died too. The company in 1895 had built a trestle across the dunes behind Little Good Harbor Beach and put up a pavilion, dance hall, vaudeville theatre, Ferris wheel, photo studio and bowling alley. The single-truck open cars, wrote historian Thomas E. Babson, "had the habit of galloping like a horse. Guard bars were let down on both sides before crossing the trestle. . . . Even so, a careless passenger was occasionally tossed off into the dunes."

The trolleys inspired a small hotel and a long boardwalk above the tide, bordered soon by a lengthening row of small summer cottages. Folks would arrive at Gloucester for the day from Boston on the snow-white excursion steamer *Cape Ann* and grab the electrics for a shore dinner and a gambol (and a gamble, some said) at the Long Beach Pavilion, encouraged, perhaps, by reassurances that North Shore trolley parks were "kept free from objectionable characters and anything that might offend ladies and children who might visit these places unaccompanied." For twenty-five years the little beach park within reach of the salt sea spray paid its way until it fell victim to its sire's bankruptcy in 1920.

For a few dollars any group could hire an open car with side curtains in case of a shower, motorman included, and go practically anywhere the tracks and the switches led. From near and far they screeched into the Willows for the fish dinners, the amusements, the concerts, the dancing, the spooning or a brush with the boys in blue—Hose Company Number 4 from Melrose in a car decorated with bunting and sunflowers, a bunch calling themselves the "Top Knots" from Gloucester, and all the way from Philadelphia in 1906 a trolley party with the reassuring word that they had passed through few cities and towns where connections were not easily made.

Ultimately their very success was their undoing. Speculation spurred expansion until the tracks, and costs, were outrunning the riders, and the farther from the city and the deeper into the country, the faster. Then began a period of consolidation. The Boston and Northern on the North Shore and the Old Colony network on the South Shore trumpeted in their joint guidebook of 1910 that the electric railway "carries the banner of progress far in advance . . . makes it possible to snap one's fingers at the gasoline tank, the turbine steamer or the soft-coal, choking steam engine." Next year the two merged as the Bay State Street Railway, claiming to be the biggest in the world, 72 former independent lines with 938 miles of track, much of it deficit-producing.

An electric trolley on Pleasant Street in Marblehead. (Beverly Historical Society, Walker Transportation Collection)

*At their peak,
just after the First
World War,
electric trolleys
provided easy
access to every
North Shore
town except
Manchester,
which banned
them. (Beverly
Historical Society,
Walker
Transportation
Collection)*

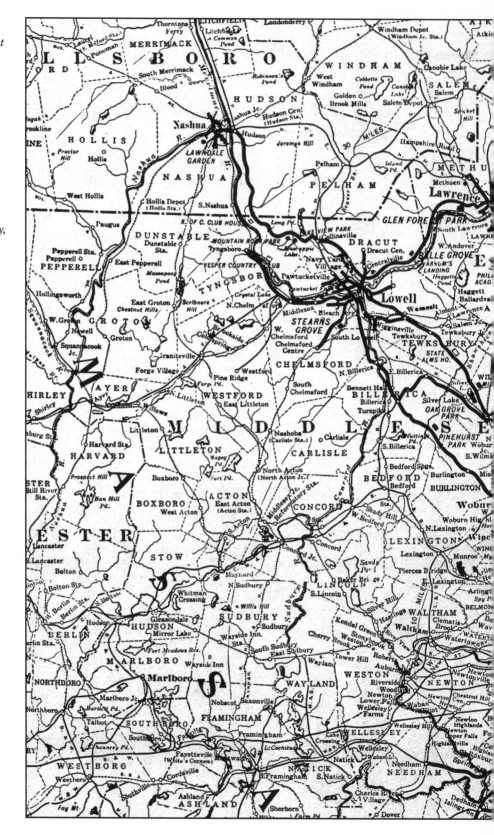

BAY STATE STREET RY. CO'S
Lines and Connections

THE
BAY STATE
STREET RAILWAY CO.
940 MILES
of LINES in
NEW ENGLAND

EXPLANATION
BAY STATE STREET RY. CO. ROUTES

Car Houses: ● Power Stations: ● Parks:

Other Electric Railways:

Steam Railroads:

Steamer Lines:

Boundaries { State
County
Town

ISSUED BY PASSENGER DEPARTMENT
15 MILK STREET, BOSTON, MASS.
(OPPOSITE OLD SOUTH CHURCH)

There were demurrers. The *North Shore Breeze* condemned the Salem-Gloucester stretch as "the roughest that we have ever ridden over . . . bump, bump, bump all the way there and back. . . . The running schedule is followed—well, it is followed, but they seldom catch up with it." The arrival of Dr. Holmes's "broomstick train" in sleepy Essex was lamented in the *Boston Herald:* "But once let the street railroad get its clutches on a town and its own peculiar and distinguishing air seems to disappear with marvelous rapidity." Manchester did something about it: jealous for their narrow streets and skittery horses, influential summer residents got the legislature to ban the trolley altogether from most of the western section of the town.

By 1906, ominously for the bouncing electrics, the *Salem Willows Budget* reported that "a big array of 'buzz wagons' commonly known as automobiles were here." In 1908 less speed from "these gasolene-driven demons" was demanded, followed by a call in 1910 for a speed limit of eight miles an hour. Not until America entered the First War, however, was there a big enough array of buzz wagons to threaten the trolleys. When peacetime mass automobile production took off after the Armistice, trolley operating profits plummeted, and the street railway industry suddenly simply collapsed with the dawn of the twenties.

Somewhere between the nickel trolley ride and the private Pullman, but rather closer to the latter than the former though they all shared a similar fate, was the *Flying Fisherman*, neither a schooner yacht nor an oilskinned aviator but a special commuter train on the Boston and Maine's Gloucester Branch that made one round trip a day for the benefit of wealthy summer subscribers only. The first Dude Train (so called by the jealous who couldn't qualify) ran into Boston from Magnolia and Gold Coast way stations in the morning and back in the afternoon in 1892; at about the same time the New York, New Haven and Hartford scheduled a similar train on its Old Colony Branch between Boston and the Buzzards Bay resorts.

Subscribers to the *Fisherman* at first paid a hundred dollars a season plus fare, an arrangement so lucrative for the B & M that in 1907 the railroad placed five big chair cars with cane seats, green leather upholstery and vestibules in service, custom-built by Pullman. By 1914 the Dude Train had four cars and about a hundred subscribers who guaranteed the B & M thirteen thousand dollars for the season, and some spoilsport on the Massachusetts Public Service Commission was questioning the legality of what were "officially called 'club trains,' implying that they are for the exclusive use of some men of social distinction who live on the North Shore or down in the Cape district during the summer." He was right, of course, but nothing, as might be expected, came of it.

Times changed, and the Dude Train, having survived the Great War, died with the peace, to the dismay of one devotee, whose chauffeur for years had been dropping him off at the Magnolia depot in the morning, then driving hell-bent over the road to Boston and picking him up at North Station and on to the office so that he shouldn't miss his game of cards en route. Presumably this mad race was reversed in the afternoon.

HORSEPOWER VERSUS HORSE POWER

The summer of 1901, a pioneer-in-reverse named F. M. Ayers chugged off from Indianapolis, Indiana, bound for Magnolia, Massachusetts, in a carriage powered by a gasoline engine. He got as far as Albany, New York, where the abominable roads at last broke the spirit of his Winton phaeton. (Alexander Winton was the first of the American gasoline automobile manufacturers of any durability and had been in production in Cleveland only since 1898.) Not too daunted, Ayers abandoned the useless vehicle and took the reliable rails of the New York Central.

Next summer the intrepid Mr. Ayers set out with two companions in a Winton touring car powered as by fifteen horses, again for Magnolia. This time he made it, in nine and a half days, declaring with justifiable self-congratulation to the gentleman from the *Boston Evening Transcript* that over the entire nine hundred miles they hadn't provoked a single horse to bolt or caused a single accident to another traveler.

The North Shore summer people had the cash and the leisure (primitive automobiling was, after all, a sport) to take to it, and Essex County had probably more Yankee tinkerers per road mile than anywhere else in the country. Amesbury was already the Detroit of the carriage trade when horse was king; the town up in the north of the county just naturally turned to automobile bodies in those pre-mass production days and in the years before World War I is said to have turned out more of them than any other place in the world.

Some fifty individuals and firms were inventing and producing motorcars in Essex County before 1915, beginning with the steam tricycle assembled by Andrew Philbrick in Beverly in 1886. The most prolific, oddly, was the General Electric Company at Lynn, with a variety of electric, steam and gasoline vehicles inspired by its guiding engineering genius, Elihu Thomson of Swampscott. Most pace-setting of all, undoubtedly, was the passenger-and-baggage-accommodating body of wood that a Beverly buggy firm introduced around 1918 as a custom option for a Model T Ford chassis that turned it into a "Beverly wagon," the first beach, or station, wagon.

In those early days, though, the motorcars that inspired really reckless enthusiasm in North Shore owners were not at first of local manufacture, but truly custom jobs, many imported and quite, and sometimes outrageously, expensive. Henry Perkins Benson of Salem bought his first, an electric, in 1898 and wrote, "I believe I was sane, normal and conservative in my sporting life as I was in business. I sailed and raced twenty-one-foot yachts out of Marblehead, played golf and tennis, and for indoor sports, billiards was my favorite. But motors did something to me. With them I was not calm or cautious or level headed. I fell for them in the most extraordinary manner."

The roadways of the time required that such passion be tempered with determination and patience. Driving raised clouds of dust in dry weather (hence the goggles and dusters of automobilists exposed entirely to the ele-

ments). Rain turned roads into thick mud concealing somewhere, anywhere, potholes invariably two inches deeper than the hubcaps. Cows wandered across the road in the middle of the night (as befell the author's father once; the cow fetched up on the hood). There were inglorious bottomings-out in downpours, busted springs, snapped steering gear, boiling radiators, burned-out clutches and flat tires, endlessly.

My father told of Bishop Lawrence, perhaps apocryphally, that while being driven somewhere along a North Shore road one day he happened upon a frustrated driver swearing profusely as he tried to pry the flat tire off the rim. "Have you tried prayer, my good man?" he inquired. The poor fellow in desperation fell to his knees, clasped his hands and lifted his eyes heavenward. He then picked up the iron, inserted it, and off popped the tire. "Well, I'll be damned!" the bishop is said to have exclaimed.

Sensible North Shore summer people with the means hired a chauffeur; equal to his ability behind the wheel, he must be a specialist in the internal medicine of his steed. Such a one was Henry Williams, a machinist for the company that built a Cleveland purchased in 1906 by Edward Williams, no relation of his but the son-in-law of Mrs. Emma Raymond, who reigned over Eastern Point's "Ramparts." Henry was loaned by the firm for a week to teach the new owner how to drive the car, then for another week to accustom the ladies to riding in it. He stayed with the paint manufacturer's family until his death sixty-three years later.

The speed limit in Beverly and Manchester was first set at eight miles an hour within the town limits and twelve outside, almost to no avail. An angry Manchester resident complained to the *Breeze* that the road hogs had so clogged the town in August that the electric trolleys might have to be admitted in self-defense—an alternative worse than almost anything to the forces of exclusiveness-by-the-sea. To the prototypical motorists, a speed limit was considered an infringement on their liberties, keenly resented and generally ignored. In 1904 the law was confounded by an epidemic of chauffeurs accidentally smearing their number plates with oil, which made them illegible under a coat of road dust.

How to catch the speeders? At first, a cop could sometimes do it on a horse. One day in the fall of 1902 Edward Parsons, the genial manager of the Moorland Hotel at Bass Rocks, drove to Boston to visit a friend. "On Commonwealth Avenue," the *Gloucester Times* reported with glee, "in endeavoring to pass a team, Mr. Parsons threw open the lever and the machine forged ahead. It had not gone far when Mr. Parsons noticed that a burly policeman on horseback was on his trail. Consequently he slowed up the auto and the guardian of the peace came up and placed Gloucester's leading practical joker under arrest, charged with traveling at a rate greater than eight miles an hour." Jailed, bailed and fined twenty dollars.

It was not until 1912 that Salem's Henry Benson observed the ladies in the driver's seat in any numbers, "thus adding a new and intriguing peril to the sport. The foot that rocked the cradle sometimes wrecked the car. Without presuming to understand their signals we gave them all the road room possible and they soon became as proficient as we were."

A year after Benson's cautious tribute the *Breeze* was raving about "chic little girls in their debutante years driving big six-cylinders with the command of a seasoned captain of a yacht, the quick decisions and proper judgments, the control of clutch and brake and gas and all the rest of it, would never have been associated with the hoop-skirt era. . . . The poise alone that it requires is a special tribute to the astonishingly clever American girl."

The big, tony watering places were natural oases for the automobilists, who frequently traveled in caravans for mutual morale and rescue, packs like the Glidden Tours rediscovering America from atop a snorting monster. The first wave of the mania struck Swampscott's New Ocean House in the summer of 1906, when its house organ, the *Reminder*, noted the presence on the grounds, among many others, of Miss Shearer's Columbia three-horse electric (the hotel was keen enough to install a battery-charging station), Colonel Wood's forty-horse Napier, a multinomial Charion, Garardon and Voigt, two Winton Model Ks, a couple of Stevens Duryeas, a Pope-Hartford, a Cleveland, a Stanley Steamer, a Rambler, a Rainier, a Pope-Toledo, a Packard, a Peerless, an Oldsmobile and a Locomobile.

Wonderful for business, but the *Reminder* had its doubts: "The terror which a puffing, dust-raising, bad-odored automobile inspires in an aged man or woman wending a slow way along the familiar road, lost perhaps in thoughts of days that were happier when walking was less difficult, can never be dreamed of by the cheerful, care-free party who so enjoy flying through space. They only laugh at the queer antics of the frightened country people and dash on to the next adventure."

Sixty years later the mid-1890s were merely yesterday afternoon in the memory of North Shore historian James Duncan Phillips, when every returning commuter train was met by "two or three spanking pairs attached to Victorias or Landaulets with coachmen in full livery on the box and a footman at the horses' heads, in which sat tightly laced dowagers under beautiful lace parasols. Surprisingly dowdy looking old gentlemen usually got into these smart vehicles and dumped some paper parcels down on the floor. A smart little trap or two might be in waiting driven by a lovely bride who prided herself on her horsemanship as much as on her young and handsome husband. The basket-work pony cart full of children and driven by the eldest was the happiest of the vehicles, especially when it was evident that father's return was the most joyous event of the day for all."

Although the afterglow lingered on, how fast the Victorian sun was set by the Wintons of the world! On the Manchester road one July afternoon of 1906, Robert C. Hooper's groom was exercising the master's steeplechaser Land of Clover, reputed to be the fastest in America and worth fifty thousand dollars. Passing a Lewandos laundry wagon, he was struck by an automobile and had to be shot. His bereaved owner ordered his forehoofs cut off and made into inkstands, and for good measure saved his tail. This was the sort of encounter between old ways and new that fired the ardor of Colonel William D. Sohier of Burgess Point in Beverly and the conscience of Walter D. Denègre of West Manchester.

Back in 1878, Colonel Henry Lee and Charles H. Dalton built the first private woods road on the North Shore from Preston Place north of Beverly Farms winding through the wilderness surrounding Gravelly, Round and Beck ponds and Chebacco Lake in Hamilton and Essex, then asked Colonel Sohier to take over the project of preserving the privacy of this primeval hinterland of the Shore. The role of Cerberus fell naturally to the doughty State Street lawyer; during the winter season in Boston he served Society as the "self-appointed major-domo for all First Family debuts," according to Cleveland Amory in *The Proper Bostonians,* and was "the all-time terror of the Boston press." He secured rights-of-way and raised money to insinuate a network of private dirt roads through the Beverly, Manchester, Hamilton, Wenham, Magnolia, West Gloucester and Essex backwoods, in some cases improving ancient ways such as the old stage road between Manchester and Essex, and Hesperus Avenue above the west shore of Gloucester Harbor.

The colonel's roads were originally ten or twelve feet wide and cost about twenty-five cents a running foot. With increased traffic they were widened gradually to eighteen feet at a dollar a foot by 1914, thirty miles of them, open to all but motorcars as a "haven of safety" for those who still clung to the saddle and the surrey seat, a ban supported, interestingly, by the North Shore Automobile Club, of which lawyer Denègre was a founder and president.

The club was started about ten years earlier, if a 1913 article in the *Breeze* can be given credence, expressly to cordon off the inner close of the North Shore from the obnoxious invasion perhaps not so much of members as of non-member outsiders. It posted Sohier's private road off limits to motor cars. "The biggest thing the club ever did was to adopt a system of 'tagging' [presumably number-plating] cars, which system grew and was later taken up by the state and by other states and has developed into the numbering system now used all over the country."

The swellest thing the North Shore Auto Club ever did was to elect Denègre president, commodore or whatever, considering the flagship he designed and had delivered in time to take on a European tour in 1907. The body was fashioned by Quinzler of Boston on a Packard chassis, in black, with family monogram on the door, wheels in English vermilion. There was an enclosure for the driver, who received his instructions through a megaphone speaking tube. The servants rode in the rear compartment, which was fitted with a revolving back step. The interior was illuminated electrically, a great luxury, and fixtures were finished in gun metal. The seats were upholstered in imported black goatskin.

By the summer of 1907, the *Breeze*, always on the lookout for trends, pronounced the North Shore auto-nutty. Motoring parties were the rage, and every evening all evening the talk in every hotel lobby and on every cottage veranda was of machines and their merits and speeds. By 1909 there were noticeably fewer horses on the roads.

Half the world was already bleeding to death when the *Breeze* looked back on the 1916 season as the best in years. All hail the motorcar, which had brought countless tourists from the Midwest and even the West Coast for their first taste of the North Shore!

Driver James Ferrara at the wheel of a 1906 Packard touring car in Beverly Farms. (Beverly Historical Society, Walker Transportation Collection)

*"No disturbing outside element" behind the formidable walls of Swampscott's
New Ocean House. (Louis A. Gallo collection)*

~12~
ARKS THAT PASS
IN THE NIGHT

Breezy piles of lumber, with verandas by the mile for the citified family

"The fog has gone!" the bell hop cried:
The guests ran out the door.
One fleeting glimpse of blue they spied:
The fog had gone—for more.
                    —*North Shore Breeze*

In its day, which was a long one, the New Ocean House at Swampscott was possibly the most disagreeably exclusive of the important summer hotels on the North Shore. George Stacy's Hawthorne Inn at East Gloucester may have been more disagreeable (his guests loved him for it) and George Upton's magnificent Oceanside at Magnolia more exclusive (and how his guests loved *him!*). But the turned-up-nose prize went to the New Ocean House.

The oldest Ocean House had been opened on Phillips Point in 1836 and was the Shore's senior summer hostelry behind the Nahant Hotel. It burned during the Civil War, reopened above Whale Beach, burned again, was rebuilt as the New Ocean House in 1884, and was sold in 1895 to the owners of the Hamilton in Bermuda. They dropped the "New," wired all 175 rooms with electric call bells, installed a telephone and an elevator, and promised prospective guests, "As the patrons of the house are among the best families in the country, the society is second to none."

Not too surprisingly, after a few years there was another fire. Two hoteliers, Allen Ainslie and Edward R. Grabow, bought in, pumped $100,000 into remodeling and enlarging and in 1902 opened as, once again, the New Ocean House. With growing prosperity they added an orchestra, subscription concerts, balls, recitations, juvenile vaudeville, bagatelle, whist, clock golf and tennis tournaments; they imported the English equestrian Arthur S. Sankey to teach riding, jumping and hunting, and started up a weekly house organ of gossip and self-admiration, the *New Ocean House Reminder.*

Ainslie and Grabow also operated hotels in Jamaica and the Tuileries,

Hotel Preston, 1926. (Louis A. Gallo collection)

as well as the Empire and Lenox in Boston. They knew how to stroke the snob. One of the *Reminder*'s early editorial campaigns, for example, was to have the letter *p* eliminated from Swampscott. The real gripe of their clientele, however, soon emerged: "the outside element." Happily, the hotel was free of it, but it was something to be watched out for, as in 1906: "No disturbing outside element . . . no objectionable parties. . . . Even on the Fourth of July, there is none of the annoying confusion that attends the day in some localities." But wait—later that season, concerning a block of sixteen tenements noxiously close to the hotel, known locally as The Acre, the publication inquired, "Why do not our people get together and look after the Italian quarter, which is certainly a disgrace to Swampscott? It is a pity that that portion of the town should not be made into a beautiful park when so little stands in the way of doing it." Elitism was selling so well that by 1907 the publication had been renamed the *North Shore Reminder*, distributed from Nahant to Marblehead, published by the Ainslie and Grabow Press, and reminding guests that "to the several exclusive resort hotels within its borders Swampscott owes that immunity from all objectionable summer patronage, which has always been one of its special claims for the select and refined class of people who seek a summer home along its cool and lovely beaches."

Chief among these others were the Lincoln House and the Hotel Preston. The latter dominated Beach Bluff with spreading piazzas and stately porte cochere through which clip-clopped turnouts spic and span and glided silent electric automobiles periodically rejuvenated at the hotel's own charging station. The elk's head surveyed the lobby with glassy gaze from above the main fireplace, every room had its own India rubber plant, and an ensemble of Boston Symphony players gave morning and evening concerts to the obbligato of the smartly struck croquet ball upon the Preston's rolling lawn.

Marblehead also had a few of these breezy piles of lumber, but nothing in the grand style. Beverly was wall-to-wall in private estates, and so was Manchester, with the solitary and memorable exception of the Masconomo. Eleven foreign ambassadors were summering in Manchester in 1904, from which may be inferred that the Masconomo's vaunted "immunity from malaria"—certainly no hazard on the North Shore—was a come-on directed at the diplomatic corps. Among these was the envoy of the Czar, and it was said that the Russo-Japanese War might have ended in the Booths' octagonal hall the next summer, except that it was not large enough for all the delegates; thus the peace was stage-managed by President Theodore Roosevelt in the larger Wentworth-by-the-Sea at Portsmouth, New Hampshire.

Manchester-by-the-Sea tolerated the Masconomo and the interesting and lively colony of actors and actresses from which it sprang in the post-Civil War era, but by 1908 the hotel was being publicly and huffily dismissed by the *Breeze* as run-down and third class. Junius had long since joined his more famous and infamous acting brothers. Aggie Booth, remarried, leased it out, and things began to look up until September of 1909, when her new manager, leaving a score of employees and a $1,600 unpaid payroll behind, was last seen running toward Smith's Point, where he allegedly put to sea in a motorboat owned by the son of his financial backer, the convicted New York "policy king" Al Adams. When Agnes died soon after, her third husband, Boston theater-owner John B. Schoeffel, bought the Masconomo from the executors for old times' sake. The once colorful old place enjoyed a brief revival during the First War, but in 1920 most of it was torn down.

High-stepping above Swampscott's Phillips Beach, 1903. (Louis A. Gallo collection)

THE OCEANSIDE

Kettle Cove and its Crescent Beach separated Manchester's Coolidge Point and Gloucester's Knowlton's Point, and still do. But when the Knowltons started selling off their pasture for summer boardinghouses in 1867, some romantic renamed the fishing hamlet Magnolia. Rapidly Magnolia was adopted by Manchester, which owned most of the intervening beach, as a convenient guest colony for its summer overflow . . . so convenient that in 1877 Gloucester had to beat back a seditious attempt by the Knowltons to get Manchester to annex its major share of Magnolia.

In 1879 George A. Upton acquired one of these bucolic boardinghouses, the Oceanside. Here was no mere dispenser of bathing suits and blueberry muffins. The man was a veritable Noah of the business; he foresaw the flood of fashion in resorts even then, and he swore to all the creatures of the summer that he and they would be borne upon it. His house grew to arklike proportions and sprouted or swallowed lesser arks until it tumbled and spread eastward from the summit of Lexington Avenue down over Magnolia Point toward the sea. Deck upon bay-windowed deck, bridge over shingled bridge rode with majesty over a vast groundswell of lawn. One day at the turn of the century, engraved in the annals of verandadom, the proprietor perambulated his piazzas with a measuring tape and discovered that he had 881 feet of them—almost exactly one-sixth of a mile.

Who knows how many rocking chairs George Upton owned? Certainly not he. His main dining saloon was 45 feet wide and 150 long, half the length of a football field, enclosed within a tenth of an acre of plate glass windows and sea-green walls. The Oceanside Casino supported a firmament of fleecy clouds drifting across a cerulean ceiling from which starlike electric lights twinkled and beamed upon the swaying dancers below.

By 1908, when this sagacious Noah sold his ark for a half a million dollars after clearing upward of sixty thousand dollars a season for the past ten, he had gathered in ten arklets and 600 rooms. The momentum of fashion surged on. In 1912 the Oceanside gobbled up the rival Hesperus on the west side of Lexington Avenue. By then the mammoth parent structure, twenty-two cottages and 750 rooms, was the biggest summer hotel in New England.

And the classiest.

George Upton was a strong temperance man, with interesting standards: he accorded his guests storage privileges under the control of his cellarer. "The single violation of the accepted rules of courtesy and politeness," shuddered John W. Black, Jr., who worked there in the Upton era, "ended the career of any employee who came in contact with the guests." That was class.

And the twenty-piece orchestra played from on top of the porte cochere every afternoon and on Sunday evenings, when the concerts were serious, if not deadly, and "absolute silence was required and obtained." That was class, and so was the rousing rendition of his own marches when that annual habitué, John Philip Sousa, borrowed the baton. And the Chinese princess dressed all in silks, with feet bound, riding the elevator in 1903 and in Black's

memory for the next fifty-three years . . . class. And his mental picture of walking down the path to "Highland Cottage" behind the ramrod figure of young Major Douglas MacArthur visiting his aunts. And glimpses of William Dean Howells and Mrs. Ulysses S. Grant, Alice Roosevelt Longworth and Mrs. J. P. Morgan, and the Turkish ambassador, and the Chilean ambassador and the Uruguayan ambassador, just drops in the ambassadorial bucket. Very classy.

The Ketchup King, Henry J. Heinz of Pittsburgh, brought his family to the Oceanside, fell for Magnolia, and in 1904 built a $240,000 mansion on the shore there. They had to sell out after the 1929 crash. The Biscuit Baron of Chicago, Jacob L. Loose, had for his house guest for most of the summer of 1906, probably in one of the Oceanside cottages that the rich rented by the season, cigar-chomping Joseph G. (Foul-mouthed Joe) Cannon, the uncouth boss of the House of Representatives, one of its less-distinguished Speakers. Smitten like Heinz, the senior partner in the Loose Wiles Biscuit Company built a mansion on the ocean side of Gloucester's Eastern Point in 1916.

And there was the Silent Partner, the slight and seemingly unassuming Colonel (Texas, that is) Edward M. House. Heir to a plantation fortune and astute enough in his own right, Colonel House was already the kingmaker of Texas politics when he discovered Magnolia in 1901. He brought his family there regularly thereafter, usually if not invariably to the Oceanside, where they were fixtures at least until 1910, often in "Breakers Cottage." House and his king of kings, Woodrow Wilson, were not to meet until 1911, although the then president of Princeton had sojourned the summer of 1903 in East Gloucester, separated by the mere length of the harbor from the man destined to be the greatest influence in his life.

And clearly it was the Oceanside with which Episcopal Bishop William

Lawrence (a Nahant summerer himself) enjoyed illustrating the social provincialism of the Harvard academic community, to wit: Upon their return to Cambridge one autumn, a dean inquired of the fabled three Palfrey sisters, all spinsters of renown, what sort of season they had had. Replied one: "We have had a delightful summer. We stayed at a great hotel in Magnolia, and met a number of really intelligent and agreeable people of whom we had never before heard." Though they had traveled far and wide abroad, Cleveland Amory claimed in a similar version of the story, it was the only occasion that they had been farther from home in their native land than Nahant.

Summering diplomats, most likely, dreamed up the truly outrageous sporting events called gymkhanas that were held for five years on Crescent Beach beginning in 1905, mainly under the aegis of the Oceanside, which concluded each one with its grand banquet and ball of the season. The word is a bastard, claiming some Hindu parentage, originating among bored English officers in India, and covering a miscellany of athletic activities involving men and horses.

The long and smoothly curving beach was the perfect arena for such goings-on, which attracted thousands of the North Shore's elite. The high point of the 1908 gymkhana was the eight-mile horseback race, requiring the contestants to dash along the beach from start to finish, dismount, toss off a bottle of ginger ale (so the *Breeze* had it, anyway), remount, gallop back to the starting line, remove coats and put them back on inside out, and charge back to the finish.

The gymkhanas ceased in 1910, perhaps because the center of Crescent Beach was being quarantined by the Manchester Bath and Tennis Club, which opened in 1912, soon to be fashionable with its pool, courts and dining room overlooking the cove and the ocean.

The Oceanside's tennis and golf tournaments, water carnivals, marshmallow toasts down on the rocks and chaperoned automobile parties to Revere Beach ("the comic-relief in the North Shore summer drama for the younger set") all fluttered through the pages of the *Breeze,* none with such abandon as the mania that struck in 1913. "If it is true that the North Shore is dance mad, then the central asylum is Magnolia, for everybody goes there."

Ah, the afternoon *thé dansant* at the Oceanside featuring the Castle walk, the trot, the maxixe, the Texas Tommy and the aeroplane glide . . . the Wednesday night hop . . . and the Saturday evening ball when, in the "sophis" patter of the *Breeze* correspondent, "fashion merrily cracks its whip. . . . The orchestra begins! A gaily gathered crowd in amazing Paris frocks trots, promenades the veranda, chats and gossips. . . . The charm of youth and the brilliancy of maturity in shadow lace and brocade, many colored chiffons and all the materials de soir, with the inevitable wide-winding girdle, with the sparkle of jewels and the prance of cut-steel-buckled slippers, dance to the rhythm of ragtime chimes, through the many variations of one-step and trots, and the maxixe, and hesitations. It is a spectacle that repays attention."

Yes, John Black, you were right: "This establishment spelled *class*." And war and taxes and automobiles and changing patterns of summer life killed and buried it. On December 11, 1958, the magnificent Oceanside burned to the ground. George Upton had been in his grave for thirty-nine years, that Noah who, when his beloved ark one time was damaged by fire, refused to accept the award of the insurance adjuster because he thought it was too high. Now *that's* class.

THE RUSTIC AND THE BEATIFIC ALONG CAPE ANN

As Magnolia whirled around the Oceanside, so East Gloucester wandered around the Hawthorne. The two Georges, Upton and Stacy, held decidedly different views regarding accommodation of guests.

The brusque and, when it suited him, genial son of a Gloucester insurance executive, George Stacy learned the hotel business from the front desk back. In 1891, at thirty-one, he built the foundation of his empire on Wonson's Point, facing Ten Pound Island across the water, and called it the Hawthorne Inn after his favorite author. Cottages sprouted until his overgrown main house, bulging with nearly thirty casinos, ells and other excrescences including a derelict lumber schooner serving as a houseboat, was a helter-skelter structure fashioned from the secondhand building materials he so dearly loved. It bedded down 450 guests in delighted discomfort.

Mrs. Blanche Butler Lane first came to the Hawthorne from New York with her mother, grandmother and nursemaid in 1902 when she was two. Her earliest memory is of an early arrival from the Gloucester depot over the dusty road by carriage after a sooty train ride down from Boston behind the coughing steam locomotive. No clean towels in their rooms, a mild remonstrance met with much muttering from Proprietor Stacy. A symbol of status among the guests was the number of trunks the delivery wagon brought from the depot for the hotel's faithful assistant, Jim Thompson, to lug in.

The popular Hawthorne had a permanent waiting list, and the only way in was said to be in the wake of a hearse. And yet, as Mrs. Lane recalled fondly, "the food was mediocre. We had one bathtub and toilet to a cottage—wash basin, pitcher, slop jar in each room. We put the pitcher outside the door at night and had hot water in the morning. We put another small pitcher out and received ice water at night." The single tub dictated a rigid ritual. In the evening the first guest in, presumably the senior occupant of the cottage, drew the water, bathed, drained and scrubbed the tub, and refilled it for the next, being allowed exactly thirty minutes from start to finish, with the result that the new visitor was lucky to be in bed before midnight.

Evidently an engaging child, Blanche was adopted as a sort of mascot by Mr. Stacy and every Fourth of July was boosted up on top of the piano and waved a little flag while five hundred or so guests sang the national anthem. This tradition endured "until we were nearly thrown out when I damn near burned the place down, leading my gang through in a game of Hare and Hounds with *live matches* as the hare's trail. Another time we played Follow the Leader, which took us up one of the old so-called fire escapes to the roof,

John Henry Twachtman, over-looking Smith Cove and Gloucester Harbor from East Gloucester's Banner Hill, undated. (Canajoharie Library and Art Gallery, Canajoharie, New York)

where we all pranced across, much to the horror of the assembled guests below." Speaking of matches, it used to be said that they were made not in heaven, but at the Hawthorne Inn.

One courageous soul informed George Stacy at breakfast that the coffee was vile, to which he replied airily, "Yes, it is. I never drink it when I'm here." Another dared to complain that the ceiling leaked over her bed. "Can't have that," said he—and had the bed moved. To a third dissident he joshed, "This is a third-class hotel run for first-class people." But a fourth habitual griper tried the Stacy patience too far: "You are very unhappy here, so Jim will put your trunk on the baggage truck at three in time for you to take the four o'clock train home."

Half sea, half country, East Gloucester and its appending Rocky Neck had picturesque charm for the summer visitor, and the Hawthorne commanded a fanatical following. Eastern Point and Bass Rocks, the ocean-clad tail and backsides of the peninsula, had been captured by the wealthy summer residents, but East Gloucester remained the stronghold of independent natives who fished, lobstered and farmed, removed from the hustle of the inner waterfront and at least some of its smell, tolerating the summer folks and a growing art colony with a mixture of amusement and imprecations.

The smart hotel keeper, like W. P. Osborne, who operated the Harbor View at the foot of Patch's Hill on Wonson's Cove, advertised that he could provide all the essential amenities of a large hotel at half the price: "But of one thing a prospective visitor [to East Gloucester] should be warned. . . . There are many who have become so enthusiastic over the charms of the place they forget that when they first came they were disappointed. The reason for this is that the resort is different from every other and its attractions are not showy but grow on one until it is a matter of affection, if not something like a passion. . . . The Harbor View is the same sort of house that East Gloucester is a resort. It is quaint, rambling, different, but it is comfortable and has many staunch friends."

Among those friends was the American impressionist painter John Henry Twachtman, who breathed his last while staying at the Harbor View in 1902, and Princeton professor Stockton Axson, host there during the following summer to his sister Ellen and his close friend, her husband, the new head of the university, Woodrow Wilson. It was a bright artistic and literary salon, almost, that the future President of the United States found there, and he joined in publishing a clever little periodical for the occasion, *The Trifler,* which naturally had to have an editorial policy: "In politics it is strictly independent but with the firm conviction that the Democratic Party is right in every particular."

Farther along the road to Eastern Point the old Fairview crowned the crest of Patch's Hill, older (1842) and no less quaint. Louisa May Alcott occupied the best third-floor room in 1868 and 1871; the father-and-son artists Stephen and Maxfield Parrish went off with their sketching kits from here in the 1880s; and for several weeks during the summers of 1895 and 1896 Rudyard Kipling and his American wife holed in while he dug into the fishing lore of Gloucester for his classic novel of the life, *Captains Courageous,* in which he wrote whimsically of the place:

"A strange establishment, managed apparently by the boarders, where the table-cloths were red-and-white-checkered, and the population, who seemed to have known one another intimately for years, rose up at midnight to make Welsh rarebits if it felt hungry."

For all his infamous frugality, George Stacy was a man with a large view. Five seasons with the Hawthorne Inn staked him to the first sizable summer hotel on the Atlantic Ocean side of the East Gloucester pastures at Bass Rocks, where he had apprenticed at the Bass Rocks House as a young man. In 1896 he went partners with Edward P. Parsons in building the three-hundred-guest Moorland on the site of the smaller burned-out Pebbly Beach Hotel.

In the summer of 1903, doubtless on the qt, Stacy had gathered unto himself several parcels of prime harbor frontage on either side of the old Niles farmhouse beyond the southerly end of Niles Beach, land from which, like the rest of the Point, commercial construction was banned until 1917 unless by special permission of the owners' syndicate, the Eastern Point Associates. How he got around the hardheaded businessmen and lawyers who were so determined to keep the public off their private preserve is a mystery.

But George Stacy built in the very heart of Gloucester's most exclusive summer resort, and for the North Shore, on an incredible scale. His Colonial Arms opened on June 25, 1904. The 175 rooms and three and a half stories first announced had swollen to 300 and five, with living quarters for 125 employees. The massive, wooden colonial–Greek Revival anarkronism spread mansard wings joined by splendid, high-columned porticoes and a super elegant porte cochere from which emanated tier upon tier of breezy porch. Three hundred feet long and sixty deep, rising full-blown from the stark ledge at water's edge, dominating all of Gloucester's glorious outer harbor, the Colonial Arms was the greatest, grandest hotel, winter or summer, ever conceived in a single stroke north of Boston.

No, Stacy the summer hotel man did not spare the horses. The Arms cost him $230,000 in 1904 money. A tremendous center lobby opened to a stunning view of Gloucester Harbor between the resplendent dining room in the east wing and the beatific ballroom in the west. There were morning room, fireplaces and antiques, professional decor everywhere, reading and writing and reference rooms, toilet parlors and suites with their own baths, seventy-five shared bathrooms besides (no pitchers outside the door here), an elevator, a six-piece orchestra (three concerts a day), a wharf for the Colonial's own steam launch to ferry guests back and forth into Gloucester (touching at the Hawthorne on the way, of course), and a great garage for the enthusiastic new automobilists. And to launch it all with the biggest possible bang, the annual outing of the Essex County Republican Club assembled to get the word from its velvet-gloved boss, Senator Henry Cabot Lodge of Nahant.

Booked solid for four seasons . . . until the night of New Year's, 1908, when a never-explained fire broke out somewhere in the part of the empty hotel almost within spitting distance of the cottage that Henry Davis Sleeper was building on the next lot. By the time the steam pumpers came flying over the frozen road from Gloucester behind their steaming horses, a half a gale of wind from the southwest had swept the flames through the whole gigantic

The construction gang who built the Colonial Arms on Eastern Point. (Lawrence Colby collection)

works, and in three and a half hours, while a great crowd watched in awe, George Stacy's dream of a lifetime, fifteen thousand square feet of it, crumbled in a smoking ruin.

There was talk that sparks from the chimney of Sleeper's cottage, where fires had been lit to dry plaster, might have been carried by the wind to the roof of the hotel, but his mason said only space heaters were in use. Whatever the *machina,* the *deus ex* must have been perfectly satisfactory to the young interior decorator, just then enclosing the nucleus of his fabulous "Beauport" in the shadow of his neighbor's monolith. And could it have been effect following cause that within three months of the utter destruction of his closest competition, George Upton across the harbor in Magnolia sold the Oceanside?

George Stacy's name is immortalized, not over the flung-open doors of a period piece of resort architecture, however grand in sweep and view, but in the graceful arc of boulevard for which he was responsible and which gives Gloucester Harbor its Bay of Naples air.

The New Ocean House, the Masconomo, the Oceanside, the Hawthorne, the Colonial Arms—all the great ones are gone in flames or torn down or shrunk to nothing worth remembering.

The great summer hotels, the arks, where the citified family was content to take a packaged vacation in immobility on the shore, invited their own destruction, and the end of a way of living, when they welcomed through their shaded portes cocheres those first gents in their goggles and ladies in their dusters in those first roaring touring cars and runabouts that put the wheels under the third American Revolution.

The ill-fated Colonial Arms, which opened in June 1904 and burned to the ground on January 1, 1908. (Ernest Blatchford photo, author's collection)

The Shurtleff Jolly Boat near Fox Creek Bridge, Ipswich, 1915.
(From Upon the Road Argilla *by Sidney M. Shurcliff.)*

~13~
"THANK GOD FOR THE GREENHEADS"

Docs from Harvard and a Prince of the Bathroom
colonize Ipswich's Argilla Road and crown Castle Hill

Geographically and geologically there is almost nothing North Shorish about Ipswich. It is the farthest from Boston and the last colonized, thanks to distance, too little water for much yachting, too much heat and humidity, too many mosquitoes and the most voracious of all the winged beasties of summer, the greenhead fly.

"Thank God for the greenheads," grinned one bite-scarred veteran of many a season on the Ipswich marsh's edge, for whom the pain was a small price for his privacy.

Ipswich is the softer variety of Essex County farmland, drifting off into marshlands riddled with creeks, mile after mile of knee-high salt grass that erupts offshore in rounded islands and necks of sand as dazzling as snow, piled up by the swirling currents into a dune-backed beach, clean-cut and surf-smoothed for as far as the eye can squint.

Castle Hill lords it over the estuary. Ancient Appleton Farms sits nobly astride rural Ipswich, a pastoral duchy of a thousand acres, the lesser part in Hamilton, granted to Samuel, the First of the Appletons, by Charles the First of England in 1638, the oldest farm continuously in one family in America, they say. Continuously renewing themselves, the Appletons extended their business and professional connections to Boston and New York and beyond, always returning and retiring to the Ipswich seat, summer and winter, to survey their fields, mend their fences and oversee their herds and herdsmen, gathering in their children and their in-laws, and their horses quite as well bred—true country squires to the last of the male line unto the ninth generation, who was Francis R. Appleton, Jr., presiding, when he died in 1974 at eighty-nine, over one of the last of the patriarchies of old.

Not so Jeffrey's Neck (or Great Neck) and its Little Neck, protected from the smashing Atlantic by the barrier bar of Plum Island—common land, so Ipswichians supposed, since the days of the colony. Then along came Alexander B. Clark in the 1890s, buying up the old shares of Jeffrey's Neck, which he sold off for summer cottages, running the road through to

Little Neck. The town followed with water mains and leased out a whole colony, all to the litigious bewilderment of feoffees, squatters, summer folk, natives and title searchers, but not to lawyers from up the line the like of Charles P. Searle of Boston. No dealer in postage-stamp lots of dubious ancestry, Searle consolidated sweeping tracts of marsh and uplands along the Ipswich River on the way to Jeffrey's Neck and nailed them down in 1906 with a mansion designed after the famous Florentine villa Belriposa. Some box for a town of saltboxes.

In the lee of the Castle Neck sandbars, the broad marshes stretching from West Gloucester to Newbury and beyond used to yield good money crops of salt hay. While important as wildlife sanctuaries, they are even more so as marine nurseries for the huge crops of ocean fish endangered by any encroachment on their earliest feeding grounds. It is as insect preserves, however, that the salt marshes have nurtured the blood-starved mosquitoes and carnivorous greenhead flies that imposed a natural selection on the summerization of old Argilla (Latin for "hard white clay") Road, which takes its time from Ipswich town for four miles along the ridge to Castle Neck. As the road saunters around Heartbreak Hill and over Labor-in-Vain Creek toward the sea, it affords pleasing vistas of the marshes quilted with the long-abandoned haycutters' drainage ditches and of the hump of Hog Island. Skirting Castle Hill, the road crosses the dunes to the Ipswich lighthouse, the only structure along the nearly five miles of Castle Neck's incredible beach.

All around here were the 250 acres of Castle Hill farm, which since 1843 belonged to Manasseh Brown, upon whose death near the end of the century it passed to his son, John Burnham Brown. The new owner had made it in railroading in Chicago and now returned to his native Ipswich to turn the farm into his country estate. There were few trees, for the drumlins were kept cropped by the livestock; J. B. made roads, added buildings, landscaped and planted thousands. Litigation is said to have reduced his fortune, and when J. B. Brown died in 1908, his dreams for Castle Hill farm were only partly realized.

THE PILLBOX COLONY

An enclave of largely Boston doctors began to take shape on Argilla Road in the late 1880s when Eugene A. Crockett, Mark W. Richardson, Charles W. Townsend, Herman F. Vickery, Francis B. Harrington and Joseph L. Goodale took to vacationing at Smith's boardinghouse about halfway out the road. All were youngish graduates of Harvard Medical School or were finishing there. Most were on the staff of the Massachusetts General Hospital and would be outstanding in their specialties. For these unpretentious spirits, not all Boston-born or Brahmins by any means, the simple saltwater farm life and setting of Argilla Road were antidote to the demands of patients and the pressures of teaching.

Here they would rusticate their growing families for the summer, the

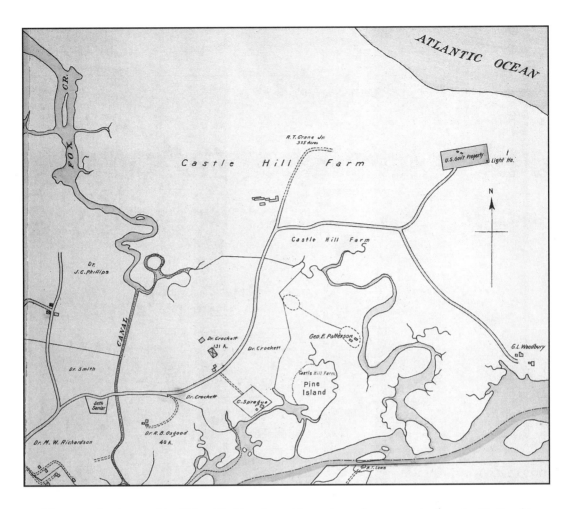

Map labels (clockwise/as positioned): ATLANTIC OCEAN; F. CR.; FOX CR.; Castle Hill Farm; R.T.Crane Jr. 375 Acres; U.S. Gov't Property; Light Ho.; N; Castle Hill Farm; Dr. J.C. Phillips; CANAL; Castle Hill Farm; Geo. F. Patterson; G.L. Woodbury; Dr. Crockett 131 A.; Dr. Crockett; Dr. Smith; Castle Hill Farm; Pine Island; Dr. Crockett; G. Sprague; Seth Senior; Dr. M. W. Richardson; Dr. R.B. Osgood 40 A.; N.T. Lowe

ambience and privacy of it all fortified by the epidermal toughness required in August to endure the absence of the cooling southwester and the descent of the carnivorous fly. Amos Everett Jewett, writing of his youthful summers "marshing" thereabouts, reminisced painfully on the season of the greenhead: "While they lasted they were probably the cause of more profanity than was anything else, although I have mowed in a cove, where there was no air, when mosquitoes and midgets made it quite entertaining. The greenhead drew blood with every bite, and if there were those who did not indulge in profanity, at least they felt like the old man in Rowley, who, when he met with an accident and some one asked him if he swore, replied, 'No! but I had very profane thoughts.'"

The nominal founder of the colony was not a pill-pusher but George Patterson, a Boston insurance man who in 1897 bought Seeby's Island, a speck in the marsh south of Castle Hill to which he retreated with his gunning pals, notably the artist Frank S. Benson. Patterson dreamed up a complex of hanging basins and mini-aqueducts to collect water from roof leaks, and one summer he imported a cowpoke from Oklahoma to teach him western-style riding, rope tricks and gunslinging.

Argilla Road in Ipswich leads through a colony of doctors to Richard Crane's Castle Hill Farm. From Atlas of the Towns of Topsfield, Ipswich, Essex, Hamilton and Wenham, *Boston, 1910. (Courtesy of Ipswich Public Library)*

The next year Dr. Crockett bought Smith's boardinghouse and soon after got married in London with the red tape–cutting help of the American ambassador, the formidable Joseph Hodges Choate. Back in Ipswich, the newlyweds heard that the great man was in Boston. Wishing to gesture thanks, they offered to ferry him out to Hog Island, otherwise known as Choate Island, to inspect the ancestral farmhouse where his quite-as-famous elder cousin, Senator Rufus Choate, was born.

To the young couple's alarm, the ambassador arrived for the voyage, which was to be by rowboat, as if for an audience with His Majesty, right up to the stovepipe hat. They rowed him out anyway. The Great Man, however, enjoyed himself so much wandering about the island that the tide had preceded them at departure time, leaving their boat high and dry. Mrs. Crockett told Sidney M. Shurcliff (author of the delightful *Upon the Road Argilla,* from which much of this account of the Pillbox Colony is borrowed) "how Mr. Choate sat stiffly and regally in the rowboat while she and Dr. Crockett jumped over the side and pulled the boat with its distinguished freight over hundreds of yards of slimy mud to deep water." Some time after, Choate again visited the family island and exclaimed, as he surveyed the view from the heights, "I would rather be governor of Hog Island than of all of Massachusetts!"

Dr. Crockett's purchase of the Smith house forced the other boarders out, and the same year, 1898, doctors Richardson and Townsend picked up some land and built a summer house they occupied with their families until 1902, when Richardson built his own, as well as a boathouse down on the Castle Neck River that served as the community landing for almost fifty years.

Bald and blackbearded, Charles Wendell Townsend was thirty-nine when he settled upon the road in 1898, a respected physician already pursuing his avocational passion, natural history, to the gradual abandonment of his profession. He called his twelve acres "Merula Farm" after *Merula migratoria,* his favorite bird, the robin. One acre he planted with saplings that grew into his "Forest," where he hammered together a lean-to from which to observe the wildlife attracted there. Here he invented the "cricket thermometer," that is, to arrive at the temperature, count the chirps in a quarter of a minute and add thirty-nine. (Crickets chirp faster as it gets warmer.)

Townsend and his first wife had four children and were great hikers and outdoor people. A few years after her death in 1917 he married her sister, but she too died soon after. He wrote his first Ipswich book on *Sand Dunes and Salt Marshes* in 1913, another on *The Birds of Essex County,* and three more on the natural history of Labrador, having once walked all the way around the Gaspé Peninsula.

As an ornithologist Charles Townsend was internationally known. As a lover of the Ipswich salt marshes, beaches, dunes and drumlins, he was gifted with a magical eye and ear, the insights of the medical clinician and the pen of the poet, writing in his book *Beach Grass* of a night spent alone on a dune above the Ipswich beach: "The laughing cry of the loon comes to his ears from the sea and the noisy clamor of a great company of herring gulls, gossiping with each other as they settle down for a night on the shore. Sandpipers and plovers whistle as they fly over, and the lisping notes of warblers, migrating from the sterile cold of the north, drop from above. Forming a continuous background to these voices are the boom and the crash of the waves on the sea beach."

After Townsend, Dr. Goodale succumbed, buying in 1900 an 1815 farmhouse and much acreage, to which in 1920 he added another house and the well-known apple orchard that has passed into other hands but retains his name. Dr. Vickery got a house and 130 acres in 1902 and the next year sold off enough to Dr. Harrington for his purposes.

Still more of the Harvard medical fraternity followed, until 1907, when a rare but congenial breach occurred. Dr. William B. Robbins and his close friend Arthur A. Shurtleff (who in 1929 changed the family name to Shurcliff), a most original and inventive young Boston landscape architect, bought a drumlin and a large field on the water side of Argilla Road, called by the natives Skim Milk Hill because it was such thin pasturage. The new owners divided, and Dr. Robbins won the toss for the lot with the ocean view. Both built summer cottages on the heights and found well water at the bottom of their hill. But how to get it up to the house? The handsome physician was one of the most popular in Boston's Back Bay, so much in demand that the routine answer to phone calls in Ipswich was "Doctor's taking a bath." To fill the tub, he had his water pumped up by an old one-lunger gasoline engine.

Not so Arthur Shurtleff, who was a tinkerer greater even than George Patterson. Wind power he would harness, but not with an ugly high farm windmill on an iron tower such as some of his neighbors employed. Shurtleff reproduced a picturesque old-timer in the Dutch style like one he had seen flailing away on Nantucket, and from this he strung wires all the way down the hill to the arm of a hand pump at the well. Occasionally this rig worked and lifted a trickle of water into the tank in the house.

Conveniently for him, he departed daily for the office and left his wife in command. A niece of the sculptor Augustus St. Gaudens, Margaret Shurtleff was a tennis player, feminist, political liberal, civil libertarian and mother of three girls and three boys including the author Sidney. She recalled in her memoirs, *Lively Days*, that when there was no wind the dishes were washed in an emergency supply of rainwater, and the guests, if they insisted, in the creek, "a long walk across the prickly marshes and, unless the tide was high, a slimy descent down a muddy bank." Tending the windmill, the energetic Mrs. Shurtleff decided, was "more of a responsibility than all the children lumped together. My first duty in the morning was to unfurl the sails on the four arms, push the big wheel that turned the hood of the mill into the wind and wait to see if the wind was strong enough to turn the arms. . . . The wind was not always cooperative."

Arthur Shurtleff was devoted to the bicycle, which he once mated with

his favorite water conveyance, the kayak. The result was the family "jolly boat," a kayak on wheels, which was towed behind a bicycle to transport children and worked better than the glider he built and tried in vain to get aloft on a run from a hilltop.

A PLUMBER IN A CASTLE

It chanced that in 1908, the year the Shurtleffs crowned Skim Milk Hill with their summer house, John Burnham Brown died, and after a few months his Castle Hill farm out at the end of Argilla Road was put up for sale. The following summer of 1909 President Taft spent on the Beverly shore, and it was persistently rumored that his brother Charles was buying the Brown estate in Ipswich.

It also chanced that summer that the President, having failed to convince his crony and Gloucester summer neighbor John Hays Hammond to accept the ambassadorship to China, instead named Charles R. Crane of Chicago, vice president of the Crane plumbing empire, who had traveled extensively in the Orient and, though a Democrat, supported Taft's Far East policy. En route to his post in China, however, Crane let fly some critical remarks about Japan, was summarily recalled by Secretary of State Philander Knox and resigned.

Charles Crane's younger brother, Richard Teller Crane, Jr., had been renting summer estates in Manchester since 1905 and was on the lookout for a spread he could call his own. Hearing about Castle Hill Farm, he inspected it one day and bought it the next. On January 14, 1910, papers were passed, and for a reported $125,000 the plumbing heir became the new owner of the farm, all of Castle Neck but the lighthouse, and Cedar

Point, eight hundred or so acres. With a stroke of the pen, a Yale man, class of '95, held the strategic high ground, most of the approaches by water and lowland, and nearly five miles of beach at the end of Harvard's Argilla Road. Had an Eli stolen a marsh on the Crimson?

Richard Crane, at thirty-six, was really an amiable and unpretentious man who carried his family wealth offhandedly enough. And yet the first thing he did was to put the Boston architects Shepley, Rutan and Coolidge to designing an Italianate mansion of about sixty-five rooms, some one hundred by three hundred feet, on the absolute crown of Castle Hill. Olmsted Brothers, the Boston landscape architects, created a matching Italian garden. Work was pushed with such speed that the next spring the Cranes and their household were able to move into their castle on Castle Hill, suddenly the lordliest and loftiest summer mansion on the North Shore. In all this may be detected the hand of Florence Crane, née Higinbotham, whose father, Harlow, rose from farm boy to partnership in Chicago with the mercantile genius Marshall Field, marrying her off to plumbing and her sister to publishing in the person of Joseph Medill Patterson. The Cranes arrived with their young son Cornelius and their daughter Florence, who would grow up to be Princess Belosselsky.

As he had swept up his tidy family fortune, Crane swept up Wigwam, Sagamore and Caverly hills, through Woodbury's Landing, around Hog (Choate) and Patterson's (Seeby's) islands and across a large farm adjoining Labor-in-Vain Creek, tearing down whatever shacks or sheds intruded on his view until he had about thirty-five hundred acres.

The Townsend family and friends were whiling away August of 1912 in one of those shanties and a spread of tents on the dunes above Castle Neck Beach, and the naturalist described in *Beach Grass* how they dined on fish,

Arthur Shurtleff's bicycle trailer, with his children Bill and Elizabeth in tow, 1913. (From Upon the Road Argilla.*)*

The Cranes' first castle on Castle Hill, new in 1911 but deemed inadequate by 1925. (From Upon the Road Argilla.)

clams and blackberries cooked over a driftwood fire, bathed in the ocean and slept, when they felt like it, under the stars. But as the Cranes gained dominion, such squatters were banished and the camps torn down or suffocated under the drifting dunes.

Still, better thus than the crowds brought to the shore by electric trolleys and motorcars, wrote Townsend. "Fortunate indeed are the birds and bird-lovers who can wander in a region unmarred and 'unimproved,' and grateful are they to anyone who can order such a state of affairs. May it always remain so!"

All did not at first share Dr. Townsend's farseeing approbation of his neighbor's territorial annexations. The gobbling-up of the five miles of Castle Neck Beach caused the *Ipswich Chronicle* to wonder why the selectmen hadn't been consulted prior to the sale, since the town claimed perpetual ownership for the public weal.

The new owner said nothing, but on the first of July of the first season of his tenure invited the entire Ipswich school population of nine hundred to his beach to celebrate Cornelius Crane's sixth birthday. Transportation was provided, and barge and boat rides. During swimming, Crane's men patrolled off the beach in his launch, and a first aid tent was pitched among the dunes, with doctor and nurses. Music by the United Shoe Machinery Company Band.

The next July, 1912, a thousand came down the Ipswich River in the excursion steamer *Carlotta* and a fleet of twenty motorboats for the occasion. After the third such beach party in 1913, an annual tradition now, the *Chronicle* was pleased to report that Mr. Crane's "controversy" with the town was being conducted most amicably, and he had made no effort whatsoever to bar the public from the beach to which he held title, legitimately or otherwise. By 1922, for Corny's seventeenth, fifteen hundred came down the river to, yes, "Crane's Beach" with their lunches; their host provided the ice cream and candy. For his twenty-first his father had the eighty-four-foot schooner *Me Gildis* built in Essex.

After President Taft's withdrawal of his ambassadorship to China in 1909, Charles Crane, in John Hays Hammond's peevish words, "in high dudgeon betook himself and his wealth to the opposing political camp where, through judicious campaign expenditures, he did much damage to his former political associates." The injured plumber first moved as far left in the Republican Party as there was room—to Senator Bob LaFollette and the Progressives—and then, as the 1912 election heated up, instead of bolting to Theodore Roosevelt and the Bull Mooses, leaped back to the Democrats as Wilson's heaviest campaign contributor. Thus in 1920 Charles Crane reached port as Wilson's minister to China, where he served, in the mining engineer's more generous estimation, with distinction.

Richard T. Crane, Sr., the blue-collar machinist who had founded the giant company and later branched out to dominate the elevator industry as well, died in 1912 at eighty. Charles succeeded him as president but in two years, preoccupied with politics and philanthropy, sold out his interests and turned over the pull chain to his younger brother—a metaphor that had earlier inspired a heraldist commissioned by the family to come up with a coat of arms (so Cleveland Amory claims in *Who Killed Society?*) which was rejected out of hand: "The shield was divided into four parts, including, in each section, a sink, a bathtub, etc. Over all was a hand gripping the handle of a chain—with the inevitable motto, '*Après moi le déluge.*'" Long before the rains descended on that dark day of 1929 the Cranes had equipped themselves with their private Pullman, *Nituna,* in which to arrive at Ipswich, fleets of shining motorcars in which to flee and, if the waters rose even unto the terraces of Castle Hill, a flotilla of arks (not hotels in their case) disguised as yachts.

ENTER THE FLIVVER

Dr. Crockett showed up with the first motorcar on Argilla Road, a 1903 Stanley Steamer that did not seduce his colleagues away from their bicycles, the colony's transport of choice to and from the Ipswich railroad depot. A very few of the Pillbox Colonists couldn't or wouldn't master the new mechanics, though they were adept enough at extracting a gallbladder, and set chauffeurs and even wives behind the wheels of a movable feast of conveyances—buggylike Stanleys, queer Hupmobiles and Pierce Arrows, a Peerless, a Napier, a Packard or two and even a Cadillac runabout purchased by the usually pedestrian Dr. Townsend. Ford flivvers predominated, befitting the rustic good life chosen by the Yankee Boston doctors.

The caravans of the family in the villa on the hill, of course, comprised huge Renaults, prepossessing Packards, overwhelming Cadillacs, gigantic

Dr. Charles W. Townsend in his new Cadillac at "Merula Farm," July 4, 1908. (From Upon the Road Argilla.*)*

Chalmerses, indescribable Rolls-Royces and even a Citroën desert half-track, with a top speed of ten miles an hour, that Crane thought would be great for dunes but never used. At the summit was Mrs. Crane's absolutely tremendous maroon Simplex, trimmed with German silver and upholstered in moleskin, which she ordered driven so sedately that her housekeeper, Mrs. Strahan, complained that one faithful family chauffeur, Alvin Johnson, "has only two speeds—DEAD SLOW and STOP!"

No chauffeur but Richard Crane himself was at the wheel of his Stevens Duryea roadster, emerging from Linebrook Road onto the Newburyport Turnpike one day in late summer of 1915. In the seat beside him was his old Yale classmate Benjamin Stickney Cable, President Taft's Assistant Secretary of Commerce and Labor, who was visiting at Castle Hill.

Suddenly they were struck by a car headed for Boston on the Pike and overturned. Crane was injured. Cable was killed. The other driver was Dr. David L. Edsall, the six-foot-four Jackson Professor of Clinical Medicine at Harvard Medical School and chief of the East Medical Service at the Massachusetts General Hospital, who was not seriously hurt, although his bride was thrown through the windshield and permanently scarred and lamed. When the case came to court, no blame was fixed, though both men were suspended from driving for six months. But Crane claimed that Edsall was indeed at fault, and there was a great stew in Boston.

In memory of his dead friend Crane built the Cable Memorial Hospital in Ipswich and never again, according to Shurcliff, took the wheel of a car. The impact on the Pillbox Colony of this tragic confrontation between their neighbor on the hill and their distinguished colleague, shortly to be the most famous dean in their medical school's history, may be judged from Shurcliff's omission of Dr. Edsall's identity from his bare account of the accident in his memoir *Upon the Road Argilla*.

TWO CASTLES FOR MR. CRANE

In his last major "private work" before World War I rendered such fancies inconsistent with the national interest, Crane had engaged his neighbor Arthur Shurtleff to design a mall dipping down from the mansion on Castle Hill and up slightly over lesser Steep Hill, then tobogganing off into the ocean—half a mile in length, 160 feet wide, of velvety grass lined with statuary and four rows of evergreens standing at arms, described in the press as "the most splendid thing of its kind in this or any country" in the fall of 1913.

With the resumption of such extravagances after the war, Crane decided he must have a superintendent, and none but the best. He interviewed Robert Cameron, who had been tending the Harvard Botanic Garden, and revealed to the Scot a bit of himself: "I don't want a man to come to Ipswich and think that I am anything more than any other man. I do not want a man to come to Ipswich that cannot get along with the people there. I want the people of Ipswich to have a kindly feeling towards my family." That understood, Mr. Cameron went to work.

To complement the magnificence of his mall, Shurtleff conceived broad avenues winding up from Argilla Road to the mansion amongst rare trees, exotic flora and native fauna for which he created a deer park, a maze, gardens and groves. His Scots spirit renewed by travels across America and back to Britain inspecting great gardens everywhere at the laird's expense, Cameron created vegetable gardens, a rose garden of six hundred varieties, ponds scalloped from the earth for watering it all and lawns without end. Crane decreed that one of his farms become the private Labor-in-Vain Golf Course, that a lake-sized swimming pool be scooped out, that there be a casino, a guest house for bachelors and cottages for Cameron, his head farmer and his gamekeeper. And all materialized.

In about 1919 Richard Crane bought up Hog Island and had the dozen or so scanty summer cottages there torn down—all but the almost two-hundred-year-old homestead on Choate Hill and a barn that he carefully preserved. He directed Cameron to provide this bald drumlin on his horizon with a headpiece of a hundred thousand trees. The word, as usual, was father to the deed.

In the spring of 1925 the plumbing king was feeling so royally flush that he ordered his Italianate villa of sixty-five (more or less) rooms torn down. It *was* fourteen years old, after all, and was believed by its owners, so reported the *Boston Evening Transcript,* to be inadequate.

Within a few months David Adler, a Chicago architect, was supervising the construction of the replacement. "The Great House" it would be called, Georgian in style, in a fashion that might or might not have elicited an ironic comment from the English satirical artist William Hogarth, whose

Richard T. Crane at the helm of his yawl Northern Light, *about 1927. (From* Upon the Road Argilla.*)*

house in London Crane bought and stripped of four rooms, which he had reassembled within the walls of Dutch brick and Ohio limestone atop remote and windy Castle Hill in the simple New England country town of Ipswich, Massachusetts.

"The Great House" was pronounced by the Cranes as quite adequate, though it contained only forty-nine rooms. Five years passed, and on November 7, 1931, his fifty-eighth birthday, the son of the machinist died.

In 1945 Florence Crane gave a thousand acres—most of Crane's Beach and Castle Neck—to the Trustees of Public Reservations, as they were then called. This nonprofit institutional device for holding on to the beautiful lands of Massachusetts, hopefully forever, had been the inspiration in 1890 of Charles Eliot, son of the president of Harvard, a young landscape architect who had sat at the feet, as had Arthur Shurtleff, of the great Frederick Law Olmsted.

Thus were the fears of the Ipswich selectmen put to rest.

When Richard Crane's widow died in 1949 she bequeathed "The Great House" and about three hundred surrounding acres to the Trustees. Having no endowment, they were about to raze it when in 1950 Harold F. Lindergreen founded a summer art school there, and the next year a series of six summer concerts was arranged by Samuel L. M. Barlow, composer and summer resident of Gloucester's Eastern Point. The Castle Hill Foundation carried on under the jocular impetus of David Crockett, son of the doctor who had led the pillbox colonization in the days of windmills and jolly boats.

Fascinated with the Far East like his Uncle Charles, slim, shy Cornelius Crane led an anthropological expedition to the South Pacific with his chum Sidney Shurcliff. In 1955 he married a beautiful and artistic Japanese girl, Mine Sawaraha, in Tokyo. "Corny" died in 1962 and was buried on the high ground of Hog Island. In 1974 his widow gave the Trustees of Reservations the Cornelius and Mine S. Crane Reservation, another seven hundred acres of marshes, dunes, and islands, including Hog.

That double-lived Argilla Roader, Dr. Charles Townsend, had summed it all up in advance in *Beach Grass:* "Growing near the edge of the dunes at the foot of Castle Hill is a willow of great age, a veteran, with split and hollow bole, unable longer to hold up its great branches which rest on the ground. In touching the ground it has renewed its life like Antaeus of old or like the banyan tree, and has taken root and sent up fresh and vigorous willow saplings."

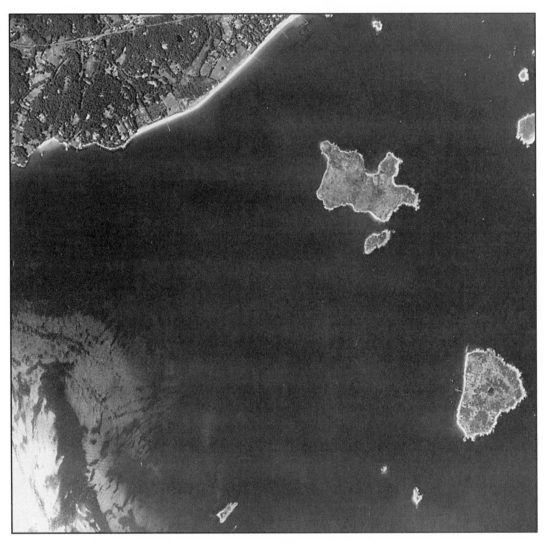

Keeping a respectful distance from West Beach (top left) while guarding the channel into Salem Harbor are Misery Island, with Little Misery tagging along, and Baker's Island. (Beverly Historical Society)

~14~
A TALE OF TWO ISLANDS

Tight little Baker's, and the company-loving Misery

Of the North Shore's thirty or so vegetative rocks and sandbars sometimes flattered by the capricious cartographer as islands, hardly more than half are even marginally habitable. Of those capable of sustaining a human toehold, six have been connected to the mainland, including Deer, which is a Boston prison colony, Winter, which is Salem's hoary chowder and marching ground, and Five Pound, literally swallowed up by Gloucester's state fish pier.

Among the remainder, only on the twin sentinels of the Salem ship channel, Baker's and Misery, has chance favored the spontaneous generation of a bona fide summer colony bearing any semblance of social organization; and that on Baker's alone has survived. With few exceptions, islands of the North Shore unlucky enough to stand in the way of the Atlantic swells are inhospitable to all but the sea birds and stray seals.

Great Misery, eighty-nine acres, with Little Misery snuggled under its southern shore, is half a mile from Beverly's West Beach. Offshore another three quarters of a mile across the main ship channel out of Salem Bay lies Baker's, shy of sixty acres, beset to the south and west by a wretched maze of rocks and ledge and shoal that makes the passage to Salem (absentee tax collector for both islands), Beverly and Marblehead a tricky trial in fog or dark, and sometimes in broad daylight too, as I once learned to my chagrin.

BAKER'S COMES INTO ITS OWN

Baker's is not so elevated but commands the bay as Misery can't, so its north shore was the logical site for a pair of lighthouses built in 1798. For the next century and a quarter they were familiarly addressed as Ma and Pa Baker; Ma, the shorter, was gracelessly dismantled in 1926. East of the lights the Salem pilots built their lookout shack with bunks and with peepholes facing out to sea so they could look for vessels needing guidance through the twisty channel. Any island with both a lighthouse and a pilothouse is off to a good start. Misery, poor Misery, had neither, nor even a clue to the origin of such a prejudicial name.

Once timbered, storm-swept Baker's never recovered from colonial cutting and went to pasture, good forage for the farmers of Salem who ferried their stock out for the summer, and themselves and their families back and forth for picnics. In the late 1870s Thomas Gilbert ran the only farm on the island, keeping hens, geese, ducks, a couple dozen cows and a bull that had the brass one day to charge no less a personage than George Dewey, the lighthouse inspector who had rowed out in his skiff. "Kill that bull!" the hero-to-be of Manila Bay screamed at keeper Walter Rogers, leaping back in his boat. "I'd rather go into an engagement any day than face that beast!"

Bracing sea air, good food and ample exercise had worked wonders for keeper Rogers, who set foot on Baker's feeling poorly and weighing 101 pounds, and retired back to the mainland at 226. The same ameliorative conditions weighed as heavily with Dr. Nathan R. Morse of Salem, induced by a patient who owned one of the ten cottages to join him in the summer of 1882. Dr. Morse was recovering from an accident and mended so miraculously that he returned the following summer with a tent, then bought one of the pilots' shacks, built his own cottage in 1885, and bought the entire island except the lighthouse reservation from its Marblehead owner in 1887.

The Salem doctor's grand plan unfolded in 1888 with the opening of the "Winne-egan" (Indian, supposedly, for "beautiful expanse of water"), a health spa that he announced as "a most delightful place of retirement from the heat of summers, the annoyance of mosquitoes, the cares of business and a sure tonic and a perfect panacea for the tired and worn-out nervous system, *neurasthenia*, so common nowadays."

The Winne-egan, Baker Island's only summer hotel. (Peabody Essex Museum)

In fact, the enthusiastic Dr. Morse was a homeopathic physician, professor of the diseases of women and children at the Boston University School of Medicine. His latest venture must have been influenced by the success on smaller Cat Island, a mile and a half toward Marblehead Neck, of the Children's Island Sanatorium, formerly the Lowell Island House, as it

was familiarly called when that rock patch of many aliases was the resort of the summer crowd from Lowell.

Joyfully proclaiming that his island air was "highly charged with ozone from the ocean," the jolly homeopathist fed his guests from the island farm, watered them from the well he dug and from the middle of the three ponds which he deepened and walled, cooled their brows with the ice that keeper Rogers cut for him in the dead of the island winter, and warmed their souls with Sunday evening "praise meetings." He got the steam ferry service from the electric trolley line extended to the island, with six trips a day. Before the first pier was built out from the western beach, passengers hitched themselves over the rail of the ferry into a scow that was hauled to shore by block and tackle, and walked a plank to dry land—exceeding dry, since the deeds for the eighteen cottage lots Dr. Morse sold off during his tenure forbade the sale or even gift of alcoholic drinks on the premises.

In 1892 the doctor turned over the active management of the Winnee-egan to his son Henry. Before he died in 1897 his pride and joy boasted an addition, seventy-five rooms, a café, a tennis court and a bulging register (1,013 guests in the peak year of 1894) that featured the signatures of former President Benjamin Harrison and actress Lillian Russell.

Dr. Morse had somehow managed to impose a six-hole golf course on terrain whose natural challenges were multiplied by the haphazard croppings and droppings of the livestock pastured thereon. This motley herd protested when the bureaucracy replaced Ma and Pa Baker's old familiar fog bell in 1907 with a compressed air siren. At the first blast, wrote De Witt D. Wise, the island's historian in *Now, Then, Baker's Island,* "they, with one exception, stuck their tails in the air and headed for the southern part of the island. One cow, intrigued by the bovine-like sounds, thrust her head through the strands of the government fence and answered it—moo for moo—until it stopped."

Taking their cue from their kine, the two-legged islanders and the more wealthy and influential mainland summerers were soon in full moo against the horrid siren themselves. They held meetings and hired a lawyer to harass the government to take it away, and to hell with fogbound mariners. Sure enough, by the end of the season Baker's fog siren had been aimed out to sea through a tremendous megaphone, to the relief of animal and man.

Unfortunately for Henry Morse's efforts to beef up his offerings with Saturday night hops and a darkroom for "fiends" of the new Kodak, the ferry *Surf City* was returning to Beverly from the island on the Fourth of July, 1898, after disembarking passengers at Salem Willows, when she was struck by one of those savage squalls that erupt so unexpectedly across Salem Bay; she swamped and sank like a stone. Though in less than seven feet of water, eight of the sixty aboard—all women and children—were trapped in the cabin and drowned. A few years after this tragedy, Henry Morse's career as a summer hotel proprietor ended as abruptly one chilly day in the early spring of 1906 when his caretaker fired up one of the stoves and then fell asleep. The room caught, the barking of his faithful dog roused the sleeper, and he fled. But the Winne-egan, after eighteen interesting seasons, went up in flames.

Burned out, Henry sold out in 1909 to his brother, Dr. Charles Morse, who collaborated with their uncle, Dr. Martin van Buren Morse, and the latter's wife in further subdivision of the family's holdings that resulted in a final building boom of twenty more cottages before America entered World War I. Martin was a homeopathist too, and he and Clara made enough money at a dollar a bottle with their home-made "Syrup of Hypophosphites" to buy themselves a grapefruit plantation down south, which they sold to pay off the Baker's Island mortgage.

The loss of the Winne-egan and sale of most of the Morse holdings left the cottage owners momentarily without the catalyst that had attracted them to the island in the first place. The hotel had been the social and religious center for a fun-loving but God-fearing summer colony, and the Morses had got things done. Faced with languishing ferry service and a rotting pier, the islanders in 1914 organized the Baker's Island Association to advance their welfare and reestablish Sunday religious services. Their object was self-government, since about all they got from the city of Salem was receipts for their taxes—and for that they had to supply their own post office, namely the old pilots' shack, "Driftwood," which had been moved hither and yon about the island behind a Model T Ford, finally coming to rest as their combination mail drop, shop, library and social center.

As the years passed, the association ensured reliable ferry and divine services, provided fire protection, kept up the roads, held up the pier, ran the store, chaperoned social events, and once, when the pond looked alarmingly low during a drought in the early 1960s, wondered about tapping a supposed subterranean stream that someone claimed ran from Rowley to

Milton by way of Baker's Island—the questionable evidence being that the levels of the island's reservoir and Wenham Lake seemed to correspond.

By the mid-1920s there were 58 snug cottages and 170 congenial summer souls on Baker's, a census and a consensus, virtually unchanged fifty-five years later. A happy and unpretentious island, an island that works, a tight little island—but a dry one—officially—as Dr. Nathan Morse had wisely decreed by word and deed.

Beverly young people's picnic at Saint's Rest Cottage, Misery Island, early 1880s. (Beverly Historical Society)

THE HEYDAY OF MISERY ISLAND

Misery Island's misery probably has to do with some dire shipwreck of colonial times like the woe of Norman's Woe, the stark hunk of rock five miles down the coast on which Longfellow cast up his mythical *Hesperus*. Because the island is rough and gouged by a shallow valley cradling a small pond, Salem leased it out for nothing better than pasturage as early as 1628. In 1705 smallpox victims were banished there during an epidemic that swept the mainland. Several generations of the Dodge family of Wenham owned Misery, carrying on with what by then appears to have become the traditional practice of rowing the spring calf out from West Beach for a free ride in the dory and letting the fatted heifer swim back astern in the fall.

Daniel Neville, an Irish immigrant who made his living quarrying stone from the islands of Boston Harbor, bought Misery in 1849 and after a while settled there with his family to farm and fish. Robert Rantoul, the Salem historian, described Neville as the affable "Lord of the Isles," who regaled visitors with the hospitality of his farm. Chief among them was Chief Justice Salmon P. Chase of the U.S. Supreme Court, who arrived in the west cove

The Hollander cottage on Misery Island with its famous thatched roof. (Trustees of Reservations)

on July 26, 1865, aboard the revenue boat *Excelsior* with his friend the state treasurer, General Henry K. Oliver, for a chowder party on the island. The jurist was a large man indeed, and his transfer to land dry-shod was in some doubt until General Oliver, who was nothing if not a classicist, supporting Justice Chase on the one side, carried the day on the other with the assistance of Plutarch: "*Ne time quicquam! Caesarem* [he pronounced it 'Chaserem'] *vehis!*" meaning roughly, "You have nothing to fear! You travel with Caesar" (or, in this case, Chase).

A more recent chronicler of the Miserys, however, Reed Harwood, had it from a descendant that Lord Neville in truth spent much of his time chasing the less distinguished off his domain. Whatever his disposition, he died in 1885. His farmhouse burned ten years later. In 1897 his widow followed him, and in 1900 Great Misery was sold by her executors for ten times its valuation of six thousand dollars to a Newton man, who sold it to a group of speculative enthusiasts, whose bites, it would all too soon turn out, were much too big for their bellies. Under the banner of Charles Stedman Hanks and Thomas W. Peirce, Boston and North Shore, the Misery Island Syndicate had hardly entered its deed in the Salem registry that spring when the members were floating out to their new holdings, blueprints in hand, on a $100,000 mortgage.

At the same time Hanks et al organized the Misery Island Club with himself as president. They issued a membership call at twenty-five dollars per annum to the select of the Shore, bought a pair of naphtha launches, *Josephine* of thirty feet and *Lizzie* of eighteen, and built a pier on the west shore of the cove opposite Beverly Farms, the idea being that a member could be ferried to the mainland, walk the five minutes to the Farms depot, and be in Boston within an hour.

The syndicate dammed a portion of the cove to make a saltwater swimming pool, erected the "Custom House" at the head of the pier, converted into a bathhouse an existing cottage moved from the west side of the island, dug a well, and raised a water tower. Guest cottages materialized, "The Governor's Palace" and "The Castle," and servants' quarters. A clubhouse rose above the west shore of the cove. A trapshooting range appeared, and a tennis court. An old boathouse was resurrected as a caddie house and locker room, and to go with it, a nine-hole golf course of 2,610 well-bent yards was squeezed with the greatest ingenuity out of the Neville pastures. Finally, another old cottage was rolled down to the cove as the Misery Island station of the Manchester Yacht Club, and a regatta committee was appointed.

The speed of the promotion was exceeded only by its dazzle. Late that same spring of 1900 the Misery Island Club published a snazzy book bound in red and green, with its hurriedly conceived pennant imprinted in gold on the cover—a seahorse on a folded anchor—and the motto: *Te salutamus miseria comitatum amat.* The first invitational golf tournament came off on June 30, with thirty-seven clubs represented. Thirty boats competed in the first three-day regatta a month later. By the end of the first season more than 260 of the better-known figures of Boston and the Shore were intrigued enough by the bizarre island setup to sign on the line.

The Misery Island Club's second season got off to a rouser of a start

Madam takes aim on the Misery Island shooting range. (Peabody Essex Museum)

The "Mystery" Island Casino and landing, probably 1912. (Trustees of Reservations)

with the combined reunions in June of the Harvard classes of 1886 and 1891. They marched boisterously up and down the new carriage road behind their band, shared an al fresco luncheon, had an unsteady round of golf, and wound up the day with a chorus of college songs to the presumed delight of the mainlanders, for, in Rantoul's words, "the wind happened to favor the shore that day, so that the music lost nothing when wafted across the water."

And yet, within a week, President Hanks was most disingenuously informing a reporter: "Here we are isolated and run little risk of intrusion. There is no temptation for display, as people cannot exhibit their expensive equipages [then why the expensive carriage road?], and those who wear expensive clothes will ruin them. There are no servants in livery or any similar indications of formal life. It is a place to rest in, and nature has done what she could to the island to make this possible. Here one finds liberty and privacy, things most desired in modern civilization." But nary a word about solvency from the president, who neglected to mention that back in January the first disagreeable dissent had been raised: the contractor who built the new clubhouse filed a lien against them for $782.87 in unpaid bills.

Nevertheless, the 1901 roster swelled to 350. Regular steam ferry service to West Beach was arranged. A second golf meet was managed, and a second regatta, with ten classes, and the Salem Cadet Band.

But 'twas all puff. The Misery Island Club survived its third season,

1902, at the end of which the city of Salem demanded $685.20 in back taxes. So it expired—golf, regattas, trapshoots, brass bands, cool July evening galas, gilded seahorse and all. For that was but the iceberg's tip; the syndicate, it seemed, owed $35,000 in notes and $45,000 in bills. For two years the miserable corpse was clobbered. Salem auctioned it off twice for taxes, and the bank foreclosed and sold the island for $5,000 to the trustees for the bondholders, who got rid of three one-acre lots for $5,000 each, with plans for more subdivision, and turned the clubhouse into the euphemistically named Beverly Farms Island Inn.

Rumors that certain creditors wanted to buy the island and make another Revere Beach of it caused a frightful stir on the porches of Beverly, which was not at all quieted by an alternative suggestion from Senator Winthrop Murray Crane, a figure to be reckoned with in Washington, that Misery be acquired for the construction of a national leper hospital.

With the transition to a compact summer colony gathering around a modest inn, the fortunes of Misery again rose. A few more summer cottage lots were sold. John H. Harwood of Brookline bought one on the west shore in 1909 and built a large double-winged bungalow named, in the spirit of the island, "Bleak House." Here his son Reed, who after fifty years wrote nostalgically and bitterly of the island's history and fate, spent the happiest summers of his childhood with his brothers and buddies.

The leading shareholder and figure in the renewed try at making Misery pay was Jacob Rogers, one of the original syndicators. Rogers put up a cottage and strove to put across the Casino, as they decided, unfortunately, to call the former club. He plumped doggedly and without success to get the island's equally invidious name changed officially to Mystery—even pushing a quixotic petition in 1911 to persuade the legislature to incorporate "Mystery Islands" and its dozen summer cottages as a separate town, since they got nothing from Salem for their taxes.

Jake Rogers survived in Reed Harwood's mind's eye as "a dapper man dressed in a blue serge jacket and white flannels, with a stiff straw hat"— hardly the type to promote, one suspects, the proposal of the Pride's Crossing contractor Daniel Linehan to erect barracks on Misery Island for his foreign-born laborers, mainly Italians and Poles, making of it a sort of private Ellis Island to which these necessary undesirables would be ferried every night after work, out of sight and smell of tender sensibilities.

These years before the storm were Misery's least miserable. The island had a summer population of a hundred. Businessmen took the ferry or their own motorboats to the West Beach landing, walked up to the Farms depot, and commuted weekdays to their offices in Boston. Gus Reugman, the Swedish caretaker, kept an eye on the Casino, ran the engine that pumped freshwater from the well up into the tank, and delivered to the cottagers ice that he had cut from the pond during the winter. When heavy supplies were wanted on the island, he towed them over behind his launch in a scow.

The Casino rocked with gaiety and parties as the war rolled across the

Atlantic. But ominously at the end of the 1915 season the trust mortgaged its seventy-seven acres against fifteen thousand dollars in debts, though the Casino opened in 1916 as usual.

But when 1917 dawned like thunder, the property again changed hands, new money was found, and the summer was spent adding an annex to sleep an expected overflow that never came. It was wartime. The Casino, alias the Mystery Island Inn, alias the Beverly Farms Island Inn, née the Misery Island Club, never again opened its doors. The foreclosure in 1918 locked the lid. Even the concrete hangar that Godfrey Cabot had built on the west shore for his experiments with refueling seaplanes in flight was abandoned when he entered active service in 1917.

A litany of miscalculation, bad luck and failure, as Dr. Harwood ruefully reviewed it. Misery had a bad name to begin with, and the shady connotations of the Casino didn't help. The carriage road was a waste of money, the golf course couldn't pay for itself, the telephone was an unreliable party line, there was no electricity, a new steam launch blew up at its mooring, and the 3,500-foot freshwater pipe laid all the way from Pride's Crossing in 1913 cracked somewhere between the shore and the island and delivered sea water to the storage tank. But least forgivably, the founding syndicate had overcapitalized this relatively inaccessible seasonal weekend operation, overestimating by far its revenue potential.

The final demise of the Casino left the seven or eight families remaining on Misery Island in 1917 the sole beneficiaries of the prized liberty and privacy Charles Stedman Hanks had so hoped to share with 350 paying kindred spirits sixteen years earlier. The golf course returned to nature, the ocean reclaimed the swimming pool, crabgrass recaptured the tennis court, and rabbits reproduced with abandon in the cool spaces beneath the deserted clubhouse. Ironically, the privacy got to be too much of a good thing for most of the cottagers, and none but the Harwoods returned for the 1919 season.

And now the three "Bleak House" boys had the whole domain of Misery from shore to shore to themselves. They worked the Harwood victory garden, raised chickens, fished and lobstered, rowed the family maids to the mainland for mass at Beverly Farms, and pitted their wits against the caretaker's successfully enough to break into the shuttered cottages for games of hide-and-seek and pillow fights.

Their last year was 1920. Mrs. Harwood had had enough of the loneliness, and the family never returned. Caretaker Reugman was left Lord of the Isles. On May 7, 1926, the Casino with all its cottages, the barn, the water tower and one of the private houses burned to the foundations when a brush fire ran out of control. The rabbits panicked, bounded into the sea, and drowned.

Again Misery was sold. Years passed, and in 1935 a Beverly oil dealer wanted to erect storage tanks for twelve million gallons of oil on the island. The Salem city council turned him down after a howl arose up and down the Shore. This time an alarmed group of citizens chipped in and once more

bought most of Misery and gave it to the Trustees of Public Reservations in perpetuity.

One cottage after another succumbed to neglect, destruction and fire, until all were gone, even Godfrey Cabot's concrete hydroplane hangar, demolished . . . all save one. Joseph B. Henderson cut his house in half and moved it by lighter to Marblehead, where he rejoined it to his satisfaction.

Today Baker's thrives, and Misery—well, Misery loves company, unrequited.

Veranda Cottage, Great Misery Island, 1912. (Trustees of Reservations)

Bryn Allan's coach-and-four in front of the old entrance at the Myopia Hunt Club in Hamilton, 1890s. (Myopia Hunt Club)

~15~
KING OF CLUBS

Is Myopia Brahminism's rowdy fringe?

> "Get to your places!" shouted the Queen in a voice of
> thunder, and people began running about in all directions,
> tumbling up against each other; however, they got settled
> down in a minute or two, and the game began.
> —*Alice's Adventures in Wonderland*

IF CLUBISHNESS IS KING ALONG
the North Shore, then Myopia by uncommon consent must be King of
Clubs. The name is as odd as the game, which consists in its most traditional
form of pursuing the fleeing fox or, for lack of one, a bag called a drag. No
other private club around, few anywhere, can touch the Myopia Hunt for
the panache with which its roster dashes faster, ever faster, across the rolling
wonderland of Hamilton and environs.

There are other suits, too, besides hunting pink, in this sometimes very
loaded deck—steeplechasers, polo players, golf addicts, tennis fiends,
backgammon nuts, boozers and even a few cards—a deck that thrives in
scornful defiance of what passes for reality all about.

The October horseman is oft the August helmsman, and the more
tightly knit King of Clubs has for a very long time shared the realm of social
governance on the North Shore with Marblehead's Eastern Yacht Club,
Queen of the Waves. Their Jack is the Essex County (a country) Club of
Manchester, whose badges of office are burnished each June by the annual
one-day laying-on of hands of Harvard's twenty-fifth reunion class.

Myopia began royally enough, not on the North Shore but on the
Winchester country estate of Frederick O. Prince, a wealthy Boston lawyer.
His four stalwart scions—Frederick H., Gordon, Charles, and Morton—reveled in the rural life, rowed and sailed, and helped Dr. Jim Dwight of Nahant
set up one of the first tennis courts in America on their property. In July
1876, while their father was running successfully for mayor of Boston, they
organized with their friends a baseball team that demanded a name. The
brothers were all nearsighted, a family trait. Hey, how about "Myopia"?

Mayor *O'Prince,* as some democratizer tagged him, pulled the table out
from under the boys when he decided to summer in Nahant in 1878 and
take his kitchen staff with him. His sons countered with a clubhouse on the
two hundred Princely acres overlooking Mystic Lake, on what came to be

MYOPIA CLVB WINCHESTER 1875 = 1881
INCORPORATED 1879
MYOPIA CLVB·RACE MEETING CLYDE PARK 1879
HOVNDS HVNTED IN BROOKLINE, WINCHESTER
AND IPSWICH 1881
MYOPIA FOX HOVNDS ORGANIZED 1882
FIRST HVNTED AT HAMILTON 1882
MYOPIA HVNT CLVB 1883, INCORPORAED 1892

known as Myopia Hill. Next year they incorporated as the Myopia Club, with an almost instant membership of 150 drawn mainly from the rosters of the exclusive Somerset and University clubs of Boston. Among their festivities, fueled by drafts of Myopia Punch, was the Myopia Landslide, which they pulled on a visiting Englishman one evening at a Lexington hotel by suddenly lifting up one end of the table. Not subtle, but effective. The table was long, and so was the landlord's bill, recalled their first president, Marshall K. Abbott, "as a successful land-slide necessitates the smashing of much crockery."

Britain took its vengeance on the Yankees by exporting the recently devised sport of fox hunting in costume, a deviate form of chase that Oscar Wilde twitted as "the unspeakable in full pursuit of the uneatable." But Fred H. Prince, a hard rider like his brothers, discovered it to his delight among Anglophilic friends at Newport and Long Island. In the fall of 1881 Prince infected his brethren o'er the bumpy hills and dales of Winchester behind a borrowed pack of hounds, and forthwith Myopia must have its own. The following spring the club's pioneer pack arrived freight-free on one of member George Warren's Warren Line steamships, purchased from Lord Willoughby de Broke, master of the South Warwickshire hounds.

The rough and wooded terrain of Winchester did not suit two particularly influential members, Charles H. Dalton, chairman of the Boston Park Commission, and William Appleton, whose ancestral Appleton Farms in Ipswich, spilling over into Hamilton, the Myopians had assayed in 1881. The two persuaded the club to rent the open, rolling acres of the Dodge farm in

George Peabody Gardner on the veranda of the old Myopia Club in Winchester, about 1882. (Myopia Hunt Club)

THIS HOVSE RAISED BY COL. ROBERT DODGE
MAY 14, 1772
SOLD BY DODGE FAMILY TO JOHN GIBNEY 1866
LEASED FROM GIBNEYS BY MYOPIA FOX HOVNDS
1882 AND BY MYOPIA HVNT CLVB 1883 - 1891
BOVGHT BY MYOPIA HVNT CLVB DEC. 16 1891
FIRST POLO GAME, GIBNEY FARM 1888
GOLF FORMALLY INTRODVCED 1894

The history of Myopia as inscribed above a fireplace in the Hamilton clubhouse. (Myopia Hunt Club)

Hamilton (the pleasant old farmhouse was raised in 1772 by Robert Dodge before he went off to fight in the Revolution) from its owner, John Gibney, a Salem leather manufacturer. Meanwhile, a group of Boston sports lovers that numbered several Myopians organized what they called simply The Country Club at Clyde Park in rural Brookline, just beginning its rise as the richest suburb in America in its day. These splinterers proposed to absorb within this first of the country clubs the Myopia Club, whose residual identity was salvaged by a simple change of name to Myopia Fox Hounds, designating its narrowed pursuits.

All this was in 1882, and for nearly ten years Milord's hounds and their heirs and assigns bayed after the genuine scent or the as irresistible anise bag dragged ahead by a rider who thought like a fox and followed at full gallop by the pink-and-canary-coated Yankees of Boston. Hill and dale they traversed, to the cry of the master's horn, through copse and thicket, over fence and stone wall, across field and stream and ditch, and wherever a run of open country presented itself, sometimes upon the invitation of the owner, sometimes not.

Winchester was forsaken in 1883, to the regret of local people who had succumbed to the color and excitement of it all, but in those days most of the towns to the west and south of Boston were not yet suburbs, and the shout of Tallyho! and crack of collarbone echoed not only through Hamilton, Wenham and Ipswich on the North Shore, but across the meadows and over the hedges of Brookline, Dedham, Westwood, Milton, Newton, Framingham, Southboro, Lexington and doubtless elsewhere.

From the offshore loftiness of Nahant, Judge Grant was mildly amused that "the beautiful inland country about Wenham, Hamilton and Topsfield has become a race-course for this hunting element, many of whom do not hesitate to risk life and limb in their almost hysterical enjoyment of the transplanted ancient sport." The farmers, His Honor had heard, "were at first inclined to resent this new invasion of redcoats as undemocratic impertinence and a legal trespass. But well-mannered tact, especially if it go hand-and-glove with liberal indemnity, will mollify the wounded pride even of a New England farmer. By degrees the hardheaded countrymen, who sniffed

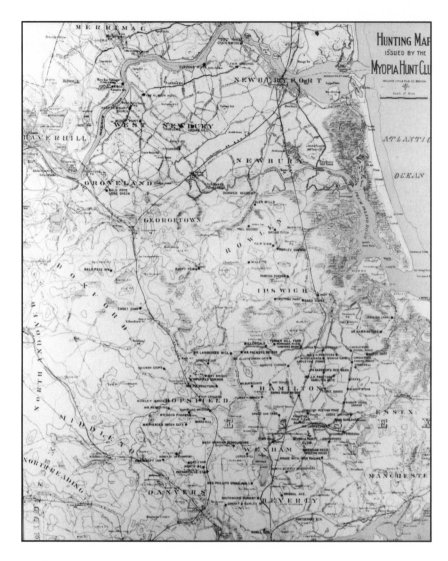

at fox-hunting as mere Anglomania, have become genuinely, though grimly, enthralled by the pomp and excitement of the show."

Among the obdurately unmollified was Louis Dodge, who prided himself on the evenness of his stone walls, over one of which the overbearing Freddie Prince was practicing jumps one day with his horses and grooms. Soon the stones were flying. The owner appeared and stood watching in grim silence. "Out of the way, my good man!" shouted Prince as he flew by . . . "And that," said Mrs. Hilda Ayer, "was the end of that!"

To smooth rural feathers, the club in 1882 staged a season's-end ball for its neighbors "at which the wives and daughters of the countryside," Judge Grant wrote, "dance with the master of the hounds and his splendid company, who valiantly, if vainly, endeavor to cut pigeon-wings in emulation of the country swains." Pigeon-wings were no match for swallowtails, however, and the annual Myopia Hunt Ball was relocated in Boston. For the neighbors left behind, the club in 1890 set up "Labor Day Sports," in which the swains were allowed limited participation, until this event, too, was refined as the Myopia Horse Show six years later. The Hunt Ball came to be considered the social highlight of the Boston season, always marked, if not distinguished, by humorous pratfalls brought on by the mixture of alcohol and arrogance.

At the successful conclusion of the hunt, Reynard was systematically dismembered, and his brush, mask and pads (that is, his tail, face and feet) were distributed to those veteran Myopians, male or female (the women superbly on sidesaddle in the early days, including Mrs. Jack Gardner, who would try anything) deemed by the master to have ridden hardest and best, in descending order; the fox blood, it is said, was smeared on the visages of the initiates. But the bag of anise seed (succeeded in recent years by a foul mixture of animal droppings, mineral oil and hot water) had pretty much replaced Br'er Fox by 1890. The ground was too broken on the inland North Shore (thirty-mile chases are recorded), the chase too often ending with the wily prey's disappearance, exhausted but intact, in Wenham Swamp.

Owner John Gibney died, and in 1891 (after almost accepting the Boston tycoon T. Jefferson Coolidge's offer of his Manchester estate, already hemmed in by shoreline development, at a rent equal to the town tax) the club bought the Dodge farm with its 150 acres from his heirs for twenty thousand dollars. The farmhouse was remodeled to suit the club's purposes.

That was the year polo came to Myopia, and with it the rivalry with the

Meeting of the Thanksgiving Day hunt, probably in 1905. (Myopia Hunt Club)

Dedham Polo and Country Club. The field was rough and the action ragged, and at the conclusion of their first match a Myopia wit commented that the best playing was done by the band. Polo was crashing, bashing madness on horseback (two players locked in combat chased the ball off the field onto the tennis courts one year, and James H. Proctor, an early veteran, proudly displayed in his home a mallet with his two front teeth embedded in it). The King of Sports deserved kingly spectatorship, and in the 1890s the coaches *Myopia* and *Constitution*, behind marvelously matched four-in-hands, leaped and lurched over the dirt roads from Manchester and Pride's Crossing, laden with top-hatted toffs and their dustered ladies, bound for the play at Hamilton.

But the hunt still reigned supreme. Presiding over all this tallyho was a succession of masters of foxhounds (MFHs) beginning with Frank Seabury, a ramrod rider who maneuvered his hunt across the farms of the yeomanry with the command of a Washington and the tact of a Franklin. His successor in 1892, Randolph M. (Bud) Appleton of the Ipswich squirearchy, consolidated Seabury's diplomatic conquests (one farmer even planted and harvested his turnips early so the club could range freely across his patches) and handed over the horn in 1901 to George S. Mandell.

Mandell ran the family newspaper, the voice of Brahminism, the *Boston Evening Transcript.* His creed: "We run no prize fights, no scandals, no divorce cases and no debasing sensational matter of any kind. We mention only the weddings and deaths of prominent people." The decade of

Mandell's mastership at Myopia passed serenely, and in 1911 he was succeeded by his predecessor's younger bachelor brother, James W. Appleton—"Mr. Jimmy"—the most popular of all MFHs and durable, for he served until 1935 with only a two-year break for World War I.

While a fox, an anise bag and even a polo ball were considered objects of horseback pursuit worthy of the true Myopian, a lump of gutta-percha, afoot, was not. MPH Bud Appleton encountered derision and dismay when in 1894 he suggested that the club follow his lead (the family had recently put in a crude course on the farm) and lay out nine holes of its own. As Edward Weeks, another journalist-Myopian (but a golfer, not a hunter) tells it in his history of the club, the only other links around, as golf swept the country in the 1890s, were a nine-holer at Pride's Crossing (long since abandoned), a six-holer at the Essex County Club in Manchester, and The Country Club's six in Brookline, all opened in 1893.

The derision of the equestrians at such pedestrian sport was exceeded only by their paradoxical dismay that the terrain was too rough for it. But the MFH won the day. The fairways were laid out and put to sheep, and a few infidels were soon whacking their unfamiliar way toward the greens.

Fortunately for the future of the game at Myopia, Herbert C. Leeds joined the club in 1896. "Papa" Leeds (a bachelor) immediately dominated the sport at Hamilton. In two more years the long faces were proved right: the terrain was rough and tough, so tough that in 1898 the first of many National Open Championships was played there. Land was bought, and more leased, and Papa himself—with a diabolical feel for the game and the terrain—laid out a new eighteen-hole course, which opened in 1900.

"Mr. Jimmy" Appleton with the hounds. (Myopia Hunt Club)

Polo for the myopic? For several years, "pushball" was played at the annual horse show. Here, in 1910, Edith Deacon, Alice Thorndike and Mary Curtis take on Catherine Tweed, Olivia Thorndike and Faith Simkins. (C. G. Rice collection)

Brilliantly conceived, Myopia's for years was regarded as among the most challenging in the country, and by the great Bobby Jones as one of the most interesting, and the more charming, as he wrote once, for its absence of artificiality, built "with trust in nature."

Some of the world's best golfers—and some of the worst—tested Myopia and found it not wanting. All teed off under the proprietary eye of Papa Leeds and his cohorts who held forth on the Male Porch, the altar of the clubhouse on which no female (banned from membership anyway) could set foot. The worst were led, or trailed, by a pair of high-stakes artists in the larger game, Henry Clay Frick and William H. Moore of Pride's Crossing, who vied in endowing Myopia with this or that (each tipped John Jones, the pro, a thousand every Christmas) and in cozying up to the heaviest hitter of them all, President William Howard Taft, when he was summering in Beverly. The tycoons and the President were bursting with expansive Edwardian egos, but not so John P. Marquand, the novelist, who a quarter of a century later took golf lessons three times a week but remained too intimidated by his fellow members to compete seriously.

Once the supremacy of the hunt had been breached by golf, tennis was bound to follow, but the game never rose above an indifferent third in the Myopian preference. The most colorful of a clutch of top players was the eccentric amazon, Miss Eleanora Sears of Pride's Crossing, and the classiest of the tennis tourneys those that pitted the best from the Myopia, Essex County and Nahant clubs, invariably topped off with cocktails, lobster Newburg and champagne.

Tales of Myopia lean to the boozy and, not surprisingly, the confrontational. Encounters between man and man, man and horse, man and mallet, man and martini, even man and woman, are legion and legend. There was the couple who lingered into the night over the hospitality after the Saturday drag, as Gordon Prince told it, then set out for Beverly Cove and home in their trap, only to reappear at the club in a short while, in a most disheveled and muddy state, on foot. "We've been in an awful accident! As we turned out of the Avenue a great motor truck, with only one headlight, crashed into us, smashing our buggy to bits, hurling us out, and the horse ran away. Lucky we weren't killed!" A reconnaissance party found the horse still in the shafts and the buggy overturned against a great stone post surmounted by an electric light marking the entrance.

And there is Ted Weeks's yarn of the Myopian who got home unexpectedly early after the annual dinner to find that "he had been preceded by a Club mate whose dogcart and horse were parked on the drive. A light on the second floor told him enough. So he shot the horse and went back to the Club."

Just before terminating in the 1929 Crash, the Era of Make-Believe culminated in an ugly clash at Myopia that left a bad aftertaste and the question in some minds: Who wins what wars on which playing fields? (Myopian George Patton's soldier-slapping temper tantrum in an army hospital in Sicily was fourteen years in the offing.) On June 26, 1929, Arthur Mason, a very hard-riding polo player, overtook Frederick H. Prince, Jr., son of one of the founding brothers, and overrode him with a terrific bump in order to make a back shot. Prince, whose fuse was shorter than ever at the age of sixty-nine, a few minutes later pounded up behind Mason at the bell and whacked him full on the head with his mallet. And when it was all over, in an even worse breach of the game's etiquette, he refused to apologize. Mason came out of it with chronic headaches and double vision, brought suit and was awarded twenty thousand dollars in damages. Fred Prince would not budge an inch; he was suspended from the club he had helped found, and resigned.

Is Myopia Brahminism's rowdy fringe? Perhaps. The more wonder that the publisher of the papyral *Transcript* should have been a Master, that the studious Allan Forbes should have penned its early history, that the satirical Marquand should have felt so put down by his fellow members, and that Weeks, that distinguished editor emeritus of the *Atlantic,* should extol its centennial.

Furthering the gentler side of the Shore, on the other hand, Myopia in its younger days attracted many Bostonians back to their Essex County roots, as Marshall Abbott observed in 1897, adding, in that time of growing class-consciousness in America, "English country life is a relic of the feudal system; but no such conditions exist in New England. Simplicity is most prominent in Hamilton. Though the leaps from city luxury to Hamiltonian simplicity are wide, all seem to land safely and to enjoy life even more on the 'landing side.'"

And the acquisition of the rolling farms by the leapers (as cheaply as the Lorings and their crowd had bought up the coast) has ensured—at least during the dynastic sway of the Ayers, Princes, Tuckermans, Searses, Appletons and their cousins, in-laws and friends—the incomparable beauty of Essex County's inland countryside.

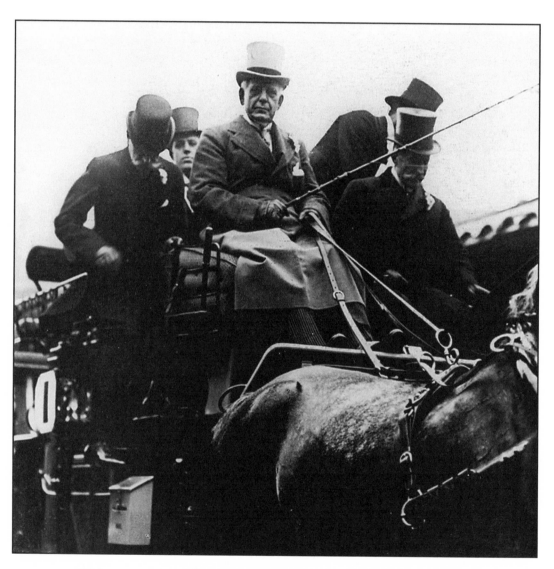

And here comes the "Judge." William Henry Moore rides into Pride's Crossing in absolute control of a four-in-hand, two-legged and four. (Myopia Hunt Club)

~16~
LOOK OUT,
MR. FRICK'S COMING!

A typhoon of tycoons hits Pride's Crossing

THE BOSTON LAWYER CHARLES Greely Loring bought his first twenty-five acres on the ocean at Pride's Crossing in 1844 for four thousand dollars and built the first summer cottage in Beverly. A long generation elapsed, the Industrial Revolution transformed America, the century turned, and Henry Clay Frick erected up above the Loring compound the greatest mansion on the North Shore, behind the longest and costliest ($100,000) fence. Presuming to improve his situation, the Pittsburgh magnate offered Miss Katharine Peabody Loring one million dollars for her house and land. C. G.'s granddaughter calmly turned her neighbor down, it was reported, with the rejoinder: "Goodness! What in the world would I do with a million dollars?"

It was the ephemeral Age of the Tycoons—those titans of finance who made America tremble during that thin stratum of time between the invention of the rolled-steel rail and the imposition of the rolling income tax. But Miss Loring did not tremble, nor did the rest of the North Shore that remained Boston's and resisted, or absorbed, every effort of the lesser Vanderbilts to gild the Gold Coast in the reflected gloss of Newport.

It is commonly supposed that the financiers, industrialists and entrepreneurs (and their wives) who bankrolled, engineered and commanded the explosive expansion were buying social status, or thought they were, when they began shoehorning their way between the shingled cottages of the Shore north of Beacon Hill. They surely were, but their mass descent upon the North Shore between the late 1890s and 1910 suggests that the herding instinct, if anything, was stronger. Not to mention the scenic attractions—a poor third, perhaps, for a Frick who had to cross Loring land to take a swim in God's ocean.

Frederick H. Prince, Boston banker and one of the horsey brothers who founded the Myopia Hunt Club, settled summers at Pride's Crossing in the early 1890s; Prince made it possible for Frick's partner Andrew Carnegie to buy the railroad that connected Carnegie's Mesabi ore with his Pittsburgh mills. T. Jefferson Coolidge of Coolidge Point in Manchester was associated with Frick in running the Atchison, Topeka and Santa Fe. Another Boston

Katharine Peabody Loring, who refused Mr. Frick's million dollars. (Beverly Historical Society)

man, John Greenough, was a railroad financier and merger expert with the Poors in New York and had one of the first summer homes on Eastern Point. Plenty more Boston money that fired the industrial furnace from the Bessemers of Pittsburgh to the looms of Lawrence was ensconced along the Shore.

No surprise, then, that one of the most powerful Republicans in the Senate, the Detroit rail and steamship magnate James McMillan, should turn up in Manchester in 1895 as the new owner, for $200,000, of the dramatic Towne estate "Eagle Head." Or that the self-sworn "Judge" William H. Moore of New York and points west, among the most brazen and astoundingly successful stock-waterers in American finance, should be found on the Shore in 1897, presumably renting, and golfing at Myopia. Next year the dapper Cleveland bachelor Henry C. Rouse, president of thirteen railroads, friend of John Greenough, bought the decommissioned Civil War fort on the heights of Eastern Point and built his "Ramparts" inside the earthworks.

In 1902 Moore and Frick, closely associated in the first failed attempt to buy out Carnegie in 1899, purchased land almost cheek by jowl at Pride's Crossing and laid plans for their mansions. In 1904 H. J. Heinz, the Ketchup King, built a house so large that years later it was converted into a famous resort hotel, the Magnolia Manor. In 1906 Richard T. Crane, Jr., Chicago's Prince of Plumbing, discovered the North Shore, renting a Manchester summer estate. Likewise Otto H. Kahn, the New York financier and art patron involved with Moore in the takeover of various western railroads; Kahn rented the Charles Head estate in Manchester for three years at ten thousand dollars a season and brought his horses and carriages in on a special train.

The invasion continued. John D. Rockefeller, Jr., tried the North Shore first in 1906 at Otis H. Luke's "Pitch Pine Hall" in Beverly Farms; the family's arrival on the private Pullman *Wyoming* in July with fourteen servants and over forty trunks was duly noted in the press: "They will live very quietly and entertain very little." The same year the enormously wealthy and powerful international mining engineer John Hays Hammond bought the Hovey estate overlooking Gloucester's Freshwater Cove for forty-five thousand dollars for his wife as a birthday present. And when Edwin Carleton Swift of the beef-packing family died at his "Swiftmoore" at Pride's, a special train of eight cars brought the bereaved from all over to the funeral.

Joining Henry Clay Frick at Pride's was Henry Clay Pierce of St. Louis, bank messenger at sixteen, son-in-law of the first refinery owner west of the Mississippi, and oil and rail multimillionaire, and Washington B. Thomas of Boston, whose fortune was in sugar. J. Harrington Walker, Detroit, whiskey, plunked his Italian-style villa down on the shore of Magnolia Point. In 1910 Richard Crane absconded with the crown jewel of Ipswich, and Hammond had a fifty-minute audience with Czar Nicholas in St. Petersburg to inform His Imperial Majesty of his plans for the investment of American capital in Russia.

KINGS OF THE CROSSING

But it was Frick and Moore, the most tyrannosaural of the behemoths of capitalism, whose thunderous descent upon Pride's Crossing caused the ground to shake. How their paths crossed, and then converged on the North Shore, is a story by itself.

Frick was fourteen when in 1863 he quit school in the farming and coal-mining country of Westmoreland County, Pennsylvania, to work in his uncle's store. That he had a fast head for figures was soon obvious, and he was made clerk and accountant in the distillery of his maternal grandfather, Abraham Overholt—"Old Overholt," who stares so sternly from the label of every bottle of his rye whiskey. The old man died in 1870 and left half a million dollars.

A compulsive worker with a fierce ambition to attain power and wealth, young Frick saw in the ground around him an unlimited potential for the manufacture of coke. Borrowing heavily with the backing of the Pittsburgh banker Judge Thomas Mellon, a family friend, he bought up mining land and built coke ovens on it right and left, not at all daunted by the panic of 1873, of which he took advantage to buy out his competitors at distress prices. With recovery, the H. C. Frick Coke Company was the major supplier of coke to the reawakening steel mills. By his thirtieth birthday Henry Clay Frick had made his first million.

Through Andrew Mellon, Frick met Adelaide Childs. And on their wedding trip he consummated another partnership—with Andrew Carnegie, who since the death of his brother Thomas had been looking for an organizational genius to run his steel mills. In ten more years—by 1892, when thirty-eight hundred workers struck their Homestead, Pennsylvania, mill over a relatively minor contract issue—Frick had engineered the acquisition of the partners' chief rival, Duquesne, imposed order on the largest segment of the chaotically mushrooming industry, and established the absolute dominance of the Carnegie Steel Company.

"The Man," Carnegie admiringly called him, and so he was—of medium height, powerfully built, authoritatively handsome, reserved, calm, private—a man who kept his counsel until he was ready to act—and then, watch out. H. C. Frick was as much as any figure of his day the high priest of corporate property rights. He beat the union at Homestead when the governor sent in the National Guard after the three hundred armed Pinkerton guards The Man imported had been routed by the strikers. At the height of it, in his office, Frick was shot twice in the neck and knifed three times by an anarchist who had no connection with the dispute. Swathed in makeshift bandages, Frick coolly returned to his desk after helping wrestle his assailant to the floor.

When Frick managed the purchase of the Oliver ore fields in the Mesabi Range, Carnegie tied them into his mills by buying the Pittsburgh, Shenango and Erie Railroad with the aid of Frederick H. Prince, who had saved it from bankruptcy. By the century's end Carnegie was ready to sell out and devote the rest of his life to redistributing his immense fortune for the betterment, as he saw it, of humanity.

Enter William H. Moore, who now offered the once-poor Scot $158 million for his holdings in the Carnegie and Frick companies, with Moore's assurance of a $5 million stake in the deal. Ten months Frick's junior, Moore came from a Utica, New York, banking family and practiced corporation law with his brother, James, in Chicago until 1887, when they decided to concentrate on the new speculative game of "corporate promotion." After reorganizing the Diamond Match Company they moved into the biscuit industry, recouping an initial $4 million loss with a merger in 1898 that created the National Biscuit Company, a ninety percent monopoly. About this time Moore tagged himself or got tagged "Judge," the sardonic sobriquet he carried for the rest of his life, like "Honest John" Jones, the used-car dealer.

Biscuits and matches were mere practice for the big move by the Moore Gang (as the brothers and their henchmen were known on Wall Street) to round up strays of steel left in Carnegie's trail until they ranked as one of the industry's Big Four. Their methods: stock-watering and overcapitalizing by puffing up expectations of future earnings, and then selling off or merging at fantastically inflated values. The result, according to the *Dictionary of American Biography,* was "the creation of monopolistic control, the contrivance of devices to avoid the operation of the antitrust laws, the reorganization of production and marketing to affect economies, and the retention of control in the hands of a small group."

In May 1899 the Moore Gang, in alliance with Frick, made its offer to buy out Andrew Carnegie. But at that moment a transient financial panic intervened, their funding was delayed, Carnegie refused to extend the option and pocketed their deposit of $1,170,000, and the deal fell through. Already differences had cooled relations between Carnegie and his Pard, as he in former times had addressed Frick. Late in 1899 he forced Frick out as chairman of his board and then bought him out for $15 million after Frick sued for the market value rather than the book value of his holdings.

The Gang went on in 1901 to organize the American Can Company. When J. Pierpont Morgan finally did buy out Carnegie that year and put together the U.S. Steel Corporation (with the essential help of Frick, who persuaded John D. Rockefeller, Sr., to sell Morgan his Mesabi holdings), Moore and his henchmen were included, though Morgan barred them from the management, he mistrusted them so. Moore's share of the new giant made him richer than ever, and so did Frick's, which was worth $60 million.

From steel Moore moved on to railroads, and by the time he landed his Pride's Crossing property in 1902 he had wrested control of the Chicago, Rock Island and Pacific. In the first decade of the new century he would add one railroad after another until his syndicate controlled fifteen thousand miles of track, and he would be wondered at and feared as "the most daring promoter in American business."

Tall, handsome and so genially glacial that they called him the Sphinx of the Rock Island, "Judge" Moore (judge of horseflesh, in a neighbor's view) first took in the North Shore in perhaps the late 1890s in company with Mr. Frick. In the autumn of 1902 Moore bought lots on Hale Street in Pride's from Francis Lee Higginson, the Boston financier, and (with ocean frontage) from Dr. Reginald H. Fitz, famed Boston pathologist who had discovered the cause of appendicitis in 1886. A month after Moore's purchase,

Here sits Mr. Frick. From Henry Clay Frick: The Man by George Harvey.

Frick bought three nearby parcels, one of which provided him with a fifteen-foot right-of-way through the intervening Loring land to a boathouse and bathhouse on the beach, his only access to the Atlantic Ocean. Moore started building his summer mansion and stables almost immediately; Frick rented the Robert S. Bradley estate at Pride's and didn't build until the end of the 1904 season, after tearing down the house of the late George Tyson of Philadelphia, from whose widow he had acquired his principal land surrounding "Eagle Rock," so called for the eagles once observed nesting there.

Horses even more than houses were Moore's passion, however, and by spring of 1904 he was having his training track near his private siding at Pride's station relaid forty feet wide and a third of a mile long. In June Mrs. Moore arrived at their rented estate with the servants, followed by her husband, then his special five-car train with thirty-eight thoroughbreds, twenty-seven stable workers and various carriages and turnouts. In November Connolly Brothers, the Beverly Farms contractors, had two hundred men spreading ten thousand yards of loam around the grounds of "Rockmarge." The Moores moved in in 1905. *Impressive.* Acres of rolling lawn. A curved drive fit for a race-track. A Grand Central Station of a mansion with a portico running the entire length of it, eight towering columns wide, topped with tiers of plain and fancy balustrades.

While one friend was thus engaged, Mr. Frick was asked by another but not a mutual one, Mr. Morgan, to help him with the world's largest corporation, which had gotten off to a shaky start. Frick demurred: he had an interest in Union Steel, and it would be unethical for him to assist a competitor. So J. P. simply bought Union, leaving The Man's conscience free to give Big Steel a hand through its crisis. Before the frost was out of the ground in 1905 Mr. Frick was ready to demonstrate his scale to his future summer neighbors. He soon had a team of three hundred doing grading and stonework.

In 1906 "Eagle Rock" was approaching completion when the *North Shore Breeze* was permitted a preview and allowed to double in print the publicized cost to "the vicinity of $1,000,000, to say nothing of the interior furnishings of the mansion, where there may be represented before it is finished, well toward another million in valuable paintings, etc."

Considerable fill was brought in to create the grand expanse on the twenty-five-acre estate from the entrances on Hale Street, along which marched the magnificent $100,000 iron fence with its handsome stone pillars. Broad avenues led up to the immense Georgian palace, which looked strikingly like the White House in Washington; at two hundred feet, however, "Eagle Rock" was thirty feet longer. Forty-eight thousand yards of fill and loam, in fact (not counting other thousands spread around neighbor Moore's yard), rolled in from West Peabody by special train onto a special spur laid for the purpose at Pride's; that amounted to two and three trains a day for two months, 1,650 carloads in all. Fifty or so maple trees were set out, perhaps not all on a scale with the elm that was moved to "Rockmarge" from Hamilton; that was seventy feet high, twenty-six inches in diameter, with an earth ball sixteen feet across, and it took ten horses two hours to get it there.

The Frick automobile house, another Georgian brick and stone pile with portico, balustrades and Palladian windows, was bigger than the mansions of most of his richest neighbors. Similarly the "Lodge," another great house of stone and shingle surmounted by waves of gables. Across Hale Street was the stable, 150 feet long and designed, like the "Lodge," in New England country estate style; a large clock and sundial adorned the front; inside, fourteen horses lolled in pampered ease, little used by their motorcar-mad master. Outbuildings, tennis court, vegetable garden and other amenities were strewn around this American Versailles.

The guest from the *Breeze* was impressed. The house up on the hill so very high above and back from the sea, but hardly visible from Hale Street, "is reached through a magnificent forecourt encircled with limestone columns, and the entrance has six immense colonial columns of limestone trimmings and fancy brick work. All of the main living rooms of the house will be finished in hand carved mahogany, expensive marbles and teak wood."

Ah, the Frick basement wherein were a hotel-size kitchen, dumbwaiters, servants' elevator to the fourth floor done in Tiffany tile, pantries right and left, refrigerator room, butchery, servants' dining room, wine vault and attached unpacking room, bellows room (yes) for the organ above, a great oak-paneled billiard room with marble fireplace, and a fresh or salt, warm or cold "swimming tank room decidedly Grecian in style, with artificial limestone, fluted columns, marble dado, moulded pilasters and architraves, and two sets of dressing and toilet rooms."

From such a basement the rest of "Eagle Rock" arose. Glassed-in loggias, den, library, drawing and sitting rooms—mahogany and marble, teak floors everywhere—more pantries right and left, housekeeper's apartment, fireproof steel-lined silver vault, dining rooms in mahogany, breakfast rooms, reception rooms for ladies.

The great hall opened onto the terraces outside through bronze doors fit for Judgment Day and, adjoining that, the staircase hall incorporating the forty-two-thousand-dollar main pipe organ (echo organ on the third floor) playable from any of three separate consoles. And on the floor above, the

bedchambers of the Fricks and their son, Childs, just graduated from Princeton, and their daughter of seventeen, Helen Clay, and governesses and guests, and servants (ten of them). And in the attic more servants' rooms and twin ten-ton water tanks.

Frick's "Eagle Rock," Moore's "Rockmarge," and Swift's "Swiftmoore," among other such Parthenons of capitalism on the North Shore, were designed by the Boston architect Arthur Little, who had graced this coast with so many mellifluous outpourings of shingle a quarter of a century earlier and was perfectly content to summer in his stuccoed union of two old barns, "Spartivento," at Beverly Farms.

Early in September 1906, the Henry Clay Fricks officially warmed the greatest mansion on the North Shore and no doubt north of Newport with an al fresco luncheon. There was a recital on the organ and a concert by Boston Symphony players, and in the evening a cotillion. All the important people were invited, and it is ungenerous to suppose that most of them were not there, if only out of the most intense curiosity, or to put much credence in the story that on this or some other occasion the Fricks gave a great party the day a local lobsterman put on his annual cookout, and most everybody turned up at the cookout. The Moores perhaps, but the Fricks . . . not likely.

While his neighbor was serenely sinking a fraction of his fortune in the North Shore's most thoroughly equipped summer camp and in his growing art collection, Moore was milking his Rock Island Line for quite a lot more than it was worth and pouring the cream into a stable considered among the best in the world. His joy was his four-in-hand, a very fancy coach pulled by four matched horses driven in tandem by the owner himself with such command and élan, in his top hat and natty greatcoat high up on the seat, that his celebrity in international equestrian circles far outshone his fame as an entrepreneur.

Late every spring a special train of up to eight cars was nudged into the Moore siding at Pride's with a few dozen horses, a few dozen more stable attendants and various equipages and motorcars. In 1908 the leader of the Gang staged the first of his annual private horse shows at his Rockmarge Driving Park. Three hundred carefully invited guests had seen nothing like it on the Shore as their host whirled by at the reins of Pride o' Prides and King of Kings, reportedly the top hackney pair in the country. Tea followed on the terrace.

About this time the "Judge" went worldwide. In 1910, as he would until the wartime high seas got hazardous for horses, he shipped forty-nine of his best to the International Show in England, where he won the twenty-five-mile coaching marathon from Windsor Castle to the Olympic Arena in London. His tallyho was the smartest on the Shore, and its regular dashes between "Rockmarge" and the Myopia Hunt in Hamilton, with a pounding of hooves, scurry of dust and clarion call, were something to behold, still ringing in the memory of Ellen B. R. Boyd, a friend of Helen Frick, fifty years later: "At the very back of this handsome and unusual carriage rode the bugler. He was dressed in striking uniform to match those of the coachman and the footman. It was this young man's duty to blow his bugle as the tally-ho neared each corner or curve in the road, so that people would know they must be on the lookout."

As for Mr. Frick, the fastest four-in-hand on earth, even at fourteen miles an hour, was a snail's pace. The arrival at Pride's of his custom Mercedes tonneau from France in the midsummer of 1904 thunderstruck the *Breeze*—seventy-four horsepower, one of the most powerful cars in America, and ten passengers! "His real hobby," wrote Frick's amused biographer, "was speed, terrific speed. . . . Motoring he found delightfully exhilarating unless hampered by road regulations, to which ultimately, after securing the most expertly daring chauffeur to be found in France, he paid little heed."

The Moore carriage house at "Rockmarge." (Beverly Historical Society)

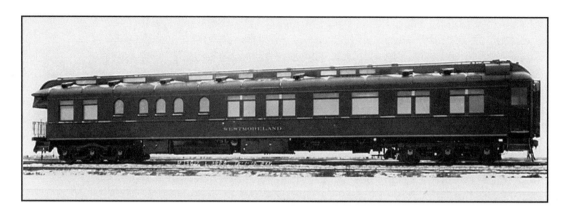

To which his West Gloucester summer neighbor, John Hays Hammond, Sr., breathed a fervent *amen*. Frick drove around one day with E. H. Harriman, the railroad financier, to pick up the engineer for a ride in his new French car. "We started on the twenty miles of narrow, winding, unpaved Cape Ann roads," Hammond wrote. "The chauffeur took the curves on two wheels and whenever we came to a village seemed to prefer the sidewalks to the streets. Hens squawked, horses reared, New England ladies scuttled into doorways." Back at Hammond's door, Frick asked of his guest, "'Harriman, how do you like the wonderful scenery of Cape Ann?'

"Harriman's trains never could travel fast enough to suit him, but now he gasped: 'To tell the truth, Frick, your French chauffeur went so fast I didn't see much of it. Another time I think I'd better ask Hammond to take me in his car. I'd really like to see the scenery!'"

THE PRIVATE VARNISH

But more than the Mercedes, more even than the blue-ribbon four-in-hand, the private railroad car—usually though not invariably built by the Pullman Company—was by 1910 the steam yacht of the landbound, the mobile mansion; and the more elaborately endowed (even unto gold plumbing), the better. A much-used dodge among rail tycoons who were not overly particular about such matters was to have the company pay for the so-called "business car," which they then simply assigned to themselves. By this means Henry Clark Rouse of Cleveland began arriving on the North Shore in 1899 in Car 36 of the Missouri, Kansas and Texas Railway, one of the numerous lines over which he presided.

The Moore Gang had ordered five "private varnish" Pullmans wholesale through the Rock Island Road in 1902, which is how their leader came by *Rockmarge,* which he named in anticipation of his mansion. Another railroad tycoon, Henry Clay Pierce, had his *Zamora* put on the books of the Mexican Central, of whose New York board he was chairman (he was president of the Tennessee Central), and luxuriated on its brocade and velvet lap while traveling between his several residences in St. Louis, New York, Wisconsin and Pride's Crossing, occasionally dipping into Mexico.

There were those, however, to whom such subterfuges were anathema. John Hays Hammond rolled in grandeur with the seasons between his homes in Georgia, New Jersey and Gloucester and back in his very own *Kya Yami*, which is Zulu for "One of My Homes." A few years later Richard T. Crane had *Nituna* built to his order for arriving at Castle Hill and elsewhere, while Albert C. Burrage of Boston acquired *Esperanzo* after the 1929 crash and renamed it *Alicia* for his wife, for more extensive travel (befitting a copper king) than the forty-minute run to Pride's.

Of course Frick had them all beat. Long after he retired from Big Steel, he charted a weekly triangular course summers between Pride's Crossing and New York and Pittsburgh on business, in various leased cars. In May of 1910, for instance, he arrived on the North Shore in the *Plymouth Rock*, which had taken first prize at the St. Louis Exposition as "the last word in luxury for travellers," then a few days later was back in the *Commonwealth* and three other special cars, one with the family baggage, one with the family automobiles, and one with his art collection, which he had decided to take with him to "Eagle Rock" for the season.

All this was mere prelude to The Man's ultimate, the *Westmoreland*, named for his native county in Pennsylvania. Pullman delivered what has been represented as the first all-steel private car in time for Christmas Day, 1910, when its owner was well on the way to owning more railroad stock than anyone else in the world.

When the Fricks glided into Pride's Crossing the following June, the correspondent for the *Breeze* was allowed aboard for an awestruck peek at kitchenette and dining room, the bedrooms of Mr. Frick and Childs upholstered in red satin tapestry, Mrs. Frick's in pink, Helen's in pale green—each with a connected bath—and the living room in brown. The silver, china and stationery bore the emblem "Westmoreland." After her husband's death Mrs. Frick enshrined *Westmoreland* in its own house on a Pride's siding and decreed in her will that after the retirement of a railroading friend to whom she subsequently gave it, it be destroyed; he died in 1967, and it was.

TWO MORTALS, TWO MONUMENTS

As early as 1908 Frick had been bringing at least a portion of his growing art collection to the North Shore for the summer. Isabella Gardner and two friends inspected his rival masterpieces at Pride's that August and then were driven around to Eastern Point in one of the Frick autos to visit the Philadelphia portrait artist Cecilia Beaux and her neighbor Henry Davis Sleeper.

Frick did seem to be gravitating more and more to the Beverly shore as his principal residence. In December 1911 the *Breeze* expectantly passed on a rumor that Frick was planning to add a wing to "Eagle Rock" for his collection, which was worth millions, that would "outdo anything in New England in the way of an art gallery," including Mrs. Gardner's "Fenway Court."

Then, as suddenly, the scene shifted. In May 1912 the North Shore

heard the news that its richest inhabitant had bought the entire Lenox Library block on New York's Fifth Avenue between Seventieth and Seventy-first streets for $2.4 million and that he would raze the library and build in its place for another $1.5 million a white marble fireproof mansion with a great art gallery. Not without precedent, this classically proportioned palace across from Central Park had cost its owner $5.4 million by the time he moved in with his family in 1914—and his collection of art another $30–40 million in pre-World War I dollars.

Amassed since 1895 by an industrialist of self-educated taste who had left school at the age of fourteen, the Frick Collection is one of the most glorious ever gathered by a private individual. In 1936, seventeen years after his death, his gallery was opened as a public museum and his monument, as he had directed in his will.

"Judge" Moore's monument, the Rock Island Railroad, slipped into receivership. The stock plummeted from two hundred dollars a share in 1902, when the Gang hijacked the trains, to twenty dollars in 1914, in spite of steadily rising earnings. Looking to erect a substitute monument to himself, and as a measure of the regard in which he held his neighbors, he offered in 1915 to build a granite depot at Pride's Crossing if the Boston and Maine (which he did not control) would change the name of the station, *ergo* the community, to Rockmarge. As a measure of reciprocation, his neighbors' protests prevailed. There was no new depot.

In 1917 Moore and his henchmen were finally ousted after a scathing condemnation by the Interstate Commerce Commission, accusing them of deliberate misrepresentation and looting. Samuel Untermeyer, counsel for a stockholders' protective committee, stated flatly that compared with the Moore Gang, "the manipulators of the old Fish-Gould days were artless children."

Moore the manipulator ignored a bad press to the end, which came in 1923. Frick the builder was aggressively sensitive: when the *Pittsburgh Leader* ran an annoying cartoon of him, he ordered a minion to buy the paper, but was relieved to hear later that a local Republican boss, similarly tweaked, had beaten him to it. When he died two weeks short of seventy in 1919, a few months after Carnegie, one Pard had as characteristically and grandly left his mark as the other.

Henry Clay Frick and William Henry Moore both left the golf links at Myopia, where Money was never in the rough, better than they found them. Yet the only Myopian anecdote of the "Judge" for the record concerns his discovery there of a cocktail called the martini. Remembrances of The Man are myriad, perhaps because Moore had no such biographer as George Harvey, who unintentionally penned *his* bearded subject's epitaph while describing his enthusiasm for golf at Myopia, "where he enjoyed special privileges, and where all stood aside when the good-natured warning was passed forward, 'Look out, Mr. Frick's coming!'"

He came and he went, as did they all, the kings and the captains, the wheelers and the dealers, before war and taxes, for a while anyway, cut the players down to more or less manageable size. "Eagle Rock" was razed by Mr. Frick's heirs, who replaced it with a compound still guarded by his $100,000 fence. "Rockmarge," too, was torn down by the descendants of its inscrutable builder, and the land sold for subdivision to . . . the ever-present Lorings.

This page from the Beverly city survey of 1907 shows the estates just west of the Pride's Crossing station (upper right corner of facing page). Included are the properties of Henry C. Frick and his nemesis Katharine P. Loring. Frederick Ayer's "Avalon" (Chapter 19) is just east of Miss Loring's property, while the location of the first summer home in Beverly (Chapter 3) is the Loring property on Plum Cove Point, west of Frick. (Beverly Historical Society)

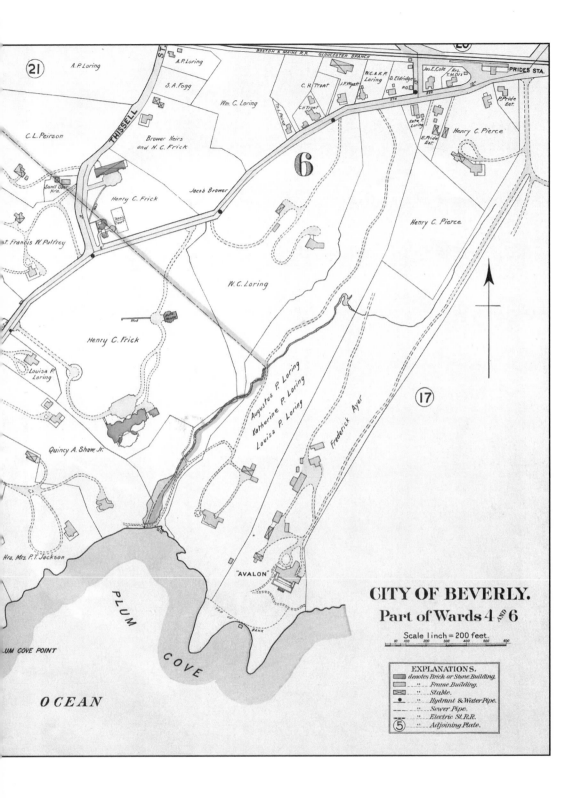

㉑

A.P. Loring

A.P. Loring

BOSTON & MAINE R.R.   GLOUCESTER BRANCH

㉖

PRIDES STA.

S.A. Fogg

Wm. C. Loring

C.H. Trant

W.C. & A.K.P. Loring

J.F. Wyatt

B. Eldridge

Jos. E. Cole   Mrs. T.M. Dix

C.L. Peirson

Brower Heirs and H.C. Frick

C.H.Trant

R.D.

Kate P. Loring

P. Pride Est.

Henry C. Pierce

Saml Ober Hrs.

Henry C. Frick

Jacob Brower

6

E. Pride Est.

st. Francis W. Palfrey

N.C. Loring

Henry C. Pierce

Well

Henry C. Frick

Louisa P. Loring

Augustus P. Loring

Katherine P. Loring

Louisa P. Loring

Frederick Ayer

⑰

Quincy A. Shaw Jr.

Hrs. Mrs. P.T. Jackson

"AVALON"

PLUM

COVE

UM COVE POINT

OCEAN

CITY OF BEVERLY.
Part of Wards 4 and 6

Scale 1 inch = 200 feet.

Continuing east from the Pride's Crossing station, this page from the 1907 Beverly survey includes the neighboring properties of Edwin C. Swift ("Swiftmoore") and William H. Moore ("Rockmarge" with its enormous carriage house). For sheer spread, however, there was no topping the Franklin Haven acreage to the east (Chapter 3). (Beverly Historical Society)

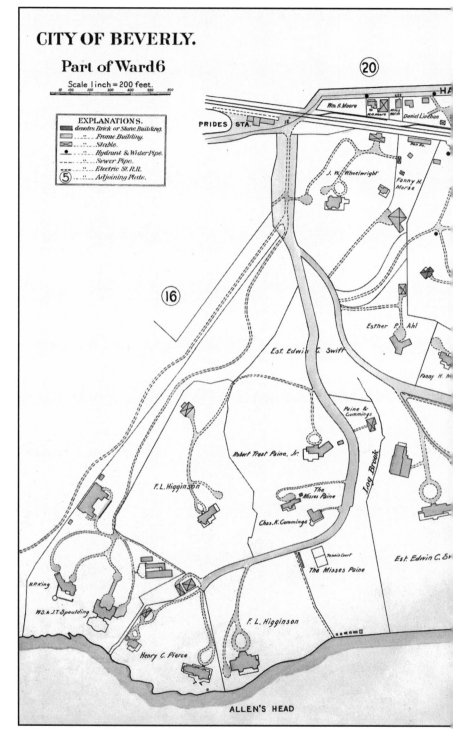

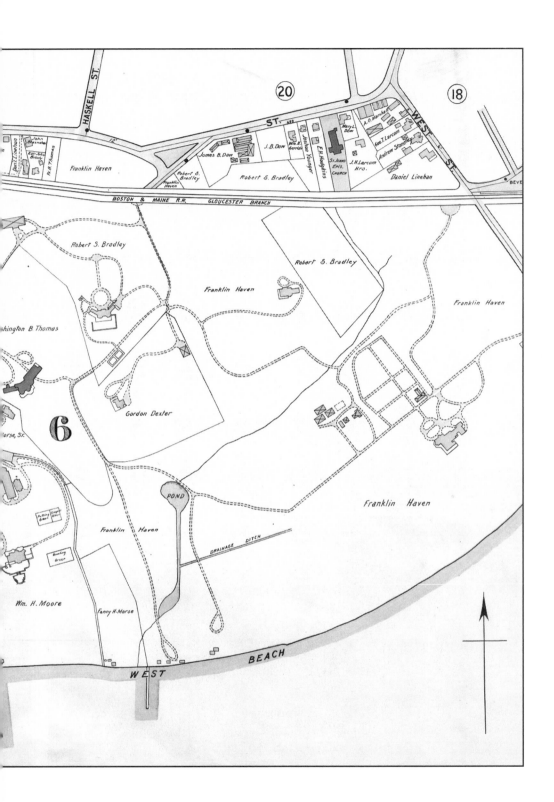

HASKELL ST.

20

18

WEST ST.

BEVE

Gen.I.Linehan
John
Bresnahe
Esq.John
Brady
N.B.Thomas
Mary L.
Dow
A.O.Marsh
Geo.T.Larcom
Franklin Haven
James B. Dow
J. B. Dow
Wm.B.
Gerrish
Joshua Younger
E.H.Hodgkins
St.JOHN
EPIS.
CHURCH
J.H.Larcom
Hrs.
Andrew Standley
Robert S.
Bradley
Robert S. Bradley
Daniel Linehan
Franklin
Haven

BOSTON & MAINE R.R.   GLOUCESTER BRANCH

Robert S. Bradley
Robert S. Bradley
Franklin Haven
Franklin Haven

shington B. Thomas
Gordon Dexter

6

orse, Sr.

Bowling
Green
Tennis
Court
Tennis
Court
Bowling
Green

POND

Franklin Haven
Franklin Haven

DRAINAGE DITCH

Wm. H. Moore
Fanny H. Morse

BEACH

WEST

"Wal!" said Uncle Sam, philosophically watching the scrap between William Howard Taft and his predecessor, Teddy Roosevelt, "I guess old friends are the best!"
(From Punch.*)*

~17~
HAIL TO THE CHIEF, AND FAREWELL

President Taft favors Beverly with his avoirdupois,
political faux pas and a fair showing at golf

H<small>E WAS SO LUKEWARM ABOUT</small> the job to which he had just been elected in November of 1908 that the ballots had barely been counted before William Howard Taft was turning over in his judicial mind how to escape from the White House and the heat of Washington the next summer.

It wouldn't do for the President of the United States to take his ease on foreign soil, even soil as friendly and fraternal as Canada's, where Theodore Roosevelt's anointed heir had been relaxing with his family for sixteen years above the broad St. Lawrence on the shore of Murray Bay halfway between Quebec City and the wild Saguenay. "A mere strawberry box of a place, but it suits me." So thought the vastly affable *petit juge,* as the inhabitants called the former jurist.

So a summer White House had to be found within the nation whose reins Mr. Taft would not very confidently take over from the dynamic driver for whom he had been Secretary of War and factotum, and whom he could never somehow quite cure himself of addressing, and regarding, as "Mr. President."

Thus it was that a couple of months before his inauguration in March of 1909 the President-elect and his strong-minded wife, Helen, were on the lookout for a summer headquarters somewhere on the New England coast, the family agreed, possibly along that breezy parapet of Republicanism, the North Shore, and near a golf links at his insistence.

Nahant, for instance, was the den of Senator Henry Cabot Lodge, Teddy Roosevelt's closest chum, who had declined, with portentous disdain, Mr. Taft's invitation to be his Secretary of State. In Manchester summered the William Boardmans, old hosts to the Tafts when they were in the Boston area, and Senator Albert Beveridge of Indiana, who would, unfortunately, turn bitterly against the President within his own party. Manchester and Magnolia already swarmed with summering embassies, at least twenty of the thirty-nine accredited to Washington, a social blessing to be regarded by a vacationing President, if not his First Lady, as not unmixed.

Inland at Hamilton, where he contentedly supervised the refinement of his "Rock Maple Farm" into one of the Shore's rural show places, resided George von Lengerke Meyer, of blood a Boston blue. TR's ambassador to Italy and Russia, and later his Postmaster General, Meyer was inherited by Taft and reconditioned as Secretary of the Navy. Cabot Lodge urged the appointment on Taft lest Meyer, out of office and chafing, take a notion to challenge his neighbor, Congressman Augustus Peabody ("Gussie") Gardner, the senator's son-in-law.

And speaking of sons-in-law, over at Pride's Crossing every season was Congressman Nicholas Longworth of Ohio, who had married Teddy Roosevelt's astonishing daughter Alice. Their romance on the Shore in 1904 had set every tongue wagging. "Alice Blue Gown" was the devilish darling of the social set, with the sharpest tongue of all.

Comfortable Republican country, the North Shore . . . if one didn't expose one's broad back.

In Gloucester, under the wings of the Colonial Arms on the harbor shore of Eastern Point, had sprung up a colony of damsels and their bachelor friends. "Dabsville" they acronymically called themselves, for Joanna **D**avidge, Virginia-born mistress of a New York finishing school; Abram Piatt **A**ndrew, young Harvard monetary expert; Philadelphia portraitist Cecilia **B**eaux of fabled hauteur; Caroline **S**inkler, Southern belle of fabled enchantment; and Andrew's close friend Henry Davis **S**leeper, the pioneering interior decorator and creator of "Beauport." Frequently Dabsville was joined in its capers by Mrs. Jack Gardner, Gussie's aunt, the capricious art collector who for several summers rented the Ellis Gray Loring cottage above Mingo Beach in Beverly. "Doc" (because professor) Andrew was the brightest brain on Senator Aldrich's team that conceived the Federal Reserve System (though the Democrats ultimately implemented it) and had so taken the fancy of the Tafts that the President was about to make him director of the U.S. Mint.

By far the strongest magnets drawing the Tafts to the North Shore, though, were their old and close friends, John Hays Hammond and his wife, Natalie. Fifty-four, only a year older than Taft, Hammond was an adventurous Californian who applied his Yale engineering studies so successfully out west that the ruthlessly ambitious Cecil Rhodes hired him to run his gold mine operations in South Africa, where he made his first fortune, ran afoul of the Boer War and Oom Paul Kruger, and was jailed, sentenced to death and ransomed for $125,000—no small thanks to the battle put up for him by his indomitable wife.

Back in the States with a whole skin, Hammond was engaged by the Guggenheims as *their* Midas at a million a year. He more or less retired in 1907 to enjoy himself and his family. Spending his summers at "Lookout Hill" above Gloucester Harbor, Hammond dabbled in public affairs, almost ran as Taft's vice president and turned down both the Navy secretaryship (before Taft gave it to Meyer) and the ambassadorship to China.

Where, then, would the President decide? The rumors flew that spring

of 1909. Emissaries had inquired about Eastern Point. Was its grandest,
"The Ramparts," for rent? Under no circumstances, declared its
redoubtable mistress, Mrs. Emma Raymond, who had inherited the fort
within a fort from the late Commodore Rouse, for whom she had kept
house. What about Harry Sleeper's rambling, eclectic "Beauport," separated
from Piatt Andrew's "Red Roof" by Miss Sinkler's amusedly nicknamed
"Wrong Roof"? "It would be difficult to imagine," chuckled a sympathetic
press, "the massive frame of the President passing through one of the small
doors of ancient make."

The choice narrowed to the Gold Coast—Manchester and Beverly. The
late Mortimer B. Mason estate in Manchester was rumored. Nellie Taft
favored the Edward Robinson cottage in Manchester, but it was too small.
The first lady settled on the green, shingled, fourteen-room cottage of the
late John B. Stetson of Boston on Woodbury Point, between Beverly Cove
and Hospital Point.

Owner of the Stetson property was Robert Dawson Evans, who had come to Boston a poor boy from New Brunswick, Canada, and bounced from the bottom of the then-infant rubber industry to the top, retiring as president of U.S. Rubber in 1898, when he turned his wits to California gold mining with his friend Jack Hammond. Possibly it was Hammond who put the Tafts on to the Stetson house, which at the time was serving as an adjunct across the lawn to "Dawson Hall," the Versailles raised by Evans for himself and his consort, whose name actually *was* Maria Antoinette.

The Taft summer got off to about as inauspicious a start as the Taft administration. The identity of the summer White House was no sooner out when several hundred (the *Boston Post* claimed five thousand) souvenir hunters invaded Woodbury Point and ripped off relics of the very house itself, leaving the grounds looking like a picnic grove on Saturday night. The *Breeze* chided: "Cut it out, Beverly, if you have any desire to make things so pleasant for the President and his family that they will want to return another season."

Less than two months after the inauguration Nellie Taft suffered a stroke that effectively put her out of action as a hostess for a year and added greatly to her husband's anxiety as he grappled with his new job. As if that was not enough, practically as the presidential train was pulling onto the special spur the Boston and Maine had laid at its depot in the Montserrat section of Beverly, landlord Evans was thrown from his horse and seriously injured. The Tafts and their youngest, Charlie, arrived on the Fourth of July in the same private Pullman *Olympia* used by the Fricks, with domestic staff, luggage, and Rosebud, the family cow, in the other cars. The President returned to Washington the next day, however, to keep an eye on the tariff bill in Congress. On July 6 Robert Dawson Evans died.

The first family was complete with the arrival of the elder son, Robert, finishing Yale, and Helen, seventeen, from Bryn Mawr. The nineteen-year-old future senator from Ohio set about golf and tennis with serious purpose. Helen drove herself in the family's electric runabout every day for tennis at the Essex County Club in Manchester. Charlie took to the water in the sailing dory *Bandit,* the gift of young Dick Hammond.

It seems unimaginable that there once was a time when a President of the United States could accept the offer of the Beverly Board of Trade of its handful of rooms in the Mason Building on Cabot Street, three quarters of a mile from the summer White House, for the conduct of the executive business of the nation. Although he did most of his work at the cottage, the *North Shore Reminder* had some fun with the prospects:

"Pretty good little rooms they are, too—for a country board of trade. One enters them by means of a marble stairway wide enough to allow two presidents to climb abreast, even though the second were of Mr. Taft's generous avoirdupois. . . . To be sure, in order to get to his room he will have to climb those marble stairs, for there is no elevator, and will have to run the gauntlet of pop corn men, candy vendors and suspender peddlers, who infest the sidewalk. Once ensconced, however, he will be all right. He can tip back in his swivel chair and enjoy the soothing strains of music, as furnished by the itinerant hurdy-gurdy man. The President has already been warned not to pay attention to any agonizing screams he may hear, for these will merely emanate from one of the dentists' offices on the same floor. It has been facetiously suggested that if the councils of state lead to uncertainty of action, recourse may be had to the wonderful powers of reading the future possessed by Mme. Zaza, occultist and palmist, whose fortune telling studio is in a nearby shop."

The tariff issue, on which he might have benefited from a session or two with Mme. Zaza, kept the President in Washington into August. Although he was not an extreme protectionist, the wall he wanted was still too high for the Roosevelt Republicans. Nevertheless, the Payne-Aldrich Bill was rammed through and signed by Taft, allowing him a few weeks of vacation. He arrived back in Beverly on August 7, three days after the city of Gloucester, on its own course as usual, had carried off a long-planned pageant in his honor, notwithstanding the absence of the honored guest. Office furniture and supplies were hauled by the wagonload to the Board of Trade, and there was set up the nation's business.

The routine of the summer White House was now taken up in earnest. The President was a keen golfer and tried both the Essex County and Myopia links. He preferred Myopia's more challenging eighteen, and its more rarefied roster. Four or five mornings a week he would be driven to Hamilton with one of his children and Captain Archibald Butt, his military aide, tee off around nine-thirty or ten, and finish within two and a half hours. "It is easier in some circumstances," observed the English writer

Maria Antoinette Evans on her Beverly estate. The Tafts' house is down the drive to the right. (Beverly Historical Society)

The caption for this cartoon described the Presidential golf stance as "more ponderous than graceful." (Beverly Historical Society)

Henry Leach, "to become president of the United States than to become a member of the Myopia Hunt Club. It is therefore all the more to the credit of Mr. Taft that he is both."

The President was surprisingly agile for one of his girth, and not a bad athlete. But he loved the pleasures of the table, which he only fitfully put from him, as in 1905 when he carved himself down from 326 to 250 pounds, though before long he was back over 300. Fat was the target of his exercise. For a while he tried horseback riding, inspiring Elihu Root to inquire politely after the condition of the horse. He was a good tennis player but followed Roosevelt's advice never to be photographed at it . . . not democratic enough, warned TR, and golf even worse. Still, his doctor had recommended golf, and the patient liked the game, and that was that. He *was* President.

A writer for *The American Golfer* followed him around Myopia with Hammond: "He stands very straight, keeps his head still and swings through the ball, sweeping it away. Possibly it is more of a baseball stroke than a golf swing, but it answers the purpose nobly." And on another morning the *North Shore Reminder* sought another opinion: "'He is a good feller,' said one freckle-nosed urchin as he unslung his sticks and wiped his grimy face after a round with the President, and after the 'good feller' had patted him on the shoulder and more substantially made known his appreciation of the boy's faithful service." The pro at Myopia merely informed Hammond that neither he nor Taft would ever make a good golfer because "the brains of both of you are always working on so many things that you can't concentrate on the game."

The inland President was no sailor. Under his feet he liked the feel of a solid deck, like that of an ocean liner. The sleek white *Mayflower* he inherited from his friend Theodore was the Scots-built yacht of an American millionaire bought by the Navy at the outbreak of the Spanish War; Roosevelt had expropriated her when he took office in 1901. She was 273 feet long, and it took a crew of two hundred to keep her in white-glove trim, including a sixteen-piece band. At that size, she couldn't get into the Potomac or visit other charming spots close alongshore, and had to anchor a half a mile off Woodbury Point. So for a few hours on the water, handy to shore facilities, Taft soon after his inauguration commandeered the smaller *Sylph*, another yacht taken over by the Navy.

And a third government vessel, Secretary of the Navy Meyer's personal dispatch boat *Dolphin*, hung around in Gloucester Harbor, where she startled the city with reverberating twenty-one-gun salutes whenever *Mayflower* or *Sylph* steamed past Eastern Point, flying the President's ensign. From her position on deck Nellie found these salvos anything but salutary. "They shake one's nerves and hurt one's ears, but they are most inspiring." And when *Mayflower* steamed through the fleet on review, and they all cut loose at once, she noted, "I think I know what a naval battle sounds like."

No, not keels but wheels were the presidential passion—swift rolling wheels under a fine presidential Pullman emblazoned with his Great Seal, and wheels under his grand and imposing White steam automobile. After his morning golf Mr. Taft would return to the summer White House for lunch, executive business in the afternoon, then almost without fail if the weather permitted, off with Nellie and frequently guests for the daily drive in the sedate open touring car, back in time for dinner. Two thousand miles of Essex County they traversed that summer. The President stuffed himself into a regulation motoring outfit with his golf cap pulled down over his forehead, and everyone in his party was equipped with goggles as protection against the clouds of dust raised on the country roads. Automobile parties were all the rage, and one Sunday afternoon several converged on Beverly for an obvious purpose. When the Tafts glided almost silently from the Evans driveway, trailing a cumulus of cottony steam puffs, they encountered a line of motor cars half a mile long on the highway in wait for them. Whether these motorized kibitzers followed the presidential party in convoy is not recorded.

Politics was politics, and the obliging President one afternoon received forty-five callers at the Stetson cottage between three and five-thirty, something of a record. There is no record of a call on that or any other occasion from a certain George S. Patton, Jr., a very brassy young house guest at Pride's Crossing of the textile tycoon Frederick Ayer, whose daughter Beatrice he was courting. Just graduated from West Point, Patton wrote his father on April 25: "I think I will have to stay at Pride's for various reasons. Mr. Taft has the house at Beverly Point where the Ayers were three years ago. It is about two hundred yards from Prides. I might meet the President and eventually get to Washington. . . . How sanguine youth is."

By displaying himself on the roads of Essex County every afternoon, Taft could keep his formal public appearances to a pleasant minimum. One such was the luncheon reception given him by the Hammonds at "Lookout

PRESIDENT TAFT AND HIS PARTY TAKING A RIDE ALONG THE NORTH SHORE IN HIS FAMOUS "WHITE STEAMER."

THIS PICTURE WAS TAKEN BY OUR PHOTOGRAPHER AT BEVERLY AT THE TURN IN THE ROAD JUST LEADING TO THE ENTRANCE OF THE STETSON ESTATE, WHERE THE PRESIDENT'S HOUSE IS LOCATED. THE OCCUPANTS ARE HELEN TAFT, CAPT. BUTT, AND THE PRESIDENT'S LIVERYMAN AND THE CHAUFFEUR ROBINSON

The motoring Tafts made the cover of the 1910 Who's Who Along the North Shore, in color. (Peabody Essex Museum)

Hill" August 28 for the Gloucester committee that had staged the day in his honor without him. Shaking hands all around, the President impressed the *Gloucester Times* reporter as "large, jovial, breezy, his face wreathed in a continuous smile, which sent the flesh up around his eyes, so that, while twinkling merrily all the time, they had the appearance of being half closed."

In ten days Commander Robert E. Peary planted Old Glory at the North Pole, only to hear that Dr. Frederick A. Cook was claiming to have beaten him to it. "Have honor place north pole at your disposal," Peary flashed his Commander in Chief on September 8. The Chief flashed back from Beverly: "Thanks for your interesting and generous offer. I do not know exactly what I should do with it. . . ."

Next day, in the interests of international amiability the President was ferried out to the *Mayflower* where he presented the Taft Cup to the American winner of the Sonder races off Marblehead. This was a class of small sailing yachts originating in Germany. Vice Admiral Barandon and Count Betho von Wedel, chargé of the German legation, stood on the quarterdeck, bemedaled and straight as pokers. Glasses were raised, first to the absent Kaiser. "I drink to the health of His Imperial Majesty, the Emperor of Germany," President Taft concluded his toast. "Long may he live to contribute to the peace of the world."

Such ironies, however, are rarely perceived except in hindsight, and it was his private rather than his public appearances that were worrying Mr. Taft's advisers, specifically down the road a piece, amid the opulence at Pride's of "Eagle Rock" with Henry Clay Frick, one of those "malefactors of great wealth" so publicly excoriated by his predecessor in office. It seems that Secretary of State Philander C. Knox was the probable go-between. Knox was a distinguished Pennsylvania lawyer, William McKinley's Attorney General, who stayed on with Roosevelt after the assassination as a trust-buster and moved into Taft's cabinet in 1909. But Knox had known Frick intimately much longer—for thirty-five years—and had been counsel for the Carnegie Company. So when the Secretary of State came on to Beverly late in August to confer with Taft, he stayed with the Fricks nearby. The evening of August 31 the President dined with Knox and Frick at "Eagle Rock," and the papers got hold of it.

A horrible blunder, in the emphatic opinion of Taft's biographer, Henry P. Pringle: "The occasion was hailed as further proof that Taft was no faithful follower of Roosevelt but a friend and intimate of the wealthy malefactors." The worst in the Frick affair was yet to come.

After entertaining their globe-trotting Imperial Highnesses, Prince and Princess Kuni of Japan, President Taft signed with Mrs. Evans to lease the Stetson cottage again next summer, bade the hounds of dissension in his administration return to their kennels (such was his vain hope), and on September 14, 1909, entrained from Beverly on the first of his annual autumn tours of a nation he wasn't terribly enthusiastic about governing.

THE SUMMER OF 1910

The first family's second summer on the North Shore got off to almost as bad a start as the first. Teddy the Great Hunter was due home from his year in Africa. Bill Taft regarded the reunion with his old friend without enthusiasm. He was having trouble carrying forward the Roosevelt reform program and was dogged by his feelings of inadequacy alongside the Man with the Big Stick; he regarded TR's predictably flamboyant return to the political scene with foreboding and was anxious to placate him if possible. Roosevelt steamed back to a tumultuous New York welcome on June 18.

The former President was to attend the Harvard commencement with Henry Cabot Lodge, then call on Taft at the summer White House in Beverly on June 30. The sitting President planned to arrive at Beverly the day before. On June 28, son Bob Taft was at the wheel of one of the family motorcars with house guests from Yale, driving through Pride's Crossing, when suddenly around a bend he encountered a gang of men oiling the dirt road. Bob slammed on the brake. The workers scattered for the ditch—all but one, Michael Grigordio, who was knocked down. He was rushed to Beverly Hospital with a fractured skull.

Notified of this bad news in Washington, the President ordered the best medical attention available, came on the next day, June 29, as planned, and was driven almost immediately to the hospital, where he found Grigordio evidently out of danger. The Beverly police did not fault Bob for the accident.

The following day, June 30, Roosevelt, Lodge and Charles Evans Hughes, the governor of New York whom Taft had named to the Supreme Court in April, drove up from Nahant for lunch at the summer White House. The principals didn't relish being alone together, and though TR proposed that he be called "Theodore" and his successor "Mr. President," the talk was awkward and punctuated with Rooseveltian "bullies" and

Taftian apologies that he just couldn't get over thinking of himself as "Bill" and Theodore as "Mr. President." Plainly the former warm friendship of the two Republican leaders was on ice. So Taft's biographer had it.

Nellie was on hand and had it differently. "Remarkably pleasant and entertaining," she recalled, finding "the old spirit of sympathetic comradeship still paramount and myself evidently proved to be unwarrantably suspicious." TR was full of amusing anecdotes of his attendance as Bill's representative at King Edward's funeral in London and convinced Helen Taft that "he still held my husband in the highest esteem and reposed in him the utmost confidence, and that the rumours of his antagonism were wholly unfounded. I was not destined to enjoy this faith and assurance for very long."

Roosevelt was soon touring the country, expounding on his "radical" position that property rights were not necessarily supreme in all cases and indicating his discontent with his understudy's emerging conservatism. At Myopia Taft was tired and tense, bursting into profanity over muffed shots and once throwing his club twenty-five feet in a rage.

On the eleventh of July Taft played at Myopia with Jack Hammond, Judge Robert Grant, and Henry Clay Frick. The Frick connection was again noted in the press as a peculiar dalliance with the right wing. But, according to Henry Pringle, Taft liked Frick: "He would not listen to arguments on the subject. He even played poker, one night, at the Frick palace. This, however, was accomplished with stealth. The President, his military aide and Secretary Norton stole past the secret service guards and went, by themselves, to the home of the steel magnate." The *Breeze* noted in late September the presence of Mrs. Frick at Mrs. Taft's luncheon table, in spite of the First Lady's misgivings about the connection.

And not only the Fricks. In mid-July, biographer Pringle found out, J. Pierpont Morgan was spirited to shore in a motorboat from his yacht "with the secrecy of some criminal conspiracy" and met stealthily with the President for an hour. Not a whisper of that rendezvous leaked to the press, nor of another with ultraconservative Senator Nelson W. Aldrich, errand man of the trusts whom Taft distrusted but had to work with, power on Capitol Hill that he was.

Compounding the potential for embarrassment, Aldrich's son-in-law, John D. Rockefeller, Jr., was vacationing at Pride's Crossing even as the President impatiently awaited the Supreme Court's okay of his uncharacteristic resolve to break the Rockefeller grip on the oil industry. Strange neighbors, that summer on the North Shore. Aldrich and John D., Jr., slipped over to Eastern Point for a visit with Piatt Andrew, and one August morning the old man himself, John D., Sr., was spotted in his limousine parked on Main Street in Gloucester while his chauffeur ducked into a store for a package.

Doing some ducking and sneaking himself, Taft and family cruised down east to Maine in *Mayflower* for ten days. They were invited to Campobello Island, off New Brunswick. The President demurred, not wishing to break the presidential tradition of territorial quarantine, but his family accepted and was entertained at the summer home of young Eleanor

Roosevelt, whose husband was just breaking into New York Democratic politics. At Bar Harbor Mr. Taft sprained an ankle golfing.

On their return, the President hastened to visit Supreme Court Justice William H. Moody, summering in Magnolia and ill from overwork. Moody admitted that his health was forcing him into resignation, and Taft found himself once again in the ironic spot of appointing others to a position to which he had always aspired more than to the Presidency itself.

Following in the footsteps of Roosevelt—would he ever get out of them?—he crossed Massachusetts Bay to Provincetown on *Mayflower* on August 5 and dedicated the Pilgrim Monument, whose cornerstone TR had laid two years earlier. Along Cape Ann, the Atlantic fleet was on maneuvers

and five battleships anchored in Sandy Bay. The colorful visit was repeated the remaining two summers of the Taft administration, reinforced with submarines and torpedo-boat destroyers.

"I love my President," wrote Cecilia Beaux after sketching TR, probably in 1902. "He sat for two hours, talking most of the time." (Pennsylvania Academy of the Fine Arts)

Always, there were the Hammonds. Golf almost daily with Jack, a clambake arranged by Natalie at Loblolly Cove in Rockport and the garden party of the ladies' auxiliary of the Gloucester Day Committee (one of her pet projects) in Stage Fort Park near "Lookout Hill," and rather more exciting, the Harvard Aero Club's meet early in September, the largest held to date in the United States. The Wright brothers had a team entered, and the daredevil Glenn Curtiss was there, as were three of the flying machines from the Marblehead factory of the yacht designer W. Starling Burgess, who only a few months earlier had fallen under the spell of flight and formed his own airplane company. His father, Edward, designer of the America's Cup defenders, had learned to sail from Woodbury Point, where the Tafts were summering. The President on this airy day congratulated Boston's mayor, John F. Fitzgerald, on "Honey Fitz's" daring flight with the star of the show, Claude Graham-White. Mrs. Taft declined the English ace's invitation to soar like a bird, and his parents forbade their eager son Charlie to do such a crazy thing.

John Hays Hammond knew every President from Grant to Franklin D. Roosevelt except Chester A. Arthur, several well, Taft intimately, although it's doubtful he had the influence with Taft that another good friend and North Shore summer neighbor of his, Colonel House, was to have with

Woodrow Wilson. Presidents, emperors, dictators and tycoons, emissaries, cabinet members, senators, congressmen, governors—Hammond knew them all, and made a point of it—and Justices of the Supreme Court.

The President stayed on in Beverly later than usual in 1910. Late in September he and Nellie dined with Justice and Mrs. Oliver Wendell Holmes in their summer cottage at Beverly Farms. Their host was still a mere fledgling of sixty-nine. Taft's elevation over the great jurist's head as Chief Justice—he saw it as just that, an elevation from the Presidency—was eleven years in the future, at the hand of Warren G. Harding, who would renominate him for the Presidency two years hence.

On another occasion, as he enjoyed telling it, Hammond and a friend motored over to the Justice's cottage on their way to Myopia for lunch and persuaded him to break away from an opinion he was hard at work on, but only with the promise to Mrs. Holmes that they would have him back by three, for her husband loathed automobiles, would never own one, and could rarely be induced to ride in one. So engrossed were the three in conversation that from Hamilton they drove to the Eastern Yacht Club in Marblehead, forgetting entirely their pledge to Mrs. Holmes. More refreshments, and then at about six they boarded the Hammond yacht and arrived at "Lookout Hill" in time for a late dinner interrupted by a furious wife who had been phoning all over the North Shore trying to locate her wayward spouse. They bolted dinner and got Justice Holmes back on his doorstep, where Hammond abandoned him to his fate and retreated shamefacedly.

The President with his frequent North Shore companion, John Hays Hammond, Sr. (From The Autobiography of John Hays Hammond)

The attempted assassination of Mayor Gaynor of Hoboken, New Jersey, on August 9 prompted the Secret Service to tighten security around the Tafts and the summer White House. Two men patrolled the Stetson cottage and the grounds day and night, and another was constantly by the President's side, riding the running board whenever he ventured out to golf at Myopia or on his daily drives. A second car of agents followed, with a large plate saying "U.S.S.S." hung below the Massachusetts plate, warning other drivers that the President was up ahead and they should keep their distance.

Of this constant surveillance Nellie Taft wrote: "The secret service men, like the poor, we had with us always, but it never seemed to me that they 'lived' anywhere. . . . They were never uniformed, of course, and looked like casual visitors. They used to startle callers by emerging suddenly from behind bushes or other secluded spots—not I am sure because of a weakness for detective methods, but because they concealed comfortable chairs in these places—and asking them what they wanted."

These measures certainly contributed to what was regarded widely as the eccentric, if not downright unpatriotic, action of Mrs. Evans in informing the most illustrious tenant in the country that he need not bother to return to her cottage for the third summer of his administration. In short, she served notice of eviction on the President of the United States, never mind that he enjoyed the setup and gave it such credit for restoring his wife to health that he had hoped to keep coming until his term was up!

Mrs. Evans's stated reason was all the more staggering: she wanted to tear the house down and plant an Italian garden in its place. Something closer appeared in the *Gloucester Times* on October 11, 1910, a week later:

"Some time after the death of her husband, a year ago, Mrs. Evans stated that this would be the last year that the President would occupy the cottage on Woodbury Point. The informant added that when Mr. Evans let the estate to President Taft, he did so much against Mrs. Evans's wish; she knew then that the estate would practically become a public place, and that practically all her own pleasure in a summer there would be spoiled. As a matter of fact, her own house, next to the cottage occupied by the President, has been closed for most of the summer, and she has been away. . . . One of her great pleasures was taking walks about her estate in the morning, but with President Taft in the estate these walks became practically impossible.

"There were other annoyances also. The beautiful avenue of elms at all times has held the automobiles of the secret service men; their telephone nailed to a tree was in constant use; newspaper men on duty lay on the grass and the secret service men at the 'dead line' [probably the protective *cordon sanitaire* around the summer house].

"Sightseers constantly drove their motors into the avenues, and these sightseers had no hesitation, being forbidden to go up to the presidential cottage, in coming to Mrs. Evans's house to ask questions about President Taft's family. This was all very distasteful to Mrs. Evans and to her sisters, Miss Belle Hunt and Miss Abbie Hunt."

The Italian garden with which Mrs. Evans replaced the President's summer home. (Beverly Historical Society)

So the Tafts set about White House–hunting again. The Hammonds wanted them at Freshwater Cove, Magnolia or East Gloucester. Nellie inspected more than forty cottages, but the location or the size was wrong, or the rent too high, and nothing had been decided when the President finally had to return to Washington on October 17, driving through Beverly between a mile of three thousand scrubbed schoolchildren cheering and waving little flags.

TWO SUMMERS AT "PARRAMATTA"

Within a fortnight, however, the Tafts had "Parramatta," the beautiful and secluded estate of the late Henry W. Peabody, Salem and Boston merchant and shipowner, from whose widow they leased it for the 1911 and 1912 seasons.

The wild setting had reminded the well-traveled Peabody, who had known Taft when he was the first civilian governor of the Philippines in 1901, of the country around the Parramatta River in Australia. The sixty-acre estate was in the section of Beverly, a little inland of Woodbury Point and Mrs. Evans's cottages, known as Montserrat, after the West Indies island that long past had been a source of salt for the local fishing industry. Peabody formed a development syndicate in 1887 and bought the tract of ninety acres they called Montserrat Highlands, from which he carved out "Parramatta." He drained and cleared a swamp for a Japanese garden, made an artificial pond, laid out tennis courts and a nine-hole golf course, and built an eighteen-room mansion nestled on a commanding ledge.

But Henry Peabody died before he had much chance to enjoy the reality of his dream—not quite as prematurely, though, as George M. Pullman. The iron-fisted creator of the Pullman parlor car and the private varnish was negotiating with Peabody for the balance of the Highlands, planning to make an estate there to rival Frick's, when he died in 1897. What howls would have gone up from the Republican insurgents if the President had moved in next door to the malefactor who precipitated the bloodiest strike in American history—regarding which the then Judge Taft wrote vehemently (and privately) that more strikers should be killed to teach labor a proper respect for private property!

As for Maria Antoinette Evans, she was better than her word. She cut the Stetson cottage in half and had it ferried on a lighter across Salem Bay to Peach's Point in Marblehead, where it was reassembled. Back in Beverly, overspreading the foundations of the departed summer White House, Mrs. Evans planted an Italian garden after all, laid out before a classical colonnaded teahouse of stone, with arbors, terraces, pools, fountains, statuary, walkways and formal plantings—a garden regarded on her passing in 1917 as probably the most elegant of its kind in the United States and preserved, after a fashion, as a public park today.

An Italian Tuileries, but she could afford it, this Maria Antoinette with all the temerity of her namesake. When her husband's estate was probated in 1910, at $10,538,103, it was the largest ever filed in Essex County, and Mrs. Evans paid the largest personal property tax in Beverly and doubtless the county—$77,352 on possessions publicly assessed in excess of $5 million. She gave Boston University $200,000 to endow a department of clinical research and preventive medicine in her husband's name. She lived to see the immense Robert Dawson Evans gallery of the Boston Museum of Fine Arts,

Half of President Taft's first Beverly home mounted on blocks, ready for ferrying to Peach's Point in Marblehead. (Beverly Historical Society)

which she built for a million dollars, dedicated as another memorial to a dedicated trustee and collector—and she endowed it for another million, and more, in her will. One of the twelve richest women in America, it was said.

A more cordial landlady than her neighbor, Mrs. Peabody painted "Parramatta" a patriotic white in readiness for the 1911 season. The President was more beleaguered than ever. As his woes mounted, he retreated into the innately conservative and apolitical depths of his nature. The Roosevelt heritage, with whose keeping he had been charged, was withering in his unwilling hands. His domestic policies fell prey to the everangrier insurgents in his own party, while his heartfelt pleas for international peacekeeping machinery fell on deaf ears in the Senate even as the House fell to the Democrats in the 1910 elections. To the east, the ascetic visage of Woodrow Wilson loomed up over the horizon; on the west, the florid face of Theodore blazed forth in apoplectic sunset.

Taft sent his family ahead to the new summer White House in Beverly but was able to escape the heat of Congress and Washington for only a few short weekends. July arrived and departed, and so did the Atlantic fleet. On August 11 the President took the train for Beverly for a three-day break.

The next day, Saturday, at six in the evening, the presidential car was rolling nonchalantly along Boston Street in Salem. The Tafts relaxed in the back seat; the presidential aide, Major Archie Butt, was up front with the chauffeur. Just as they turned into Essex Street, William A. Jepson, a Boston coal dealer out for a spin with his wife, rounded the other way. "The two met on the turn," the *Gloucester Times* reported. "While the chauffeur of the President's car jammed on the brakes Mr. Jepson locked the wheels of his own machine. The two skidded for a short distance, and struck, locking together. The impact was not hard, and while it jarred the occupants of both cars, did not injure any one in either. Major Butt leaped out at once. He went around to Mr. Jepson as soon as he saw that President Taft, after the first scare of the collision had turned to reassure Mrs. Taft, who was manifestly uninjured, and took the matter calmly." When the unfortunate coal dealer "endeavored to back he found that his machine had been crippled," the report continued. "The impact had broken the springs, and disturbed the gearing so that the car could not be driven."

So the nation's First Car had to give way and back off, which was getting to be a familiar story with the President, who ordered a seven-passenger, sixty-six-horsepower 1912 model Pierce Arrow touring car, his third, in dark blue with a brown stripe. His seal was affixed to the door, and it was ready for him when Congress mercifully adjourned and allowed the executive branch to set up summer shop in "Parramatta" and the now-famous rooms of the Beverly Board of Trade on August 24. Also ready and waiting back at "Lookout Hill" were the Hammonds, whom the President had dispatched as his personal envoys to the coronation of King George V and Queen Mary of England in June. His friends smilingly hailed Jack as "Your Excellency" and Her Majesty addressed him as "Mr. Hays Hammond."

The foreshortened summer routine of golf, motoring and hobnobbing was resumed. Taft took the occasion of the Essex County Republican Club's outing at Congressman Gardner's "Sagamore Farm" in Hamilton to lambaste the unholy congressional alliance of progressive Republicans and Democrats who had forced him to veto their recent tariff cuts. The speech was regarded as the opening salvo in his campaign for reelection—a prospect for which he had little stomach. On September 21 he left Beverly for his annual autumnal swing around the country.

A month passed, and on October 26 his Attorney General, George W. Wickersham, fired the salvo that opened the final act of the Taft administration's self-immolation, an antitrust suit against the U.S. Steel Corporation. This was in the Roosevelt tradition, except that back in 1907, when it looked as if a financial panic would result if the overextended brokerage of Moore and Schley collapsed, Frick and Elbert H. Gary had proposed to TR to save it by having U.S. Steel buy the $5 million in Tennessee Coal and Iron stock the brokerage held for $45 million. Roosevelt had agreed not to regard the purchase as grounds for antitrust action.

But now, here was Taft's Attorney General four years later on a trust-busting binge, claiming in a suit that Henry Frick and Gary had deceived Roosevelt in order to gain control of Tennessee at what proved in time to be a bargain price. Taft was so insensitive politically that he apparently was unaware of the invidious implication. But Roosevelt was furious and never forgave him. Frick, on the other hand, rather reluctantly contributed fifty thousand dollars to Taft's campaign in 1912.

The President's troubles were piling up. On April 14, 1912, the liner *Titanic* struck the infamous iceberg and went down, and with it Major

President Taft addresses the town before laying the cornerstone for Beverly's YMCA, August 31, 1911. (Beverly Historical Society)

Archibald Butt, his faithful aide. Roosevelt was now savaging Taft, who responded like a wounded hippo. In June the two fought for the nomination at the Republican convention in Chicago. Taft steamrolled through on the party machinery. Roosevelt shouted "Thief!" and bolted, and the delirious Democrats nominated Woodrow Wilson in Baltimore.

Hence the arrival of the Tafts at Montserrat on the Fourth of July, 1912, was for them the more bittersweet than ever, in the hauntingly Far Eastern setting of "Parramatta." They were hardly settled when the next day the papers broke the news of Piatt Andrew's explosive resignation as Assistant Secretary of the Treasury, the idol of Dabsville utterly exasperated in his relations with Secretary of the Treasury Franklin MacVeagh, a grocery wholesaler by occupation. Caught between the least popular member of an unpopular cabinet and the brilliant bad boy who was the brains behind the front man, the President stuck with his establishment and fired Andrew. In Nahant Senator Lodge came to Doc's defense, as did the Roosevelt wing in general. The consensus: another family squabble miserably handled by Taft.

For the rest of July the President spent a weekend or two in Beverly before delivering a lukewarm acceptance speech in Washington on the first of August. On the fifth, the Bull Moose Party convened in Chicago. Theodore Roosevelt was nominated, splitting the Republicans, and the battle was joined, to the absolute delectation of the Democrats.

Through the soft North Shore September and most of its golden October, President Taft lurked in his summer retreat, golfing at his exclusive clubs, off on his afternoon drives with Nellie, but without the familiar figure of Archie Butt up front. Everything was the same, and nothing. Old friend Theodore barnstormed the land, badmouthing old friend Bill. Cabot Lodge agonized and stuck with Taft against his closest pal and almost lost reelection to the Senate for his political loyalty. Gussie Gardner remained loyal, and so did Doc Andrew in spite of his wounds. Nick Longworth, conservative to the bone, felt constrained finally to come out for Taft against his own father-in-law and lost his seat in Congress.

The Taft-Lodge alliance was never better than an uneasy one, and later they broke over the League of Nations, which Lodge fought in the Senate and Taft supported as the only hope for postwar peace. (How the tables would be turned thirty-three years later, when in 1952 Henry Cabot Lodge's grandson and namesake, a fervent internationalist, swept General Dwight D. Eisenhower through to the Republican nomination over Taft's son, the isolationist Senator Bob Taft from Ohio, and lost his own seat in the Senate to John F. Kennedy as Taft and the bourbon Republicans of Massachusetts knifed him in reprisal!)

A loyal old friend and supporter visiting "Parramatta" assured Helen Taft that her husband would be reelected. "Well," she said, "you may be right, but just the same I intend to pack everything up when I leave Beverly, and I shall take the linen and silver home."

It was a less-than-grand fall for the Grand Old Party, and on the fifth of November, 1912, Woodrow Wilson swamped Theodore Roosevelt, who swamped the incumbent, much to the lesser of the losers' relief. "What a dismal petering out for Taft," Caroline Sinkler, the Lavender Lady of Dabsville and Eastern Point, wrote her neighbor Doc Andrew. "But I do rejoice in thinking of that jealous and spiteful and small-brained MacVeagh returning without honor to his grocery or whatever they called it."

President William Howard Taft relinquished "the burden" to the lesser of the devils, he was certain, in March of 1913 and retired with a sigh to Yale to teach law—and that summer and every one thereafter to his "strawberry box" above the sweep of the St. Lawrence. His good humor returned, and his game. He wrote Henry Clay Frick from Murray Bay in that dark year of 1914: "I hope Myopia Links still give you the pleasure you used to derive from them when I was at Beverly. These links at Murray Bay are by no means so difficult as you may judge from the fact that I have been around once in 82 and once in 83."

President Taft's military aide, Captain Archibald Butt, who went down with the Titanic. *(Peabody Essex Institute)*

All was forgiven, after all. Frick read this note at a Myopia luncheon with the comment: "Eighty-two and eighty-three! Pretty good, I should say. And I used to wonder why I couldn't beat him. I ought to. I am eight years older than he is. I wonder if he would have mentioned the scores if they had been 102 and 103. I guess he would. There's nothing small about Taft. I must get up a game with Mr. Rockefeller. He is ten years older than I am and I may have a chance." Years later he did, and lost.

The next June the Parramatta Inn opened to the public on the rise of ground between the Montserrat station, with its weed-grown presidential siding, and the superb Italian garden of Maria Antoinette Evans. Nothing much had changed since the place was the nerve center of the nation. Each arriving guest, of course, was reverentially shown the oversize armchair said to have been custom-made for President Taft.

What does she see? Frank W. Benson, Summer, *1909.*
(Museum of Art, Rhode Island School of Design)

~18~

A CERTAIN AIR
OF UNCERTAINTY

*As war looms, diplomats confer, women conquer,
and time, momentarily, is held in abeyance*

Aweek before Mr. Taft and the Republicans formally handed the country over to Mr. Wilson and the Democrats, the Sixteenth Amendment to the Constitution was adopted, raising the first tax on private and corporate income in the history of the federal government, dropped by the foxes of capitalism as a bone to the hounds of redistribution.

The income tax was one end of the beginning of the end, not only of the Edwardian era as misapplied to the United States and the age of the tycoons, but also belatedly of the nineteenth century. The other end occurred three months afterward with the unremarkable arrival for the summer of 1913 at Norton's Point in Manchester's diplomatic enclave of His Excellency Constantine Dumba, the ambassador from Austria-Hungary. Within a year the heir to the throne of his artificially conjoined nation's throne had been assassinated at Sarajevo, and the Emperor of Germany, awaiting the merest of pretenses, took up arms against the Emperor of Russia.

If the crowns of Europe had rested as easy as their envoys on the Gold Coast of the North Shore, it all might have been sorted out over a few rounds of gin and bitters on one of the porches of the Oceanside, for there were more summering foreign ambassadors to the running foot of veranda on the Shore than any comparable stretch anywhere. Among the first was the Siamese legation, which discovered Bass Rocks and Eastern Point in Gloucester in the 1890s and took summer residence in cottages and hotels for decades after.

Toward the end of this interlude of illusion, when most were still on fairly cordial speaking terms, Baron Hermann Speck von Sternberg, the Kaiser's envoy, and Youssouf Zia Pasha of Turkey occupied Beverly Farms, Baron Mayor des Planches of Italy held down Manchester, and Baron Moucheur of Belgium had staked out Hamilton. Others of like pinstripe represented France, England, Brazil and a spectrum of colors on the map, trying to relax hither and yon between Beverly and Magnolia. One of the more popular of the barons was Roman Romanovich Rosen, representing the Czar in

America, usually at Coolidge Point in Manchester, where he arrived by motorcar in 1907, he jovially told the press, "without even killing a chicken."

The old-time, year-round natives tended to regard the peerage-in-residence with amused or not-so-amused tolerance. There was the Sunday morning when the Argentine ambassador drew up before Floyd's News Store in Manchester in a victoria drawn by a smart span of horses. His son came running in and so pestered for the ambassadorial newspaper that the busy proprietor finally wheeled on him in exasperation with: "I don't give a God damn if the Ambassador is waiting; put your ass on that stool and wait until I get ready to give it to you!" And there was the day the Manchester police nabbed and grilled two members of the Brazilian embassy as suspects in a housebreak. Ultimately convinced (perhaps reluctantly) that they had the wrong parties, they released the diplomats, who swore the State Department would hear about it.

The hiatal tone of this score of years preceding the War to End War—all loose ends and bewildered beginnings and everybody ever so certain about everything in between—was established at the right time, on the Fourth of July, 1893, in the right place, Nahant, as if contrived by Sigmund Romberg, and described in the right medium, the *Boston Transcript*. Several warships from the visiting Russian navy had anchored offshore, and the Nahant Club was entertaining a boatload of officers. The place was jammed. "The Russian band was playing with all its might and main. The Russian officers were scattered everywhere about the grounds, talking to the ladies, watching the tennis, playing pool and struggling with the English language, when suddenly a loud clanging of bells brought everything to a stop.

"At once there was a cry of 'Fire!' and in one mad helter-skelter stampede officers, band, ladies, guests and children rushed across the lawn down to the Nahant Road. In this free-for-all, go-as-you-please run, Lieutenant Something-or-Other of the Russian fleet won 'hands down,' and the spectacle was presented of a tall man in scarlet breeches, a long brown coat, a white fur cap, silver belt and silver dagger, leading a motley crew of Russians and Americans down across the lawn of the Nahant Club."

'Twas but a roof fire up the road, and a feeble one at that, but the international brigade, filled with the spirits of amity, made short work of it, and broke most of poor Herv Johnson's windows in the fray.

A beach of pebbles suits Cold Roast Boston at Nahant's Forty Steps, 1913. (Nahant Historical Society, Hammond Collection)

Nahant was in a fair way of becoming Cold Roast Russia. Senator Lodge and Governor Curtis Guild, year-round and summer residents respectively, were as political flypaper to dignitaries buzzing about the honey pot of the Gold Coast, especially Russians touching base with Ambassador Rosen at Manchester. In July 1908 the Guv held court in his summer State House for a certain Count Dobrinskay, touring the States with a certain Dr. William D. Carlisle, court dentist of all things at St. Petersburg—not Florida, but Russia. All in due course, Governor Guild was made Ambassador to the Czar by his summer neighbor, President Taft, in 1911.

All the same, Nahant held coldly to its roast, distinctly so from the rest of the Shore. "The compact social world was just as adroit, just as assured, and even more secure than a European group of the same size," Eugenia Brooks Frothingham, granddaughter of George and Mary Crowninshield Mifflin, reflected on the summer of 1904. "Sure of our loyalties, a forced departure for any social indiscretion—provided it was at all discreetly contrived—was unthinkable. In our midst were about three married couples who liked to hear themselves called the 'Gutter Club' and justify the name by their actions. They were all distinguished by birth, intelligence and education, so their chosen sobriquet was only partly descriptive. We thought them amusing. . . . The whole of that summer is a pretty picture, but I was not especially happy. I knew myself to be outside of a circle within which were the idioms of a social temperament which was strange to me. It had a thinness, a gayness, a sort of necessity for continuous enjoyment that I could only carry with effort to ultimate defeat."

This from a Mifflin, a Crowninshield, a Frothingham!

Needing to go nowhere, being already there, Nahant remained Nahant as the centuries turned. On the other hand, the Gold Coast from Beverly Cove through Manchester, principally, grew ever more golden, though still woven with threads of Old Boston sterling.

Fred Prince kept forty-five horses and seventeen miles of bridle paths on the fifteen hundred acres of "Princemere"—and sixty more in his stables in France. More and more mansions: Oliver Ames and his palace with its formal gardens the envy of a prince; William Amory Gardner's stone shack of twenty-three rooms and eleven baths above Mingo Beach; Quincy Shaw's, parlayed from a mining fortune; and Francis Bartlett's, from his father's forays into mines and rails.

High on a Manchester hill commanding 260 acres, 150 workers employed by Philip Dexter in 1910 blasted solid ledge for the building of his cottage, leveling ground for tennis courts, dredging for a pond—and still not as grand as the grandest on Coolidge Point, where T. Jefferson Coolidge, Jr., one-upped his old man, the tycoon, in 1904 with a monument to dynastic riches 230 feet in length that people promptly dubbed "The Marble Palace." *His* son tore it down in the late 1950s and replaced it with one as consuming but less conspicuous.

In West Manchester, Eben D. Jordan's prodigious pile was as much as Coolidge's a temple to family wealth. He was not a Brahmin, never could

be; his father came down from Maine at fourteen with the mandatory $1.25 in his pocket, founded Jordan, Marsh and Company, the massive department store, and bought a piece of the ground floor of the *Boston Globe*. Nothing inconspicuous about the younger Jordan's consumption in the dawn of the Age of Consumerism, or about his generosity: he built the Boston Opera House and added Jordan Hall to the New England Conservatory in honor of himself, and composed summer houses on an operatic scale—"The Forges" near Plymouth on the South Shore, where he kept his stables, and "The Rocks" at West Manchester.

Length serving as good a yardstick as any, "The Rocks" at 185 feet stretched halfway between Coolidge and Dexter. Completed about 1905 when the owner was forty-seven, it was Neo-Elizabethan Department Store inside and out, crushingly deposited upon the landscape, overpoweringly ornate in oak panel, mahogany and cypress, marble and fancy plasterwork, with the essential billiard rooms, stableman's cottage and the rest. When wearied of the environs of Boston, the Jordans leased estates and castles in Scotland. All rather well done on buttons, lingerie and Morris chairs.

Eben Jordan's summer neighbor on Smith's Point across Manchester Harbor was George Robert White, who had humbled along as a chore boy for the Boston druggists Weeks and Potter until they admitted him as a partner in 1888. In no time he had organized the Potter Drug and Chemical Corporation, biggest of its kind in the country; he invested heavily and wisely in real estate and by his prime was the heaviest, and wisest, taxpayer in Boston.

Bachelor White bought and tore down one of the original summer places overlooking Manchester's Long Beach in 1898, and built on the

T. Jefferson Coolidge, Jr.'s, "Marble Palace" in Manchester. (Manchester Historical Society)

heights a spacious shingled summer cottage he called "Lilliothea." By 1912, like Jordan, he hankered for a change. But instead of relocating, he set to work enclosing "Lilliothea" within a brick and stone shell, leaving a three-inch airspace between the old and new walls. That winter, as this fancy overcoat rose around the simple shingle, the eccentric soap maker (Cuticura was his brand) ordered the contractor to enclose the entire project within a second, temporary epidermis, heated so that his more than three hundred workers could continue uninterrupted by the weather.

Thus insulated in what his neighbors called his "Cuticura Soap Palace," George Robert White lived the remaining summers with his sister and brother-in-law, Mr. and Mrs. Frederick T. Bradbury, until his death in 1922. In his will this self-made soap king established the philanthropy he is remembered for, the George Robert White Fund for the benefit of the people of Boston, but left nothing to his adopted Manchester, which disgruntled some of the natives.

LEISURE'S PURSUITS

"With all the society columns of the summer papers filled with stories of what society is doing in its pursuit of personal pleasure, it is refreshing to note that not all its devotees are purely selfish in their activity," editorialized the *North Shore Reminder* in 1907. "Palatial summer homes are opened to the public for their functions, which though fashionably attended, are to result in funds for the happiness of less favored fellow beings. Society women, though wearied by their innumerable social duties, unselfishly give up an off day much needed for rest, and go up to town to superintend an outing of their pet charity. Others with a commendable desire to share the blessings which the gods have bestowed on them, invite properly escorted parties of children from city tenement districts to come for a day of delight in the beautiful grounds of their summer estates. . . . The inter-dependence of humanity's widely differing strata is coming into prominence as the problems of human existence are being taken up by the great minds of the day. . . . "

This was eight years after the publication of Thorstein Veblen's uncomfortably (to those members who chanced to read it) trenchant *Theory of the Leisure Class,* wherein he identified the "conspicuous consumption" that has since been embraced by all classes as "consumerism."

The pursuit of leisure had so far been institutionalized—in no season more so than summer, when it laid claim to all outdoors—that society women were finding that wealth and its uses and misuses imposed a drudgery as taxing as the domestic slavery from which the suffragettes were marching toward liberation. Social duties bred more social duties and the escalation of pretense. An American petty aristocracy was in the making, contrived and effete—not in Nahant, perhaps, where the blood lines had long been drawn—but along the Gold Coast without a doubt. Witness the *Breeze,* May of 1908:

> *Coachman*
> English, wants situation, thoroughly experienced in the care and training of horses, total abstainer, highest of references, with some experience in autos. 16 years in last situation, well acquainted with North Shore.

Society women, wearied by their duties, pleading in the public print for tutors, French teachers, French lady's maid, French dressmakers, laundress, chambermaid, seamstress, parlormaid, governess, gardener . . . For the North Shore matron who was longer on pretension than on staff, the Bureau of Social Requirements in Boston advertised that *its* staff was prepared to handle the purchase, sale and leasing of summer property, to close and open city and country residences, interior-decorate, shop market, pack trunks by the hour or day, provide visiting stenographers and amanuenses by the hour, mend and repair, shampoo and manicure at the patron's residence, and, wrapping it all up, fill mourning orders promptly.

The ultimate in hired elegance that made every matron an Adelaide Frick for a day was provided by William J. Creed, who in 1908 established in Beverly the catering business without whose total takeover no function could be considered quite de rigueur. Before striking off on his own, this Englishman raised in the Wodehouse tradition of domestic service buttled for the family of Robert G. Hooper in West Manchester; before that, in the 1890s, he was Henry Clay Pierce's steward in St. Louis and Pride's Crossing.

The help question, if a summer resident of sensitivity thought about it overly, could bring on a migraine. Perhaps taking a preliminary reading on his readership, young J. Alexander Lodge sent out an editorial feeler when his *North Shore Breeze* was but a month old in June 1904. The leading summer hotels of the Shore had announced that they would no longer employ blacks: "While we do not object to the negro and have no race prejudice, we believe this is a step in the right direction. The attitude of the negro servant in our summer hotels along the shore has become so overbearing that it has become a nuisance and we might say almost insulting." So much for that.

A problem of another complexion was presented by the servant population explosion. By 1906 recreational rooms euphemistically called "clubhouses" had been found for male and female servants in Magnolia who hitherto, the *Breeze* sympathized, had no off-duty amusements except to "sit, or walk, or go to bed." In 1909 the Men's Club House was built in Magnolia out of a fund subscribed by summer cottagers and hotel guests, with rooms mainly for "the rapidly rising class of chauffeurs" at least fifteen of whom (and here's the rub) had to be boarded by their employers at the Oceanside at sixteen dollars a week. Such was the craze for one-upmanship that servants were being imported faster than quarters could be provided for them, indeed were simply left to fend for themselves. A trained nurse had to hire an apartment for a year in order to occupy it two months in the summer, and the second gardener on a West Manchester estate was forced by his boss's frugality to hike seven and a half miles every day just to eat.

One of the select shops catering to the well-heeled on Robbers Row in Magnolia. (From the North Shore Breeze, *July 4, 1917.)*

By 1911 editor Lodge had had a change of heart and was taking the landowners of Manchester and particularly Beverly Farms to task for demanding such exorbitant prices for open property that thrifty and industrious domestics could not possibly afford to build homes for themselves; hardly one small cottage a year had been put up in the Farms in the last ten. "The bane of the North Shore has been its unwise and un-American class distinctions," chastised the *Breeze* in February. "The peril works damage to the best interests of all and the dreadful housing condition does more to irritate honorable men and women worthy of better opportunities for decent living to discontent and unhappiness than any other one thing. That there is not a single first class public house where a stranger can find a place to lay his head for a night at Beverly Farms, or where a party could obtain a simple meal, served with ordinary decency, is an unfortunate truth. . . . It is peculiarly lamentable when one considers the other side of the North Shore life with its splendid mansions, costly display and luxurious ease."

Within four years the Great Leveler was solving the servants' housing shortage forever.

MAGNOLIA: STYLE CENTER OF AMERICA

One should not retire from the field of domestic service on the North Shore without paying respects to a collateral amenity, Robbers Row, so designated by those who could and those who could not afford to patronize it. This consisted of the score or so of Boston, New York and Paris specialty shops that sprang up almost overnight on the Magnolia land of Miss Frances H. Stearns, an astute Boston business-woman who in about 1906 built a charming colonnade shading a blockfront on Lexington Avenue. These she added to and anchored with the leading night spot north of Boston, the North Shore Grill

Club, before she died in 1911. Their names were enough to send a cold chill down the backs of the men with the checkbooks, even on the hottest day of summer: Grande Maison de Blanc, Dreicer, Bonwit Teller, DePinna, A. Schmidt and Sons, Cammeyer, Harlow and Howland, and Mme. Mogabgab, to select a few, and they offered the fashionable everything from trousseaus, linen and jewelry to imported objets, furs and antiques.

Advertisement in the North Shore Breeze, *September 15, 1916.*

The exclusive integrity of Robbers Row was maintained even unto the Second War, when it dwindled bravely if pathetically. But in its snobby glory in the months before America entered the First War, the Colonnade, Lexington Row, the Colonial and the Arcade, shading their haute-couture storefronts, throngs of sophisticates and curbside lines of shining limousines, chauffeurs liveried and waiting, were thus hyperbolized in the *Breeze:*

"For years Magnolia has been acknowledged the premier style center of America and second only to Paris. . . . It has been the fate of many splendid resorts that hordes of lesser personalities have followed in the wake of the more select groups whose names and persons first graced the resorts and made them famous. In turn other multitudes of vacationists have swarmed to these centers to bask in the light shed by the socially prominent. The result has always been the same; society has sought new haunts. . . . Having prevented the incursions of crowds, which would make this section 'popular,' by the establishment of large estates and the exclusion of the cheap hotels, the North Shore—particularly Magnolia and vicinity—has become the headquarters of American society in summer."

THE QUEEN, ELEO, AND MRS. JACK

And then there were those—led off, perhaps, by a trio of *femmes formidables*—who could care less.

First, "The Queen," Louise Evelina du Pont Crowninshield, the Grande Dame of the North Shore from her marriage in 1900 to Francis Boardman Crowninshield ("Keno," the short and not too prepossessing last of his line) until her death fifty-eight years later, regally rich, fabulously fat and egregiously eccentric to the end.

Keno had his 109-foot schooner yacht *Cleopatra's Barge II,* updated from his ancestor's. His Queen had her jewels, her packs of Pekinese, her raucous pet macaw, her limousines, her charities, her antiquing (she dropped $175,000 casually one afternoon in a Maine shop; the owner's life was never again the same), her various stunning family estates to descend

Louise Evelina du Pont Crowninshield. (Peabody Essex Museum)

upon at will, her hats and her two million a year. Myriad are the stories, most of which she surely relished, concerning Louise—such as the great occasion when she presented the Peabody Museum of Salem with a handsome replica of the main cabin of the original *Cleopatra's Barge.* She acknowledged, from the audience, the president's fulsome praise of her as a veritable institution by quipping, "I presume you're referring to my size." Unabashed, she would bathe in the buff off Peach's Point in Marblehead, and for a joke had a chemical covertly added to her swimming pool to teach peeing children a lesson, when "at once," as Crowninshield in-law and biographer David Ferguson passed the story along, "purple streams issued forth from a couple of Boston's best old dowagers in tank suits."

As much the Talk of the Shore in

her own right was Eleonora Sears, and as self-liberated. Eleo (always Eleo) was the improper daughter of proper Frederick R. Sears, Jr., of Boston and Beverly Farms, granddaughter on her mother's side of T. Jefferson Coolidge of Manchester and the most famous female "jock" in a day when that sort of thing just wasn't done, not in the best of circles, anyway.

Eleonora Sears. (Beverly Historical Society)

Even as she was leaving all in her wake as a prodigious distance swimmer, by 1908 she was the eastern tennis champion in women's singles, doubles and mixed doubles. Betwixt dashes among Beverly, Magnolia, Boston, Newport, New York, California and Europe at tennis, golf, riding, swimming, squash, skating, backgammon and driving fast cars, Miss Sears announced in 1910 that she would defy the previous season's male outcry against her latest projected invasion. "Those who have seen her give an exhibition of whirlwind polo," the *Reminder* applauded with glee, "feel that she is quite capable of taking care of herself and will give some of the crack polo players of the opposite sex a good run for the honors." With her "berry-brown skin and twinkling blue eyes" she is "a busy and tireless example of the up-to-date society girl. At the same time, in evening clothes, she is as charming and womanly as the most feminine of her sex and carries herself with ease and grace."

But she shocked Propriety by striding along Beacon Street in riding britches and by turning up, on a dare, on the stage of the Majestic as a matinee extra. Over the years Eleonora Sears presided with haughty horsiness over her stables at Beverly Farms, ever the more eccentric exhibitionist. She plodded along on well-publicized hikes from Boston to Providence, followed by her limousine in low gear, chauffeur at the ready with restorative drafts of

hot chocolate; she fired guns over the startled heads of beachcombers who had the gall to pollute her beach with their presence, formed committees against the income tax, demanded the impeachment of President Truman, and that sort of thing. Bitchy, ruthless and unreasonably rich, yet richly endowed in the bursting bloom of her youth, peremptory, one of the first of the modern playgirls, this super Amazon smashed the sports barriers against her sex right and left, and in those (relatively) innocent years before the Great War—before she had left most of her grace behind—imparted to the North Shore an air of her own special snappy coolness.

The famous—and to some, infamous—Isabella Stewart Gardner, by contrast, was subtle, seductive, soulful, direct, supremely manipulative and quite as center-stage, the secret of which is the entrance.

The Gardners of Boston were old summerers of Beverly, and one day at the height of the 1891 season, being sports, they reserved seats on the maiden run of a new tallyho from Pride's Crossing to the Myopia Hunt Club in Hamilton. They missed the train at Boston, however. An hour later, as the gala coach-and-four was about to pull out, down the track thundered a locomotive of the B & M, belching smoke and steam, whistle screaming, bell urgently clanging. This apparition screeched to a grinding stop at the Pride's station, and out of the cab jumped Jack to help his Mrs. down from her seat in the nick of time. Arriving at North Station to a missed train, the Gardners had hired a spare engine on the spot, which was something you could do in those days if you had the right connections.

Isabella Stewart Gardner (right rear) sits beside Piatt Andrew on his terrace at "Red Roof," overlooking Gloucester Harbor, October 6, 1910. Sharing the view are the Japanese artist-scholar Okakura-Kakuzo; the pensive Lavender Lady, Caroline Sinkler; and Henry Davis Sleeper. (Andrew Gray collection)

In seven years Jack Gardner was dead, leaving his widow with the jack to create his and their memorial, "Fenway Court," for their growing art collection . . . and to perfect another institution, herself, as Boston's grandest and gayest of dames.

By 1907 Isabella had abandoned summering in the shingled Gardner cottage, "Alhambra" at Beverly, and her car too, and set upon an unashamedly regal progress of visiting around her North Shore friends and bumming rides from them, for she was feeling frugal; "Fenway Court," her palatial chef d'oeuvre, had opened to a stunned Boston in 1903, and it is doubtful that even she knew how much it had cost her. Around 1910, however, bank accounts were back in perspective, and Mrs. Jack commenced building "Twelve Lanterns," a cameo replica of a Spanish villa, above the shore on the ocean side of Marblehead Neck. The place had all the haunting otherworldliness of "Fenway Court," and its creator similarly supervised every detail, touched every corner with her intuitive taste. But if she planned to make this aerie her new North Shore base, she never did. In 1911 she presented it outright to one of her stable of handsome protégés, now no longer quite so young, the talented but lazy pianist George Proctor, on the occasion of his marriage to a former pupil, Margaret Burtt.

Another protégé—no, a *friend*—was the magnetically handsome, aquiline-featured Harvard economist Abram Piatt Andrew, who was to rise and fall so rapidly in President Taft's Treasury Department and personal favor. Soon after it opened, "Doc" was introduced to Mrs. Gardner at "Fenway Court" by their mutual friend Cecilia Beaux, the portrait artist summering on Eastern Point. Bachelor Andrew in 1903 was just occupying his dark and Gothic cottage "Red Roof," honeycombed with secret rooms,

Eleonora Sears's motorcar. (Beverly Historical Society)

hidden passages, bedchamber peepholes and unexpected mirrors, and hosting such favored Harvard economics students as Franklin Roosevelt. His neighbor Joanna Davidge, the proprietress of Miss Davidge's Classes for young ladies in New York, was moving into hers, with her mama.

"Bo" soon bought land beyond Joanna (both were ten years older than Doc, who was thirty-three years younger than Isabella) and moved into her "Green Alley" in 1906. That was the year Bo's friend Caroline Sinkler bought her cottage on the other side of "Red Roof." And that same spring, 1906, the soft-faced interior decorator with the hatpin wit, Henry Davis Sleeper, met Piatt Andrew, same age, same nonmarital status, and was invited down to "Red Roof" for the first time. Within three years Harry had bought an Eastern Point lot and moved with *his* mama into the core of what would become the great house-museum "Beauport."

Mrs. Gardner was invited down in September 1907 by Piatt Andrew for her first visit to Dabsville (Davidge-Andrew-Beaux-Sinkler-Sleeperville) on the magic shore of Eastern Point. On returning to her Brookline estate, "Y" (as soon she would be to all in her relation to Andrew) wrote "A" (as he would be to her) a gushing note: "In a few hours, what a change! The land change does not make one into something rich & strange—alas! Your village is Fogland with the sea's white arms about you all. Don't let outsiders crawl in—Only me! For I care. I love its rich, strange people, so far away."

Again and again "Ysabella" returned to the rich, strange people of Dabsville and their rich, strange guests—the James brothers, novelist Henry and psychologist William, the amiable editor Richard Watson Gilder, the imperious John Singer Sargent—with the sea's white arms about them all, as if . . . as if on the fourteenth of April, 1910, she wouldn't, couldn't, be seventy. But she was, and for four more years time stood still, or nearly so, in Dabsville, on Eastern Point, and the length and breadth of the North Shore, until that fatal June day in far-off Sarajevo.

Not the sea's white arms but the "sea howl and the sea yelp"—that and the salt-scented brier rose, the rusty granite and the song sparrows—drew the boy Tom Eliot back each summer to Eastern Point until he was twenty-three, when in 1911 he exchanged forever those impressionable summers for the seasoning summers of England. Time—that time sailing, tramping, staring at the blue sea and the blue sky, curled up with some arcane volume on the piazza of the Eliot cottage above Niles Beach, from 1896 until this so-cerebral son of the St. Louis brick manufacturer graduated from Harvard in 1909—clamored and clanged in the poet's memory of fog in fir trees and "the heaving groaner / Rounded homewards," so hauntingly evoked in *The Dry Salvages*.

Out of the Great War emerged *The Waste Land*, and out of that waterless watershed of modern poetic expression were expunged seventy-one lines describing the outward-bound trip of a Gloucester fishing schooner and her fatal collision with an iceberg, a voyage canceled in the manuscript on the urging of Ezra Pound. And in total contrast, the lightheartedness of

the bird-lover in that concise panegyric *Landscapes* with the surprise ending, "Cape Ann."

Although many the literary laborer has found the North Shore hospitable to his muse, few have drawn inspiration from their surroundings as directly as the artists have; far fewer have succeeded in universalizing their perceptions of the place and the people. Eliot's immersion along a particular shore of the Shore was granted him during his formative years. The imprint remained as fresh in his mind's senses as the fog in the firs. Nearly fifty years after he left, this alienated soul returned one summer day to sniff it out and was gone again, satisfied or not, as suddenly as he had reappeared.

A child of fogs and fancies. Tom Eliot on his family porch at Eastern Point. (Sawyer Free Library, Henry Ware Eliot collection)

Godfrey Lowell Cabot at the controls of his Burgess-Dunne seaplane, The Lark, *doing all in his considerable power to ward off the Kaiser. (Cabot family collection)*

~19~
TOUS ET TOUT POUR LA FRANCE

*War sweeps across the sea and engulfs the Shore,
from an eager Patton to a reluctant President*

> It was during this summer that the then Italian
> Ambassador, Marquis Cusani, was established in the
> neighborhood and often came to the studio at [Eastern
> Point]. I did a drawing of him and it was from him, on
> that splendid summer afternoon when the news came, that
> we heard it. His view, in his clear and perfect English,
> would have been interesting to remember—but how little
> we guessed that we—we—were just entering the most
> awful moment of History.
>
> —Cecilia Beaux, *Background with Figures*

EUROPE WAS A TIME BOMB THAT
spring of 1914, ticking away while the world waited and trembled.
Woodrow Wilson sent Colonel Edward M. House across to see if cool
American reason could disarm disaster. In May the President's Silent Partner
met with Kaiser Wilhelm in Berlin and reported back on the twenty-ninth:
"It is militarism run stark mad. Unless someone acting for you can bring
about a different understanding, there is some day to be an awful cataclysm.
No one in Europe can do it. There is too much hatred, too many jealousies."

A month later the fuse was touched at Sarajevo. House sailed with
heavy heart, arriving at Boston on July 29, and went straight to the cottage
he had rented for the season at Pride's Crossing. On the first of August, that
"splendid summer afternoon," the bomb exploded with Germany's declaration of war, sooner even than he had feared. On that day House wrote
Wilson, hoping he would cruise up to the North Shore on the presidential
yacht *Mayflower* for relaxation and talk, but it was not to be.

Pouncing on Belgium while Austria-Hungary held off the Russians,
Germany aimed for the heart of France. In far-off Beverly French chauffeurs
gave notice and booked passage *pour la patrie*. Fifth Avenue's Grande
Maison de Blanc's Magnolia shop announced that a shipment of children's

coats and bonnets in the latest mode had fortuitously arrived from Paris before hostilities had broken out. Anxieties were expressed about the safety of friends and relatives abroad, and the sanctity of foreign business connections. Even the weather frowned. Fewer found solace upon the beaches, or in their clubs. There was a temptation to retrench.

Two weeks after the armies of Europe marched, the Royal Hungarian Orchestra was the popular dancing attraction in the North Shore Grill's new outdoor garden. Well offstage, however, the *Breeze* sounded an uncertain trumpet: "It is impossible for the new world to entirely forget the conflict in the old world, but it is a rare spirit that has the ability to find rest and peace of mind in the midst of this martial conflict."

THE AMERICAN FIELD SERVICE

Piatt Andrew had loved France ever since his graduate studies had taken him there, had Frenchified his house and everything in it. Though a native Hoosier, he was a Princeton graduate, a noted economist and an internationalist. In September of 1914, as the German army advanced on the Marne, he ran in the Republican primary for Congress against, of all people, Isabella's favorite nephew, Gussie Gardner, the incumbent, and was beaten.

Stinging from defeat, burning for the great cause he knew his country must sooner or later join, Doc organized the American Field Service to help the French evacuate their casualties from the front . . . and as a ploy, he hoped and prayed, for drawing America into the war. Inspector General Andrew, chief of the Field Service, sailed for France in December of 1914, leaving loyal Harry Sleeper behind in charge of raising money for ambulances and recruiting idealistic young college men to drive them.

By early 1915 what began as a North Shore project was siphoning off the first young adventurers from the college campuses of America for the battlefields of France. Andrew set up his headquarters in the small hospital in Neuilly-sur-Seine supported by the American colony in Paris. Henry Ford had invented the moving assembly line in 1914 and the next spring was shipping across the first of the twelve hundred chassis ordered by the Field Service to put under its French-built ambulance bodies. Mr. Crane stood for three, Mr. Frick for two, and Mrs. Gardner's had a cryptic Y painted on the door.

And then the flood of hellbent volunteers shuttling between the trenches and the shellholes and the *postes de secours* with their bounding burdens of the maimed and dying, and dying themselves, and "busily writing and agitating in terms that were not neutral," in Andrew's words, "sending to their families and friends throughout the Union, to their home papers, to their college publications, and to American weeklies and magazines the great story of France and her prodigious sacrifice. . . . Herein lay by all counts the greatest contribution which the men of the Field Service could make and did make to France. . . . The epic and heroic quality of France's whole history,

and especially of that chapter of which we were eye-witnesses, the quench-less spirit and unfaltering will of her people, the democacy, the comradeship, and above all, the calm, unboasting, matter-of-fact courage of her troops, kindled something akin to veneration in all of us. The Field Service motto was 'Tous et tout pour la France.' We all felt it. We all meant it. It is forever ours."

Among the graphic, horrifying eyewitness accounts to find their way into wider print were the letters sent back to his Gloucester friends in Dabsville and his special friend Jack Hammond, Jr., by the good-looking young English émigré-actor Leslie Buswell, holder of the Croix de Guerre; they were published as *Ambulance No. 10*, edited and prefaced by Sleeper and Andrew. After his return in 1916 Buswell and Hammond were "extended guests," as the *Breeze* phrased it, at Sleeper's "Beauport."

The younger Hammond had his father's genius if not his hail-fellow sociability, having followed him through Yale's Sheffield Scientific School, where he developed such an interest in radio, then in its infancy, that the senior staked him to a $250,000 laboratory on "Radio Point" below "Lookout Hill" in 1911.

Soon Jack, Jr., was startling fishermen with an unmanned, radio-con-trolled motorboat that he raced around Gloucester Harbor from his lab. In March of 1914 his remote-controlled radio-gyroscope steered the experi-mental *Natalia* to Boston and back with a naval observer aboard. Here in action was the brain behind the brain behind the autopilot and the guided

Inspector General Piatt Andrew of the American Field Service (right) in France with ambulance driver Leslie Buswell. (Andrew Gray collection)

missile and the space shuttle. Then he went on to 128 patents for radio-controlled torpedoes that he sold the government for $750,000 in 1916. As a side venture in 1914 Jack invented a light incendiary aerial bomb that was rejected by both the United States and Britain. But when such bombs fell on London, he was accused of having peddled the design to the Germans and was not cleared, so it is said, until a former employee admitted stealing and selling the plans to the enemy.

Italy's entrance into the war against the Austro-Hungarian Empire on May 23, 1915, dealt another rude reminder to the North Shore of Old World troubles. Italians, as the *Breeze* had remarked only six weeks earlier, had replaced the Irish as the dominant laboring class in the area, making less than two dollars a day, living accordingly, some well trained, most unable to speak English. "It is true that they are selfish in their desires to learn English, but on the other hand there is a moral and economic reason why the New England towns and cities should try to do something for them."

This uplifting advice came too late. As the French chauffeurs had responded to the call, so now did the Italian reservists, and in such large numbers that in August the John Hays Hammonds were persuaded to sponsor at "Lookout Hill" an Italian fiesta for the benefit of the families of these patriots under the patronage of the Marquis Macchi di Cellere, the ambassador summering at Beverly Farms. It was the social event of the season.

A home *front* would violate the President's strictures on neutrality—except that the North Shore branch of the French Wounded Emergency Fund met twice a week in Mrs. Walter Denegre's coach house at West Manchester and turned out more than fifteen thousand medical supplies a month. Not bad for unpaid piecework in a dowager's summer cottage industry.

Something was happening to home and hearth. For five years the suffragists and those who could not suffer them had been having at it in the letter columns of the *Breeze* when Lillian McCann, a not dull observer of the summer scene, awoke one day in July 1916, as Europe lay bathed in blood, with a sense of elevated awareness:

"Do you know how the women of the most exclusive homes of America, gathered on the North Shore for the summer, are toiling to make life pleasanter for the soldier at the front, to help the nurse in the hospitals, and to aid the family at home, left without its breadwinner? The ability to do something worth while—to stand for something, is gaining many a society woman a new zest in life. The ability to open and build up such workrooms as are on the North Shore might spoil any woman for the life she has always been supposed to lead, by men. Before the war, the world seemed made for the comfort of the well to do and travel was as safe as staying at home. But all that seems tame and uninteresting now. Action is the word, and practically all of our women have interests vastly more important than golf, tennis or tea."

Action *was* the word, male and female, neutrality be damned. First the

Field Service and now at long last another return of favors to the Marquis de Lafayette. It came about this way:

W. Starling Burgess, son of the North Shore's late, great yacht designer, had in due course picked up the paternal torch and was a successful fashioner of boats of beauty in Marblehead when in 1909 he was asked by Augustus M. Herring, an irascible but pioneering airplane designer who had fallen out with Glenn Curtiss, to build a biplane for him in his yacht yard.

Flying Fish emerged from this mix of creative juices and skittered a few hundred wobbly feet low over the sands of Plum Island on April 17, 1910. Among the aviation nuts on hand were two scions of rock-ribbed North Shore families, Norman Prince and Greely S. Curtis, Jr. A Grottie and Harvard 1908, Prince was a compact, rugged, clean-cut student of twenty-two at the Harvard Law School whose distinguishing mark was a yellowish moustache. He was a chip off Frederick H. Prince, cofounder of Myopia, and grew up on "Princemere," the family acres at Wenham. Curtis was pushing forty, a son of General Greely Curtis, commander of the First Massachusetts Cavalry in the Civil War, who had come up from Boston and built "Sharksmouth," the first of the truly grand summer mansions, on the Manchester shore in 1868. With some background in aeronautics at Cornell, Curtis persuaded Burgess to let him take the controls of *Flying Fish* a few days after the Plum Island trial and immediately cracked her up. Herring took a perhaps understandable dislike to him, quit the company in a huff, and was replaced as Burgess's partner by his nemesis.

Meanwhile, Burgess, being Burgess, just naturally had to work a boat in there somewhere and that year built his first hydroplane; the Navy began ordering his improved model in the spring of 1913. A year later the Burgess Company produced a radical new hydroplane under the patents of the English designer I. W. Dunne, the Burgess-Dunne, and by the end of that first war year, both the Army and the Navy were taking delivery.

Piatt Andrew, campaigning for Gussie Gardner's congressional seat in June, was flown up one day, cap on backward, to land on the Merrimack River in this open-aired contraption, leaning out with his camera on the way to snap the first aerial photo ever taken of Cape Ann.

THE LAFAYETTE ESCADRILLE

Europe had been hardly a month at war when Greely Curtis's younger brother, Frazier (though thirty-eight and with limited flying experience), sailed on September 2 on the *Arabic*, hoping to enlist in the Royal Flying Corps—the first Yank to volunteer abroad as an aviator. Politely rejected on account of his age and his citizenship, which he would have had to renounce, he returned to the States with the notion that he might be accepted if he bought a Burgess-Dunne and brought it back with him. But first he had to learn to fly it, so he enrolled in the school Burgess had established with the object of turning out pilots as fast as planes.

It happened that Norman Prince was back in Marblehead from practicing law in Chicago with the same object as Curtis's, much against the wishes of his father. The two now conceived the idea of getting up a volunteer Yank squadron to take to the air against the Boche. Norman knew France intimately, spoke the language, loved the people. Still, flight training, let alone actual combat, in those pioneer days of flimsy flying machines with wings of fragile fabric held together by struts and wires, and uncertain engines, was by the seat of the pants, and a father rightly worried for a son. Indeed, in one year at a Texas training field more than forty students were killed in crashes, and at least two hundred more were injured.

After another battle with his father, Norman sailed for France on January 20, 1915, to organize an American *escadrille* (squadron) to fight alongside the French. Frazier Curtis returned to England, where his offers were again declined, and then joined his friend in Paris. Prince tackled the French bureaucracy, which only after months of his insistent argument began to sense the potential of his proposal. At last both men, with Elliott C. Cowdin of New York (a year behind Prince at Harvard), hung on to U.S. citizenship by enlisting in the French Foreign Legion along with scores of their countrymen ready to fight in the trenches if necessary.

The three aviators shifted to Pau, in the lower Pyrenees—Prince family horse country—for flight training, joined by Bill Thaw, a seasoned pilot already flying with the French forces. Injured in several crashes and not an adept airman, Frazier Curtis washed out, returned to the States, and organized the Harvard Flying Corps. In the meantime, Prince got the financial backing of William K. Vanderbilt.

That December of 1915, Prince, Cowdin and Thaw inveigled eight-day leaves back to America in time for Christmas. With her son home for the holidays, Abigail Prince was suddenly possessed with the terrifying thought that she might never see him again, and on January 2, two days before his departure, determined to have his portrait painted. The Princes engaged Frank W. Benson, the noted Salem artist, reportedly for ten thousand dollars. Benson took the train that same night to New York, where a room at the Hotel Vanderbilt was improvised as a studio. There he painted the young flyer all the next day. At dusk the portrait was done. The following day Norman, with his older brother Frederick H. Prince, Jr., who wanted to enlist in the French Army, sailed for France.

On April 20, 1916, *L'Escadrille Américaine* was officially organized and assigned to the worst of the Western Front, the slaughterhouse of Verdun. Headquartered in the ironically idyllic village of Luxeuil-les-Bains, they were to provide fighter escort for a French bombardment squadron. While they waited for their planes they borrowed a trainer, and Prince, whose faulty depth perception should have disqualified him at the outset, flew it through the hangar wall on his first try and wrecked it.

Six new disassembled French Nieuport single-seat fighters arrived by van at Luxeuil the first week in May, and the entire squadron pitched in putting together their *bébés,* as the French aviators affectionately called them. On May 13, eleven months before the United States entered the war, the volunteers of *L'Escadrille Américaine* flew their first mission against Germany.

Even as Norman Prince and his Escadrille flew their baptismal missions over the tortured earth of Verdun that verdant May morning of 1916, another Brahmin of an age to be their sire, Godfrey Lowell Cabot, was organizing his own private squadron back on the North Shore. One of the wealthiest and healthiest (he died at 101 in 1962) men in Boston, America's leading manufacturer of carbon black was only fifty-four when he learned to fly the Burgess-Dunne at Marblehead in the spring of 1915. In a year he bought the western end of Misery Island, directly offshore of his Beverly Farms summer estate, and erected a

Lieutenant Norman Prince, a founder of the Lafayette Escadrille. (From New England Aviators, 1914–1918.)

hangar for the B-Ds he got a few rich younger fellow patriots to buy and learn to fly and fight in, against the day when he foresaw that America would make Europe's war its own. He leased Gooseberry Island, a chunk of rock southwest of Baker's Island, as a target for gunnery and bombing practice.

For all his crusty Bostonism, Cabot had the soul of the innovator: in the course of announcing these plans for his Massachusetts Independent Aviation Corps he proposed that for less than four million dollars the Navy could equip twenty-four warships with torpedo, fighter, spotter and patrol planes, and the catapults to launch them with. After a year, American belligerence and his own commissioning as a Navy pilot ended the private Cabot air corps. Lieutenant Cabot patrolled Boston Harbor in his seaplane, *The Lark*, and went on to invent the technique of in-flight refueling.

Starling Burgess quit his own company when he was commissioned in charge of the Navy's Bureau of Construction and Design in Washington in December 1917, and when his airplane plant burned on November 7, 1918, it never reopened.

Over in France, the myopic Prince vision dogged Norman on the ground and in the air, drawing from one historian of the Escadrille the mournful comment that his "notoriously poor depth perception had caused him to wreck more Nieuports than any other man in the squadron." Frustrated by many misses, he for a while settled on being the first in the Escadrille to down a German observation balloon with a battery of electrically fired Fourth of July skyrockets. Finally, on August 23, 1916, he picked off the machine gunner in an Aviatik six miles behind the enemy lines and herded the Heinie pilot triumphantly back to earth and captivity. On September 9 he downed a Fokker. On the morning of October 12, still in the Verdun sector, the Escadrille convoyed a bombing raid across the Rhine. Prince shot down an attacking E-III, his third confirmed victory out of 122 engagements.

As he approached a patch of an emergency field in Corcieux at dusk, his eyes deceived him again. Coming in too low, he struck a high tension cable with his landing gear and flipped. His seatbelt snapped, and he was flung to the ground with such impact that both legs were badly broken. Two days later Norman Prince died of an embolism in the field hospital. Croix de Guerre. Legion of Honor. His place was taken by his waiting brother, Fred, Jr. Two months later, on the suggestion of its ambassador in Washington, France changed the name of *L'Escadrille Américaine* to *L'Escadrille Lafayette*.

The premonitions of a mother . . .

THE UNITED STATES JOINS THE ALLIES

Back on the North Shore for the summer of 1914 after his fruitless intermediary mission to Europe, Colonel House continued proselytizing for peace among the vacationing diplomatic colony, several times in September with Ambassador Dumba of Austria-Hungary. In spring of 1915 he sailed again for Europe, on the *Lusitania*. But when a German U-boat torpedoed her on May 7 on the return trip, with the loss of 1,198 lives, many of them Americans, all chance of an American-negotiated cease-fire sank too. House returned to America on June 5, determined to persuade President Wilson to prepare for inevitable war with Germany.

House was still at sea when a cabal of like-minded alarmists organized the Conference Committee on National Preparedness under the influential industrialist Henry A. Wise Wood, a summer resident of Annisquam. Wood was one of the sixteen children of that interesting New York City mayor and congressman, Fernando Wood—wealthy inventor and manufacturer of newspaper-printing machinery, an early aviation editor, yachting enthusiast and all-round gadfly on behalf of the causes that arrested his attention, including the considerable challenge of awakening America.

As keen a Democrat as his summer friend and neighbor John Hays Hammond was a Republican, Wood from the beginning of the war had deprecated the President's see-no-evil, hear-no-evil policy of neutrality and put Hammond up to pressuring his neighbor Ed House to urge on Wilson the political importance of armament.

However, House was unable to push the President as far or as fast as the preparedness advocates urged, in spite of the horror of the *Lusitania*. He met openly and secretly several times with the British ambassador, Sir Cecil Spring-Rice, who had a cottage at Beverly Cove. The pacifist Secretary of State, William Jennings Bryan, had resigned in a difference of policy after the *Lusitania* crisis, and his successor, Robert Lansing, late in July traveled up to Manchester to talk with Wilson's kitchen cabinet minister. Navy Secretary Josephus Daniels visited House and Hammond and seemed to be coming around to beefing up the fleet, but quarter-steam ahead was too slow for Henry Wise Wood, who in December walked off the Naval Consulting Board in disgust, went over to the Republicans, and after the war wanted to impeach Wilson for his advocacy of the League of Nations.

The Wilson-haters on the dominantly Republican North Shore were rabid on the issue of his apparently doctrinaire attitude of neutrality, a stance he had of course inherited from his Republican predecessor. Godfrey Cabot fumed that Wilson didn't have the ability to run a peanut stand. Young Lieutenant George S. Patton, Jr., wrote his father, who was campaigning as a Democrat for the Senate in California in 1916, "I would like to go to hell so that I might be able to shovel a few extra coals on that unspeakable ass Wilson. . . . He has not the soul of a louse nor the mind of a worm. Or the back bone of a jelly fish."

Colonel Edward House and President Woodrow Wilson. (From The Intimate Papers of Colonel House.)

In the spring of 1916 Colonel House made the rounds of the belligerent capitals for the third time, returning to Sunapee, New Hampshire, for the summer to escape the incessant interruptions at the North Shore, which had become, Hammond wrote, "a veritable 'hub of the universe': every important diplomat who came from Europe was sent by President Wilson to consult with the colonel." As the year dragged on and the nightmare deepened, hope for peace talks glimmered once more, only to be doused altogether by Germany's sudden decision to attempt to bring Britain to her knees with unrestricted submarine warfare in February 1917.

Visions of U-boats prowling off the beaches of the North Shore had a thrilling effect in certain quarters. The President was two weeks away from declaring war when the *Breeze* rejoiced over prospects of a boom season—practically every available cottage had been rented (at $2,500 to as high as $6,000 that summer): "Jocular references to submarine attacks on this side of the water have little terror for residents of the North Shore, as is evident by the number of early arrivals this season. . . . In the minds of city dwellers there is confidence that on the North Shore there is security from any of the sufferings incident to the war."

Then on April 6 Woodrow Wilson abandoned the role of peacemaker, and the United States, prepared or not, jumped in. The early exodus to the "safe haven" of the Shore, the *Breeze* decided just a little nervously the same day, was inspired by widespread fear of disorder and sabotage around munitions plants and naval bases. "The chance of a German submarine picking its way among the hidden reefs and jagged rocks of the North Shore to get near enough to land to fire a shot, is about as remote as the possibilities of the German fleet itself being able to get out of its 'bottle' into the Atlantic Ocean."

Lieutenant Patton, the abrasive West Pointer who had dreamed of attracting President Taft's approving attention in the summer White House days, had won beautiful Beatrice Ayer—his first important victory—when they joined forces and fortunes one triumphal May day in 1910 before the flowered Episcopal altar in Beverly Farms. A jeweled throng attended, many by means of a special train from Boston commanded thence by the snowy-bearded father of the bride, Frederick Ayer, eighty-eight, patriarch of the Ayers and of the giant, sprawling, smoking, whirling American Woolen Company. Georgie honeymooned Beat to Europe, prophetically on the *Deutschland*.

They arrived on leave from Texas at palatial "Avalon," her family estate in Pride's Crossing, some days after the "jellyfish" declared war. Patton

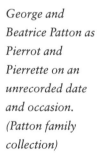

George and Beatrice Patton as Pierrot and Pierrette on an unrecorded date and occasion. (Patton family collection)

wrote General John J. Pershing, whose aide he had been in the Punitive Expedition against Mexico, that "all the people here are war mad and every one I know is either becoming a reserve officer or explaining why he can't. It looks to me as if we were going to have too many reserve officers many of whom are meer children." This more than faintly Prussian-type cavalry officer of thirty-one must have noticed that at the family club, Myopia, fewer than six of the usual thirty started a meet that season.

In pursuit of rare amusement, *Mayflower* steamed into Gloucester Harbor and dropped anchor off Hammond's "Lookout Hill" on the ninth of September, 1917. A Navy launch ran the Wilsons in to the public landing, where they were met by the Houses. It was Sunday, and the Commander-in-Chief and his party drove through the streets of the fishing port almost unrecognized, on along the western harbor shore, past Hammond's estate and through Magnolia to Coolidge Point, where they paused briefly at the House cottage and the Coolidge mansion to inspect memorabilia inherited by T. J. from Thomas Jefferson. Then on a two-hour drive along the North Shore, they stopped to inspect the marvelous Italian garden that Mrs. Robert Dawson Evans had planted at Burgess Point in place of the summer White House from which she had summarily evicted the President's predecessor. That evening the Houses dined with the Wilsons aboard *Mayflower*.

On Monday morning the men golfed at the Essex County Club. In the afternoon, another motor tour from Salem to Ipswich. Back aboard

"Avalon," the Pride's Crossing mansion of Frederick Ayer. (Patton family collection)

Mayflower for dinner, and on Tuesday morning the President headed back for Washington and the burdens of the war he had sought for three years to keep his country out of, an effort that rewarded him with narrow reelection in 1916.

RIGHT HERE AND OVER THERE

Now that the nation was in the thick of it, the *Breeze,* North Shore society's conscience in such matters, predicted that summer activities would assume "a more serious tone." Mrs. Congressman Gardner of Hamilton signed a summit agreement with eight other Washington socialites: "1. No meal to exceed three courses. 2. One meatless day a week. 3. Simplicity in dress and entertainment." Yachtsmen organized a Coast Guard auxiliary patrol out of Marblehead, where the Navy was taking over the Eastern Yacht Club as headquarters for its submarine-chaser fleet. And suddenly the *benefit* took center stage as entertainment. There were house and garden tours, readings, concerts, musicales, specialty dog shows and so on for hospitals, surgical dressings, the Red Cross, and even a song recital at the Gallery-on-the-Moors in East Gloucester by the Duchess de Richelieu on behalf of the French Tuberculous Soldiers' Relief Fund.

Albert C. Burrage offered his own brand of assistance. This small-town boy from Ashburnham had piled up a fortune speculating in Chilean copper. He summered at "Seahome" in West Manchester, grew prize orchids by the tens of thousands in his Beverly Farms greenhouses, cared for sick and crippled children by the hundreds by building Burrage Hospital on Bumkin Island in Hull Bay, and entertained guests by the score aboard his steel 260-foot schooner-rigged steam yacht *Aztec,* one of the ten biggest in America. Now Burrage offered Uncle Sam the use of his personal hospital for sick and wounded sailors, proposing to stand the expense of it up to four thousand dollars a month . . . and *Aztec* as a hospital ship up to eight thousand dollars a month—both for a minimum of four months.

Over at Pride's a patriot of a different stripe, William H. ("Judge") Moore, was moved to admit the public for the first time to his private horse show for the benefit of the Red Cross. In Ipswich the Cranes opened the gates of Castle Hill (or at least the casino at one end of their vast swimming pool) to help the Scottish Women's Hospitals for Foreign Service.

Frederick H. Prince, Sr., had by then stood behind a son, and in another step he sacrificed the heating of the greenhouse to the coal shortage and a flower garden or two to vegetables under the "Hooverizing" of federal food administrator Herbert Hoover. The *Breeze* sacrificed space every week for the explicit instruction of the Irish cooks on the Shore as to the exact number of jars of this or that to be put up from the vegetable (ex-flower) plots.

Forty society girls, as the war dragged into planting time in 1918, sacrificed nine hours a week in the four acres of vegetable gardens on the Dudley Pickman estate at Beverly Cove—equal, it was proudly claimed, to the labor of eight men. The North Shore Garden Club organized a service auxiliary of

"Farmerettes" to grow produce for the Beverly Hospital. Estate owners supplied land, horses and manure; the girls brought their own seeds, tools and automobiles, with and without chauffeurs. Most wore the national garb of the Farmerettes—khaki smocks, bloomers and leggings designed by Miss Gregg of the exclusive Winsor School for Girls in Boston.

In her library at Pride's, Mrs. Bayard Warren taught her friends how to machine-knit socks for the doughboys. At Beverly Farms Mrs. George Lee permitted the folding of surgical dressings in her garage. At Manchester Miss Charlotte Read borrowed a car from the local Ford dealer, took it apart in *her* garage, and taught herself how to put it back together again. Then she hied herself overseas in January of 1918 and signed up with the Hackett-Lowther ambulance unit of twenty-three English and two other American women drivers. They were attached to the French army, rated as *poilus,* and won the Croix de Guerre.

Relief work and rest from the arduousness thereof, soothed the *Breeze,* would be the summer's theme for 1918. And though the U-boats had sunk more than a score of merchant vessels off the coast, the sensible Shoreite need hardly take notice, "for there is good reason to believe that our resorts will not be molested. . . . They would hardly waste time or valuable ammunition killing a summer boarding house or a cottage that costs less than one of their torpedoes."

Inspector General Andrew the while was directing twelve hundred volunteers and a thousand ambulances in thirty-one sections spread across the entire Western Front and in the Balkans. So magnificently did the men of the American Field Service perform that the initially skeptical French asked him to organize an adjunct of transport camions after America got into the war,

Charlotte L. Read on the running board of her British ambulance, somewhere on the French front, 1918. (Peabody Essex Museum)

and soon another eighteen hundred of Sleeper's recruits were trucking ammunition and supplies to the lines. The ambulance sections and camions wound up in the U.S. Army, Doc wound up a colonel, and Harry wound up in Paris running the headquarters.

In June, Helen Clay Frick returned to Pride's Crossing after seven months with the Red Cross in France putting her slender shoulder to the reconstruction of villages retaken after the devastation of the first German offensive. Destined never to marry, this compassionate soul in 1909 had bought H. H. Melville's twenty-five-acre "House with the Iron Railings" summer estate in Wenham as a country retreat for the poor girls from the mills owned by her millionaire neighbors. The estate was to be known variously as the Iron Rail Vacation Home or The Frick Rest, and eventually, when she made it the National Camp of the Girls' Clubs of America in 1954, simply as The Iron Rail. Miss Frick spent the summer of her return from France producing *Home Fires,* an amateur motion picture filmed by Norman McClintock that she planned to show at the Red Cross canteens in Europe as a morale-booster for the boys.

On July 18, 1918, the French and Americans launched the counterattack that drove the exhausted Germans back across the river in the second Battle of the Marne and turned the tide of the war. On August 8 the British opened the Allied offensive at Amiens that never again let up. A week later President and Mrs. Wilson, accompanied by the White House physician, Admiral Grayson, arrived at Manchester, this time wisely by special train, which stood by for them at the Magnolia depot, for a few days of rest with the Houses at Coolidge Point.

The President was pale and tired. Mrs. T. Jefferson Coolidge turned over the "Marble Palace" to the Wilsons and their aides—servants, automobiles and all—and moved in with her mother, Mrs. C. W. Amory, in a small cottage on the estate. Thirty-three Marines pitched their tents on the grounds, and heavily armed guards were all about.

The tense atmosphere and tight security were contagious, taxing the credulity even of the usually phlegmatic Manchester police. The second day of the visit the Wilsons and the Houses drove over to the nearby home of the latter's son-in-law, Randolph Tucker. "A policeman on the beat eyed us with suspicion," the colonel recorded in his diary. "After remaining in the house a few minutes the President, Grayson, and I walked out the back way, strolling along the grounds and taking a walk in the neighborhood. We did not know until after we returned that the policeman had followed us and had stopped one of the Secret Service men to tell of his suspicions. He said he knew the owners of the house were away, and having seen us drive up to the front door with two machines, one of which he thought was for the 'loot,' and then come out the back way bareheaded, he was convinced something was wrong and was about to put us under arrest. The Secret Service man had some difficulty in making him believe that it was the President of the United States he had under suspicion."

The Silent Partner had for some time been cerebrating over the implications of the war's impending end and drafting—with deep skepticism—a Covenant for a League of Nations that would incorporate the President's determination that all nations, large and small, should have an equal voice. The two discussed the dilemma in depth on the loggia of the "Marble Palace" overlooking the Atlantic, with flaming, ruined Europe out of sight somewhere beyond the shimmering horizon. Sir William Wiseman, Chief of British Intelligence in the United States, who chanced to be visiting House, was sympathetically impressed.

"I remember one afternoon in particular the President and Colonel House sat on the lawn in front of House's cottage with maps of Europe spread out before them, discussing ways and means of organizing Liberal opinion to break down the German military machine, and how the nations which had suffered from oppression might be safeguarded in the future. The Allied embassies in Washington were keenly interested and somewhat disturbed about the conferences at Magnolia. Rumours of peace overtures were flying around, and, with one excuse or another, various embassies tried to reach that part of the North Shore where they felt the destinies of Europe were being decided."

For the rest of it, there were walks, auto rides, golf at the Essex County and Myopia clubs, and plain loafing. Mrs. Wilson knitted socks for the soldiers, almost without letup. After five days, the sunburned savior of democracy departed for Washington with his party. Admiral Grayson said it had done him a world of good.

George Patton was General Pershing's boy, and when Black Jack sailed for France with the first units of the American Expeditionary Force in May 1917, he took him on his staff. George wanted to get Beatrice over too, but Pershing had already put the ban on wives overseas. In September Beat wondered if John Hays Hammond's pull with Colonel House mightn't get her over, but nothing came of it. The "unspeakable ass" evidently was wired into neither the Ayers nor the Pattons.

Bored with staff work, itching for action, intrigued by the mechanized tin cans that the French had been using in the field with some success, George got Pershing to put him in charge of the tank school at Langres in December. He was promoted to major. Training, training, training in the horseless cavalry . . . plans, plans, plans.

Colonel George S. Patton, Jr., led the First Brigade of the Army Tank Corps into battle at St. Mihiel on September 12, 1918, under the commander of the IV Corps, a general by the name of Douglas MacArthur. Never before had American tanks been under fire: "Passed some dead and wounded. I saw one fellow in a shell hole holding his rifle and sitting down. I thought he was hiding and went to cuss him out, he had a bullet over his right eye and was dead. As my telephone wire ran out at this point I left the adjutant there and went forward with a lieutenant and 4 runners to find the tanks, the whole country was alive with them crawling over trenches and into woods."

Patton was still looking for his first good tank fight four days later when, an ocean away in Pride's Crossing, Helen Frick's morale movie *Home Fires* flickered across the greensward of her father's "Eagle Rock" in its benefit premiere before an appreciative audience of the patriotic elite. To remind the doughboys that the nation was behind them, there were shots of school letting out in Manchester, the GAR parade in Beverly Farms, Farmerettes plying their hoes, and classes in surgical dressings, sock-knitting and canning. To remind the Yanks of what they were fighting for, Miss Frick had selected vignettes of the beloved "Bunny" Woods's outing classes for little boys and girls of the North Shore summer colony, a tennis match between Eleo Sears and Alice Thorndike, hunting and golfing at Myopia, polo at "Princemere" and whippet racing on the private track at Charles G. Rice's "Turner Hill" estate in Ipswich. More than four thousand dollars was raised for the Red Cross.

As if exhausted by the effort, with the Germans on the run, editor Lodge suspended publication of the *North Shore Breeze* on the first of October for the duration (plus a few months, as it turned out). He blamed high costs and went to work on Henry Ford's assembly line in Detroit.

Lieutenant Samuel P. Mandell II. (From New England Aviators, 1914–1918)

It would be the last American air raid of the war, this morning of November 5, 1918. Argonne-Meuse sector, 20th Aero Squadron of the First Day Bombardment Group. Objective: railroad and warehouses at Mouzon. The Armistice was six days in the offing. Piloting one of the Liberties was

Lieutenant Samuel P. Mandell, St. Mark's and Harvard, polo, in every feature "the facial type of the young American of today of the best race," son of George S. Mandell (publisher of the *Boston Evening Transcript* and Master of Fox Hounds emeritus, Myopia Hunt) and Emily Proctor Mandell, and summer resident of Hamilton, on the North Shore of Massachusetts Bay. The previous day, on his seventeenth bombing raid, Lieutenant Mandell shot down his first Fokker.

They prayed for rain, but no dice. Returning from Mouzon after dropping its bombs, the 20th was attacked three times by Fokkers. On the third pass, German tracers knocked out an aileron, and Mandell's engine. Out of control at 12,000 feet, his Liberty "sank in great spiral vrilles from which its occupants managed to right it about every 1000 feet. The last recovery was less than 100 feet from the ground. It fell within a few yards of the canal at Martincourt. Lieut. R. W. Fulton, of N.Y., his observer, was practically unhurt; Mandell's leg was badly broken. The exact details of his other injuries are doubtful. The Germans marched Fulton away, and left the wounded pilot propped against his plane.

"The rest of the story is gleaned from the inhabitants of the town. About 4 o'clock in the afternoon, a German captain of infantry came to the bank, took a rifle from one of the guards, and deliberately fired a number of shots into the helpless American."

Lieutenant Mandell was twenty-one.

Total of dead, wounded, missing and prisoners (rounded off): 37,494,000 . . . plus one.

Anna Coleman Watts was a sculptress married to Dr. Maynard Ladd of Boston. They summered on the North Shore in Manchester. Toward the end of the Great War they went to France for relief work with the Red Cross. Making the rounds of

A Bit of Unintentional "Acrobatics"

(Courtesy of the Lynn Item)

Fighter pilot Sam Mandell of Hamilton dove to get a shot at the same German scout plane his observer, Lt. Gardner H. Fiske of Weston, was peppering, with the results pictured back home in the Lynn Item. *After the Armistice the lucky Fiske married a North Shore girl, Constance Morss, and summered in Manchester. (From* New England Aviators, 1914–1918.)

the wards with her husband, appalled at the wreckage of humanity, she got the idea of creating artificial faces for the disfigured soldiers. Her method was to make first a plaster cast from what remained of the patient's features, upon which she sculpted his likeness in plastic as nearly as she could project it from old photographs and her own imagination. After coppering this mask in a galvanic bath, Mrs. Ladd trimmed it to fit exactly the portion of the face that had been shot away, enameling it in flesh color, painting in an eye where one was missing.

Anna Watts made face masks for five American and seventy French soldiers. Two *poilus* in particular had refused to go on the street in daylight because of the horrified stares they attracted; the American sculptress masked them and went out with them for a stroll, and hundreds passed them by without a glance.

Back home again, the gentle lady let it be known that she would make a new face for any American soldier who had left his over there.

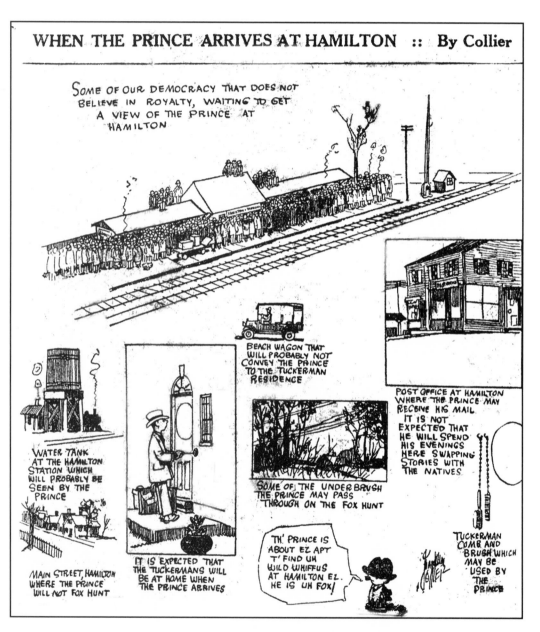

Boston newspaper columnist Collier is unruffled by the pending arrival of the Prince of Wales on the North Shore in the autumn of 1924.

(Tuckerman family scrapbook)

~20~
PROHIBITION, A PRINCE
AND A PRESIDENT

*The Twenties roar, gallop and stroll through an
enclave of slightly diminished privilege*

After the defeats of the
Kaiser and Woodrow Wilson, destiny decreed a reversion to Republicanism
in the person of Warren G. Harding. The new President's promised "return
to normalcy" could not arrive soon enough for the nation and most particularly for the summer colony spread along the North Shore of Boston
which, having enjoyed a fuller measure of leisure than the rest of America
before the war, naturally felt the more keenly the sacrifices incident thereto.

The first of the future's distressing waves had been of immigrants, eastern and southern Europeans for the most part, millions from the turn of the
century until the flood was shut off by the war. And the most ominous alien
of all, the income tax, had elbowed in on the land of the free and the enterprising, just before the war began.

In the years before the hated levy many of the more pretentious spreads
on the Shore were built out of surplus untaxed income by the plentiful,
cheap and therefore welcome labor of Italian immigrants. Then the new tax
began to skim off the thickest cream, then the inconvenience of the war.
Patriotic estate owners bit their lips and cut back on maintenance and work-
force. Many of the Italian laborers had returned home to fight. Many more
remained, welcome at first but now regarded with hostility. The *Breeze*
considered them unfair competition for the returned boys "strong and
true," living as these foreigners did under conditions "in marked contrast to
the general prosperity of the Shore . . . a shifty, unreliable element . . . a distinct menace when they are interested only in prosecuting their own pleasures and interests according to old world ideals."

In response to such alarms, Congress adopted the first quotas in 1921,
limiting immigration in any one year to three percent of each nationality
according to the 1910 census, up to 357,000. On the eve of the adoption of
a far more restrictive new quota, the *Breeze* chose the Fourth of July, 1924,
to suggest that "any community has a right to resent being ruined by such
an admission of aliens that our institutions and customs are endangered."
As early as 1920, editor Lodge had perceived an even more insidious peril

from within, citing "the appalling increase in the number of men in the colored race." His views went unchallenged in his letters column.

The postwar depression occasioned by all the national and international gear-shifting—and the rediscovery of the wheel under the influence of gasoline, and the self-loss of the war generation under that of bootleg booze—augured the moribundity of most if not quite all of the patriarchal estates of summer and of the way of life they had sheltered on the Shore since the Civil War—and their dismemberment and division, or, as with the inevitable matriarchies, their demise and distribution.

Henry Clay Frick exited with his era, on December 2, 1919. There would be no more "Eagle Rocks" on the North Shore. Still, if the fortune was great enough and properly trusted, as the most Bostonish ones were, it was almost impervious to death, war and even taxes, and quite a few held their feudal grip on the land unscathed. The polo field at "Princemere" reverted to the pounding hoof and swinging mallet in 1919—a hundred auto parties on the sidelines there one Saturday—thirty horses in the stables, thirty hounds in the kennels; that September the Princes returned to Pau for the hunting, taking twelve and twenty of each with them on the boat now that the seas were clear. Soon "Princemere" had grown to a thousand acres in Beverly, Manchester, Wenham and Essex.

The dowager queens of the Shore had the postwar problem of cooks who had been welcomed in munitions factories now indignant at offers of fourteen a week with room and board, as were maids at ten. The women's vote was in, the new quotas were choking off the supply of young innocents from abroad, and suddenly a red-blooded American girl was finding that she could command twice as much in a steaming North Shore summer kitchen as her business college counterpart in a steaming city office. The war had liberated more than bleeding France.

Now that the silliest law ever passed by Congress over a President's veto and adopted by the states was on the books, Society was bound to drink itself silly in the flouting of it. Between them, the Eighteenth and Nineteenth Amendments to the Constitution worked to liberate both spirit and libido. And now that Detroit put wheels under her (by 1924 at a mere $265 for a Model T Ford runabout), the goofy, garish day of the red-blooded American flapper—the first abortively liberated female—clattered in all its transient dizziness along the shore at three in the morning, with all the boozy bedlam of a tin lizzie laden with loaded lads and lassies.

Still the mecca for the smart set, the North Shore Grill in Magnolia was bought in 1918 by Joseph P. Del Monte, Boston hotelier, who promised his young patrons the best avowedly liquorless meals and the best dancing to the rhythms of the best jazz on the Shore, and he was as good as his word on all counts. In 1924 Del's four-piece band was featuring a youthful violinist named Ruby Newman. Next year Ruby had his own orchestra, playing for *thés dansants* in the late summer afternoons and evenings from eight until midnight.

Liberation appalled and occasionally amused convention. "Petting par-

BONWIT TELLER & CO.

The Specialty Shop of Originations

FIFTH AVENUE AT 38TH STREET, NEW YORK

DISTINCTIVE BEACH FASHIONS~

ties, without even the cover of a sunshade, girls smoking cigarettes and baseball were popular pastimes," the *Lynn Item* observed of Nahant's Short Beach one July Sunday in 1922. "The sight of two young women parading the beach attired in men's trousers and swimming jerseys, nonchalantly puffing cigarettes, entertained hundreds in the early afternoon."

Ah, the confrontations between the old hair shirts and the new shirtless, the itchy black woolen bathing suits (shot through with moth holes after one season) and the rubber caps, unisexed and sexless . . . and the beach flapper in her wetless getup of voiles, cheesecloth, nets, cretonnes, stockings, ballet slippers, scarf, feather boa and coyly carried sunshade! A "perfect figure" of a girl strolled along a North Shore beach, marveled Marion Dodge one July day in 1924. "She wore a brilliant red woolen bathing suit, no cap, but her hair, curly and bobbed, was as red as her suit. A pair of red, white and blue stockings were on her legs and around her neck a white fur. In one hand, she had a cherry ice cream cone and in the other she held a huge red parasol over her ruddy Fourth of July self."

The new sexual freedom inside the curtained flivver, the feast rollable from the woods to the beach and back, was neither to be marveled or laughed at, however, by those who knew a woman's place. The goings-on and takings-off on Long Beach by midsummer of 1923 so alarmed the clubwomen of Lynn that they planned an antipetting drive against the hated flappers and their naughty escorts. The churches got up a purity league. The minister of

Advent Church, Mr. Frederic Brooks, hurled a thunderbolt from the *Item*'s paper pulpit: "This splendid gift from God's hand has been used by Satan as a spawning place for the propagation of his species. Not only are the lecherous libertines and the painted vamps there seeking prey, a menace to our virtuous youth; but the sons and daughters of some of our so-called respectable homes are there in attire and posture that give convincing evidence of moral dereliction. I have not dared, personally, to allow my wife and daughters to frequent the beach because of what I have witnessed when riding by."

Stretched along a coast of covert coves, bits of beach and involuted inlets suited for the midnight rendezvous, the North Shore imported and exported, it seems likely, even more illicit beverage than it consumed. Bill McCoy, a towering Florida boatbuilder and master mariner, turned up in Gloucester early in 1921 looking for a fast fishing schooner, which he found in the *Henry L. Marshall*. Captain McCoy refitted the *Marshall* for a liquid cargo and started running the best stuff he could get—"The Real McCoy"—from Nassau to New York, where he hovered just outside the territorial limit and unloaded into speedboats fast enough to outrun anything the Coast Guard then had in service. Thus he founded "Rum Row," the floating wholesale hooch business that kept the Atlantic seaboard and the Feds occupied until Repeal.

A few months after acquiring the *Marshall*, McCoy wooed and won the love of his life, the beautiful Gloucester schooner *Arethusa*, which he registered with the British as *Tomoka* and moved squarely into the big time . . . for a short time. In 1923 she and he were captured. Big Bill served *his* time in Atlanta, briefly—relieved to be gotten out of the business just as the gangsters were getting in. He never did realize his dream of sailing *Tomoka* to the South Seas and died in 1948, the most legendary and innovative of all the personages of Prohibition in its heyday. They made him an honorary Gloucesterman, you might say, and while ashore between trips he dearly enjoyed to sneak in a round or two at the Bass Rocks golf course with his fellow businessmen and a customer or two.

On the land side, the mansion of rubber magnate Lester Leland on Boardman Avenue in Manchester was raided while the family was in Europe

by a man identifying himself as William McCarthy, Supervisor of Prohibition Enforcement in New England, and eight others one March day in 1921. While butler, housekeeper, servants and a crew of workmen stood gaping, the raiders trooped down to the basement, picked the lock on the wine cellar door, politely loaded 146 cases of rye whiskey and fifty-seven of gin into their truck, and drove off. When the Manchester cops got hold of Supervisor McCarthy on the phone he was understandably fit to be tied.

Two years passed, and investigators in Nahant arrested Edward (Big Ed) Furey of New York at gunpoint. Known in the West as 270 pounds of confidence man, he was wanted on various counts in various places. Big Ed, who drove a Cadillac and possessed several guns, was indicted and found guilty of numerous raids on North Shore clubs and homes in the guise of a federal Prohibition officer, seizing caches of liquor or extorting substantial hush money for his silence.

A common practice on the Ipswich Bay side of Cape Ann was to torch a summer cottage at Folly Cove, and while everyone rushed to the scene, land a load of hooch on the other side of Halibut Point in the quiet of Pigeon Cove—or, for variety, vice versa. On the other hand, more than one summer resident of the North Shore arrived in June to open up and find an anonymous bread-and-butter note and a wad of thank-you bills on the kitchen table.

And then there was "Blighty."

Among those unaffected by the rather severe postwar recession were Arthur Leonard, stocky builder of the Union Stockyards in Chicago (financed by Frederick H. Prince), and John Wing Prentiss, suave senior partner in the investment banking house of Hornblower and Weeks, who profited prodigiously by buying up deflated Liberty War Bonds on margin and waiting it out. Son of Irish immigrants, Leonard fought to the top from railroad office boy, found and fell for Eastern Point, and in 1921 moved his family into "Druimteac" (*drum-hack*), Gaelic for "House Back of the Ledge," a solid summer mansion of remarkable elegance that was quarried from the ledge itself.

Always "Colonel" (a staff lieutenant colonel in the War), Prentiss began the climb from Harvard as a three-dollar-a-week Boston Stock Exchange messenger. Twenty-five annual rungs later, in the mid-1920s, he had the sublime satisfaction of offering Henry Ford, not once but three times in a row, a cool billion dollars in cash for his company on behalf of sundry interests he represented—and of course the sublime disappointment of being turned down. By then Colonel Prentiss owned the twenty wild acres of shore between Leonard's and Brace Cove and had built his own self-quarried manse, christened "Blighty," or in the language of the blighters, "one's home place." They moved in down the shore from "Druimteac" the year after the Leonards, in 1922, to an estate complete with tennis courts, bowling green and an abbreviated six-hole golf course.

Once in "Blighty," the Prentisses established two institutions now indelibly of the lore: the Fourth of July and Labor Day all-day buffet, golf and tennis tournaments, which opened and closed the season at Eastern Point for the sixteen years of the Prentiss primacy. All the Point was invited. The luncheons were sumptuous. As for the tennis and the golf (and bowling on the green for those so inclined), everything was provided, including liquid fuel. The courts and the links were maintained as if with whisk broom and manicure scissors, and if one had arrived unequipped, racquets, clubs and plenty of balls were available in the hall closet.

Andrew Volstead might as well have saved himself the trouble, for the Prentissdom of "Blighty" recognized no twelve-mile limits. After the buffet and during the afternoon's play the popping of corks mingled with the crackle of distant firecrackers, and every spirit lifted on the flooding tide of champagne. There was always a bottle of champagne presented for a hole in one. All summer the courts and the links were crowded, and on weekends from noon until suppertime the "Seventh Hole" was open, a terrace room at the end of "Blighty" with Teachers Highland Cream, soda, ginger, ice and glasses on the table. Every afternoon Marie Prentiss presided at tea, warm and gracious, everyone invited.

Fanning (just Fanning) was the Prentiss chauffeur, mechanic, jack of all trades, arbiter of the fourteen servants, keeper of the Prentiss mutts Hooch (an English bull) and Booze (an Airedale), and steward. In the latter capacity this factotum kept a spacious and seaworthy power dory moored off the estate in Brace Cove; by means of this modest craft he filled the liquid needs of the household on periodic nighttime cruises to some well-laden schooner out on Rum Row, financed with two or three of his master's numerous crisp thousand-dollar bills.

"We got our alcohol in a drugstore on the Main Street of Gloucester" (Blanche Butler Lane speaking, the grown-up little girl who perched on the piano and waved the flag at the Hawthorne Fourth-of-July parties) "and brought the gallon jug home and 'aged' it by rolling it across the kitchen floor several times. Gad, what days *those* were! A wonder any of us are still alive!"

A wonder indeed.

THE PRINCE AND
THE HAM SANDWICH

Midway in this daring and decadent decade of the tinseled Twenties the North Shore was visited by a prince long on names (Edward Albert Christian George Andrew Patrick David) but short on the stuff it took to cut the "figger" that his grandfather Edward VII did. Sacrificing his throne on the altar of love was sadly anticlimactic. But princes are not born to be pitied.

The whole of *the* North Shore, and possibly some of the rest of the country, had been in a tizzy since the word was handed down that during his second tour of the former colonies in 1924 (he had visited the States and Canada, where he bought a western ranch on the spur of the moment in 1919), His Highness Edward Albert (Eddie to the American press), Prince of Wales and heir to the throne of

His Royal Highness, the Prince of Wales, up on Desert Queen, derby and all. (Tuckerman family scrapbook)

England, age thirty, would pause for a day at the Myopia Hunt Club. He would be the houseguest of the Bayard Tuckermans at their beautiful "Savin Hill Farm," and not only that—he would ride to the hounds. It was absolutely the most extraordinary coup since Harpo Marx had actually played a harp in a musicale one evening inside the broodingly Gothic stone penitentiary on Eastern Point built by Evelyn Ames, the shovel heiress.

The Tuckermans, it was revealed, had met "Wales" two years earlier while they were in residence with their horses at Melton Mowbray in the Leicestershire hunting district of England. They had gone over with Tuckerman's cousin, the Myopia master of foxhounds, Jimmy Appleton. Phyllis Tuckerman was a Sears, and her husband was in the insurance business in Boston.

An awful lot of people agreed that the Prince, though not brilliant, was amiable company and enjoyed a good time as much as the next chap. The question of a number of lifetimes, of course, was: Who would be invited? Or more to the point: Who wouldn't?

Edward's destination on his second tour of the New World was his once-seen ranch in Alberta. But first he swung through Washington for an unusually awkward luncheon at the White House with the Coolidges on August 31. HRH was dressed with his usual startling informality. Evidently this faux pas, combined with the usual taciturnity of the President, so

The derby-topped prince takes North Shore walls in stride. (Phyllis Tuckerman Cutler collection)

unnerved him that his usual sense of presence evaporated, and the royal guest was so painfully ill at ease that Silent Cal surprised his wife, his cabinet and his staff with a sympathetic torrent of unusual, if monosyllabic, volubility.

Then on to Long Island for the polo matches between America and Britain, and the round of house parties and swell times that produced the famous headline "Prince Gets in with the Milkman" that so annoyed his father, King George V. From Syosset, Edward resumed his royal progress to Canada and the ranch, planning his return to Olde England via the New England hunting country. Originally he was to arrive in Hamilton on October 22, but he came down with a chill in Montreal that threatened to cancel the entire affair.

A day late, his special train puffed into the Lowell station at ten in the morning of Thursday the twenty-third, and Edward descended the steps behind his white-coated valet, followed by his aides, Brigadier General G. F. Trotter, known to his intimates as G; Major Edward D. (Fruity) Metcalf; and Captain Alan Lascelles. The general was twenty years his liege's senior but so close, nevertheless, that the later Duke of Windsor wrote of him, "I learned from 'G' Trotter that life should be lived to the full." Genial Fruity Metcalf, almost lifelong companion and accomplished rider, was particularly in charge of the none-too-expert though game equestrian side of the boss's life. Lascelles was a bit of a stick, admittedly smarter by far than his charge; his principal function seems to have been, wherever possible, to keep the reins on a chap he disliked the more he knew him.

The royal entourage was greeted effusively by Tuckerman, Mr. Jimmy in a great bearskin coat, Charles S. Bird, Jr., and Dudley Rogers. All immediately departed the Lowell station in the host's "high-powered motorcar" for the imposing English-style brick mansion house set upon the prime crest of the two hundred acres of "Savin Hill Farm" off upper Asbury Street, where they were welcomed by Mrs. Tuckerman and her awed household. The grounds and buildings of the Tuckerman estate were crawling with local police and state troopers, mounted and afoot, Secret Service men and, so it was said, private detectives.

Light refreshments were served, after which everyone drove over to Myopia for a tour of the clubhouse and stables. Dashing headlong into the clubhouse before the others, the Prince found himself alone for a few moments with Blanche Wheeler, the telephone operator, who told an inquiring reporter later that "he just stood there and dropped his eyes, fingered his cap around nervously and then started walking toward the pool room. I think he's nice, but he's too bashful, I'd say."

Wales struck a reporter from the *Salem News* as slender and of medium height, giving "the curious impression of being boyish and at the same time utterly sophisticated. . . . The Prince's sartorial equipment created a deal of interest. The initial impression of his clothes was that they were striking, not to say loud; at least they would have been loud if worn by an American. He wore a black derby hat, set jauntily on one side of his head. When he half raised it at a feeble cheer from the crowd, a white silk livery could be seen. His loose knee length overcoat was made of tweed, with astounding black and white checks, and was garnished in front with four large brown buttons." Light blue shirt and "razor-creased" checked tweed trousers topped off the outfit.

Edward and his hosts returned from the Myopia clubhouse to "Savin Hill" and sauntered down to the Tuckerman stables, where three horses were saddled and waiting. The Prince mounted Desert Queen, a nine-year-old chestnut mare he had seen his hostess ride at Melton Mowbray. The Salem reporter observed that Desert Queen, "sensing that she was carrying a noted guest for the day, proved equal to the honors and with her sleek body aquiver from tip to tail, loped away with her royal charge. Mrs. Tuckerman followed on Old Bachelor and Mr. Tuckerman on Buckskin."

Accompanied by Major Metcalf, James W. Parker, the president of Myopia, and Dudley Rogers, guest and hosts proceeded across the lovely October countryside to Appleton Farms, the oldest and greatest of New England family spreads, as guests of the Francis R. Appletons for the start of the long-awaited hunt.

And now tallyho! The course was to be across Appleton Farms, through the Blair and Adams estates into Nancy's Corner at the junction of Cutler Road and Highland Street in West Hamilton. The corner was named for Lady Nancy Astor, who for three years or so had occupied a house there (no longer standing) when as just plain Nancy Langhorne of Greenwood, Virginia, she was married to her first husband, polo-playing Robert Gould Shaw II of Boston. From Nancy's Corner Chuck Haley had dragged the anise bag (lifting it twice to provide breaks for the hounds) through the Burroughs estate over Vineyard Hill into the Smith Farm, through the Sargent and Hobbs estates and on to the finish at "Savin Hill."

Fifty or so of the best and most socially impeccable horsemen and horsewomen on the North Shore were gathered at the Appleton stables, as Leicestershire-looking as could be in brilliant hunting pink—all but Wales, whose style was his international hallmark: namely, light britches, brown coat and that same black derby. The pack yelped and strained in a furious wagging of tails and scuffing of dust, salivating with excitement. The horses pranced and pawed and shook their handsome heads and whinnied with the contagion of it—the unaccustomed human air of deference, the pungent smells of manure and sweat and leather, the soft afternoon sun, the fiery foliage, the slight autumnal snap to the atmosphere. What an astounding and anachronistic, playfully class-ridden tableau! Yet how perfectly, how movingly, was it all carried off! What style! What theatre! How deliciously was belief suspended!

Unhappily, it was the visitor, the monarch of all that he might have surveyed had his ancestors prevailed, who was not entirely at his ease for all the wishful thinking of his loyal countrymen, the grooms. Edward was gracious to the pushing photographers and willing to pose if an American hunter posed with him, which presented no problem. And as the master's horn signaled the start, and Royalty touched Desert Queen into motion, he did smile and wave to the crowd of some three hundred—"mostly," Salem smiled, "pretty girls of the flapper type."

And yet the Prince of Wales seemed nervous and ill at ease, his smiles perfunctory. For he *was* rather out of his class, and he knew it. So too, without a doubt, did the owner of the last name on the roster of the hunt, Major (back to his regular army rank) George S. Patton, Jr., who with Beatrice was wintering in "Sunset Hill" at Beverly Cove where they had a string of polo ponies.

Early in the chase, while the crowd was still in sight, Edward appeared to take the jumps easily enough and was seen to glance back over his shoulder repeatedly at the other hunters and to spur his mount when his lead was threatened. But it was clear to the watchers—so contended the *Salem News* correspondent, at any rate—that the royal guest held the lead by the courtesy of his hosts. He kept his seat, though he twice nearly lost it taking high walls.

The ever-gallant Gordon Prince, who succeeded Mr. Jimmy as Master, recalled that "unfortunately the Prince preferred to ride with a snaffle bit, which was not what Desert Queen was accustomed to. Of course the Prince was supposed to ride up front with the Master, and this he had no trouble doing whatsoever as Desert Queen, with that in her mouth, could 'take quite a hold.'" The one Prince called the other's "a flawless performance under most difficult circumstances."

Unexpectedly as generous was North Shore sportswoman Eleonora Sears, Phyllis Sears Tuckerman's cousin, whom one Boston paper pitted

against her rival "bachelor girl," demure Olivia Ames of Pride's Crossing, for the royal attention. Although at the last minute she elected not to join the drag (she had a superb sense of timing), Eleo gained the day in an interview that made a point of her long acquaintance as both riding and dancing partner of the Prince. "Slight accidents that would never be mentioned were he not the Prince of Wales are repeated over and over until people believe that he only gets on a horse to fall off," snorted Miss Sears. "He is a daring rider and rides as if born to the saddle."

The Salem reporter thought otherwise. "Edward of England took punishment, though, on the last two miles of the drag hunt in the late afternoon that even the chivalry of the red-coated Myopia hunters in drawing rein to let him come first into the public view could not conceal from the thousands who lined the back roads and filled the seven hills of the Tuckerman estate. . . . The hunt had to wait for him at the check back of Vineyard Hill, two thirds of the way from the start. The Prince was all blown when he came in, almost last of the nearly fifty riders he had led over the Appleton Plains for the early, very public jumps. They made it a very long check on his account. . . . And the courteous Myopia riders held back for him as they faced the colorful throng along the finish."

Two thousand spectators were all over the lawns and stables of "Savin Hill" at the finish, and they sent up a rousing cheer as the Prince of Wales panted in. Salem noted hundreds of pretty girls in the crowd, "all dressed in their Sunday best, with an extra dab on their cheeks. Some of them tried to give the impression that they were members of the exclusive set—and some of them succeeded."

Well, he had carried it off in the American limelight that fascinated and repelled him, and he had kept his seat. Edward climbed the terrace to the mansion with his host, changed rather wearily, one supposes, and then descended to meet "the neighbors," as the Tuckermans cozily referred to them—two hundred of them—and tea to the tunes of a small orchestra.

And then—for the royal day was not yet done, nor could the princely bones yet rest—it was off to Topsfield for dinner at their "Gravelly Brook Farm" with the John S. Lawrences and fifty-four other extra-honored guests—and yes, oysters, lobster, chicken and gigantic pots of Ayrshire cream for the princely stomach so recently indisposed.

And then—dancing in the Lawrence ballroom to the strains of William Boyle's Copley Plaza Orchestra—dancing first, His Highness, with Isabel, the Lawrences' nine-year-old, whence Cinderella was packed gently off to bed—and then dancing, dancing, dancing until three in the morning, when the most socially acceptable visitor the North Shore had *ever* entertained felt he must call it quits.

The high-powered motorcar was there at the door. Good-bye! Good-bye! Jolly good time! Jump in! And Wales and his aides were driven by their elated hosts back to Lowell in time for his special train to get under way for New York and the liner *Olympic,* sailing for England later that very day.

As he was leaving the dance Edward did something that struck one of his American cousins as . . . oddly democratic? The memory stuck, and came unstuck in print eleven years later in 1936, just a fortnight after he had ascended the throne of Great Britain and Ireland as His Royal Majesty, Edward VIII. Dashing for the waiting motorcar, "the Prince refused the food that was proffered, the finest and most select that could be procured, and whispered into the ear of Creed, the caterer, that he would like a ham sandwich that he might eat as he scurried along."

And, as all the world knows, the Duke of Windsor and the American divorcée for whom he would forsake his throne, did not live especially happily ever after.

"WHITE COURT"

President Calvin Coolidge was everything America thought it was bored with but was good for it, like prune juice for a hangover, as the Prince of Wales was a bit of what it thought it envied but didn't want steadily, like double martinis before lunch. Both were throwbacks to the times, the values, the misguided views of reality that had led the nations one presided over, the other would reign over so transiently, into a tragic war and an aftermath fraught with folly.

Coolidge, the marbliest of Vermonters, was so indifferent a rider that for a while, until he was laughed off it, he resorted to a hobby horse for exercise in the White House. So it was not the chase that drew him to Swampscott for the 1925 season but the escape from it, from the most distasteful aspect of his Presidency—people, just too damn many of them.

The agent for this second Republican summer White House on the North Shore was his strangely devoted, self-appointed President-maker, Frank W. Stearns, son of the founder and head of the well-known Boston dry goods firm of R. H. Stearns, Tremont Street opposite the Common, who fit the picture to a T—dry, good, short, pleasantly paunchy, gray hair and moustache, unassuming, vest sprinkled with cigar ashes. The perfect Colonel House or Jack Hammond for a Calvin Coolidge . . . except that, quite consistent with their unusual relationship, the President cautioned his mentor, who was sixteen years his senior, "Mr. Stearns, an unofficial adviser to a President of the United States is not a good thing and is not provided for in our form of government."

The caveat was faithfully honored by the devoted merchant, who conceded to an admirer once that he had some fair influence with his lofty pro-

The Swampscott summer home of President and Mrs. Calvin Coolidge in 1925. (Swampscott Historical Society)

tégé, then governor of Massachusetts, "but it will last just as long as I don't try to use it, and not one minute longer."

The two Amherst alumni first met in 1912 concerning some legislation affecting their alma mater when Coolidge was in the Massachusetts Senate. In 1915 Frank concluded that Calvin was the cool star for the wagon that would carry him beyond a place in the dry goods hall of fame. So he spent the balance of his prime marking up Coolidge's political price tag with extraordinary acumen, devotion, persistence, selflessness and success, to the astonishment of those who couldn't believe good old Frank Stearns wasn't getting anything more out of it all than vicarious satisfaction.

The Stearns family had summered in Hull on the South Shore but moved out with other wealthy cottagers in disgust after the garishness of Paragon Park was imposed above Nantasket Beach in 1905. After the First War Frank rented "Red Gables" on Little's Point in Swampscott, entertaining Calvin and his wife, Grace, for several weekends in the summer of 1920. Meanwhile, Governor Coolidge's star was rising as the result of his coolness in dealing with the Boston police strike of the previous September. That winter Stearns bought the sprawling place. Vice President and Mrs. Coolidge were planning to weekend at "Red Gables" on August 2, 1923, when President Harding suddenly died. They remained at the old family home in Plymouth, Vermont, where Cal took the oath from his father, Colonel John, in the famous lamplight scene.

The first presidential visit to Swampscott was to get away from it all after the death of the Coolidges' younger son, Calvin, Jr., of blood poisoning on July 7, 1924. In November this tight-lipped image of old-fashioned Yankee values so engaged the conscience of a nation scandalized by the excesses committed in the name of his predecessor (and encouraged by signs of recovery from the postwar depression) that he was swept back into office, in his own right, with the greatest Republican majority in history.

The inauguration stand had not yet been taken down in March 1925 when it was revealed that Mr. Stearns had leased "White Court," the stately estate next door to "Red Gables" on Little's Point, as the summer White House for the coming season. Standing on a six-acre knoll behind four hundred feet of ocean frontage, "White Court" commanded a view to the southward toward Nahant and Graves Light at the entrance to Boston Harbor. It had been built about 1905 by the late Frederick E. Smith of Dayton, Ohio, and was up for sale by his heirs. The executive offices for the summer would be located on the seventh floor of the Security Trust Company in Lynn.

The announcement set great social wheels in motion. North Shore real estate brokers were swamped with demands for estates where one could make a splash in the hope that the Coolidges would show up. All at once anyone of any importance in the country expressed an interest in visiting Swampscott that summer. The New Ocean House, where most of the White House crowd stayed, and the Preston were booked solid for the season.

A certain awkwardness among the summering diplomatic corps, lately

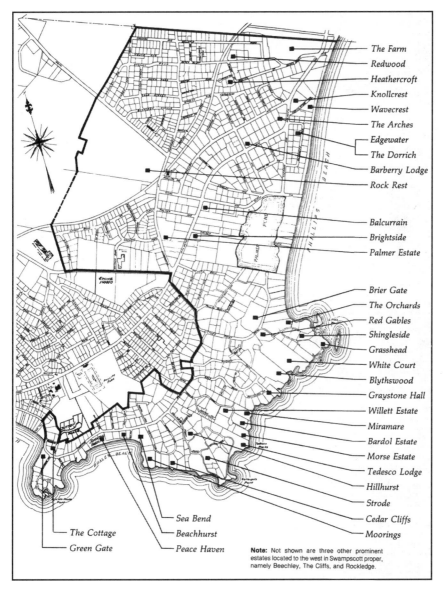

The Farm
Redwood
Heathercroft
Knollcrest
Wavecrest
The Arches
Edgewater
The Dorrich
Barberry Lodge
Rock Rest

Balcurrain
Brightside
Palmer Estate

Brier Gate
The Orchards
Red Gables
Shingleside
Grasshead
White Court
Blythswood
Graystone Hall
Willett Estate
Miramare
Bardol Estate
Morse Estate
Tedesco Lodge
Hillhurst
Strode
Cedar Cliffs
Moorings

The Cottage
Green Gate
Sea Bend
Beachhurst
Peace Haven

Note: Not shown are three other prominent estates located to the west in Swampscott proper, namely Beechley, The Cliffs, and Rockledge.

"White Court" was just one of more than three dozen estates in Swampscott during its summer heyday. (From The Era of the Summer Estates by Dorothy M. Anderson)

at official swords' points, had been cleared up to everyone's relief, and the embassies were back on their favorite North Shore in full panoply. The Right Honorable Sir Esme Howard, the British ambassador, and Lady Isabella, already exposed to the social frigidities of the administration in Washington, did choose to forgo their usual sojourn on the Shore this of all seasons, it is true, but the new German envoy, Ago von Maltzan, Baron zu Wartenberg und Penzlin, manfully brought up the rear in a manor in the Magnolia woods.

If the President pleased State by choosing to summer on Embassy Row, he caused Treasury no end of aggravation by selecting an ocean view of Rum Row. Or so it was joyously claimed by certain newspaper correspondents who swore the fleet could be observed from the rocking chairs on the

The Coolidges with Rob Roy at "White Court." (Lynn Public Library)

piazza of "White Court." Bootleggers for some time had outnumbered bathers on the beaches of Swampscott after sundown. On June 21 fourteen of the Coast Guard's fast new rum-chasers steamed into Boston, with more expected, along with a couple of Navy destroyers and a hydroplane. For the rest of the summer the closest Rum Row got to Swampscott was thirty miles. The Coast Guard denied that there was any connection between the arrival of this task force and the impending arrival of the President, who was most certainly in favor of vigorous enforcement.

Two days after the show of dry force, June 23, 1925, the Coolidges arrived at Salem from Washington in three Pullmans and a baggage car. They were greeted by a local delegation, including the now Republican congressman A. Piatt Andrew, who had entertained Vice President Coolidge at "Red Roof." The President was dressed with his accustomed ascetic precision and emerged from the train, according to the wide-eyed reporter from the *Lynn Item,* with "an actual smile on his face and a friendly nod for all around him." Almost at the same time, the presidential yacht *Mayflower* arrived quietly at Marblehead and anchored off the Corinthian Yacht Club, back in familiar North Shore waters.

On June 27 Mr. Coolidge held his first press conference of the summer. That is, it was held on his behalf. The press was summoned and permitted to submit written questions fifteen minutes in advance. At the stated hour an aide appeared and responded to those selected by the President for a reply. No questions allowed.

Two days later Colonel John Coolidge was operated on in Vermont, and the Coolidges were driven up to be with him for the day. On the way the cavalcade of twelve cars was stopped near Charlestown, New Hampshire, by a large lady gate tender in a sunbonnet, who refused to let the President of the United States across her toll bridge until a Secret Service man came up with fifteen cents.

Thus the summer White House lapsed into routine. The President was there for a rest, period. He occasionally walked about the grounds, now and then went for a drive, did some reading and worked. He wasn't interested in sports or games, didn't fish, ride, swim, sail, golf or play cards. His single recreational weakness was the jigsaw puzzle, to which he was said to be addicted.

Grace Coolidge, a pleasant and rather outgoing Vermonter, bore her husband's creed of the tight lip with resignation, declining all invitations, to the bitter disappointment of the North Shore set. She enjoyed being driven over the shore roads at ten miles an hour so that she could take in the scenery and ocean views, and she walked briskly every morning, once almost at her cost when four state troopers on motorcycles came roaring around the bend into Little's Point, forcing her to leap into the ditch. Sunny mornings she swam in the natural rock pool down on the shore. Reported the *Breeze:* "Mrs. Coolidge prefers to wink at the sun from under a broad white hat, rather than let him toast her to a ruddy brown. Passing up the lane between the hedges surrounding the Mitton and Brush estates on either side, Mrs. Coolidge only has to wander across the field, humming happily to herself after her refreshing dip, through the gap in the hedge and she is on the green lawn of White Court, her Secret Service escort with her as always."

The Brush estate, "Shingleside," was one of Arthur Little's early shingled creations and had been acquired in the early 1900s by Charles N. Brush, a most sedate and distinguished-looking merchant of Boston. His grandson, William R. Brush, a boyhood chum of mine, was told that one spring—surely not the spring of 1925—"Grandfather arrived at 'Shingleside' with his entourage only to find rather threatening rum runners present. At their suggestion, he returned to his home on Longwood Avenue, giving them time to complete their work, and found on his return some rather elegant champagne awaiting him."

Yes, that *must* have been another spring, for all agreed that during this season on Little's Point, quiet was the word. The high point of the day was the lowering of the flag at the Marine encampment—a brace of color sergeants and a bugler. With the first flash from Graves Light across the water, down came Old Glory and as the plaintive notes of "Taps" trilled along the shore, likewise the flags of the cottagers. A moving sight and sound for the guests on the spreading porches of the New Ocean House.

President-watching was a calm and rarely rewarding pastime, as discovered by a crowd of Baker's Islanders whose destination one late July afternoon aboard the good launch *Melba* was the Swampscott shore. "A halt of 15 minutes was made in front of President Coolidge's summer home, giving the party ample opportunity to take in all the surroundings, observe the sentries pacing about the grounds and finally to cap the climax, receiving a friendly wave from the group on the piazza." As exciting as watching the grass grow on the "White Court" lawn, or the President having his portrait painted inside by Edmund Tarbell.

Underwhelmed by the presidential presence was my uncle Phil Lewis's great-aunt Emma Ireson Newhall, one of seven Ireson sisters of Lynn. Ever since anyone could remember, Emma had been driven out around Little's Point on her daily outing. (If they happened to be on the sunny side of the road, which she abhorred, she ordered James to drive in the shade on the left, oncoming traffic be damned.) One late June morning the carriage halted at the entrance to the Point. "Why are we stopping, James?" "There's a Marine at the gate with a gun, Ma'am." "A Marine? Drive on, James." And he did . . . and the astonished guard stepped aside.

Calvin Coolidge, son of the soil, had been at Swampscott eleven days before he set careful foot on *Mayflower*. On the Fourth of July, his birthday, he and Grace were driven to Marblehead for dinner in the main saloon, at anchor in the harbor. A week later they assayed their first voyage beyond the mouth of the Potomac, which until then had been the extent of the Coolidge cruising ground. The stunning white yacht steamed presidentially the few miles down to Boston for a tour of the harbor defenses. Mr. Coolidge, in an admiral's hat, was seen on the bridge. His spouse spent the round trip knitting a pair of socks.

The photographers for some reason were excluded from this first venturing forth in *Mayflower* and raised a cry. To make up, they were the only press taken on the second cruise, July 15, to Quincy, when the Landlubber-in-Chief posed patiently in his nautical cap. Another week, and the presidential yachting party plunged valiantly across the bay twenty-five miles to Hull and back in seas rough enough for the press corps forced to follow *Mayflower*'s boiling wake in a twenty-four-foot launch that was nearly swamped by every swell, taking on water that threatened to douse the engine, pumps going, most of them hanging over the rails interviewing the fishes.

Twice more *Mayflower* poked out of Marblehead, for the Charlestown

The living hall at "White Court." (Louis A. Gallo collection)

Navy Yard and the South Shore. Insouciantly that summer she would steam through the starting line of whatever race was forming outside the harbor, as she did one Saturday when Phil Lewis was crewing for Alfred Chase, scattering the fleet, almost capsizing the contestants in that wake. Mr. Coolidge was seated up in the bow in his seagoing cap, all by himself, pre-occupied perhaps with the ins and outs of his tax cut program, the coal crisis, regarding which he had lunched with Mr. John Hays Hammond, or an especially challenging jigsaw puzzle. "Fact is," Uncle Phil recalled, "we rode her bow wave, got a head start across the line, and it was the only race we won all season."

Somehow, some silver-tongued politician persuaded the President to make one public showing that summer to raise the flag on what was touted as the highest wooden flagpole in New England, just erected on Lynn Common. On August 28 twenty-five thousand converged for a glimpse of their nation's leader. It was a regular mainsail of a flag, and the President had a little trouble managing the halyard as it flapped furiously in the breeze that rattled his coat and ruffled the always carefully brushed Coolidge hair. But when it was done, and the banner waved proudly aloft, and the thousands of schoolchildren massed around the reviewing stand lifted their voices in patriotic respect, the Chief Executive turned to Mrs. Coolidge and was heard by those near him to say:

"That's a wonderful sight."

Labor Day was around the corner, and the week after, the nation's business would revert to Washington. The President, a spokesperson earnestly declared, had made every effort to be impartial in his relations with the communities of the North Shore—residing in Swampscott, maintaining his offices in Lynn and his yacht in Marblehead, and attending divine services in Salem.

Mr. Coolidge was paid a call on September 4 by Donald H. Smith, owner of "White Court," setting off a flurry of speculation that he might be considering the estate as his permanent summer residence. It was not to be. The matter was not brought up, Smith told reporters. Early in the summer the press had reported that friends of the President had pledged $125,000 to buy "White Court" for him. He had demurred, so it was said, with his usual finality: "I might not like it."

On September 9, 1925, the Coolidges motored to Salem and boarded the night train for Washington, even as *Mayflower* raised anchor and steamed for the last time out of Marblehead. Whether or not Calvin Coolidge in fact liked "White Court," his neighbors or any of the North Shore at all, he wasn't talking. But then, why should he?

John Hays Hammond, Jr., strikes a pose in his theatrical castle.
(Hammond Castle Museum)

~21~
PAINTED PLACE AND
PAINTED FACE

*Old Fishtown, of all places on the Shore, tolerates
knights of the brush and idols of the boards*

As the 1921 season opened,
W. Lester Stevens, an artist and sometime writer of Gloucester, made an off-the-cuff survey and announced that there were more representations of Cape Ann in more styles in more museums and private collections than of any other place in America. He calculated that six hundred artists had already invaded the cape for the season, and all the more buyers with cash to burn, some of whom were attracted to the North Shore's famous art colony as simple lovers, some because it was the thing to do, "while a few, whose Ford incomes of 1916 have grown to Rolls-Royce proportions in 1921, come here that they may absorb and carry back to their woman's clubs in White Horse Junction, Arkansas, or some similar locality, the message of the 'Moderns.'"

Thus did Master Stevens, traditionalist among traditionalists, with one fell swoop dismiss both the patrons *and* the moderns, of whom there were precious few, for at that moment Gloucester's single brief experiment in modernism, the Gallery-on-the-Moors, was on the brink of collapse. Not that there wasn't a stray comet still in the offing for a firmament that had glowed to a Lane, a Homer, a Hunt, a Duveneck, a Twachtman, a Hassam and a Sloan. But quantity had clearly won the day, and by the end of the decade, in the rueful words of art historian James F. O'Gorman, the country's most prolific art colony was trademarked by "a kind of rubber-stamp Impressionism."

The first was Fitz Hugh Lane who, though crippled by polio in childhood, captured the beguiling, elusive vitality of Gloucester as no other. And though he was well appreciated by his knowing contemporaries before his death in 1865, Lester Stevens mentioned every name but his. Today Fitz Hugh Lane is hailed—with and without Winslow Homer—as the greatest of American marine artists. Homer certainly knew Lane's work as painter and lithographer when he painted Gloucester as early as 1871, returning for longer stays in 1873 and 1880. At almost the same time William Morris Hunt, of bald pate and flowing beard, was roaming the North Shore for subjects, sometimes in his painting van behind a span of horses, sometimes

Frank Duveneck galvanizes an audience, 1909. (Duveneck House, Covington, Kentucky)

accompanied by a clutch of worshipful female students, seventeen of whom invaded Annisquam in his wake to immortalize the apple blossoms of 1875. Two years after that, Hunt bought an old barn in Magnolia and converted it into a studio.

Lane and Homer were as intimate with Gloucester as Hunt was detached. Somewhere between these extremes of impressionability was the best teacher of them all, the one who came closest in his diffident way to fathering a school, the German-born Cincinnati painter-etcher-sculptor Frank Duveneck. A large, fair fellow with a drooping moustache who liked good talk, Duveneck when he was twenty-seven produced a most successful show of his red-blooded colors in Boston in 1875 and got a huge boost from Hunt. He returned to Europe for more study and then teaching there mostly American students—the "Duveneck boys," including the early American impressionist John Henry Twachtman.

Although Duveneck's biographers don't place him in Gloucester until 1899, his son stayed with him in a rented house on Eastern Point as early as 1893. Lester Stevens wrote that he sketched on Cape Ann in the mid-1870s with Hunt and rented the Niles farmhouse on Eastern Point for the season before 1880, while his local obituary in 1919 had him summering in Gloucester for more than forty years. William Niles, an avid amateur painter, ran the farm after his father's death in 1872 and may have been the agent of Duveneck's tenancy.

Several other artists rented the picturesque old homestead on Gloucester Harbor, beginning with Reginald Cleveland Coxe, the etcher and illustrator, in 1890, and including one "Eisham" in 1895, no doubt the critic and historian who knew them all, Samuel Isham. The amiable Duveneck for many years kept studios at both Bass Rocks and Rocky Neck to take advantage of the morning and evening light across sea or harbor. His canvases are evocative and full of color and light. He painted Brace Rock, off the back shore of Eastern Point, ten or twelve times at different hours, as Lane did, for the effects of the light.

As an aesthetic chauvinist at a time when collectors in this country were still buying third-rate European over first-rate American, this co-rediscoverer of Lane's Cape Ann with Hunt and Homer introduced a number of painters, who would be widely influential in their own right, to its always shifting theatricality as an arena of nature, one of the world's great basins of the *plein air*, a nursery of American art on no less a scale than the Hudson River valley and the Southwest.

Among the disciples who followed Duveneck to Cape Ann were Joseph R. De Camp, Theodore Wendell, Edward H. Potthast and Lewis H. Meakin. De Camp and Wendell settled in Boston as landscapists (the former a portraitist as well), Potthast in New York specializing in bright beach scenes, Meakin remaining in the Midwest to produce landscapes and still lifes. Ross E. Turner trailed De Camp to Boston from Munich in 1882, taught thousands of students over a long career, settled in Salem, and came

"The Ten." Front: Edward Simmons, Willard L. Metcalf, Frederick Childe Hassam, J. Alden Weir and Robert Reid. Rear: William Merritt Chase (who replaced John H. Twachtman after the latter's death in 1902), Frank W. Benson, Edmund C. Tarbell, Thomas W. Dewing and Joseph R. De Camp. (Peabody Essex Museum)

early to Cape Ann to sketch, as did the flamboyant, innovative, emancipative William Merritt Chase, who studied with Duveneck and Twachtman in Venice. Twachtman was twenty-two when the two traveled to Munich to study in 1875. He didn't return to America to settle until 1889, when he joined the coterie of painters infected with the work of Monet and the new European Impressionism and that summer was drawn to Gloucester, probably by Duveneck.

Frederick Childe Hassam and Twachtman developed a supportive friendship. One, Maine-born, athletic, a devotee of the outdoors, was as physically dynamic as the other was ostensibly enervated, temperamental and unstable in all but what his inner eye conveyed to him. The two drank too much together and painted the New England shore together, with a common partiality for the Connecticut coast around Greenwich and for Gloucester. Twachtman was joined in the *plein air* and in 1895 at the classes of Charles A. Winter for the first of many summers by another rising luminist, Willard L. Metcalf of Lowell.

In 1898 Twachtman, Hassam, De Camp, Weir, Metcalf and Edmund C. Tarbell (Boston portraitist and pillar of the Museum School, then painting in Annisquam on occasion) broke away from the Society of American Artists, itself a splinter from the National Academy, and with four friends— Frank W. Benson, Salem portraitist and etcher of waterfowl; Thomas W. Dewing of Boston, limner of dreamy damsels; and the muralists Robert Reid of Stockbridge and Edward Simmons of Concord—organized as the "Ten American Painters," commonly "The Ten," showing more or less together for another twenty years, William Merritt Chase replacing Twachtman on the latter's death in 1902.

Childe Hassam had a studio in East Gloucester up the dusty road from the old Fairview Inn, where in the 1880s the Philadelphia etcher Stephen Parrish boarded with his teenage son Maxfield (illustrator-to-be) and his chum Charles Adams Platt (artist and architect-to-be). They sketched and etched and painted the bustling harbor. Coincidentally or not, the portraitist Cecilia Beaux, the future "female Sargent," had taken a room at the Fairview in 1879 to paint, nine years before she built her summer home, "Green Alley," on Eastern Point; her studio in Philadelphia was next to the elder Parrish's, but she was too awed to introduce herself.

After the turn of the century the influx gathered impetus until the independent folk of East Gloucester and its pendant Rocky Neck looked around one fine luminescent morning to find themselves, to their surprise and sometimes dismay (pocketbooks excepted), harboring *the* art colony north of Boston, perhaps *the* summer art colony of America.

Here was the heart of it all, the wharves stalling the patient schooners in still waters, the helter-skelter sprawl of fishing establishments and shoreside emporia and acres of flake yards of pungent salt codfish spread to dry, the cozy inner harbor contrasts of bustle and serenity, the comings and goings of gray canvas in the breeze, the snug clapboard houses, Five and Ten Pound islands, lighthouses, salt ships from Sicily airing out patched squaresails in the sun, steam-puffing tugboats, lobstermen, dorymen, beachcombers and bathers, sailing yachts and naphtha launches, tall rows of trees, upland meadows, Dogtown scrub and boulder, the Back Shore in an easterly, wild as the coast of Maine.

Above all, literally, the light over and around, enveloping, permeating, insinuating, suffusing the Olympian amphitheater of Gloucester Harbor and the very water itself, as if *under* . . . that evanescent, airy, heaven-sent light almost as palpable, it strikes one who has dwelled within its embrace for forty years, as the hard rock shore. Not infrequently this almost landlocked bowl of the heavenliest light you ever experienced, in its thousand shifting nuances from day to night and night to day, scowl to smile, season to season, has been compared with the Bay of Naples alone. And many the traveler has rounded the world, only to return, gaze about him, breathe a deep sigh, and announce as if he had the tablets in hand at last that there was nowhere, anywhere, for that interplay of land and sea and sky and inhabitants to surpass the old, old fishing port of Gloucester, on the North Shore of Massachusetts Bay.

Portrait of Fanny Travis Cochran, 1887, by the "female Sargent" of Dabsville, Cecilia Beaux. (Pennsylvania Academy of the Fine Arts)

Here Maurice Prendergast was drawn back summer after summer to dip and dab on paper the dreamy colors of an open-air tea party above the harbor (a *dauber,* scoffed the traditionalists). Also came the solid marinists Walter Dean, Frederick Mulhaupt from far-away Missouri, Swedish-born Theodore Victor Carl Valenkamph and A. W. Bühler, painter and etcher, who shifted his ground from Annisquam in 1898 because there was more to paint over at East Gloucester and Rocky Neck. To Annisquam was magnetized the Vermonter William L. Picknell—fresh, strong, uncomplicated landscapist—and tourists, invited by a trolley guidebook to kibitz over

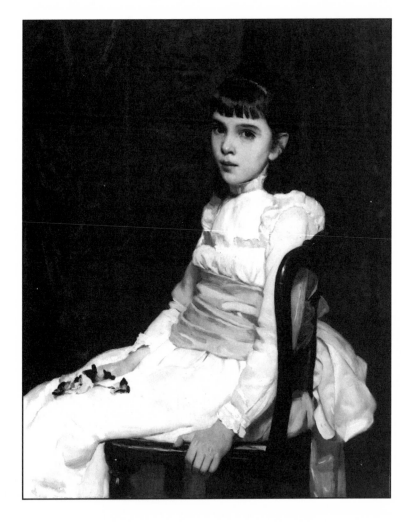

Rockport Harbor and especially the fishing shack dubbed "Motif Number One" (behind the mainmast of the schooner at center) were already attracting painters in 1896. (Sandy Bay Historical Society)

"a score of artists at work on the beach, sketching some of the gray-bearded old followers of the sea who work away on their nets apparently unconscious that they are attracting attention." Not so unconscious, some of them. One learned that his portrait had fetched a good price during the winter and declined to pose again for the artist "'cause prices has ris'."

East of Annisquam and the granite quarries of Lanesville, near Folly Cove on broad, blue Ipswich Bay, settled Charles Grafly in 1904, Cape Ann's first summer sculptor, foremost in his day, escaping from Philadelphia winters. Considered the leading portraitist of men, Grafly was mentor of George Demetrios, Paul Manship and Walker Hancock, who all stayed and worked their roots into the ledges of Lanesville. And of course Leonard Craske, sculptor and sometime photographer/lecturer, whose noble bronze colossus, *The Man at the Wheel*, has dominated the fisherman's harbor since Gloucester's three-hundredth anniversary in 1923.

Farther east yet, to Pigeon Cove in the north of Rockport in the 1880s, came John Joseph Enneking, Cincinnati-educated Impressionist, early influence on the young Hassam, getting the hang of the New England landscape that would bring him fame. But Cape Ann's far shore was rough and sparked inspiration in only the sturdiest of souls.

For the more easily inspired in these frontier days of the art colony, the quaint fising and lobstering and quarrying village of Rockport lay compla-

cently ahead. Down on the shore in 1873 a self-taught young fellow of twenty-one, Gilbert Tucker Margeson, set up his easel in a shack, sharing with Homer the rediscovery of Cape Ann if not the honors, and he was still at it seventy-two years later, bringing up the rear of the parade he had led.

The day came when the fishermen could not afford not to sell their shanties on Bearskin Neck to that parade, the originality of whose marching song was emblazoned on the marching mile of canvas as the too-familiar red wharf shed derided by one bored art teacher as "Motif Number One." And the day would come, too, in 1978, when the Rockport colonists and their symbiotic swarm of crafts- and tradespersons could not afford not—so they swore—to replace this too-common trademark of the lowest denominator with an exact copy (the measurements had already been taken against such a catastrophe) when the "Motif" disintegrated at the height of a storm. But of course alluring Rockport, like picturesque Provincetown and charming Rocky Neck, has attracted many the fine artist impassive or private enough to shrug off such stigmata of the market.

For all its visual attractions, its intimacy, its undoubted paintability, Rockport has so far not been gifted with the chemistry for greatness. Gloucester was, and is. She was and is dirty, dazzling and dynamic.

After the mists of impressionism had receded, along came "The Eight" in 1908 in a single show assembled by the progressive New York art teacher Robert Henri. What a contrast to The Ten! The Ashcan School had arrived. "What shocked the world of art was a preoccupation with types, localities and incidents to which Americans were conveniently deaf and blind," art historian Oliver W. Larkin has written with a nice irony. "A degree of strenuousness could be forgiven in the days of Teddy Roosevelt; but to paint drunks and slatterns, pushcart peddlers and coal mines, bedrooms and barrooms was somehow to be classed among the socialists, anarchists and other disturbers of the prosperous equilibrium."

And again, there was the common thread of Gloucester. Of The Eight, mild Maurice Prendergast, with a foot in both camps, had to be the sentimental favorite. Three of the others as well, John Sloan and his pal William Glackens and Ernest Lawson (who absorbed his technical nuances from

Twachtman and Weir), were influenced to varying degrees of profundity by their exposure to the land of light, whose effects, if any, on George Luks, Arthur Davies, Everett Shinn and Robert Henri are moot.

And then, along came Europe again—always Europe—disarticulating in the buff down an abstract tumble of steps at the Armory Show. Fixed in the popular eye by Marcel Duchamp's *Nude Descending a Staircase,* that bombshell of modernism exploded in mid-Manhattan in 1913, and in the back alleys of John Sloan's head, clearing his visual landscape in one clean sweep that propelled him to Gloucester.

Square-jawed John and Dolly Sloan, and Charles Winter (old teacher of Twachtman, bridge to The Eight) and his artist wife Alice, took for the 1914 season a cottage that is still standing on East Main Street in East Gloucester above the causeway to Rocky Neck. Next summer they were joined by the much younger Stuart Davis, even more mind-blown by the Armory Show, for the first of his many years in Gloucester with his wild brush and poster colors. Sloan spent but five summers in Gloucester, spanning the war in which he was too old to serve, but they were the most productive of his life, the fork in a career that led him from the monotones of the big city to the full spectrum of land and sea at Cape Ann and finally of desert and mountain in the Southwest.

There is noble irony in the appearance on the East Gloucester scene in the middle of the Great War—the Great Divide—of a pair of patrons, dedicated to forward movement in the arts, whose very intentions bore the seeds of their disappointment. These were William Atwood, a civilized Connecticut textile manufacturer and amateur artist, and his gracious wife, Emmeline. Finding the artists trying to seduce the muse (and the custom) in waterfront warrens of "dark little lofts, old outhouses, chicken coops, stables, tiny rooms, poorly lighted and unattractive," the Atwoods took the extraordinary step of buying upland above the Sloan-Davis-Winter cottage and engaging the Boston architect Ralph Adams Cram to design and build the medieval-revival "Gallery-on-the-Moors," and nearby, their own summer home, "House-on-the-Moors." In the midwar year of 1916 the Gloucester colony's first genuine gallery opened, with high promise. A Duveneck was the centerpiece. The Atwoods would accept no commissions. All was for the artists' sake.

As so frequently is the reward for Samaritans, the benefactors within a couple of seasons were being roundly muttered at by many of the colonists who found their work excluded from the new gallery by the well-intended efforts of the owners to observe certain standards. Sloan is said to have sold one painting before he came to Gloucester, and more at the Atwoods'. The market was seeking its own level. East Gloucester was alive with artists . . . or dying from them, the new bungalows elbowing out the old fishing colony. For the solitary painter there was hardly anywhere left to be alone. Even gregarious Lester Stevens pined for his boyhood when he and his art teacher "would wander all day through the fields, or along the shore, and never meet another painter."

Sloan gave up painting in the streets of Gloucester after a disagreeable encounter with a drunken fisherman, complaining to Van Wyck Brooks that he had no use for art colonies (though he could not stay long away from them), that "there was an artist's shadow beside every cow in Gloucester, and the cows themselves were dying from eating paint-rags."

By the summer of 1919 the war was over. John and Dolly Sloan abandoned Gloucester forever for Santa Fe. Stuart Davis took off for Cuba. Frank Duveneck died, and so did Alden Weir, the third of The Ten to pass away. And the Atwoods surrendered. The show that season was hung by a jury selected by the colony and dominated by landscapes executed, according to one caustic critic, "to catch the eye of the wealthy tourist." For three more seasons the Atwoods compromised their tastes. There would be lonely exceptions wandering across the landscape—Edward Hopper, Marsden Hartley and a few others. But Gloucester was overrun with the Pharisees of the familiar, of the endless surf upon an endless shore, of the seagull and the saccharine. In 1922 the artists organized the North Shore Arts Association and bought a hulking old warehouse on Reed's Wharf with acres of walls. The Gallery-on-the-Moors tiptoed out with a last small show. Deftly, the victors installed the Samaritan as their first president.

But of course painters paint to be hung, as writers who are not critics write about painters to be drawn and quartered!

ALL THE SHORE'S A STAGE

As for the Atwoods, defeated in their Quixotic tilt with the windmilling jury system of the Gloucester art establishment, they carried, as luck would have it, a spare lance. By 1918, they were planning a community theater in their Gallery-on-the-Moors, rather in the forefront, too, of the summer theater movement, close behind Ogunquit and Detroit.

Happily for Cape Ann and the theater at large, Florence Cunningham, a Gloucester-born graduate of Vassar College then teaching spoken English at Smith, heard of their plan, offered to take charge, and was gratefully taken up. With the catching enthusiasm that carried her through a long and distinguished career, she recruited a local cast behind Leslie Buswell, the young English actor returned from ambulance-driving in France and residing, for the nonce, with his friend John Hays Hammond, Jr.

After getting off to a patriotic start that final summer of the war with an outdoor pageant for the benefit of "Bundles for Britain," the Playhouse-on-the-Moors presented three one-act plays, beginning with *Land of Heart's Desire* by Yeats. Success overnight. Cunningham had a knack for matching types with roles, such as the Gloucester policeman she followed on his beat one day until she screwed up the courage to recruit him for the cop in *Two Crooks and a Lady.*

Eastern Point's Dabsville and friends, naturally, patronized this so interesting experiment. Buswell had been one of Mrs. Jack Gardner's favored young men ever since she saw him in a juvenile lead. She got Leslie to read aloud to her to improve her diction, not that it needed it, and he got the players to put on a pair of one-acters as a delayed birthday present in the Gothic Room at "Fenway Court" on the eleventh of June, 1922; she had been eighty-two for two months.

Recalled Florence Cunningham: "On the dot at 2:25 we began our show before an elite audience. Harvard's President Lowell, also Henry Cabot Lodge, I believe, and a few others of their stature. Mrs. Gardner wore a lovely white gown and the Catherine of Russia pearls. Everyone had a front seat as there were only about a dozen guests." A thunderstorm had obligingly swept across the Fenway during the storm scene in Maeterlinck's *Monna Vanna.*

Magnet as it was for a mixture of amateur and professional talent, the Playhouse-on-the-Moors was strong up front but weak backstage. Always resourceful, Cunningham rang in Florence Evans, Boston diction teacher and drama coach. The two Florences rented the huge paint shop of the Rocky Neck Marine Railways and opened the Gloucester School of the Theatre in this old place of interesting odors in the summer of 1919.

Annisquam summer resident Russel Crouse responds to applause as his 1939 classic Life with Father *opens at Rocky Neck's Little Theatre in 1952. (Cape Ann Historical Association)*

Like its companion playhouse, which the indefatigable Cunningham continued to direct by day, the Little Theatre—as everyone was soon calling it—was by night one of the first of its kind in the country. One-act plays on the ground floor at first to a small audience, then on to full productions when the upper stories were removed for a regular stage and a whitewashed auditorium seating two hundred.

The firetrap of a paint shop was projected partly on piles over the reeking inner harbor. From a deck, the enchanted patrons had cool, summer-

evening-wafted smells and views and sounds of the water, the lit city across the channel, the riding lights of the fishing vessels and the twinkling stars above. Usherettes wore sailor suits, and the curtain was raised like a sail to the nautical clang of a ship's bell. One night, as if responding in some ghostly fashion to O'Neill's stage directions for *Anna Christie*, the fog rolled in and a passing schooner's blast sent spine-tingling thrills through the audience. 'Twas magic, pure magic.

Although the Little Theatre catapulted no great names onto the marquees, Russel Crouse, summer resident of Annisquam, hung around productions of his plays, and so did Thornton Wilder his. The poet May Sarton braved the footlights.

Four legends: playwright Russel Crouse; Florence Cunningham, director of the Gloucester School of the Theatre; Life with Father; and America's premier summer playhouse. 1952. (Cape Ann Historical Association)

The pioneering Gloucester School of the Theatre was a force on the American summer drama workshop circuit for thirty-two years. The smaller playhouse, given up as an art gallery by the Atwoods, closed after eight seasons. Florence Cunningham was summoned to Hollywood as a dramatic and linguistic coach for stars and was ninety-two when she died in 1980.

HAMMOND'S CASTLES

Again the scene changes. In 1923 young John Hays Hammond, Jr., sold patent rights worth half a million to the Radio Corporation of America and put architects to work on a sort of castle, a donjon at any rate, adjacent to his "Bungalow" to house the gigantic organ taking shape, pipe by pipe, in his imagination.

His friend Leslie Buswell, meanwhile, acquired thirty-three acres of the wooded height directly above the Hammond estate, dammed the brook to make "Buswell Pond," and was soon overseeing the construction of a rambling reproduction of a seventeenth-century English country home on the crest of the hill, with a manorial command of Gloucester Harbor, Eastern Point and the sea beyond.

Early in 1924 Benito Mussolini, now Il Duce and the dictator of Italy, summoned America's electronic genius to create for him a secret radio communications system to help consolidate his authority.

In April Hammond and his Buswell sailed for Rome. In three months the job was done. The deviser admitted to *True* magazine thirty-six years later that "I was really sold on dictatorship as a way of running a government efficiently." Jack was not alone of course, but almost immediately he was disillusioned: the network's first major mission, in reality, was to entrap important anti-Fascists, "and among those who were snared by the system were a good many of Hammond's friends."

In Gloucester that fall, Buswell's Jacobean estate, practically completed in his absence, was opened for inspection by the press while Hammond's donjon rose stone by stone above the high-tide mark. Meanwhile, Jack "wooed and won" Irene Fenton, an artist; after her divorce they were married in the summer of 1925, incurring such disapproval from the inventor's parents, as historian James O'Gorman reconstructs the scene (and it must have been some scene), that he had to abandon altogether any thoughts of bringing a divorced woman to live on Hammond family turf. Work on the donjon organ house ceased abruptly, and a mile and a half toward Magnolia, above Norman's Woe Rock, Jack purchased on the very brink of a Wagnerian cliff a rocky tract to which he transferred his castellar ambitions.

Hammond Senior, friend of Presidents, was dismayed: "I dropped in to see the site of your new house and I fear you do not realize the *staggering* sum you will have to provide. [By 1928, with twenty years of work still ahead, young Jack had spent more than $350,000.] This is a very costly site to develop—You should go slowly! A small, inexpensive house with money in the bank is better than a costly house mortgaged to death!!! I am very much worried about you and your affairs." It may be noted that the father had built his own costly battlemented stone tower to Arthur Shurtleff's design three years earlier at "Lookout Hill" and was not a man to be upstaged lightly, least of all by a precocious offspring.

The summer of 1925 dropped the final curtain on the Playhouse-on-the-Moors. The next April Leslie Buswell's mother died in England. She was the daughter of Admiral Henry Croft of Stillington, Yorkshire, and a cousin of Lord Plummer, the King's Master of the Rolls. Her son called his new turf "Stillington." In July Buswell completed an addition, Stillington Hall, a vaulted manor hall with a stage at one end, professionally equipped in every respect, seating 170. While doing so, he organized his own amateur troupe, the Stillington Players.

Summer theater on Cape Ann in the dramatis personae of the Stillington Players, without the lapse of even a season, reopened in 1926 in the hills of West Gloucester, in the most Gothic setting imaginable, with the French comedy *She Had to Know*. The heavy cream of North Shore society was packed in behind Governor and Mrs. Alvan T. Fuller, who had been entertained at dinner across the harbor on Eastern Point in his slightly spooky "Red Roof" by Congressman Piatt Andrew and doubtless the doyens of Dabsville.

Leslie Buswell, torchbearer, trouper, producer, director, host and star, was never more magnetic. A week later the musical side of "Stillington" burst harmoniously upon the dream world of the North Shore with a recital by the virtuoso violinist Ephraim Zimbalist. For his second season as impresario Buswell presented the American Opera Company in *Faust, The Barber of Seville* and *I Pagliacci,* among others, while the Players introduced *The*

Intimate Stranger with the Manchester socialite actress Mrs. Fitzwilliam Sargent in the female lead. A stuffed house every night. The in thing on the Shore.

Buswell's coup of the decade came in 1929 with the world premiere of *Christopher Rand* by Mrs. August Belmont and her collaborator on an earlier success, Harriet Ford. Leslie knew where the choirs of angels sang. An actress once herself, this grandest of the New York and Newport dames, wife of the ridiculously rich financier, was already long a legend in society, charity, music and the arts, and she had a long way to go, for she died in 1979 at a hundred.

Mrs. Belmont stayed at the Oceanside in Magnolia for rehearsals and the opening. The critic for the *North Shore Breeze* ventured, concerning *Christopher Rand*, that "certainly, with the exception of the rather infelicitous curtain of Act II, it is difficult to see how any company could have done more for this drama of the mines, and this is the more noteworthy, when one realizes that practically all of Mr. Buswell's previous productions might roughly have been classed as 'society plays.'" One can almost imagine Mrs. Belmont descending into one of her husband's coal mines, researching her play. She had ascended some distance since that day when the beautiful young actress Elizabeth Robson, hardly more than an ingenue, was beckoned by the maid from the window of a Beacon Street town house as she passed. She paused. And Mrs. Jack Gardner appeared at the door,

Trying out Jack Hammond's invention for extracting new tonal effects from the piano at the "Bungalow" in 1925: Leslie Buswell, now manager of the Hammond Laboratories; Hammond; conductor Leopold Stokowski; and painter Lester Donahue. (Hammond Castle Museum)

declared, "Walk erect, young woman!" and disappeared back inside. Mrs. Jack had been dead five years when her young man Leslie premiered Eleanor's latest.

Collapsed the stock market upon the land, and in 1930 so did the curtain upon the cameo stage of "Stillington." Always, though, there was someone to pick up the torch—this time a carpenter at the Oceanside who with a few other Buswell veterans started up the Oceanside Theatre with a series of one-acters that were still wowing 'em in 1935.

The castle that issued stone by stone from the solid-state imagination of John Hays Hammond, Jr., above Longfellow's sacred Norman's Woe—"Abbadia Mare," Abbey-by-the-Sea—was one of the truly unauthentic architectural anachronisms of the North Shore. He built it around a great hall right out of Camelot, the sort and size at one end of which his friend Mussolini would have set himself on an elevated dais, if he had only thought of it first. A hundred feet long and sixty high, his Great Hall was designed to amplify to the limit of aural tolerance the product of every one of the ten thousand pipes of his magnificent organ that would take twenty years to complete.

But this organ (no relation to the electric make of the same name), one of the universe's more pretentious musical instruments, was not the only bizarre feature of Hammond's moated, drawbridged, portcullised, battlemented, parapeted and towered castle, home and, after 1930, museum as well. Jack had great sport working into it all sorts of the secret passages and bedrooms, peepholes, peekaboos, naughty niceties and narcissistic knickknacks first favored by his friends Doc Andrew and Harry Sleeper. What acronymic antics they engaged in, those four—Buswell, Andrew, Sleeper, Hammond—what BASHes!

Further, the inventor incorporated "art treasures and architectural specimens that today are almost priceless museum pieces." So instructs the *Hammond Museum Guide Book,* which explains as ingenuously as it can that "he brought these treasures from Europe as he collected them in his travels." The provenance of the treasures of Italian origin, anyway, is raised by the "immediacy" of Jack Hammond's recollected disillusionment with Il Duce after the entrapment of his anti-Fascist friends. In 1927, after installing Mussy's radio network, Hammond was praising the dictator to the heavens in an interview in the *Breeze*. Nine years after, in 1933, a *Breeze* article revealed all—or almost all—stating that if Benito Mussolini ever visits America, Jack Hammond's "will be one of the first roofs to shelter him. . . . Hammond was thrown in close contact with the powerful Premier. They shared a common enthusiasm for Italian antiquities. Masonry, furniture and bibelots of medieval birth have been brought to Gloucester to give the stamp of authenticity to Hammond's portcullised home."

Twelve years after the rendition of the son's considerable favor to the Fascisti, in 1935, John Hays Hammond, Sr., wrote in his *Autobiography* of his own interview with the "beneficent" dictator in 1926. He described the Duce and his movement and methods with enthusiasm as heroic bulwarks against Communism in Europe, observing proudly that Mussolini had made Jack, Jr., a Grand Officer of the Crown and added: "I have not seen him since but have kept directly in touch with him through my son, Jack, who installed for him a selective system of radio which he uses in communicating with his representatives in Italy and Africa." Thus is history made, and written, and rewritten. Visitors to the Hammond Castle Museum in search of the treasures of Italy, *nota benito*.

On a terrace overlooking the North Atlantic Ocean, Jack Hammond erected a much-larger-than-life statue of himself, heroically posed in the buff, gazing in bronze condescension over the sea. He died in 1965 at seventy-six, lord of quite a lot he had surveyed, at that, and had himself buried a few feet away. Though not a Catholic, he left his castle to the Archdiocese of Boston, which in a while found it too much of a secular care and sold it. Most of Jack's library went to the Sawyer Free Library in Gloucester. En route, it was stored in the basement of the First Baptist Church in the next block until shelf space could be found. None of his own particular taste in "blue" books in the collection made it to the library, which would have given him a chuckle, for like his father, he was a bit of a rascal at heart.

The patriarchal Frederick Ayer with grandson Frederick by his first marriage (left) and son Frederick by his second, holding his own son Frederick. Behind, a Gloucester bed hammock made by sailmakers in their spare time. "Avalon," Pride's Crossing. (Patton family album)

~22~
CONTINUITY

. . . all things considered

By the 1920s the North Shore had survived ten decades since Colonel Perkins opened Boston's summery window on the sea with the Nahant Hotel, a century of much change (the "American Century") and some progress (a lot of it either deplorable or excitingly revolutionizing in nature and direction). Three generations and the beginning of a fourth had witnessed the opening up of the West and the attendant (and causative) shift of culture and control from the increasingly effete (so Westerners thought) East, the disruption (and rejuvenation) of two major wars, the desolation of income taxes, waves of ethnic adulteration from across the sea and inundations of motor cars whose presence on Route 1A was a curse or a blessing, depending on who was behind the wheel.

Cold Roast warmed over? A hundred years later a summer census of "leading families" surprised no one who already knew: Nahant contained 106 from Boston, five from Washington, one each from New York and Chicago, one from Philadelphia, and one each from indeterminate locations in Connecticut, Illinois, Ohio and Florida. Greater Boston continued to dominate every colony on the Shore while tolerating, if not exactly welcoming, hinterlanders from the vast unknown beyond Dedham, and the postwar trend toward year-round suburban living of a sort was gaining favor.

There was a characteristically cautious feeling by 1928 that the depression (we would call it a "recession" today) following the Armistice was finally being overcome and that business conditions were improving. To all this the *North Shore Breeze* was tempted to "almost yell hurrah!" It voiced careful optimism, however, that house sales were picking up but thanked God the Shore had been "spared from the aggressive ruinous propaganda of real estate exploiters and boomers."

Caution, Boston caution, resisted the temptation (not always, but often enough) to sell off the family acres acquired by Great-Grandfather from families who couldn't resist the temptation to make, they had thought, a killing. Caution built the dynasties that built Boston's North Shore, and cautious trust funds of bonds, and maintained its grip on the coast for a hundred years—and would for another fifty after all came Crashing down around it, and perhaps another fifty after that . . . well, Cold Roast Caution

transfused regularly, lest we forget, with the hot blood of the patriarchal gamblers from Perkins to Prince.

Caution built continuity—that and a proper marriage, to be sure. Caution, and Concern for the Customer.

The firm of S. S. Pierce, which provided every proper pantry in Boston By Appointment, inaugurated "City Service at the Seashore" in the early Twenties. Salesmen would call for orders regularly, in person, or they could be phoned or mailed in. The company's own motor trucks, with facilities for icing perishables, would deliver anywhere between Boston and Cape Ann and even beyond. H. A. Hovey, "The Oldest Butterhouse in Boston," with headquarters at the Faneuil Hall market, was a little more chary and promised delivery of the choicest butter and eggs on standing order, from Nahant to Bass Rocks. Langley-Wharton guaranteed fresh Russian Beluga caviar via your North Shore service entrance, packed in ice at twenty-eight degrees Fahrenheit.

And after all was cleared away ("So many covers were laid at Mrs. So-and-So's 'Atavistic Acres' in Beverly Farms on Tuesday," the *Breeze* never tired of regaling its readers), the man from the Pilgrim Laundry would pick up and deliver without fail, while Lewandos—with its feline laundress and her children painted so amusingly on the panel of every truck—packed milady's "good" linens separately in blue tissue.

For a coming-out party, Jefferson-Johnson Orchestras on Tremont Street in Boston advertised in *The North Shore Blue Book and Social Register:* "Superior Colored Players—Jazz Bands and Entertainers." While for cautious continuity of a less bouncy cadence, summer as well as winter, the *Boston Evening Transcript* with uncharacteristic belligerence (perhaps feeling so comfortably buffered within the cold, fraternal pages of the *Blue Book*) termed itself "as nearly perfect a daily newspaper as it is possible to print."

Caution, Continuity—and Bunny Woods.

Bernard J. Woods—"Bunny" to thousands of North Shore, Boston-based, Best-of-Brood "Chicks," as he called the children lovingly placed under his wing—was to their instruction in the manly and womanly ways of the outdoors what Marguerite Souther, the dreadnaught proprietress of the Eliot Hall dancing school in suburban Jamaica Plain, was to their indoctrination in the arts of the anteroom. Both were pillars in the institutional structure of Boston Society, Miss Souther for fifty-five years, Bunny Woods from 1899 until well into the 1930s.

The Cement of Continuity. There *are* rules governing social intercourse. The formidable Souther, a perfect flagship on the dance floor, once commanded a certain unnecessarily shy young fellow, with a twinkle in her eye: "LEAD me! As if I were FLESH and BLOOD, not a cigar store INDIAN!" And an ex-chick of the male sex wrote Bunny late in his career "first of all to tell you how wonderful I think you are, and second, to say that I would give a good deal to be back at that age myself, for nothing ever comes up to the fun I had with you in those days, and I don't believe you ever realize how much you did for me. You may not remember how I suffered from shyness at first, but I'll never forget how kind you were to me, nor will I forget a party at George Lyman's when I won my first cup. I have always felt that was a turning point in my life, and nothing has ever been so hard again, and I attribute that all to your help and tact. One of the regrets of my life is that you haven't had a hand in bringing up my boys, for I consider it a rare and lasting privilege."

This benign Pied Piper started instructing children in sports and gymnastics at a New York State resort and was inveigled to Boston during the winter, inevitably following his chicks summers to their North Shore habitat, where the contagion for him was such that before long estate owners were vying for the privilege of hosting his "outing classes," and mothers from far-off New Jersey were pressuring their spouses to summer on the North Shore of Boston and pulling strings to get their babes enrolled with him.

Early patrons were the Charles G. Rices in Ipswich. Pupils from as far as Nahant would be conveyed to the Beverly depot, nearly filling the coach that tumbled them out at Ipswich, where all piled into carriages and wagons for the bumpy ride to "Turner Hill." The Rices turned a floor into a gym. Sixty or seventy happy chicks splashed in the pool and gobbled their lunches at a long outdoor table presided over by the gentle Bunny.

Games, folk dances and "stunts" designed to teach chicks to be "real true sports" were the fare for the under-six classes on the lawn of the Beverly Cove estate of Dr. and Mrs. Henry F. Sears, their own children included. Opening day, each initiate was brought up to Mr. Woods and shook hands or curtsied. "Some told their names, but usually the nurses helped out in answer to Bunny's question, 'What little chick is this?'" Hard to believe, but in 1919, after only twenty years of it, Bunny thought he might have taught over 100,000 children.

Kindergartenmeister, all-around athlete, coach and trainer, innovator in physical education and therapy, builder of character, but above all a kindly referee between the generations, Bunny Woods coaxed his little ones, as he had their fathers and mothers, from the Rice barn and the Sears lawn and the Higginson hayfield and the icy waters of West Beach to Harvard Stadium, the battlefields of France and the United States Senate.

For every wholesome intergenerational influence of a Bunny Woods on the more thoughtful, and stable, of the privileged families of the North Shore there were dozens of yacht club stewards and sailing instructors instilling respect for the sea, joy in the mastery of the wind and the fervor of the race into these same chicks, noses peeling, sun-bleached hair stiff with salt.

There was something about the Twenties, the confused, crazy—not so often roaring—*childish* Twenties that was especially of and for and perhaps by the children—children of the Great War, children like fresh poppies forever springing from a thousand Flanders fields—innocents in the linen, lace and ribbons of the summer—the great-grandchildren of Victoria—the children Prendergast and Beaux and Sargent could not resist putting on canvas, wide-eyed and cherry-lipped. How many of the children of the Twenties would be children always—puzzled by the shady corners of their elders, heads aswim with bathtub gin, crowded by the gathering social, political and philosophical catastrophe toward the only conceptual precipice left, economic calamity?

The North Shore of Boston was after all a mere veranda above an enchanting sea, a veranda to a veranda to a certain hotel, long gone, built by a cynical old man who loved his little grandson.

There is a continuity to verandas, and a caution.

In April of 1929 Bill Swan, the dean of New England yachting writers, checked forty-three boatyards along the North Shore and reported that they were building 325 yachts of respectable dimensions at a total cost of more than eight million dollars. The Shore was moving into the biggest yachting season in history. Swan had to admit, however, that ninety percent of the activity in the yards was in pleasure craft and "very little construction for commercial purposes can be found."

Who now can say how many of that great armada of dreams were launched on a sea of watered stock?

It was midsummer of the last year of the Lost. Absolutely everybody

Anne Steele (Proctor) Rice leads the way at a Turner Hill outing class, and Archie White, head of the house, brings up the rear, 1920s. (C. G. Rice collection)

and everything were on the rise, without a shadow of a doubt. Spirits, prices, real estate, elevators, stocks, heels, murders, indices, savings and the bubbles in the bootleg champagne.

For weeks the great secret had been the fantastic bash in the making at "Rocklea," the summer mansion of the Lyon Weyburns (he was a Boston lawyer) at Pride's Crossing. In dubious honor of the dubious hotel that glowered sootily over the B & M yards from on top of North Station, the Weyburns cast the party to end all parties as "Opening-Closing Night of the Manger Night Club" and turned over the vast carriage room of their barn for it. Not a word leaked out. But you could tell from the hour on the invitation that it was one of those late starters that portend a red, white and blue wing-ding.

The cabaret got under way at eleven-thirty with a "screamingly funny skit that completely brought the house down." (The *Breeze* was there—who else?) Then everyone out on the floor for a tango and a waltz to Ruby Newman's orchestra, after which "a most amusing playlet in which Mrs. Daniel Comstock from her chaise longue carried on a typical society matron telephone conversation with Mrs. Lloyd Nichols seated at her desk. It brought gale after gale of laughter, as the indiscretions and idiosyncrasies of one person after another on the Shore were blandly discussed over the wire."

Two society dames in little girl outfits belted out four numbers, followed by Mr. Edward A. Weeks of Montserrat leading his partner "through the intricate steps of a maxixe, and several interpretive dances—in fact he danced all around her with great agility, accompanied by the roars of laughter from the onlookers. His partner was a coquettishly painted broomstick."

More dancing, more acts, more of the joys of the Twenties until somewhere around four-thirty the lights of the Manger Night Club faded into the dawn as the first wide-awake milkman came clip-clopping briskly down Hale Street.

That summer a gaily anonymous contributor to the *Breeze,* which has insinuated so much of the vitality of the times into this chronicle, penned unintentionally, innocently, eloquently, their obituary:

"Seven-thirty! Cocktail hour! The 'clear call that may not be denied' is sounded, and from all up and down the shore, from Marblehead to Rockport, the nightly hegira of the Faithful has begun.

"Turning out from spacious driveways, from tiny side-streets, from country estates, cars of every description join the ever-growing procession on the highway.

"At Del Monte's, the first cars draw up to the door—the thin wail of a violin being tuned floats out through the night. From across the quiet water, lights on the Burrage yacht *Aztec* flare up—launches, hurrying back and forth from shore to ship, like water bugs, carrying dinner guests—gay voices, laughter, music!

"In front of a beautiful Tudor home two policemen have taken their stand. A car stops—saxophones, a violin, drums, are lifted out. The orchestra. The Jack Clunies are giving a dance! Some jovial members of a patriotic war organization, climbing the stairs to the second floor of a barn—later the strains of 'Sweet Adeline' will make the night hideous in Beverly Farms.

"Down in a little cove, past Pride's, a loving father and his four-year-old son have anchored a speed-boat, and hand in hand, the tall man and the little boy climb the hill, through the fast gathering dusk, to a long, low, white house.

"The group of languid gentlemen who hold up the front of some of the shops in Manchester are slowly assembling. Never do to miss any of the passing show! Legend has it that they sleep like the bears all winter, and it must be true, for they never put in an appearance until the first daffodil and the first Rolls-Royce come out in the spring!

"At Calderwood's boat yard, the Lloyd Nichols, with a gay party, are starting for their boat, *Stornaway,* out in the harbor—a moonlight sail is on!

"A huge lavender machine with 'New York City' written in large and impressive letters across the front, purrs by—exactly the shade of the Sen-Sen tablets we used to chew in order to disguise the odor of nicotine from watchful parents, in the far-off days before the Emancipation of Youth.

"Betty Barrell, Connie Percival and two young men turning in at Essex—the most utterly dilapidated Ford touring car, churning along with a young couple, apparently oblivious to the incongruity of evening dress, in such a contraption!

"And so they go. The whole world is on the move, for it's cocktail hour along the North Shore."

After three and a half more months of such engaging giddiness, on October 29, 1929, the stock market collapsed.

Boston's North Shore survived rather well, all things considered. Not too surprisingly, either. And it survives to this day, not surprisingly, even charmingly in many places.

But since Black Friday, it has been, somehow, déjà vu, don't you agree?

Sailing out of Gloucester *with Winslow Homer, 1880.*
(Canajoharie Library and Art Gallery, Canajoharie, New York)

EPILOGUE

Still about as good as it gets

This whole modern trend of having one's friends in business is simply harrowing to anyone who contemplates buying anything whatsoever. Mention that you enjoy reading a particular magazine and you'll find a half dozen acquaintances selling it. Admit your gown is shabby and you'll learn your neighbor is running a "shoppe." Stores are employing post-debutante saleswomen in the expectation that their friends will purchase there.

—*North Shore Breeze*, 1933

WITH THE UPHEAVALS OF THE Depression that followed the stock market crash of 1929, World War II, and the postwar era that grips us to this day, the North Shore has endured but not yet entirely submitted to the erosion of its geographical and sociological distinction. Economic and political turmoil, domestic governmental activism and New Deal populism, and the further social leveling of the war lowered a few bars and bent a few boundaries. The egalitarianism and relative prosperity of the second half of the century have smothered some of the old social snobbery, effectively done away with the domestic service class, for instance, and brought many of the amenities formerly the guarded prerogatives of those on the upper rungs within reach (Europe in six hours on your credit card) of the rest of the ladder.

How to get there, horizontally and vertically, has been a recurrent theme of the transformation of the North Shore of Boston into Boston's North Shore, and since 1934, back to the North Shore of Boston. That is the year Sumner Tunnel under Boston Harbor linked the city's North End with East Boston, the growing Boston Municipal Airport and, beyond these, with Winthrop, Revere, Lynn and the rest of the Shore via Route 1A, opening up the vulnerable flank to the penetration of the motor vehicle, a sort of penance, surely, for the demise of the old ferry and the Narrow Gauge.

Two more years, and the North Shore's northern flank was exposed, a mere flick, but a portentous one; in 1936 the modern Route 128 was born in the rustic countryside of Peabody, a brief stretch of highway and a bridge over Lowell Street—the "Road to Nowhere," the skeptics derided.

The old 128 had been no more than a meander of connected streets between Quincy and Peabody. The new was rather offhandedly planned as a four-lane link through the farmland in twenty-seven Greater Boston communities that would supposedly provide easier access, as a dividend, to recreational areas to the north and south of the city. In 1956, twenty years and $118 million later, the last link in this fifty-eight-mile belt highway from Quincy leapfrogged the Annisquam River to Gloucester proper over the A. Piatt Andrew Bridge.

Vast tracts of farms, woods, wetlands and residential areas in the countryside beyond Boston had been destroyed to feed an insatiable project innocuously embarked upon that had taken on a seemingly out-of-control life of its own. Then in 1957 the Soviets launched the satellite Sputnik and the space age, and our race to catch up launched the colonization of the new 128, drawing on probably the densest concentration of scientific talent in America. Almost overnight The Road to Nowhere was Technology Highway, and the exploding new electronics community and its satellites wanted to locate beside it, work beside it, live near it, shop by it, and of course tear along it until a couple of hundred thousand fuming vehicles and drivers a day were roaring frenetically at seventy or eighty miles an hour or more almost bumper-to-bumper over an expanse of blacktop designed for a tenth the load.

To paraphrase the mossback who decried the arrival of the railroad a hundred years earlier, a new giant had stretched forth its arm and laid, literally, a hand of tar upon the bosom of Essex County.

Now the entire flank of the northern main body of the North Shore was accessible (or exposed, depending on one's vantage) within a few driving minutes of the vast, pulsing, crash-ridden Technology Highway and its connections: Peabody, Beverly, Salem, Manchester, Magnolia and the rest of Gloucester all the way to Rockport via routes 128 or 127, with Wenham, Hamilton, Essex and Ipswich easily reached from 1A, 22 and 133. Only Nahant, Swampscott, Marblehead and Baker's Island remained remote enough to give pause to the relentless day-tripper.

Meanwhile, in 1950 the Mystic River Bridge (in due course, as these things happen, renamed for the late Governor Maurice ["Mossy"] Tobin) spanned Boston's northern inner harbor to Charlestown and Chelsea, with a reconstituted Northern Artery and Route 1 linking with the old Newburyport Turnpike to speed (in the off hours) the new-found commuters from the distant new-found Boston suburbs east of Peabody to the ocean and as far north as Ipswich and New Hampshire.

Finally, but not necessarily ultimately, the Massachusetts Turnpike in 1957 was thrust like its logo arrow across the Commonwealth from Route 128 in Waltham to the New York Thruway and the rest of America, seven years later in the opposite direction into the heart of Boston.

No longer was the North Shore a mere spoke of the new Hub. Now it belonged to the Universe!

At the lower end of this coast, once so impossibly distant by land, Winthrop by the 1920s was beginning to wonder if it was rather too close by sea. A rival peninsula, the Boston Municipal Airport, was creeping out from East Boston into the harbor, drying up the waters that had always laved the southwesterly on its way to cool the brow of Pullen Point. As Boston grew, so did its flying field into the Logan International Airport. Belle Isle Inlet and its flats were partially filled for the Suffolk Downs race track and the million-gallon silos of that wry euphemism, the "Oil Farm." The debris from all this filling ruined Winthrop's salt marshes and shoaled its harbor and the channel of Shirley Gut. Not that it mattered; the excursion steamers were long gone, and the Army built a causeway across to Deer Island, where Boston maintained a house of correction.

Before a more civilized means of disposal was forced upon the authorities the Metropolitan District Commission dumped the combined sewage of forty-one communities off the penal island; the vapors peeled the paint from Winthrop's trim cottages. But the fumes of oxidized kerosene from the jet aircraft screaming over the rooftops still drift down on a small summer community whose golden day in the sun shimmers on the rim of memory.

Meanwhile, at its easternmost protrusion into the Atlantic, the boldest bastion of the North Shore, old Gloucester, was breached in 1956 by Technology Highway in that dramatic leap across the Annisquam River, which for 333 years had denied access to the world from the west except by rowboat, drawbridge and, for ninety years, rail. The once greatest fishing town in the Western Hemisphere (and to a much lesser extent Rockport, which had long since surrendered to tourism and the summer trade) would never be the same, nevermore an island. The precipitous decline of the over-fished and probably overpolluted fisheries from the 1960s on, the search for new high-tech industries, gentrification of the old residential sections and the extension of the city sewers into ledge-ridden West and North Gloucester, hitherto thought impervious to development, faced the city with a daunting identity crisis in 1998 as it observed the 375th anniversary of its settlement by that brave band of English fishermen clinging to the very verge of the North American wilderness.

Fortunately for our heritage, New Age environmentalists and old-time conservationists in the tradition of Agassiz and even Tudor of Nahant, Sawyer and Babson of Gloucester, Crane and Townsend of Ipswich, Sohier of Beverly, and many others of lower profile, including numerous back-country estate owners, have made common cause with such as the Trustees of Reservations, Essex County Greenbelt, the Massachusetts Audubon Society, Greenpeace, the Gloucester Civic and Garden Council and responsible representatives of government to preserve and protect a broadening patchwork of our North Shore fields, woods, salt marshes and wetlands, drumlins, shore front and ocean habitat.

Amusement parks, trolley cars, outdoor movies, beach wagons, chauffeurs, *thés dansants,* starched and stuffed shirts, croquet and professional sailing crews are out. Flea markets, diesel-belching buses, the Internet, sports utility vehicles, stretch limos, tailgate parties, dungarees, aerobics and the National Park Service's Essex National Heritage Area for the preservation and enhancement of the North Shore by overrunning it with tourists are in—at least for the moment.

The passenger trains, diesel now, still run in and out of Boston's North Station (with a subsidy), and Beverly has an airport. Everywhere are more and better restaurants. Theatre is with us, joined by dance in Rockport and a world-class magic show in Beverly, and symphony and chamber music and chorus too, and the art colonies are alive and well, and the museums are multiplying and growing. A splendid arc of concrete has replaced the old Beverly-Salem bridge inspected by President Washington himself. On the other hand, the last vestige of Maolis Gardens still stands stark and weatherworn near a street corner in Th' Haunt, and so does the storm-lashed *Man at the Wheel,* peering down to the sea beyond the inner arc of Gloucester Bay, unblinking in the light of a thousand flash bulbs.

Myopia still reigns, the king of clubs. And the country clubs and county clubs, golf clubs and yacht clubs that have survived the hard times thrive in the good ones. But the pleasures of the courts and the links and the plastic sloops have gone proletarian, and there are no more *North Shore Breezes* to waft aloft the self-esteem of the self-baked upper crust.

Still, more money than ever will still buy you a piece of the seashore of which the Reverend Bartol was canny enough to discover the good Lord was making no more—and an especially more costly, if not stately, mansion to build thereon.

To my north, when all's said and done, the lovable old fishing town looks about the same as it did in 1929 when I was a lad of seven. To the west across the harbor, the sun tends to set less vividly but more in the vein of Fitz Hugh Lane since they stopped burning the city dump at dusk. And down along the Shore past Magnolia and Manchester, beyond Baker's Island and off to the east'ard of Newcomb's Lodge and Halfway Rock, Marblehead still sprinkles the horizon on a glowing summer afternoon with a sifting of spectral spinnakers.

Life here on the North Shore of Boston can still be about as good as it gets, and I believe I may just duck out for a little sail down around Ten Pound Island and back before supper if the tide's up when I'm done with whatever I'm doing.

BIBLIOGRAPHY

Abbott, Katharine M. *Trolley Trips on a Bay State Triangle.* Lowell, Mass., 1897.

Abbott, Marshall K. *Myopia Songs and Waltzes.* Cambridge, Mass., 1897.

———— *Along the North Shore.* Boston and Northern Street Railway Company. Boston, 1905.

Addison, Daniel D. *Lucy Larcom: Life, Letters and Diary.* Boston, 1895.

The American Heritage History of Notable American Houses. Ed. Marshall B. Davidson. New York, 1971.

Amory, Cleveland. *The Last Resorts.* New York, 1952.

———— *The Proper Bostonians.* New York, 1947.

———— *Who Killed Society?* New York, 1960.

Anderson, Dorothy M. *The Era of the Summer Estates.* Canaan, N.H., 1985.

Andrews, Wayne. *Architecture in New England.* Brattleboro, 1973.

Appleton Farms Tercentenary, 1638-1938. N.p., 1938.

The Articulate Sisters (letters and journals of the daughters of President Josiah Quincy of Harvard University). Ed. M. A. DeWolfe Howe. Cambridge, Mass., 1946.

Aub, Joseph C., and Ruth K. Hapgood. *Pioneer in Modern Medicine: David Linn Edsall of Harvard.* Boston, 1970.

Babson, John I. *History of the Town of Gloucester, Cape Ann, including the Town of Rockport.* Gloucester, Mass., 1860. Reprinted, with introduction and historical review by Joseph E. Garland. Gloucester, Mass., 1972.

Babson, Thomas E. "Evolution of Cape Ann Roads and Transportation." *Essex Institute Historical Collections,* October 1955.

Bacon, Edwin M. *Walks and Rides in the Country Round About Boston.* Boston, 1898.

Baedeker, Karl. *The United States.* New York, 1893.

Barrett, Richmond. *Good Old Summer Days.* Boston, 1941.

Beaux, Cecilia. *Background with Figures.* Boston, 1930.

Beebe, Lucius. *The Lucius Beebe Reader.* New York, 1967.

———— *Mansions on Rails.* Berkeley, Calif., 1959.

"Belle-Life at Nahant." *Harper's Weekly,* August 28, 1858.

Benjamin, S. G. W. "Gloucester and Cape Ann." *Harper's New Monthly Magazine,* September 1875.

Benson, Henry Perkins. "Half Century of Motoring in Essex County." *Essex Institute Historical Collections,* July 1949.

Bentley, William. *The Diary of William Bentley, D.D.* Salem, Mass., 1905. Reprinted Gloucester, Mass., 1962.

Bergan, William M. *Old Nantasket.* Quincy, Mass., 1969.

Beverly Farms Island Inn (flyer). N.p., 1905.

Blumenson, Martin. *The Patton Papers 1885–1940*. Boston, 1972.

Bollman, Henry. "The Little Theatre." Gloucester, Mass., *Daily Times*, Sept. 27, 1956.

Boston Looks Seaward: The Story of a Port, 1630–1940. WPA Writers Program. Boston, 1941.

"Boston, Revere Beach & Lynn." *Trains*, January 1946.

Boswell, Charles. *The* America: *The Story of the World's Most Famous Yacht*. New York, 1967.

Bowen's Picture Book of Boston. Boston, 1838.

Boyd, Ellen B. R. *Adventures in Sharing*. Newburyport, Mass., 1964.

Boyle, Richard J. *American Impressionism*. Boston, 1974.

Bradlee, Francis B. C. "Boston, Revere Beach & Lynn Narrow Gauge Railroad." *Essex Institute Historical Collections*, October 1921.

——— *The Eastern Radroad: A Historical Account of Early Railroading in Eastern New England*. Salem, Mass., 1922.

——— "Some Account of Steam Navigation in New England." *Essex Institute Historical Collections*, January 1919.

Brainard, John G. C. *Occasional Pieces of Poetry*. New York, 1825.

Brann, E. H. *Sketches of Nahant*. Nahant, Mass., 1911.

Brooks, Van Wyck. *John Sloan, A Painter's Life*. New York, 1935.

Bunting, William H. *Steamers, Schooners, Cutters, and Sloops*. Boston, 1974.

Burgess, Edward. *American and English Yachts*. New York, 1887.

Buswell, Leslie. *Ambulance No. 10*. Boston, 1916.

Butler, Benjamin F. *Butler's Book*. Boston, 1892.

Carroll, Thomas. "Bands and Band Music in Salem." *Essex Institute Historical Collections*. October 1900.

Carter, Robert. *Carter's Coast of New England*. Boston, 1864. Reprinted Somersworth, N.H., 1969.

Chamberlain, Allen. *Pigeon Cove: Its Early Settlers and Their Farms, 1702–1840*. Pigeon Cove, Mass., 1940.

Channing, Walter. *A Topographical Sketch of Nahant*. Salem, 1821.

Choate, Craig Cogswell. "New Life on Old Cape Ann." *Boston Herald*, July 16, 1895.

Clark, William H. *The History of Winthrop, Massachusetts, 1630–1952*. Winthrop, 1952.

Clarke, George C. "The Story of Revere Beach." Part I *of Kiwanis History of Revere*. Mimeographed, 1966. At Revere, Mass., Public Library.

"Coast Rambles in Essex." *Harper's New Monthly Magazine*, May 1878.

Cobb, Albert W. "The Town of Winthrop." *New England Magazine*, July 1892.

Coffin, R. F. "The History of American Yachting," in Fred S. Cozzens et al., *Yachts and Yachting*. New York, 1887.

Cole, Adeline P. *Notes on Wenham History, 1643–1943*. At Wenham, Mass., Historical Association, 1943.

Collins, Lou, and George Hardy. "Salem Willows for Mine Waltz." Salem, Mass., 1919.

The Conductor (guidebook). Boston [ca. 1849].

Copeland, Melvin T., and Elliott C. Rogers. *The Saga of Cape Ann*. Freeport, Me., 1960.

Crawford, Mary Caroline. *Romantic Days in Old Boston*. Boston, 1910.

Crowninshield, Bowdoin, B. *Fore-and-Afters*. Boston, 1940.

Curtis, Caroline G. *Memories of Fifty Years in the Last Century*. Boston, 1947.

Curtis, George William. *Lotus-Eating: A Summer Book*. New York, 1852.

Cushing, John Perkins. "Diary." Manuscript at Boston Athenaeum, Boston.

A Descriptive Guide to the Eastern Rail-Road, from Boston to Portland. Boston, 1851.

Deveney, James J. "History of Bass Point, Nahant." Series in Lynn, Mass., *Item*, June 1953.

Dictionary of American Biography. New York, 1964.

Donaldson, Frances. *Edward VIII*. Philadelphia, 1974.

Dow, George F. *History of Topsfield*. Topsfield, Mass., 1940.

Dow, Mary Larcom. *Old Days at Beverly Farms*. Beverly, Mass., 1921.

Drake, Samuel Adams. *Old Landmarks and Historic Personages of Boston*. Boston, 1906.

Duveneck, Josephine W. *Frank Duveneck—Painter-Teacher*. San Francisco, 1970.

Dwight, James. "Lawn Tennis in New England." *Outing*, May 1891.

Eastern Ramblings. Eastern Railroad. Boston, 1879.

Eastman, Ralph E. *Pilots and Pilot Boats of Boston Harbor*. Boston, 1956.

Eliot, T. S. *Four Quartets*. New York, 1943.

Emerson, Ralph Waldo. *Journals*. Boston, 1909–1914.

Estaver, Paul E. "Castle on the Coast." *The Shoreliner*, July 1952.

Falt, Mary Taylor. "Rocky Neck's Development as a Summer Resort." *North Shore Breeze*, Sept. 29, 1911.

Fein, Albert. *Frederick Law Olmsted and the American Environmental Tradition*. New York, 1972.

Felt, Joseph B. *History of Ipswich, Essex and Hamilton*. Cambridge, Mass., 1834.

Ferguson, David L. *Cleopatra's Barge: The Crowninshield Story*. Boston, 1976.

Floyd, Frank L. *Manchester-by-the-Sea*. Manchester, Mass., 1945.

Forbes, Allan. "Early Myopia at Winchester." *Essex Institute Historical Collections*, January 1942.

——— "Early Myopia at Brookline, Dedham, Framingham, Southboro and Milton." *Ibid.*, April 1942.

——— "Early Myopia at Hamilton." *Ibid.*, July 1942.

——— "Early Myopia Festivities." *Ibid.*, October 1942.

Forbes, Robert Bennet. *A Discursive Sketch of Yachting; Forty and More Years Ago*. Boston, 1888.

——— *Personal Reminiscences*. Boston, 1882. Reprinted New York, 1970.

Foster, Charles H. W. *The Eastern Yacht Club Ditty Box*. Norwood, Mass., 1932.

Foster, Mrs. E. G., and Alice W. Foster. *The Story of Kettle Cove*. Magnolia, Mass., 1899.

Frank Duveneck. Chapellier Gallery, New York, n.d.

Fraser, Mrs. William S. "Manchester Becomes a Resort." Manchester, Mass., *Cricket*, serialized 1961.

Frothingham, Eugenia B. *Youth and I.* Boston, 1938.

Fuess, Claude M. *Calvin Coolidge: The Man from Vermont.* Boston, 1940.

Gallup, Donald. "The 'Lost' Manuscript of T. S. Eliot." *The Times Literary Supplement,* Nov. 7, 1968.

Gardner, William H. "The Town of Winthrop." *The Bostonian,* September 1895.

Garland, Joseph E. *Beating to Windward.* Gloucester, Mass., 1994.

———— *Eastern Point: A Nautical, Rustical and Social Chronicle of Gloucester's Outer Shield and Inner Sanctum, 1606–1950.* Dublin, N.H., 1971.

———— *The Eastern Yacht Club: A History from 1870 to 1985.* Marblehead, Mass., 1989.

———— *The Gloucester Guide: A Stroll through Place and Time.* Rockport, Mass., 1990.

Gibson, Sally. "How Presidents Enjoyed the North Shore." *North Shore '74,* Nov. 2, 1974.

Glen Magna Farms: Gateway to Historic Essex County. Danvers, Mass., Historical Society report, 1963–1964.

Gott, Lemuel, and Ebenezer Pool. *History of the Town of Rockport.* Rockport, Mass., 1888.

Gould, Bartlett. "Burgess of Marblehead." *Essex Institute Historical Collections,* January 1970.

Gove, Charles E., Jr. *Queries of Old Nahant.* Manuscript at Nahant, Mass., Public Library.

Grant, Robert. *Fourscore: An Autobiography.* Boston, 1934.

———— *The North Shore of Massachusetts.* New York, 1896.

Grattan, Thomas C. *Civilized America.* 2 vols. London, 1859.

Green, Eleanor. *Maurice Prendergast.* College Park, Md., 1976.

Hammond, John Hays. *The Autobiography of John Hays Hammond.* 2 vols. New York, 1935.

Harbor View Hotel (brochure). Gloucester, Mass., n.d.

Harmond, Richard. "The Time They Tried to Divide Beverly." *Essex Institute Historical Collections,* January 1968.

Harris, Leslie. *150 Years a Town.* Essex, Mass., 1969.

Hartt, Hildegarde T. *Magnolia Once Kettle Cove.* Magnolia, Mass., 1962.

Harvey, George. *Henry Clay Frick: The Man.* New York, 1928.

Harwood, Reed. "The History of Misery Island." *Essex Institute Historical Collections,* July 1967.

Hawes, Charles Boardman. *Gloucester by Land and Sea.* Boston, 1923.

Heerman, Norbert. *Frank Duveneck.* Boston, 1918.

Here and There by Trolley from Salem. Boston and Northern Street Railway Company. N.p., n.d.

Herreshoff, L. Francis, *Capt. Nat Herreshoff: The Wizard of Bristol.* New York, 1953.

Heuvelmans, Bernard. *In the Wake of the Sea Serpents.* New York, 1968.

Hill, Benjamin D., and Winfield S. Nevins. *The North Shore of Massachusetts Bay* (guidebooks). Salem, Mass., 1879–1894.

History of the American Field Service in France. "Friends of France" 1914–1917. Told by its members. 3 vols. Boston, 1920.

History of Essex County, Massachusetts. Ed. D. Hamilton Hurd. 2 vols. Philadelphia, 1888.

Holmes, Oliver Wendell. *The Autocrat of the Breakfast-Table.* In *Works.* Boston, 1892.

—— *Our Hundred Days in Europe.* In *Works.* Boston, 1892.

—— *Pages from an Old Volume of Life.* In *Works.* Boston, 1892.

Holzman, Robert S. *Stormy Ben Butler.* New York, 1954.

Homer, James L. *Nahant, and Other Places on the North Shore.* Boston, 1848.

—— *Notes on the Seashore; or Random Sketches by "Shade of Alden."* Boston, 1848.

House, Edward M. *The Intimate Papers of Colonel House.* Ed. Charles Seymour. 4 vols. Boston, 1926.

Howard, Channing. *Stage Coach and Early Railroad Days in Winthrop.* Mimeographed. At Winthrop, Mass., Public Library, 1938.

"The Ill-fated Misery Islands." *Yankee,* August 1966.

Jewett, Amos Everett. "The Tidal Marshes of Rowley and Vicinity with an Account of the Old-Time Methods of 'Marshing.'" *Essex Institute Historical Collections,* July 1949.

Kenny, Herbert A. *Cape Ann: Cape America.* Philadelphia, 1971.

Kenyon, Paul B. "The Playhouse and the School of the Little Theatre." Gloucester, Mass., *Daily Times,* March 20, 1976.

Kidney, Walter C. *The Architecture of Choice. Eclecticism in America, 1880–1930.* New York, 1974.

Kimball, F. R. *Handbook of Marblehead Neck.* Boston, 1882.

King, Caroline H. *When I Lived in Salem, 1822–1866.* Brattleboro, 1937.

King's Handbook of Boston. Ed. Moses King. Cambridge, Mass., 1878.

King's Handbook of Boston Harbor. Ed. Moses King. Cambridge, Mass., 1882.

Kipling, Rudyard. *Captains Courageous.* New York, 1896.

Kline, Naomi Reed. *The Hammond Museum—A Guidebook.* Gloucester, Mass., 1977.

Lamson, D. P. *History of the Town of Manchester, Essex County, Massachusetts, 1645–1895.* Boston, 1895.

Larkin, Oliver W. *Art and Life in America.* New York, 1966.

Later Years of the Saturday Club. Ed. M. A. DeWolfe Howe. Boston, 1927.

Lawrence, William. *Memories of a Happy Life.* Boston, 1926.

Leonard, Henry C. *Pigeon Cove and Vicinity.* Boston, 1873.

Lewis, Alonzo. *The Picture of Nahant.* Lynn, Mass., 1855.

—— and James R. Newhall. *History of Lynn, Essex County, Massachusetts: Including Lynnfield, Saugus, Swampscott, and Nahant.* Revised ed. Boston, 1865.

Lodge, Henry Cabot. *Early Memories.* New York, 1913.

—— *An Historical Address Delivered at the Celebration of the Fiftieth Anniversary of the Incorporation of the Town of Nahant, July 14, 1903.* Nahant, Mass., 1904.

Long, H. Follansbee. "The Newburyport and Boston Turnpike." *Essex Institute Historical Collections,* April 1906.

Lord, Priscilla Sawyer, and Virginia Clegg Gamage. *Marblehead: The Spirit of '76 Lives Here.* Philadelphia, 1972.

Loring, Katharine Peabody. "The Earliest Summer Residents of the North Shore and their Houses." *Essex Institute Historical Collections,* July 1932.

Lowell, James Russell. *Letters of James Russell Lowell.* Ed. Charles Eliot Norton. New York. 1894.

Lynn and Boston Horse Railroad Company Annual Report, 1861.

Lynn Yacht Club 34th Annual Ball, with history. Lynn, Mass., 1912.

McCauley, Peter. *Revere Beach Chips.* Revere, Mass., 1979.

Manchester-by-the-Sea, 1645–1970. Town of Manchester, Mass., 1970.

Mansur, Frank L. "Swampscott, Massachusetts: The Beginnings of a Town." *Essex Institute Historical Collections,* January 1972.

Marblehead Neck Bulletin (brochure). Marblehead, Mass., 1889.

Masconomo House (brochures). Manchester, Mass., 1899 and 1906.

Mason, Edward S. *The Street Railway in Massachusetts: The Rise and Decline of an Industry.* Cambridge, Mass., 1932.

Mason, Herbert N., Jr. *The Lafayette Escadrille.* New York, 1964.

Massachusetts: A Guide to Its Places and People. Works Progress Administration, Federal Writers Project. Boston, 1937.

Memoranda Relating to Nathaniel Souther. Springfield, Ill., 1886.

Miller, Richard H. "John Hays Hammond: Electronic Sorcerer." *True,* November 1960.

The Misery Island Club. *Announcement of the Second Annual Regatta.* N.p., Aug. 7, 1901.

The Misery Island Club (flyer). N.p., 1900.

Montserrat (brochure). N.p., 1897.

Montserrat Highlands (brochure of Montserrat Syndicate). Np., 1910.

Morison, Samuel Eliot. *The Maritime History of Massachusetts, 1783–1860.* Boston, 1921.

Morse, John T., Jr. *Life and Letters of Oliver Wendell Holmes.* Boston, 1896.

Mumford, Lewis. *Sticks and Stones.* Revised ed. New York, 1955.

"Nahant." *Boston Monthly Magazine,* July 1825.

Nahant. Nahant, Mass., Public Library. Lynn, Mass., 1899.

Nahant: And What Is to Be Seen There. Boston, 1868.

Nahant, or A Day in Summer. N. p., May 1811. At the Essex Institute.

Nahant, or "The Floure of Souvenance." Philadelphia, 1827.

Nason, Elias. *A Gazetteer of the State of Massachusetts.* Boston, 1874.

New England Aviators 1914–1918: Their Portraits and Their Records. Intro. A. Lawrence Lowell. 2 vols. Boston, 1919.

The North Shore Blue Book and Social Register. Boston, 1893 on.

Northend, Mary H. "The Summer Home of Mr. Eben D. Jordan." *Town and Country,* June 10, 1905.

Ocean House (brochure). Swampscott, Mass., 1896.

Official Encyclopedia of Tennis. United States Lawn Tennis Association. New York, 1971.

O'Gorman, James F. "Architectural Action Was His Disease." Gloucester, Mass., *Daily Times,* Feb. 17, 1979.

——— *Portrait of a Place: Some American Landscape Painters in Gloucester.* Gloucester, Mass., 1973.

——— *This Other Gloucester.* Boston, 1976.

——— "Twentieth-Century Gothick: The Hammond Castle Museum in Gloucester and Its Antecedents." *Essex Institute Historical Collections,* April 1981.

Old Shipping Days in Boston. State Street Trust Company. Boston, 1918.

Other Merchants and Sea Captains of Old Boston. State Street Trust Company. Boston, 1919.

Parks, Groves, Seashore Resorts. Boston and Northern and Old Colony Street Railway companies. Boston, 1903.

Peabody, Robert E. "Peach's Point, Marblehead." *Essex Institute Historical Collections,* January 1966.

Phelps, Elizabeth Stuart. *Chapters from a Life.* Boston, 1896.

Phillips, James Duncan. "Commuting to Salem and Its Summer Resorts Fifty Years Ago." *Essex Institute Historical Collections,* April 1944.

Picturesque Cape Ann (booklet). Gloucester, Mass., 1909.

Pierce, Patricia Jobe. *Edmund C. Tarbell and the Boston School of Painting, 1889–1980.* Hingham, Mass., 1980.

——— *The Ten.* Hingham, Mass., 1976.

Pigeon Cove House (pamphlet). N. p., 1880.

Pittee, Charles R. "The Gloucester Steamboats." *The American Neptune,* October 1952.

Pleasant Rides and Pleasure Spots on the Lynn and Boston Railroad. Lynn, Mass., 1897.

Pratt, Walter Merriam. *Seven Generations: A Story of Prattville and Chelsea.* Boston, 1930.

Prendergast, Maurice. *Watercolor Sketchbook, 1899* (facsimile). Notes by Peter A. Wick. Cambridge, Mass., 1960.

Preston Hotel (brochure). Swampscott, Mass., 1907.

The Priceless Gift (Wilson letters). Ed. Eleanor Wilson McAdoo. New York, 1962.

Prince, Warren. "The Pioneers of the Seashore." Beverly, Mass., *Citizen,* serialized 1884.

Pringle, Henry F. *The Life and Times of William Howard Taft.* 2 vols. New York, 1939.

Pringle, James R. *History of the Town and City of Gloucester, Cape Ann, Massachusetts.* Gloucester, Mass., 1892. Reprinted with index, 1997.

Procter, George H. "How Bass Rocks Became a Summer Resort." Gloucester, Mass., *Daily Times,* August 23, 1911.

——— "Reminiscences of the Annisquam River." Gloucester, Mass., *Daily Times,* April 3, 5, 7, 13, 1909.

——— "The Summer Boarder Industry." Gloucester, Mass., *Daily Times,* August 9, 1911.

Pulsifer, David. *Guide to Boston and Vicinity.* Boston, 1871.

Rantoul, Robert S. "The Misery Islands and What Has Happened There." *Essex Institute Historical Collections,* July 1902.
———— "Some Notes on Old Modes of Travel." *Essex Institute Historical Collections,* April 1871.
Revere: 100 Years, 1871–1971. City of Revere, Mass., 1971.
Rhys, Hedley H. *Maurice Prendergast, 1859–1924.* Cambridge, Mass., 1960.
Roads, Samuel, Jr. *The History and Traditions of Marblehead.* Boston, 1880.
Robinson, Morris B. "Some Artists Who Called Squam, Lanesville and the Folly 'Home.'" Gloucester, Mass., 1973. Typescript at Sawyer Free Library, Gloucester.
Roscoe, Theodore. *The Web of Conspiracy* (the Booth family). Englewood Cliffs, N.J., 1959.
Rowsome, Frank, Jr. *Trolley Car Treasury.* New York, 1956.
Ruggles, Eleanor. *Prince of Players* (the Booth family). New York, 1953.

Salem Willows Anniversary Booklet. Salem, Mass., 1958.
Santayana, George. *Persons and Places.* New York, 1944.
Scully, Vincent J., Jr. *The Shingle Style and the Stick Style.* New Haven, 1971.
Seaburg, Carl, and Stanley Paterson. *Merchant Prince of Boston: Colonel T. H. Perkins, 1764–1854.* Cambridge, Mass., 1971.
Searle, Richard W. "History of Catta Island off Marblehead." *Essex Institute Historical Collections,* October 1947.
———— "Marblehead Great Neck." *Essex Institute Historical Collections,* July 1937.
Shaw, O. J. "The 'Sea Breeze': Polka Brillante." Boston, 1857.
Shepley, Hayden. *Automobiles Built in Essex County.* Toughkenamon, Pa., 1976.
Shurcliff, Margaret H. M. *Lively Days.* Taipei, 1965.
Shurcliff, Sidney N. *Upon the Road Argilla.* Boston, 1958.
Shurtleff, Benjamin. *The History of the Town of Revere.* Revere, Mass., 1937.
Solley, George W. *Alluring Rockport.* Manchester, Mass., 1924.
Some Merchants and Sea Captains of Old Boston. State Street Trust Company. Boston, 1918.
Souvenir of Bass Rocks. Bass Rocks Improvement Association. Boston, 1905.
Souvenir of Salem Willows. Salem Willows Merchants Association. Salem, Mass., 1929.
Standard History of Essex County, Massachusetts. Publ. C. F. Jewett, Boston, 1878.
Stephens, William P. *American Yachting.* New York, 1904.
———— *Traditions and Memories of American Yachting.* New York, 1942.
Stetson, Helen L. "Sketch of Nahant." *Lynn Item,* March 22, 1902.
Stevens, W. Lester. "Cape Ann: An Artist's Paradise." *North Shore Breeze,* April 29, 1921.
Stone, Edwin M. *History of Beverly.* Boston, 1843.
The Story of Essex County. Ed. Claude M. Fuess. 4 vols. New York, 1935
Streeter, G. L. "The Story of Winter Island and Salem Neck." *Essex Institute Historical Collections,* January-June 1897.
Sturges, Walter Knight. "Arthur Little and the Colonial Revival." *Journal of the Society of Architectural Historians,* May 1973.

Swan, William U. "A Century of Yachting at Marblehead," in Joseph S. Robinson, *The Story of Marblehead*. Salem, Mass., 1936.

Tapley, Charles S. *Country Estates of Old Danvers*. Danvers, Mass., 1961.

Tapley, Harriet S. *Chronicles of Danvers (Old Salem Village) Massachusetts, 1623–1923*. Danvers, Mass., 1923.

Taft, Mrs. William Howard. *Recollections of Full Years*. New York, 1914.

A Testimonial to Charles J. Paine and Edward Burgess from the City of Boston, for Their Successful Defense of the America's Cup. Boston, 1887.

Tharp, Louise Hall. *Mrs. Jack: A biography of Isabella Stewart Gardner*. Boston, 1965

Thompson, Waldo. *Swampscott: Historical Sketches of the Town*. Lynn, Mass., 1885.

Thompson, Winfield M., William P. Stephens, and William U. Swan. *The Yacht "America."* Boston, 1925.

Ticknor, George. *Life of William Hickling Prescott*. Boston, 1864.

Truax, Rhoda. *The Doctors Warren*. Boston, 1968.

Tompkins, Eugene. *The History of the Boston Theatre, 1854–1901*. Boston, 1908.

Townsend, Charles W. *Beach Grass*. Boston, 1923.

———— *The Birds of Essex County, Massachusetts*. Camhridge, Mass., 1905.

———— *Sand Dunes and Salt Marshes*. Boston, 1913.

Trolley Trips. Bay State Street Railway Company. Boston, 1912.

Trolley Trips. Boston and Northern and Old Colony Street Railway companies. N.p., May 1910.

Tryon, W. S. *Parnassus Corner* (James T. Fields). Boston, 1963.

Tucker-Macchetta, Blanche Roosevelt. *The Home Life of Henry W. Longfellow*. New York, 1882.

Van de Water, Frederic F. *The Real McCoy*. New York, 1931.

Varrell, William M. *Summer-by-the-Sea*. Portsmouth, N.H., 1972.

Waters, Harold. "King of Rum Row." *The Compass*, Fall 1974.

Waters, T. Frank. "Candlewood." *Ipswich Historical Society Publications*, 1909.

———— "A History of the Old Argilla Road." *Ibid.*, 1900.

———— "Ipswich in the Massachusetts Bay Colony." *Ibid.*, 1917.

———— "Jeffrey's Neck and the Way Leading Thereto." *Ibid.*, 1912.

———— "The Old Bay Road from Saltonstall's Brook and Samuel Appleton's Farm." *Ibid.*, 1907.

Webber, C. H., and W. S. Nevins. *Old Naumkeag: An Historical Sketch of the City of Salem, and the Towns of Marblehead, Peabody, Beverly, Danvers, Wenham, Manchester, Topsfield and Middleton*. Salem, Mass., 1877.

Webber, John S., Jr. *In and Around Cape Ann*. Gloucester, Mass., 1885.

Weeks, Edward. *Myopia, 1875–1975*. Hamilton, Mass., 1975.

Welch, William L. *Walk around Salem Neck and Winter Island*. Salem, Mass., 1897.

West, Richard S., Jr. *Lincoln's Scapegoat General* (Benjamin Butler). Boston, 1965.

Wheildon, W. W. *Letters from Nahant*. Charlestown, Mass., 1842.

——— *The Willows*. Boston, 1900.

Whitehill, Walter Muir. *Boston: A Topographical History*. Cambridge, Mass., 1968.

——— *Museum of Fine Arts Boston: A Centennial History*. Cambridge, Mass., 1970.

Whitehouse, Arch. *Legion of the Lafayette*. New York, 1962.

Who's Who Along the North Shore. Manchester, Mass., ca. 1907ff.

Williams, John. *The Other Battleground: The Home Fronts—Britain, France and Germany, 1914–18*. Chicago, 1972.

Willoughby, Malcolm F. *Rum War at Sea*. Washington, 1964.

Willow Park Pavilion (broadside). 1882. At the Essex Institute.

The Willows (brochure). Salem, Mass., 1900.

Wilmerding, John. "Interpretations of Place: Views of Gloucester, Mass." *Essex Institute Historical Collections*, January 1967.

Wilson, Fred A. *Some Annals of Nahant*. Boston, 1928. Reprinted by the Nahant, Mass., Historical Society, 1977.

Winsor, Justin. *The Memorial History of Boston*. 4 vols. Boston, 1881.

Wise, DeWitt D. *Baker's Island Now and Then*. Salem, Mass., 1940.

——— *Now, Then, Baker's Island*. Salem, Mass., 1964.

Witham, Corinne B. *The Hammond Museum Guide Book*. Gloucester, Mass., 1966.

Woodbury, C. J. H. "The Floating Bridge at Lynn on the Salem and Boston Turnpike." *Essex Institute Historical Collections*, January–June 1898.

Newspapers and Periodicals

Boston Globe

Boston Herald

Boston Post

Boston Transcript

Cape Ann Weekly Advertiser

Essex Institute Historical Collections

Gloucester Daily Times

Gloucester Telegraph

Harper's Weekly

Ipswich Chronicle

Lynn Item

Magnolia Leaves

New Ocean House (later *North Shore*) *Reminder*

New York Times

North Shore Breeze

Revere Journal

Salem Gazette

Salem News

Salem Willows Budget

Town and Country

Willows Budget

INDEX

Bennett, James Gordon, Jr., 77, 78
Benson, Frank W., 203, 274, 296, 331, 332
Benson, Henry Perkins, 183, 185
Bent, Luther S., 142
Bent, Quincy, 142
Bentley, William, 3, 4, 5, 69, 70
Bethlehem Steel, 142
Betho, Count von Wedel, 262
"Betsy's Inducement," Manchester, 119
Beveridge, Albert, 255
Beverly, xi, xv, 5, 26, 104, 114, 120, 121, 122,
    124, 166, 184, 191, 215, 223, 224, 234,
    237, 278, 287, 310, 354, 355, 356;
    earliest summer residents, 33–40 ; maps,
    34–35, 250–253; Taft summer White
    Houses, 255, 257–273; yachting, 77, 80;
    See also Beverly Cove, Beverly Farms,
    Pride's Crossing
Beverly Board of Trade, 258, 259, 270
Beverly Cove, 38, 77, 177, 234, 257, 278, 299,
    302, 318, 348
Beverly Farms, 20, 41, 86, 96, 103, 104, 105,
    124, 176, 186, 187, 224, 238, 242, 244,
    266, 275, 282, 285, 294, 297, 300, 303,
    306, 347, 351; earliest summer residents,
    33–40; secession movement, 121–124
Beverly Farms Island Inn, 223, 224
Beverly Harbor, 26, 69
Beverly Historical Society, ix, 36, 39, 123, 158,
    179, 184, 187, 214, 219, 238, 243, 245,
    250, 252, 257, 259, 268, 269, 271, 285,
    287
Beverly Hospital, 303
Beverly Point, 261
Beverly Yacht Club, 80
Beverly-Salem bridge, 33, 356
"Big Heater," Gloucester, xiii, 114
Bigelow, Sturgis, 90
Bird, Charles S., Jr., 317
Birds of Essex County, The (Townsend), 204
Black, John W., 192, 194
"Black Ben." *See* Forbes, Robert Bennet
Black Bess Point, Gloucester, 137
Black Cove Beach, Manchester, 41
Blake, Alpheus P., 152, 154, 157, 161
Blanchard, Jesse, 57, 63
Blanchard farm, 58
Blaney's Beach, Swarnpscott, 29
Blatchford, Ernest, photo, 51, 199
"Bleak House," Misery Island, 223, 224

"Blighty," Gloucester, 313, 314
Blueberry Hill, Annisquam, 142
Blynman Canal, Gloucester, 114, 139
"Blythewood," Swampscott, 30
Boardman, B. G., 42
Boardman, William, 255
Boardman, William H., 72
Bodin, Fred, ix
Boer War, 256
Bonette, Professor, 171
Booth's Theatre, New York, 110
Booth, Agnes Perry, 108, 110, 111, 112, 191
Booth, Edwin, 107, 108, 110, 111
Booth, John Wilkes, 107, 108
Booth, Junius Brutus, 107, 191
Booth, Junius Brutus, Jr., 63, 107, 108, 110,
    111, 112
Bossidy, John Collins, 89
Boston, *passim*
Boston and Gloucester Steamboat Company,
    133
Boston and Lowell Railroad, 26, 37
Boston and Maine Railroad, 26, 33, 182, 249,
    258, 286, 350
Boston and Northern Railway, 178, 179
Boston Athenaeum, 13
Boston Boat Club, 71
Boston Church, Nahant, 10, 11, 12, 14, 17, 90
Boston Daily Advertiser, 27
Boston Evening Transcript, xi, 167, 183, 211,
    232, 235, 306, 347
Boston Globe, 279
Boston Harbor, xii, 3, 33, 71, 72, 88, 152, 219,
    297
Boston Herald, 76, 182
Boston Land Company, 151
Boston Municipal Airport, 353, 354
Boston Neck, 27
Boston Opera House, 279
Boston Park Commission, 228
Boston Pioneer Seashore Club, 45, 46, 47
Boston Post, 258
Boston Public Library, Print Department, 27
Boston, Revere Beach and Lynn Railroad,
    152–156, 158, 159, 161, 353
Boston Society of Natural History, 142
Boston Stock Exchange, 314
Boston Symphony Orchestra, 190, 244
Boston Theatre, 106, 107, 108, 110
Boston University School of Medicine, 216, 269

Harvard University, 13, 14, 21, 23, 71, 83, 90, 98, 116, 120, 194, 227, 263, 287, 288, 296, 306, 314, 338, 348
Harvey, George, 241, 249
Harwood, John H., 223
Harwood, Reed, 220, 223, 224
Hassam, Frederick Childe, 329, 331, 332, 334
Haven, Franklin, 38, 39, 252
Haven, Franklin, Jr., 38
Haverhill (Mass.), 26
Hawks, Edward C., 140, 149
Hawks, James D., 140
"Hawksworth Hall," Gloucester, 140
Hawthorne Inn, East Gloucester, 189, 195–199
Hawthorne, Nathaniel, 103, 105
Hayes, Rutherford B., 104
'Headers, 56, 65, 66, 79
Heard, Augustine, 77
Heard, John, 77, 78
Heartbreak Hill, Ipswich, 202
Heinz, Henry J., 193, 238
Helen, sloop, 55, 145
Hemenway, Augustus, 83, 116, 121
Hemenway, Mary, 121
Henderson, Joseph B., 225
Henn, William R., 85
Henri, Robert, 335, 336
Henrietta, schooner, 77
Henry Clay, brig, 71
Henry L. Marshall, schooner, 312
Herreshoff, John, 84
Herreshoff, L. Francis, 87
Herreshoff, Nathanael G., 83–84, 87
Herring, Augustus M., 295
Hesper, sloop, 83
Hesperus (ship of Longfellow poem), 219
Hesperus House, Magnolia, 128, 129, 130, 192
Higginson, Francis Lee, 241
Higginson, Henry Lee, 118
Higginson, Thomas Wentworth, 35
"Highland Cottage," Magnolia, 193
highways, 353–355
Higinbotham, Harlow, 207
Hingham (Mass.), xii, 4
Hinkley Farm, 58
His Snakeship, 2, 4, 8, 11
History of Catta Island off Marblehead (Searle), 56
History of Lynn (Lewis), 10, 31
History of the Boston Theatre, 109

Hoar, George Frisbie, 123
Hodgkins Cove, Gloucester, 143
Hog Island, Essex, 202, 204, 207, 211, 213
Hogarth, William, 211
Holmes, Amelia, 95, 104, 105
Holmes, Edward, 105
Holmes, Fanny (Mrs. Oliver Wendell, Jr.), 105, 266
Holmes, Oliver Wendell, Dr., 18, 20, 23, 35, 86, 95, 96, 98, 103, 104, 105, 106, 122, 182, 266
Holmes, Oliver Wendell, Jr., 105
Home Fires, film, 304, 306
Home for All; or, the Gravel Wall and Octagon Mode of Building, A (Fowler), 118
Homer, James L., 5, 11, 29
Homer, Winslow, 132, 329, 331, 335, 352
Homestead (Pa.) rail strike, 239–240
Hood, Abner, 5
Hood, Mrs., 19
Hood family, 11
Hoop Pole Cove, Rockport, 146
Hooper, Robert C., 186
Hooper, Robert G., 281
Hooper, William, 41
Hoover, Herbert, 302
Hopper, Edward, 337
horsecars, 66, 122, 136, 150, 151–152, 156, 162, 163, 165, 166, 176
Hospital Beach, Salem, 165
Hospital Point, Salem, 38, 163, 172, 257
hotels: Baker's Island, 216–218; Beverly, 273; Gloucester, 52, 134, 149, 178, 195–197; Eastern Point, 138, Magnolia, 128–130, 192–195, 238, 275; Manchester, 110–112; Marblehead, 56–57, 58, 64–65; Nahant 6–11, 13, 23, 27, 88, 89, 90, 91, 92; Revere, 155, 156, 158, 168, 170; Rockport, 145–147; Swampscott, 28, 61–62, 185, 188, 189–191
Hotel Preston, Swampscott, 190, 191
Hotel Vanderbilt, New York City, 296
Houghton Mifflin, 90
Housatonic, steamer, 10
House Island, Manchester, 116
"House with the Iron Railings," Wenham, 304
House, Edward M., 193, 265, 291, 298, 299, 301, 304, 305, 321
"House-on-the-Moors," East Gloucester, 336
Houses of American Authors (Hunt), 32

King's Beach, Swampscott, 39
Kipling, Rudyard, 197
Knowlton, Allen, 128
Knowlton, James, 128
Knowlton family, 127, 128, 192
Knowlton Point, Gloucester, 191
Knox, Philander, 206, 262, 263
Kruger, Oom Paul, 256
Kuni, prince and princess of Japan, 263
Kya Yami, Pullman car, 247

Labor-in-Vain Creek, 202, 207
Labor-in-Vain Golf Course, 211
Ladd, Dr. Maynard, 307
Lafayette, Marie Joseph, Marquis de, 295
Lafayette Escadrille, 295–298
LaFollette, Bob, 209
Lamson, D. F., 125
Land of Heart's Desire (Yeats), 337
Lands End, Rockport, 149
Lands End Association, 149
Landscapes (Eliot), 289
Lane, Blanche Butler, 195, 314
Lane, Fitz Hugh, 44, 132, 329, 331, 356
Lanesville, 133, 334
Langley-Wharton, 346
Lansing, Robert, 299
Lapwing, cutter, 83
Larcom, Lucy, 104
Lark, The, seaplane, 290, 297
Larkin, Oliver W., 335
Lascelles, Alan, 316
Lawlor, Dennison J., 18
Lawrence, Abbott, 12, 98
Lawrence, Amory, 90
Lawrence, Amos A., 12, 89, 90
Lawrence, Isabel, 320
Lawrence, John S., 39, 320
Lawrence, Sarah Appleton, 90
Lawrence, William ("Bill") (later bishop), 89, 90, 95, 97, 184
Lawrence family, 18, 95
Lawrence, A. & A., textile firm, 12
Lawrence (Mass.), 59, 149
Lawson, Ernest, 335
Leach, David, 116
Leach, Henry, 260
League of Nations, 272, 299, 305
Lee, Henry, 38, 186

Lee, Mrs. George, 303
Lee, Robert E., 107
Leeds, Herbert C., 233
Leland, Lester, 312
Leonard, Arthur, 312, 313, 314
Leonard, Henry C., 146
Lewandos, 186, 347
Lewis, Albert, 138
Lewis, Alonzo, 10, 15, 28, 30, 31, 119
Lewis, John V., 138
Lewis, Lloyd, 141
Lewis, Phil, 141, 325, 327
Lewis Wharf, Boston, 25, 26, 33, 138
Lexington (Mass.), 229
Life With Father (Crouse), 338, 339
Lillie May, ferry, 65
"Lilliothea," Manchester, 280
Lincoln, Abraham, U. S. President, 95, 107
Lincoln, Alice Towne, 114
Lincoln House, Swampscott, 61, 62, 190
Lindergreen, Harold F., 212
Linehan, Daniel, 223
Linnaean Society of New England, 4
Linzee, John, 14
literary figures. *See* Bryant, Dana, Eliot, Emerson, Fields, Hawthorne, Higginson, Holmes, Larcom, Longfellow, Lowell, Motley, Prescott, Taylor, Whittier
Little, Arthur, 119, 120, 121, 244
Little, James L., 30, 120
Little Good Harbor Beach, Gloucester, 147, 178
Little Misery Island, Salem, 214, 215
Little Neck, Ipswich, 201, 202
Little Theatre, 338–339
"Little Wiggler." *See* Boston, Revere Beach and Lynn Railroad
Little's Point, Swampscott, 30, 120, 322, 325
Lively Days (Shurtleff), 205
Lizzie, launch, 221
Loblolly Cove, Rockport, 149, 265
Lobster Cove, Annisquam, 141, 142
Lobster Cove, Manchester, 117, 120, 125
Lodge, Anna Cabot, 89
Lodge, Elizabeth, 89, 91
Lodge, Dr. G. H., 30
Lodge, Henry Cabot (grandson), 175
Lodge, Henry Cabot, 23, 89, 96, 97, 100, 198, 255, 256, 263, 272, 278, 338
Lodge, J. Alexander, 177, 282, 309, 310

Puritan, compromise cutter, 82, 83, 84, 85, 86
Puritan Cup, 84
Puritan Road, Swampscott, 29

Quarry Point, Gloucester, 138
Queen of the Air, hot-air balloon, 76, 77
Quincy, Eliza, 8
Quincy, Josiah, 8
Quincy, Margaret, 8
Quincy (Mass.), xii, 326, 353, 354; granite quarries, 25
Quinzler, early motorcar maker, 187

Radcliffe College, 21, 23
Radio Corporation of America, 339
"Radio Point," Gloucester, 293
railroads, 24, 25–26, 28–30, 33, 37, 38, 41, 47, 48, 56, 58–59, 60–61, 63, 83, 129, 133, 136, 147, 151, 164–165, 182, 195, 241, 286, 350, 356; private car (varnish), 238, 239, 242, 245, 246–247, 248, 249, 269, 353
"Ramparts," Eastern Point, 238, 257
Rantoul, Robert S., 26
Rantoul, Robert, 30, 219, 222
Raymond, Emma, 184, 257
Read, Charlotte, 303
real estate investment: Beverly Farms, 36–37; Cape Ann, 126, 149; Gloucester, 47, 48–49, 127, 140, 147–149; Eastern Point, 136–138; Ipswich, 201; Magnolia, 128; Manchester, 42–43, 110, 113–118, 120; Marblehead, 56, 63–64, 66, Nahant, 11; Revere, 151, 154–156; Rockport, 144; Salem, 164
Rebecca, schooner, 78
Record, Boston, 135
"Red Gables," Swampscott, 322
"Red Roof," Gloucester, 257, 286, 287, 288, 324, 340
Reed, Benjamin Tyler, 29, 30
Reid, Robert, 331, 332
Reugman, Gus, 223, 224
Revere, xi, xii, 151–152, 154–162, 167–171, 353. *See also* Revere Beach
Revere Beach, xiii, 94, 150, 152, 155, 157, 159–163, 166–171, 177, 178, 194, 223
Revere Electric Street Railroad, 167
Revere Journal, 160
Revere Public Library, 150

Revolutionary War, 26, 45, 48, 69
Rhea, Madeline Berlo, 155
Rhodes, Cecil, 256
Rice Anne Steele, 349
Rice, C. G., ix, 234, 346, 349
Rice, Charles G., 306, 348
Rice, E. E., 118
Richardson, Henry Hobson, 119, 121, 130
Richardson, Mark W., 202, 204
Richelieu, Duchess de, 302
Rindge, Frederick Hastings, 57
Rindge, Samuel B., 57, 62
Rise Of the Dutch Republic, The (Motley), 19
Rivals, The (Sheridan), 108
"River," Manchester, 120
Riverhead Beach, Marblehead, 57, 60
Riverhead House (later Atlantic House), Marblehead, 60
Robbers Row, Magnolia, 282, 283
Robbins, Edward H., 13, 15
Robbins, William B., 205
Robinson, Edward, 257
Robson, Elizabeth, 341
Rock Island Railroad. *See* Chicago, Rock Island and Pacific Railroad
"Rock Maple Farm," Hamilton, 255
Rockefeller, John D., 241, 264, 273
Rockefeller, John D., Jr., 238, 264
Rockholm, Annisquam, 143
"Rocklea," Pride's Crossing, 350
"Rockmarge," Pride's Crossing, 242, 244, 245, 246, 249, 252
Rockport, xi, xv, 40, 81, 265, 354, 355, 356; artists, 334–335; earliest summer residents, 133, 139, 144–147, 149; map, 124. *See also* Pigeon Cove, Sandy Bay
Rockport Harbor, 334
"Rocks, The," West Manchester, 279, 280
"Rockwood," Saugus, 14
Rocky Neck, Gloucester, 45, 51, 57, 134, 136, 178, 196, 331, 332, 333, 335, 336, 338
Rocky Neck Marine Railways, 338
Rogers, Daniel, 48
Rogers, Dudley, 317
Rogers, George H., 48, 147, 148
Rogers, Jacob, 223
Rogers, John Kimball, 48
Rogers, Sarah McClennen, 49, 136
Rogers, Walter, 216, 217
Romberg, Sigmund, 277

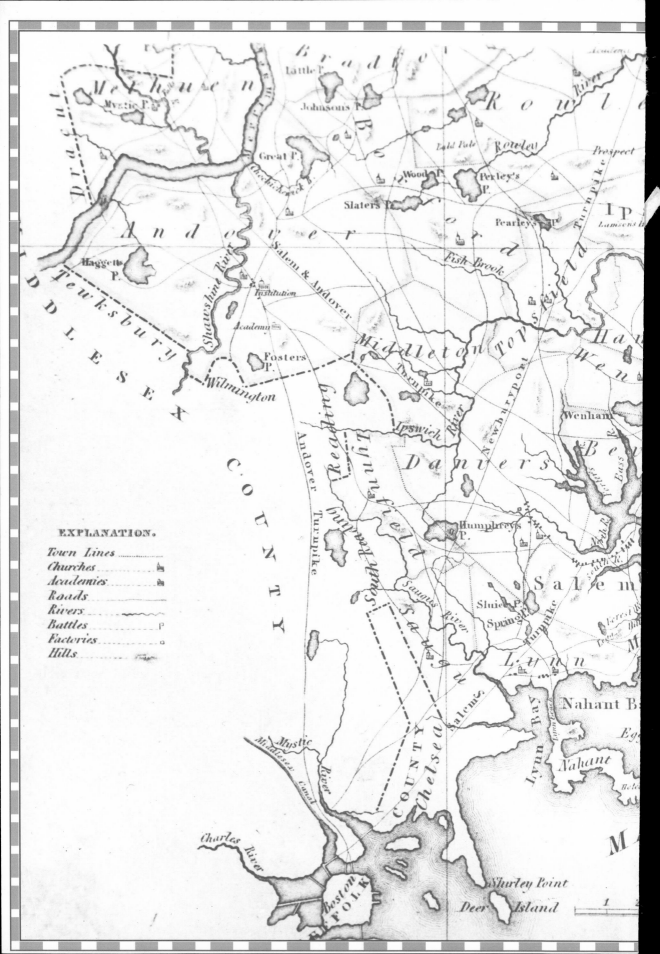

EXPLANATION.

Town Lines ....
Churches ....
Academies ....
Roads ....
Rivers ....
Battles .... P
Factories .... □
Hills ....